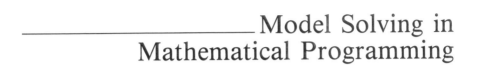

Model Solving in
Mathematical Programming

Model Solving in Mathematical Programming

H. P. Williams

University of Southampton, UK

JOHN WILEY & SONS

Chichester · New York · Brisbane · Toronto · Singapore

Copyright © 1993 byJohn Wiley & Sons Ltd,
Baffins Lane, Chichester,
West Sussex, PO19 1UD, England

Other Wiley Editorial Offices

John Wiley & Sons, Inc., 605 Third Avenue,
New York, NY 10158-0012, USA

Jacaranda Wiley Ltd, G.P.O. Box 859, Brisbane,
Queensland 4001, Australia

John Wiley & Sons (Canada) Ltd, 22 Worcester Road,
Rexdale, Ontario M9W 1L1, Canada

John Wiley & Sons (SEA) Pte Ltd, 37 Jalan Pemimpin #05-04,
Block B, Union Industrial Building, Singapore 2057

Library of Congress Cataloging-in-Publication Data
Williams, H. P.
    Model solving in mathematical programming / H. P. Williams.
        p.   cm.
    Includes bibliographical references and indexes.
    ISBN 0-471-93581-6 (cloth)
    ISBN 0-471-93722-3 (paper)
    1. Programming (Mathematics)   I. Title.
QA402.5.W52   1992
519.7–dc20   92–1648
                                                        CIP

British Library Cataloguing in Publication Data

A catalogue record for this book is available from the British Library

ISBN 0-471-93581-6 (cloth)
ISBN 0-471-93722-3 (paper)

Typeset in 10/12pt Times by
Mathematical Composition Setters Ltd, Salisbury, Wiltshire
Printed and bound in Great Britain by
Biddles Ltd, Guildford and King's Lynn

To

Eileen, Anna, Alexander and Eleanor

Contents

Preface

This book is a sequel to *Model Building in Mathematical Programming* (Williams, 1990a) (subsequently referred to as *MBMP*) although the present text can stand alone. That book was written in the belief that *problems* should come first to be followed by *models* representing them. It did not address the issue of how these models were to be solved, apart from the use of computer packages. This is the aim of this book.

There are a number of possible approaches to writing a book on the mathematics of solving mathematical programming models. Firstly one can write a fairly abstract book on the subject with a rigorous treatment using theorems and proofs. At the opposite extreme one can list a number of computer routines for the standard algorithms written in a real or simplified programming language. Both approaches have their place. In this book, however, I adopt a third, somewhat unconventional, approach falling between the two extremes. My aim is one of *explanation* even if at the expense of mathematical rigour or immediate implementation. I feel understanding must come first, hopefully to be followed later by rigour and implementation. Therefore the methods of mathematical programming are explained through numerical examples solved independently of any computer system. My experience is that this is how the methods are usually *first* understood. Such an approach is, of course, controversial. For example, proofs of the finiteness of algorithms and their complexity are sometimes ignored or left as exercises. Numerical examples do, of course, deal with special cases and can ignore general cases, which need to be dealt with more abstractly. Nevertheless, abstract treatments can often evade the awkward issues that numerical examples may reveal.

The approach here is therefore to use numerical examples together with a commentary on the nature of the methods. The examples are intended to *motivate* the discussion and help with understanding. Also definitions are introduced *in context* rather than formally, again as an aid to understanding. It is also my experience that it is better to treat the same example by different methods rather than to use different examples. The temptation to tailor examples to methods is then avoided. Also the numerical examples (some taken from *MBMP*) are sufficiently small to be solvable by hand. This is deliberate in order to remain independent of any computer system. It is, however, helpful, particularly in the exercises, to make use of computer packages. We do not list these as they are widely available and constantly changing.

In Chapter 1 we discuss the nature of mathematical programming in general terms. Relatively little attention is paid to application areas and formulations as these are widely covered in *MBMP*. We do, however, pay some attention to the underlying algebraic and geometric structures of the different types of model. Also we discuss computer data structures needed for implementing the algorithms as well as the concepts of computational complexity.

The main aim of this book is to describe methods for solving the *general* models of linear programming (LP), separable non-linear programming (NLP) and integer programming (IP). This is done in Chapters 2, 5 and 6 respectively. Also we consider their practical computer implementation in Chapters 4 and 7. The material in Chapter 4 is rather more specialised and may be skipped by those not concerned with questions of numerical analysis. It is sometimes desirable to take account of specialist structures. This is the case in Chapter 3, for network flow models. For IP it is even more the case that account must sometimes be taken of specialist structures. This is done in Chapter 8.

This book is a personal one. Some topics are emphasised here much more than in other texts, while others are given less emphasis. Ideas are explained in ways that the author finds most illuminating. Above all, it is intended that the book be *readable* as well as stimulating questions worthy of further investigation.

The book is aimed at both undergraduate and postgraduate students in mathematics, operational research, business studies and computer science as well as software engineers and consultants who wish to understand the subject. It is recommended (but not necessary) that the book be used in conjunction with *MBMP*.

It is highly recommended that the reader attempts the exercises at the end of each chapter. Those which are more difficult are marked with an asterisk. Also some of the exercises can, with benefit, be done in conjunction with a computer package.

At the end of each chapter there is a short discussion of the origins of the material in the sections with selected references and sometimes indications of future directions of work. These references are deliberately selective. Many workers in the field have not been quoted. By following the references, however, the readers should have indirect access to all work.

Many people have helped in the preparation of this book through suggestions and the reading of part of the manuscript. In particular, I would like to acknowledge the help of Alistair Fitt, Ken McKinnon and Alan Munford. Norman Thomson of IBM helped with the solution to numerical examples using APL, and Vic Baston meticulously read and checked the whole manuscript. I am very grateful to them all. Finally, I would like to thank Diane Taylor of John Wiley & Sons for her help and patience, Anna Anderson, who did the typing, and Alexander Williams, who produced the diagrams.

Paul Williams
Winchester, England
April 1992

Chapter 1
The Nature of Mathematical Programming

In this introductory chapter we describe what a mathematical programme is from both an algebraic and a geometric point of view. We describe the three main types of mathematical programmes (MP), namely linear programmes (LP), non-linear programmes (NLP) and integer programmes (IP), as well as some important special types within these categories.

The purpose of this chapter is primarily to describe problems and concepts in general terms as a basis for the more detailed coverage given in later chapters. Many of the numerical examples are taken from *Model Building in Mathematical Programming* (Williams, 1990a), which will subsequently be referred to simply as *MBMP*.

1.1 LINEAR PROGRAMMING

A linear programme (LP) is a type of mathematical problem of which the following is an example.

Example 1.1 Example of a Linear Programme
Find values of x_1 and x_2 among the real numbers so as to

$$\text{Maximise} \quad 3x_1 + 2x_2 \tag{1.1}$$

subject to

$$x_1 + x_2 \leqslant 4 \tag{1.2}$$

$$2x_1 + x_2 \leqslant 5 \tag{1.3}$$

$$-x_1 + 4x_2 \geqslant 2 \tag{1.4}$$

$$x_1, x_2 \geqslant 0. \tag{1.5}$$

Although we have referred to the above as a "mathematical problem", we will in future usually restrict the term "problem" to the practical context in which it arises and refer to its mathematical form as a "model" or "programme".

All LP models have the following features:

(i) *Variables*, e.g. x_1, x_2, etc., the values of which are to be determined from among the real numbers. In practice we shall assume that all the coefficients are rational numbers. This then allows us also to restrict the values of the variables to rational numbers.

(ii) An *objective function*, e.g. (1.1), whose value is to be *maximised* (in this case) or *minimised*.

(iii) *Constraints*, e.g. (1.2) to (1.5). We have expressions that must be less than or equal to ($\leqslant$), equal to ($=$) or greater than or equal to ($\geqslant$) some given constants. For our example we only have *inequality* ("$\leqslant$" and "$\geqslant$") constraints present. We could equally have had *equations* ("$=$") present.

(iv) The expressions arising in (ii) and (iii) are all *linear*, i.e. they involve sums of coefficients multiplied by variables. Nowhere, in LPs, do we get terms such as x^2, $x_1 x_2$, log x, etc.

For most LPs arising in a practical context, the variables are restricted to be non-negative by constraints such as (1.5). Indeed, non-negativity of the variables is sometimes assumed implicitly. This assumption should, however, be stated explictly in the formulation if necessary, since there are circumstances in which some variables are not so restricted. These are then known as *free variables*.

It should, however, be recognised that linear programming is essentially concerned with *inequality* systems. If there are no inequalities present in the model, i.e. all constraints are equations and all variables are free, then either (a) the objective function can be optimised (maximised or minimised) without limit, or (b) its value is fixed uniquely by the solution of the equations, or (c) there is no solution. Our model then becomes one for which optimisation is inappropriate. We will simply be concerned with the easier problem of solving simultaneous equations.

It is possible to convert any LP model into the *standard form* of a maximisation where all constraints (apart from non-negativity of the variables) are of the "$\leqslant$" form and all variables are non-negative. In order to do this we can:

(i) Convert a minimisation to maximising the negated objective function.

(ii) Convert "$\geqslant$" constraints to "$\leqslant$" by negating both sides.

(iii) Convert "$=$" constraints to a "$\leqslant$" and a "$\geqslant$" and apply (ii) to the resulting "$\geqslant$" constraint.

(iv) Represent a free variable as the difference of two non-negative variables.

This standard form is of theoretical, rather than practical, value. It makes it easier to prove and understand certain fundamental results. On the other hand, for computational purposes, there is no value in converting to this form. For example, a free variable is a simpler entity to process than a non-negative variable.

Some of the history of how this type of mathematical model arose, and came to be studied, is discussed in section 1.8. The use of the name "programming" should, however, be explained now since there is widespread confusion between its use in this context and in computer programming. Within mathematical programming, and linear programming in particular, "programming" means "planning". One of the first applications of an LP was to planning in the American Air Force. Here, planning was referred to as "programming" and the first phrase to be applied to the LP type of model and its associated methods of solution was "programming within a linear structure". This cumbersome phrase got truncated to "linear programming". The term "mathematical programming" (MP) became applied to the extensions and modifications of LPs resulting from changing some of the features (i) to (iv). There is, of course, a close relationship between MP and computers arising from the need to solve the models, but this relationship should not cause the use of the term "programming" to be misunderstood.

A Geometrical Interpretation

Although the nature of LP has been described above *algebraically*, it is also very informative to describe this type of model *geometrically*. In order to do this, we let the values of the variables represent the coordinates of points in space. For a model with n variables, we need to consider space of n dimensions. Fortunately, our example above only has two variables x_1 and x_2. Therefore, we can represent this model in the two-dimensional plane as is done in Figure 1.1.

Since constraints (1.5) hold, we are only concerned with points in the positive quadrant shown. Constraint (1.2) restricts us to points on AB (or its extension) or below. Similarly, constraints (1.3) and (1.4) restrict us to points below BC, on BC or on CD or above respectively. Taken together we are restricted to points within the region ABCD known as the *feasible region*. The coordinates of any point within this region give a *feasible solution*, i.e. one that satisfies all the constraints (1.2) to (1.5).

If there had been an equality constraint present, this would have restricted us to points on the line corresponding to the equation, effectively taking the feasible region into a space of one lower dimension.

This example demonstrates a model with an infinite number of feasible solutions. From among these solutions we wish to find those which maximise the objective function (1.1). If we set $3x_1 + 2x_2$ equal to some trial value of (say) 10, then the points giving rise to this trial value can be seen to lie on the line

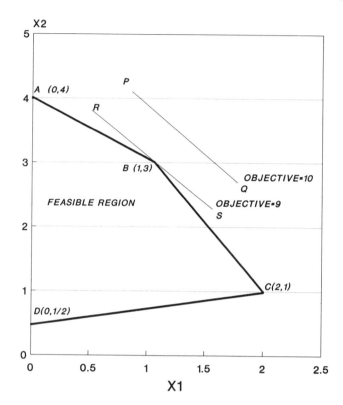

Figure 1.1 Geometric representation of a linear programme

PQ. Clearly there are no points in common with the feasible region, demonstrating that the value of 10 is unattainable. Setting the objective to other values gives other lines parallel to PQ. The higher the value, the higher the line. Therefore, the maximum such value that can arise from a feasible solution corresponds to the highest such line that intersects the feasible region. In this case, this line is RS, which intersects the feasible region at B. B has coordinates $x_1 = 1$ and $x_2 = 3$, giving the (unique) optimal solution with objective value 9.

This somewhat elementary and simple example has been discussed in order to exemplify more general properties of LPs. In practice, of course, LPs would have many more than two variables (often tens of thousands of variables) and would not, therefore, be representable in a visible geometric form. For a model with n variables, this corresponding feasible region will be a *polytope* in n or less dimensions.

This will be bounded by *facets* of one less dimension than the polytope. Different values of the objective function give rise to spaces (*hyperplanes*) of dimension $n - 1$. Typically the optimal solution lies at one of the vertices of the polytope where the objective hyperplane just intersects the polytope. Hence, with LP models we are usually concerned with looking for vertices of polytopes. We illustrate the situation for three dimensions by another example.

Example 1.2 A Geometrical Representation of an LP

$$\text{Maximise} \quad -4x_1 + 5x_2 + 3x_3 \qquad (1.6)$$

subject to

$$-x_1 + x_2 - x_3 \leqslant 2 \qquad (1.7)$$

$$x_1 + x_2 + 2x_3 \leqslant 3 \qquad (1.8)$$

$$x_1, x_2, x_3 \geqslant 0. \qquad (1.9)$$

Figure 1.2 illustrates this model. The feasible region, defined by the

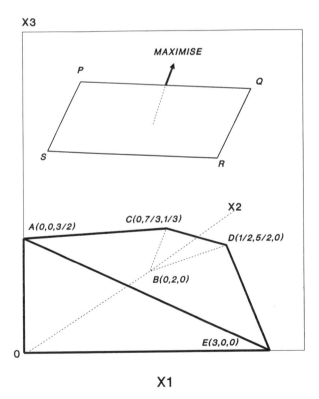

Figure 1.2 Geometric representation of a three-variable linear programme

constraints (1.7) to (1.9), is a three-dimensional solid OABCDE bounded by two-dimensional facets OACB, OAE, OBDE, BCD and ACDE. Different values of the objective (1.6) give planes parallel to PQRS. The optimal solution arises from vertex C, giving $x_1 = 0$, $x_2 = 7/3$, $x_3 = 1/3$ and objective value $38/3$.

Different Types of LP Model

Although Examples 1.1 and 1.2 illustrate typical models where there is a unique optimal solution arising from a vertex of a closed polytope, we should be aware of the possibility of other situations. Satisfactory methods of solving LPs should be able to deal with all such eventualities. These will also be illustrated by numerical examples.

There may be alternative optimal solutions

If, in Example 1.1, the objective function were

$$\text{Maximise} \quad 4x_1 + 2x_2 \tag{1.10}$$

then, from Figure 1.1, we can see that the coordinates of any point in the line BC give equally good optimal objective values of 10. It is important to note, however, that among these alternative optimal solutions are the *vertex solutions* at B ($x_1 = 1$, $x_2 = 3$) and C ($x_1 = 2$, $x_2 = 1$).

Similarly, in Example 1.2, an objective function:

$$\text{Maximise} \quad -4x_1 + 4x_2 - 4x_3 \tag{1.11}$$

allows any point in Figure 2 on the facet BCD to provide an optimal solution of value 8. *Vertex* optimal solutions are provided by B ($x_1 = 0$, $x_2 = 2$, $x_3 = 0$), C ($x_1 = 0$, $x_2 = 7/3$, $x_3 = 1/3$) and D ($x_1 = 1/2$, $x_2 = 5/2$, $x_3 = 0$).

The polytope representing the feasible region may be open

This situation is illustrated by an example.

Example 1.3 An LP With an Open Feasible Region

$$\text{Maximise} \quad x_1 - x_2 \tag{1.12}$$

subject to

$$x_1 + 2x_2 \geqslant 5 \tag{1.13}$$

$$2x_1 - x_2 \leqslant 2 \tag{1.14}$$

$$x_1, x_2 \geqslant 0. \tag{1.15}$$

Figure 1.3 illustrates the model.

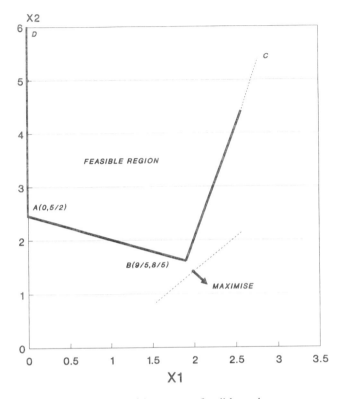

Figure 1.3 A linear programme with an open feasible region

When a polytope (in any number of dimensions) is closed, we will sometimes refer to it as a *polyhedron*. The name "polytope" will be applied to both situations.

In this example the optimal solution lies at B, giving $x_1 = 9/5$ and $x_2 = 8/5$ with an objective value of $1/5$.

If, however, our objective had been (say)

$$\text{Maximise} \quad 3x_1 - x_2 \tag{1.16}$$

then it is easy to see that this can be increased without limit. The solution at B ($x_1 = 9/5$, $x_2 = 8/5$) gives an objective value of $19/5$ but (non-vertex) solutions going up the line BC give increasing values for the objective. In such a situation the LP is said to be *unbounded* as the objective has no (finite) maximal value.

For open polytopes, such as that in Figure 1.3, when optimising an objective, we are not always only interested in vertices (A and B) but we may also be interested in *extreme rays* (the lines BC and AD). If the model has a finite optimal solution, then one such solution may be found from the vertices. On the other hand, we must examine solutions on the extreme rays to investigate the possibility of the model being unbounded.

Instead of a polytope being defined by a set of constraints, it can also be defined by its sets of vertices and extreme rays. Extreme rays will (in any number of dimensions) generally be *half-lines* starting at a vertex but having no terminal point in the other direction. There are, however, circumstances in which a polytope has no vertices. Then extreme rays may not exist or, if they do, they will have no terminal points. This is illustrated by the next discussion.

The polytope representing the feasible region may have no vertices

This situation is again illustrated by an example.

Example 1.4 An LP With No Vertex Solutions

$$\text{Maximise} \quad -4x_1 + 5x_2 + 3x_3 \tag{1.17}$$

subject to

$$-x_1 + x_2 - x_3 \leqslant 2 \tag{1.18}$$

$$x_1 + x_2 + 2x_3 \leqslant 3. \tag{1.19}$$

This example appears very like Example 1.2 but the non-negativity constraints (1.9) have been omitted. Therefore the facets OACB, OAE and OBDE in Figure 1.2 will not be present and edge CD can be extended without limit in both directions. The resultant polytope will therefore be the wedge shape illustrated in Figure 1.4.

This polytope has no vertices but CD (extended in both directions) provides an extreme ray. The associated LP, with the objective (1.17), is unbounded since we can make the objective value as large as we like by choosing the coordinates of points on CD in the direction of C. The only way in which an LP associated with a polytope, such as that in Figure 1.4, can have a finite optimal solution is if the objective hyperplane is parallel to the extreme ray. If, for example, the objective were

$$\text{Maximise} \quad -2x_1 + 4x_2 - x_3 \tag{1.20}$$

then it can be verified that the coordinates of any point on the line CD give the maximal objective value of 9.

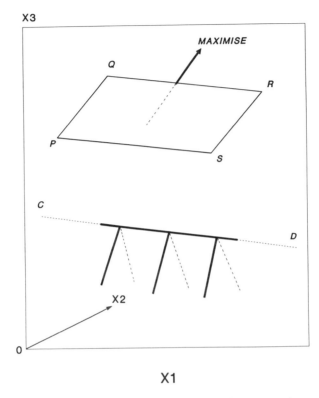

Figure 1.4 A linear programme whose feasible region has no vertices

A polytope that has a vertex (unlike Example 1.4) is known as *pointed*. Notice that if all variables in an LP are restricted to be non-negative, then the associated polytope must be pointed.

It may be the case that a polytope has no vertices, or extreme rays either, as illustrated by the next example involving a single constraint.

Example 1.5   *A Polytope With No Vertices or Extreme Rays*

$$x_1 + x_2 + 2x_3 \leqslant 3. \tag{1.21}$$

Here we have left out the first constraint of Example 1.4. The feasible region is now the *half-space* below the plane ACDE in Figure 1.5. Plane ACDE stretches to infinity in all directions on its surface. A, C, D and E are marked in order to define the plane.

The only objectives that would provide a finite maximal solution with

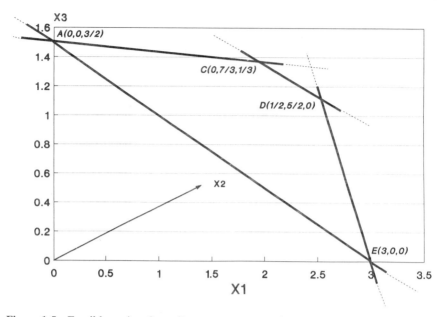

Figure 1.5 Feasible region for a linear programme with no vertices or extreme rays

constraint (1.21) are parallel to ACDE, such as

$$\text{Maximise} \quad 3x_1 + 3x_2 + 6x_3. \qquad (1.21a)$$

Any point on ACDE gives the maximal objective value of 9.

In all the previous examples the optimal solutions, so long as the model is not unbounded, lie on the boundary of the feasible region. It should be pointed out that even this property is not necessary, as is demonstrated by the following (somewhat pathological) example.

Example 1.6 An LP With Interior Optimal Solutions

$$\text{Maximise} \quad 0x_1 + 0x_2 \qquad (1.22)$$

subject to

$$x_1 + x_2 \leqslant 4 \qquad (1.23)$$

$$2x_1 + x_2 \leqslant 5 \qquad (1.24)$$

$$-x_1 + 4x_2 \geqslant 2 \qquad (1.25)$$

$$x_1, x_2 \geqslant 0. \qquad (1.26)$$

The constraints are the same as those of Example 1.1 illustrated in Figure 1.1 but the coordinates of any point in the feasible region (not just those on the boundary) provide optimal objective values of 0.

An LP model may have no feasible solution

Example 1.7 An LP With No Feasible Solution
The constraints are

$$x_1 + 2x_2 \leqslant 3 \tag{1.27}$$

$$x_1 + x_2 \geqslant 4 \tag{1.28}$$

$$x_1, x_2 \geqslant 0. \tag{1.29}$$

No values can be found for x_1 and x_2 that satisfy (1.27) to (1.29) simultaneously. If we were to attempt to draw the feasible region corresponding to these constraints it would be found to be empty. Notice that the objective function is irrelevant in these circumstances since there is no feasible solution, let alone an optimal one.

LP models may therefore take one of the following forms. They may be *unbounded* or *infeasible*, otherwise they are said to be *soluble*, i.e. they possess one, or more, feasible solutions giving a finite optimal objective value. When an LP is soluble, we may be sure that, among its (possibly more than one) optimal solutions, there will be some on the boundary of the feasible region. Therefore, we may normally restrict our attention to such *extreme solutions* in the knowledge that we will find an optimal solution if the model is soluble. Indeed, we often assume the existence of vertex solutions and restrict our attention to them, since, if the model is soluble, and the corresponding polytope is pointed, then there will be a *vertex optimal solution*.

1.2 NON-LINEAR PROGRAMMING

An MP model is said to be non-linear if non-linear expressions appear in the objective or the constraints, or both. The following is an example resulting from a modification of the feasible region of Example 1.1.

Example 1.8 A Non-Linear Programme

$$\text{Maximise} \quad 2x_1 + 3x_2 \tag{1.30}$$

subject to:

$$6x_1 + x_2^2 - x_2 \leqslant 12 \qquad (1.31)$$

$$-x_1 + 4x_2 \geqslant 2 \qquad (1.32)$$

$$x_1, x_2 \geqslant 0. \qquad (1.33)$$

Figure 1.6 illustrates this model. Analysis of this model would demonstrate that the optimal solution is given by the coordinates of A where $x_1 = 0$ and $x_2 = 4$, giving an objective value of 12.

The important point to notice is that the optimal solution occurs when the objective contour PQ just touches the feasible region. In methods described in Chapter 6, we will approximate non-linear functions by *piecewise-linear* functions. That is, we will approximate a curve, such as AC in Figure 1.6, by a series of straight lines, such as ABC in Figure 1.1. This procedure can obviously create some inaccuracy, but the approximation by straight lines can be made as close as we like.

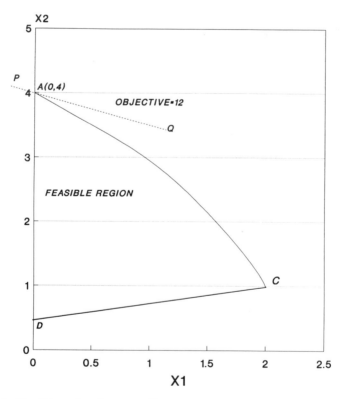

Figure 1.6 Feasible region for a non-linear programme

Convex and Non-Convex Models

Example 1.9, however, illustrates a situation where this procedure cannot be guaranteed to work.

Example 1.9 A Non-Convex Non-Linear Programme

$$\text{Maximise} \quad 2x_1 + 3x_2 \tag{1.34}$$

subject to

$$-x_1 + 4x_2 \geqslant 2 \tag{1.35}$$

$$5x_1^3 - 14x_1^2 + 11x_1 + 2x_2 \leqslant 8 \tag{1.36}$$

$$4x_1 - 4x_2^2 + 20x_2 \leqslant 29 \tag{1.37}$$

$$x_1, x_2 \geqslant 0. \tag{1.38}$$

This is illustrated by Figure 1.7. Some solution methods would again

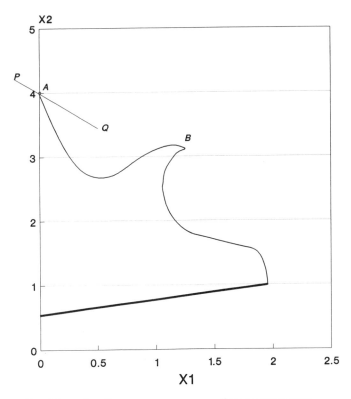

Figure 1.7 Feasible region for a non-convex non-linear programme

result in the solution at A giving an objective value of 12. There is, however, a better solution at B where $x_1 = 1.41$ and $x_2 = 3.16$, giving an objective value of 12.29. The difficulty arises because the feasible region in Figure 1.7 is *non-convex*.

A region (in any number of dimensions) is said to be *convex* if the line joining any two points within the region lies entirely within it. By this criterion the feasible region of Figure 1.6 is convex but that of Figure 1.7 is not. Figure 1.8 illustrates when a region is non-convex.

Notice that in Figure 1.7 in particular PQ would re-enter the feasible region if extended beyond Q. It is often very difficult to distinguish between convexity and non-convexity.

The difficulty arises because while, *locally* in the region of A, in Figure 1.7, A appears optimal, looked at *globally* B can be seen to provide a better solution. A would be known as a *local optimum* (i.e. only optimal for a part of the feasible region), while B would be said to be a *global optimum*.

Even if the feasible region is convex, if the objective function is non-linear, local optima can still result. This is demonstrated by the following example.

Example 1.10 A Non-Linear Programme With Local Optima

$$\text{Maximise} \quad 4x_1^3 - 3x_1 + 6x_2 \quad (1.39)$$

subject to

$$x_1 + x_2 \leqslant 4 \quad (1.40)$$

$$2x_1 + x_2 \leqslant 5 \quad (1.41)$$

$$-x_1 + 4x_2 \geqslant 2 \quad (1.42)$$

$$x_1, x_2 \geqslant 0. \quad (1.43)$$

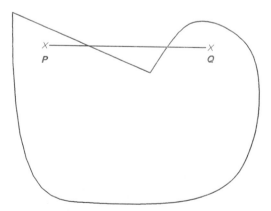

Figure 1.8 A non-convex region

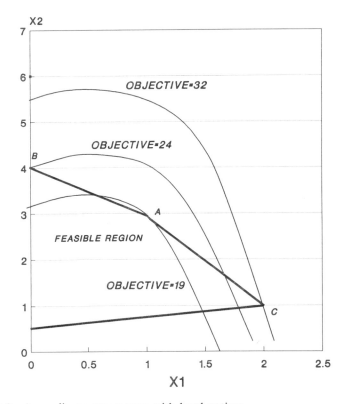

Figure 1.9 A non-linear programme with local optima

Different values of the objective function (1.39) give rise to the curved contours shown in Figure 1.9. A and B both give rise to local optima. The global optimum is at C.

On the other hand, the following example can be guaranteed to produce a global optimum.

Example 1.11 A Non-Linear Programme With One (Global) Optimum

$$\text{Maximise} \quad -x_1^2 + 4x_1 + 2x_2 \qquad (1.44)$$

subject to

$$x_1 + x_2 \leqslant 4 \qquad (1.45)$$

$$2x_1 + x_2 \leqslant 5 \qquad (1.46)$$

$$-x_1 + 4x_2 \geqslant 2 \qquad (1.47)$$

$$x_1, x_2 \geqslant 0. \qquad (1.48)$$

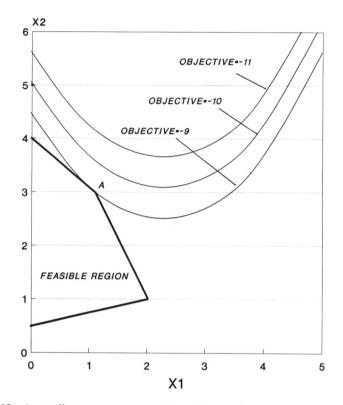

Figure 1.10 A non-linear programme with a global optimum

In Figure 1.10 the objective contours "curve away" from the feasible region, demonstrating that A provides the *global* optimal solution.

If treated as a minimisation, the objective function in Example 1.10 would be

$$\text{Minimise} \quad x_1^2 - 4x_1 - 2x_2 \tag{1.49}$$

This function is said to be *convex*. A *function* (as opposed to a region) is said to be convex if the region above the surface which it defines is a convex set. Figure 1.11 illustrates this for the objective function (1.49).

A *mathematical programme* such as Example 1.11 is then said to be convex if it is equivalent to *minimising a convex function over a convex set*. Convex programming models can be guaranteed to produce globally optimal solutions (to some degree of approximation) when we make piecewise-linear approximations to the non-linear functions if we use methods based on a local search.

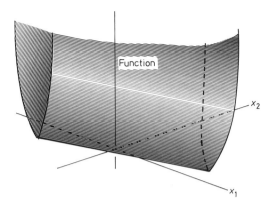

Figure 1.11 A convex function

Although we do not cover calculus-based methods for non-linear programming in this book, we should remark that they all use local search methods. Hence they can only be guaranteed to produce locally optimal solutions to non-convex models.

The reader should verify that if the objective function (1.39) in Example 1.10 were converted to a minimisation, it represents a non-convex function by drawing the appropriate surface. To produce globally optimal solutions to non-convex programming models requires methods based on *integer programming* (IP). This topic will therefore be discussed again in section 1.3 and methods described in section 7.3.

A further example of a non-linear programming model is given below to illustrate that the optimal solution may not even lie on the boundary

Example 1.12 A Non-Linear Programme With an Interior Optimal Solution

$$\text{Maximise} \quad -8x_1^2 - 16x_2^2 + 24x_1 + 56x_2 \quad (1.50)$$

subject to

$$x_1 + x_2 \leqslant 4 \quad (1.51)$$

$$2x_1 + x_2 \leqslant 5 \quad (1.52)$$

$$-x_1 + 4x_2 \geqslant 2 \quad (1.53)$$

$$x_1, x_2 \geqslant 0. \quad (1.54)$$

This is illustrated in Figure 1.12. The objective contours are as shown, demonstrating that the unique optimal solution does not lie on the boundary (in contrast to LP). It is at $x_1 = 1.5$ and $x_2 = 1.75$, giving an objective value of 67.

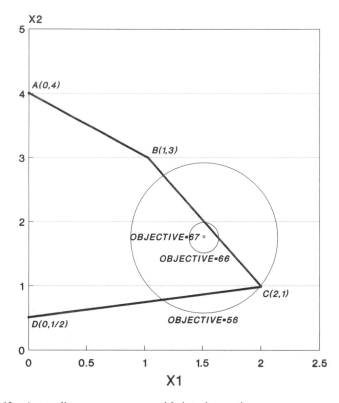

Figure 1.12 A non-linear programme with interior optimum

It should be remarked that LP models can be regarded as a special case of convex programming models. The feasible regions will always be convex, as will the (linear) objective functions. Therefore, the important distinction could be said to be between *convex* (including LP and some non-LP models) and *non-convex* models, instead of between LP and non-LP models. LP methods can be used to produce (global) optimal solutions to the former, but IP methods are needed for the latter.

1.3 INTEGER PROGRAMMING

An integer programming (IP) model superficially looks like an LP model except for the fact that all, or some, of the variables are restricted to take *integer* values. In the former case the model is said to be a *pure* integer programming (PIP) model and in the latter case a *mixed* integer programming (MIP) model.

The optimal solution to an IP may bear little relation to the optimal solution to the corresponding LP, as is demonstrated by Example 1.13. We refer to the LP corresponding to an IP as the *LP relaxation* since we have "relaxed" the integer variables allowing them to take continuous values.

Example 1.13 A Pure Integer Programme

$$\text{Maximise} \quad x_1 + x_2 \tag{1.55}$$

subject to

$$10x_1 - 8x_2 \leqslant 13 \tag{1.56}$$

$$2x_1 - 2x_2 \geqslant 1 \tag{1.57}$$

$$x_1, x_2 \geqslant 0 \quad \text{and integer.} \tag{1.58}$$

This is clearly an example of a PIP model and is illustrated by Figure 1.13. The triangle ABC represents the feasible region of the LP relaxation,

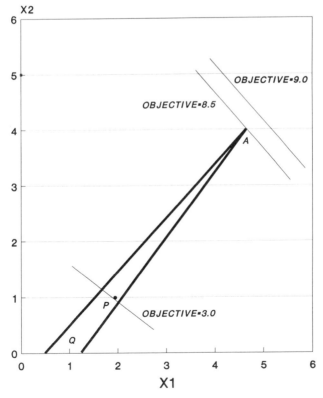

Figure 1.13 Geometric representation of an integer programme and its linear programming relaxation

demonstrating that the optimal solution to this LP is given by A where $x_1 = 4.5$ and $x_2 = 4$, giving an objective value of 8.5.

The optimal solution to the IP is, however, given by P where $x_1 = 2$ and $x_2 = 1$, giving an objective value of 3. The solution clearly cannot be derived from that above by any simple procedure such as rounding to the nearest integer.

In general, the set of feasible solutions to an IP will no longer be a single region as with an LP but will be a disconnected set. In the PIP case it will be the lattice of points with integer coordinates within the LP feasible region. For the MIP case it will be a set of regions defined by integer coordinates in some directions. Figure 1.13 demonstrates that the feasible solutions to Example 1.13 are given by the two points P $(2, 1)$ and Q $(1, 0)$. This illustrates two important differences from LP:

 (i) The set of *feasible solutions* to an IP is *disconnected*.
(ii) There may be *no solutions* to an IP *on the boundary* of the feasible region of the LP relaxation.

These two features sometimes cause IP to be classed as a special case of non-convex programming. The feasible region is seriously non-convex insofar as it is disconnected.

Linear IP does, however, have so many special features that it is useful to distinguish it from general non-convex programming, although we do discuss the connection further, in section 5.3, in relation to IP providing a satisfactory means of globally optimising non-convex models.

The *discrete* nature of the solution set of an IP sometimes causes the name *discrete programming* to be used in place of IP. In some ways, this is a better name. For many aplications it is the discrete nature of the problem that we are trying to capture. Integer variables are used only as a means to this end.

Zero−One Programming

The majority of practical applications of IP restrict the integer variables to the two values 0 and 1, giving rise to the name *0−1 programming*. Example 1.14 gives a small *mixed* 0−1 IP model.

Example 1.14 A Mixed 0−1 Integer Programme

$$\text{Maximise} \quad 2x_1 + x_2 \tag{1.59}$$

subject to

$$x_1 + x_2 + 5\delta_1 \leqslant 9 \qquad (1.60)$$

$$x_2 + \delta_1 \leqslant 4 \qquad (1.61)$$

$$-x_1 + x_2 + 4\delta_2 \leqslant 4 \qquad (1.62)$$

$$3x_1 - x_2 + 7\delta_2 \leqslant 15 \qquad (1.63)$$

$$x_2 + 3\delta_3 \leqslant 4 \qquad (1.64)$$

$$x_1 \leqslant 5 \qquad (1.65)$$

$$\delta_1 + \delta_2 + \delta_3 \geqslant 1 \qquad (1.66)$$

$$x_1, x_2, \delta_1, \delta_2, \delta_3 \geqslant 0 \qquad (1.67)$$

$$\delta_1, \delta_2, \delta_3 \leqslant 1 \quad \text{and integer.} \qquad (1.68)$$

This is taken from *MBMP* as a model with a non-convex region in the space of x_1 and x_2.

It is common to represent 0–1 variables by means of the Greek letter "δ". By giving the (non-negative) δ variables upper bounds of 1 and restricting them to integer values, we obviously restrict them to be 0 or 1.

Applications of MP and IP in particular are discussed at considerable length in *MBMP* and are not the main subject of this book, although they are briefly covered in section 1.4. It is, however, worth remarking on the nature of Example 1.14 since the *structure* of IP models can be very important in determining solution procedures. Constraint (1.66) forces at least one of δ_1, δ_2 or δ_3 to take the value 1. The effect of this, combined with the other constraints, is to force the values of x_1 and x_2 to be the coordinates of points in the feasible region shown in Figure 1.14.

This *non-convex* feasible region has been split into three discrete components by means of δ_1, δ_2 and δ_3 respectively. If we could have represented the model in the five dimensions of x_1, x_2, δ_1, δ_2 and δ_3 then we would have had three disconnected regions.

Another term is worth introducing here. If we consider each of the convex components of ABCDEFGO separately, we have the *disjunction* (i.e. involving the "or" relation):

$$x_2 \leqslant 3 \qquad (1.69)$$

$$x_1 + x_2 \leqslant 4 \qquad (1.70)$$

or

$$-x_1 + x_2 \leqslant 0 \qquad (1.71)$$

$$3x_1 - x_2 \leqslant 8 \qquad (1.72)$$

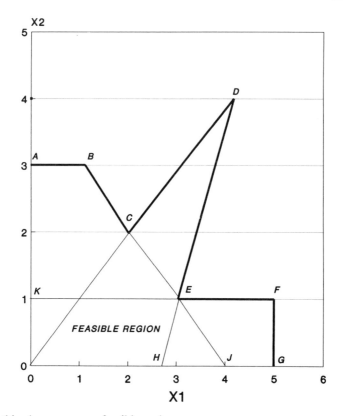

Figure 1.14 A non-convex feasible region

or

$$x_2 \leqslant 1 \tag{1.73}$$

$$x_1 \leqslant 5 \tag{1.74}$$

together with

$$x_1, x_2 \geqslant 0. \tag{1.75}$$

LP can only deal with a *conjunction* (i.e. involving only the "and" relation) of constraints in continuous variables. The discrete stipulation of this disjunction has been modelled by extra *integer* variables in order to create a conjunction of constraints.

A further example is given in order to demonstrate the discrete nature of IP applications.

Example 1.15 A Fixed-Charge Integer Programme

$$\text{Maximise} \quad 12x_1 + 4x_2 + 3x_3 - 4\delta_1 - 5\delta_2 - 16\delta_3 \qquad (1.76)$$

subject to

$$2x_1 + 3x_2 - 7\delta_1 \leqslant 0 \qquad (1.77)$$

$$x_2 + 4x_3 - 8\delta_2 \leqslant 0 \qquad (1.78)$$

$$3x_1 + x_3 - 5\delta_3 \leqslant 0 \qquad (1.79)$$

$$x_1, x_2, x_3 \geqslant 0 \qquad \delta_1, \delta_2, \delta_3 \in \{0, 1\}. \qquad (1.80)$$

Such a model could arise from a *discontinuous* (a serious case of non-linearity) objective function in an otherwise LP model. The objective would arise if there were *fixed charges* associated with certain activities giving

$$\text{Maximise} \quad 12x_1 + 4x_2 + 3x_3 - F_1 - F_2 - F_3 \qquad (1.81)$$

where

$$F_1 = 4 \quad \text{if } x_1 \text{ or } x_2 \text{ (or both)} > 0 \qquad (1.82)$$

$$F_2 = 5 \quad \text{if } x_2 \text{ or } x_3 \text{ (or both)} > 0 \qquad (1.83)$$

$$F_3 = 16 \quad \text{if } x_1 \text{ or } x_3 \text{ (or both)} > 0 \qquad (1.84)$$

otherwise the corresponding F_i are 0.

A typical overall cost function related to the first activity would then be given by Figure 1.15.

Such a situation cannot be modelled by LP. The use of 0–1 variables is needed to distinguish between the absence or presence of an activity (however small). Notice that this cost function is non-convex (and discontinuous).

Sometimes there are alternative approaches to the explicit use of integer variables in a number of important applications. Nevertheless the methods used to solve such models can all be regarded as IP methods. Hence the expression "IP" will be used to cover such models. For example, we could have referred to the stipulation of the conditions of Example 1.14 in the form of contraints (1.69) to (1.75) as a *disjunctive programme* and tackled the model as such.

Special Ordered Sets of Variables

An alternative formulation of Example 1.14 is given below.

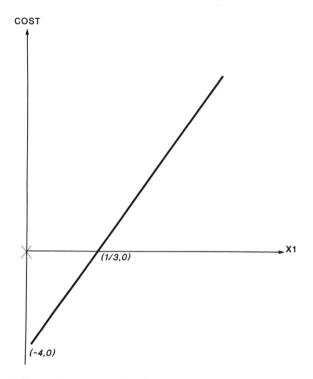

Figure 1.15 A discontinuous cost function

Example 1.16 Alternative Formulation for an MIP

$$\text{Maximise} \quad 2x_1 + x_2 \tag{1.85}$$

subject to

$$\lambda_B + 2\lambda_C + 4\lambda_D + 3\lambda_E + 5\lambda_F + 5\lambda_G - x_1 = 0 \tag{1.86}$$

$$3\lambda_A + 3\lambda_B + 2\lambda_C + 4\lambda_D + \lambda_E + \lambda_F - x_2 = 0 \tag{1.87}$$

$$\lambda_A + \lambda_B + \lambda_C + \lambda_D + \lambda_E + \lambda_F + \lambda_G \leqslant 1 \tag{1.88}$$

$$\lambda_A, \lambda_B, \lambda_C, \lambda_D, \lambda_E, \lambda_F, \lambda_G, x_1, x_1, x_2 \geqslant 0 \tag{1.89}$$

$$\text{at most two adjacent } \lambda_i \text{ can be non-zero.} \tag{1.90}$$

In order to understand this formulation we refer to Figure 1.14. The λ_i variables are interpreted as "weights" to be attached to the vertices $A, B, ..., G$. Condition (1.90), in conjunction with constraints (1.86) to (1.89), forces the values of x_1 and x_2 to be the coordinates of points within one of the triangles OAB, OBC, ODE, etc.

It is possible to deal with the condition (1.90) by introducing 0–1 variables as is demonstrated in *MBMP*. Alternatively the condition can be dealt with algorithmically as is described in section 7.3. A set of (continuous) variables such as $\{\lambda_A, \lambda_B, ..., \lambda_G\}$, together with the stipulation (1.90), is known as a *special ordered set of type 2* (SOS2). Similarly a set of variables $\{x_1, x_2, ..., x_n\}$ with a condition

$$\text{at most one of } \{x_1, x_2, ..., x_n\} \text{ can be non-zero} \qquad (1.91)$$

is known as a *special ordered set of type 1* (SOS1). Condition (1.91) can also be dealt with algorithmically through the methods of IP rather than introducing 0–1 variables to represent it.

It is convenient to refer to integer variables and SOS1 and SOS2 sets collectively as *discrete entities*.

SOS1 sets commonly arise when we wish to stipulate that exactly one of a set of variables is 1. As an alternative to making the variables 0–1 integers, we can simply say they belong to an SOS1 set and specify the constraint

$$x_1 + x_2 + \cdots + x_n = 1. \qquad (1.92)$$

SOS2 sets usually arise in NLP when making a piecewise-linear formulation of a non-linear function. If, in Figure 1.14, we had wished to restrict x_1 and x_2 to points on the line ABCDEFG, then we could have stipulated equations (1.86) and (1.87) together with condition (1.90) and the constraint

$$\lambda_A + \lambda_B + \lambda_C + \lambda_D + \lambda_E + \lambda_F + \lambda_G = 1. \qquad (1.93)$$

It is sometimes helpful to regard an SOS1 set as a generalisation of a 0–1 variable. Instead of a general integer variable as a generalisation, the expression

$$a_1 x_1 + a_2 x_2 + \cdots + a_n x_n \qquad (1.94)$$

is a broader generalisation, which can take one of the $n + 1$ discrete values $0, a_1, a_2, ..., a_n$ if the x_i are 0–1 variables and form an SOS1 set.

Combinatorial Optimisation

Another way of viewing IP models is to consider them as formulations of *combinatorial optimisation* problems. Combinatorial optimisation problems are concerned with the assignment or ordering of discrete objects. Frequently, although not always, there are a finite number of such objects. Nevertheless this number may be very large, making it impracticable to "try every possibility". IP constraints provide a way of modelling many such problems. Even when not so modelled, the methods of IP are applicable. Even when there is no obvious objective, optimisation may provide a means of directing the combinatorial seach for solutions purposefully. Hence it is valuable to regard the subject of combinatorial optimisation within IP. In section 1.4 we list some examples of combinatorial problems that can be treated through IP models. The modelling and applicability aspect is covered more fully in *MBMP*.

It should, however, be pointed out that the apparent similarity between a combinatorial problem formulated as an IP and the LP relaxation can be deceptive. Combinatorial problems can be very difficult to solve, unlike LP models. There are important exceptions, particularly regarding some combinatorial problems involving graphs and networks. These are discussed in sections 1.5, 3.1, 3.2, 3.3 and 8.3.

Further Considerations

In all the examples considered in this section the integer variables have been restricted to a *finite* set of values. Frequently they have been restricted to the values 0 or 1. It is pointed out by the next example that this need not necessarily be the case.

Example 1.17 An IP With an Infinite Set of Feasible Solutions

$$\text{Maximise} \quad x_1 - x_2 \tag{1.95}$$

subject to

$$x_1 + 2x_2 \geqslant 5 \tag{1.96}$$

$$2x_1 - x_2 \leqslant 2 \tag{1.97}$$

$$x_1, x_2 \geqslant 0 \quad \text{and integer.} \tag{1.98}$$

The LP relaxation of this example is Example 1.3 illustrated in Figure 1.3. Here x_1 and x_2 are not restricted to a finite range of values. For certain solution methods discussed in Chapter 6, it is necessary to restrict the integer variables to finite ranges. A model in the form of Example 1.17 would not be amenable to solution unless remodelled. An indication of one of the difficulties that might arise is given by the following example.

Example 1.18 An Infeasible IP With an Unbounded LP Relaxation

$$\text{Maximise} \quad x_2 \tag{1.99}$$

subject to

$$6x_1 - 9x_2 \leqslant 14 \tag{1.100}$$

$$4x_1 - 6x_2 \geqslant 9 \tag{1.101}$$

$$x_1, x_2 \geqslant 0 \quad \text{and integer.} \tag{1.102}$$

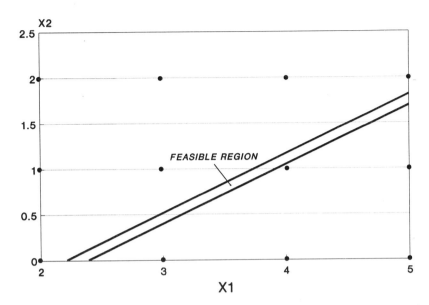

Figure 1.16 An infeasible integer programme with an unbounded linear programming relaxation

Figure 1.16 demonstrates that the associated LP relaxation is unbounded but that the IP is infeasible. It may be impossible to detect this using some solution methods, particularly if no geometric intuition is possible.

If all the integer variables in a model are restricted to a finite range (as is usually the case in practice), then it is possible to convert the model into a form in which all variables are 0–1. Suppose we have

$$0 \leqslant x \leqslant u. \tag{1.103}$$

We may replace x by the expression

$$x_0 + 2x_1 + 4x_2 + \cdots + 2^{\lfloor \log_2 u \rfloor} x_{\lfloor \log_2 u \rfloor + 1} \tag{1.104}$$

where $\lfloor \log_2 u \rfloor$ stands for "the next integer less than or equal to $\log_2 u$". This "binary" expansion might be worth while if a specialist solution method restricted to 0–1 IPs were to be used.

Pure 0–1 IP models occur in a number of applications. The following example is an illustration.

Example 1.19 A Set-Covering Integer Programme

$$\text{Minimise} \quad \delta_1 + \delta_2 + \delta_3 + \delta_4 + \delta_5 + \delta_6 \tag{1.105}$$

subject to

$$\delta_1 + \delta_2 + \delta_5 \geqslant 1 \qquad (1.106)$$

$$\delta_1 + \delta_3 + \delta_6 \geqslant 1 \qquad (1.107)$$

$$\delta_1 + \delta_2 + \delta_4 \geqslant 1 \qquad (1.108)$$

$$\delta_2 + \delta_3 + \delta_5 \geqslant 1 \qquad (1.109)$$

$$\delta_2 + \delta_3 + \delta_6 \geqslant 1 \qquad (1.110)$$

$$\delta_1, \delta_2, ..., \delta_6 \in \{0, 1\}. \qquad (1.111)$$

This model clearly has a special structure, which is discussed in *MBMP*. It is an example of a *set-covering* model. Superficially one might suppose that the LP relaxation would provide an integer optimal solution. This is, in fact, not the case. The optimal solution to the LP relaxation is

$$\delta_1 = \delta_2 = \delta_3 = 1/2 \qquad \delta_4 = \delta_5 = \delta_6 = 0 \qquad \text{objective} = 3/2 \quad (1.112)$$

whereas an optimal solution to the IP is

$$\delta_1 = 1, \quad \delta_2 = 0, \quad \delta_3 = 1 \qquad \delta_4 = \delta_5 = \delta_6 = 0 \qquad \text{objective} = 2. \quad (1.113)$$

IP models that do have the property of yielding integer optimal solutions to the LP relaxation are discussed in sections 1.5, 3.1, 3.2, 3.3 and 6.1.

Before concluding this section we return to the relationship between IP and LP. Although the feasible region associated with an IP will be disconnected, there is virtue in considering the *convex hull* of feasible solutions to an IP. This is the *smallest* convex set containing the feasible solutions and is illustrated by an example.

Example 1.20 The Convex Hull of an IP

$$\text{Maximise} \quad x_1 + x_2 \qquad (1.114)$$

subject to

$$2x_1 + 2x_2 \geqslant 3 \qquad (1.115)$$

$$2x_1 - 2x_2 \leqslant 3 \qquad (1.116)$$

$$2x_1 + 4x_2 \leqslant 19 \qquad (1.117)$$

$$x_1, x_2 \geqslant 0 \quad \text{and integer.} \qquad (1.118)$$

In Figure 1.17 the feasible region associated with the LP relaxation is marked as ABCD. The feasible solutions are therefore given by the 12 integer points inside and have the convex hull given by the region PQRSTUV.

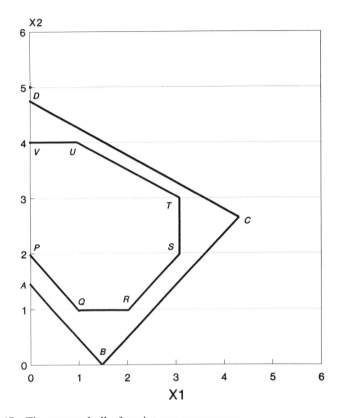

Figure 1.17 The convex hull of an integer programme

If we were to replace constraints (1.115) to (1.118) by those defining the region PQRSTUV, we could treat Example 1.20 as an LP. Constraints that do this are

$$x_1 + x_2 \geqslant 2 \tag{1.119}$$

$$x_2 \geqslant 1 \tag{1.120}$$

$$x_1 - x_2 \leqslant 1 \tag{1.121}$$

$$x_1 \leqslant 3 \tag{1.122}$$

$$x_1 + 2x_2 \leqslant 9 \tag{1.123}$$

$$x_2 \leqslant 4 \tag{1.124}$$

$$x_1 \geqslant 0. \tag{1.125}$$

Although the feasible region of this LP is larger than that for the IP (which consists of disconnnected points), restricting our attention to vertex solutions guarantees that the optimal solution is one of the integral points. In this case we would obtain the optimal solution at T where $x_1 = x_2 = 3$, giving an objective value of 6.

It should be intuitive that this concept generalises to IPs with any number of variables. The convex hull of feasible integer solutions will itself be a polytope bounded by facets. It can therefore be represented by linear inequalities and LP applied. Unfortunately the number of "facet constraints" may, in practice, be astronomically large and difficult to calculate. For *some* classes of model *some* facets are, however, easily obtainable. This topic is considered further in sections 6.3, 6.4 and 8.3.

For Example 1.13 the convex hull consists of the line between P and Q. In the case of Example 1.14 we need five dimensions to represent the convex hull, but we can represent its *projection* into the space of x_1 and x_2 in Figure 1.14. This will itself be the convex hull of the region ABCDEFGO. In Figure 1.18

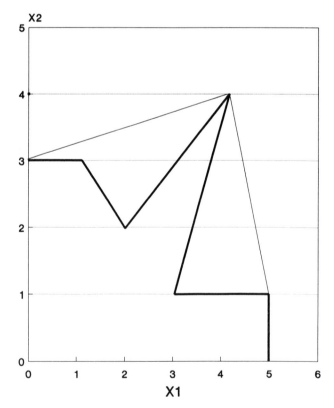

Figure 1.18   The convex hull of a non-convex region

we redraw this region giving its convex hull as the original region together with that included by the new lines.

Again LP could be applied to the resultant model to yield the feasible optimal solution.

It should be recognised that the LP relaxation associated with an IP depends on the *representation* by equations and inequalities, not on the inherent problem. Ideally we would like this to be as constrained (or as "tight") as possible, i.e. the convex hull of feasible integer solutions. Hence it is not possible totally to separate the solution methods of IP from the modelling aspect, which is considered in detail in *MBMP*.

1.4 APPLICATION AREAS

Although our emphasis, in this book, is on the *mathematical* nature of MP models and the methods of solving them, we give a brief discussion of application areas. Sometimes the nature of the application affects the structure of the model in a way that can be exploited by the methods of solution. This is particularly true of the structures considered in section 1.5. A much fuller treatment of application areas and how the resulting models may be built is given in *MBMP*.

The major application of LP is to problems of *resource allocation*, e.g. allocating resources such as productive capacity, raw materials and labour force to different activities. Such problems arise in a variety of industries, one of the most important being the petroleum industry, where it is used for *refinery optimisation*. The resultant models often involve tens of thousands of variables and constraints. Problems of resource allocation to which LP can be applied also occur in the chemical industry, agriculture, health, mining, energy and water resources as well as general manufacturing.

Another important application is to problems of *distribution*. The food and drinks industry as well as the energy industry are users of LP for this reason. Often the resultant models have a network structure, which is discussed in section 1.5. The large models in the petroleum industry often involve planning distribution (e.g. crude oil from the oilfields to refineries) as well as optimizing the operations of the refineries.

Manpower planning is another area of application resulting in multiperiod models (described in section 1.5).

Many other applications arise in industries as diverse as paper (recycling and trim loss), defence (military deployment) and forestry.

NLP models usually arise from non-linear relationships complicating otherwise LP models. This often happens when it is necessary to incorporate physical or engineering relationships into a model. It also happens when costs are non-linear functions of an activity involving discrete changes or economies of scale. Applications of NLP models occur in this way in engineering design and control engineering. They also occur in finance (portfolio selection), ecological and urban planning and advertising (media scheduling).

As explained in previous sections the distinction between LP, NLP and IP is not clear-cut. Like NLP, IP models usually arise from complications to otherwise LP models. This often happens when IP is used to find globally optimal solutions to non-convex models or to deal with fixed costs. Such applications occur in facility location (depots, factories and utilities). Other applications arise in investment, energy (power systems loading), scheduling and sequencing, and political districting. Many problems that might be described as combinatorial can be formulated as IPs. These include the famous travelling salesman problem and its extension, the vehicle scheduling problem. Another difficult combinatorial problem is the quadratic assignment problem arising in locational problems and computer circuit design, which can be formulated as an IP. Other such problems that can be tackled by IP are job shop scheduling, crew scheduling (the set-covering problem) and assembly line balancing.

1.5 SPECIAL TYPES OF MODEL: NETWORKS, ECONOMIC MODELS, STRUCTURED MODELS, GAME THEORY MODELS

LP models are applicable to a wide range of problems. The simplex algorithm, which is described in sections 2.3 and 2.4, provides an almost universal practical means of solving such models. Nevertheless, it is still sometimes worth distinguishing certain *structures* that arise in particular applications. It can be more efficient to use specialist methods for such models or to adapt the simplex algorithm to exploit the structure. Sometimes these specialist models have also been studied independently of LP before the relationship to LP was recognised. In these circumstances it may still be worth while considering different conceptual frameworks within which they can be viewed.

Network Models

Problems involving networks arise frequently in operational research. Application areas and methods of expressing problems as networks are discussed extensively in *MBMP*. The numerical examples used here are taken from there. Here we will consider two classes of network model, the *minimum-cost network flow* and the *maximum-flow* models, as well as special cases of these giving rise to the *assignment* and *shortest-path* models. Other network models arise in Chapter 8.

Example 1.21 Minimum-Cost Flow Through a Network

Express the problem of finding the flow of minimum total cost through the network in Figure 1.19 as an LP model.

The costs of each unit of flow in each arc are given by the associated numbers. It is assumed that there must be *material balance* at each node, i.e. total flow in equals the total flow out. Certain nodes, i.e. A and B, have external flow in and are known as *sources*. Some other nodes, i.e. F, G and H, have external flow out and are known as *sinks*.

The formulation of the problem as an LP is straightforward. The flow in each *arc* will be represented by a variable x_{ij} where i is the predecessor node and j is the successor node. In order for there to be material balance at each *node*, we specify a constraint.

It is convenient to adopt the accounting convention among variables that flow in to a node is regarded as positive and flow out of a node is regarded as negative. The following model results:

Minimise $\quad 5x_{AC} + 4x_{BD} + 2x_{CD} + 6x_{CE} + 5x_{CF} + x_{DE} + 2x_{DH} + 4x_{EC}$

$$+ 6x_{EF} + 3x_{EG} + 4x_{HG} \quad (1.126)$$

subject to

$$-x_{AC} = -10 \quad (1.127)$$

$$-x_{BD} = -15 \quad (1.128)$$

$$x_{AC} - x_{CD} - x_{CE} - x_{CF} + x_{EC} = 0 \quad (1.129)$$

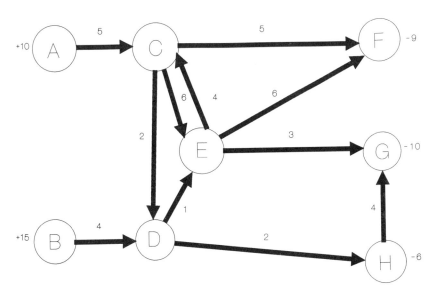

Figure 1.19 A minimum-cost network flow problem

$$x_{BD} + x_{CD} - x_{DE} - x_{DH} = 0 \qquad (1.130)$$

$$x_{CE} + x_{DE} - x_{EC} - x_{EF} - x_{EG} = 0 \qquad (1.131)$$

$$x_{CF} + x_{EF} = 9 \qquad (1.132)$$

$$x_{EG} + x_{HG} = 10 \qquad (1.133)$$

$$x_{DH} - x_{HG} = 6 \qquad (1.134)$$

$$x_{ij} \geqslant 0 \quad \text{all } i, j.$$

This model has a number of features on which it is worth remarking.

(i) Each arc gives rise to a variable. Hence there are the same number of variables as arcs, i.e. 11.
(ii) Each node gives rise to a constraint. Hence there are the same number of constraints as nodes, i.e. eight.
(iii) Each variable has exactly two coefficients in the constraints, a -1 coefficient (flow out) in the constraint corresponding to the predecessor node and a $+1$ coefficient (flow in) corresponding to the successor node.

Property (iii) demonstrates that any set of equations where the variables have coefficients with this property gives rise to a network representation. A *matrix* of detached coefficients with the property is known as the *node–arc incidence matrix* of the corresponding network.

An important result of property (iii) is that so long as the coefficients (external flows) on the right-hand side are integers and the model is soluble, then there will be an optimal solution involving *integral flows*. The reason why this is so will become apparent in section 3.1, where the simplex algorithm is applied to this example and interpreted in terms of the network. This important property is known as the *integrality property* for an LP.

Example 1.22 Maximum Flow Through a Network

We will suppose that we want to maximise the *total flow* through the network illustrated in Figure 1.19, ignoring the unit costs on each arc. Each arc has a maximum (and sometimes a minimum) capacity. For our example we will specify only maximum capacities in Table 1.1.

In order to model this problem as an LP, we will replace the external flows in equations (1.127), (1.128), (1.132), (1.133) and (1.134) by variables x_A, x_B, x_F, x_G and x_H. The objective can be formulated as

$$\text{Maximise} \quad x_A + x_B. \qquad (1.135)$$

The capacities give extra "simple bound" constraints on variables x_{AC}, x_{BD}, etc.

Table 1.1

Arc	Capacity
AC	12
BD	20
CE	3
CF	6
DC	6
DE	7
DH	9
EC	2
EF	5
EG	8
HG	4

Models with this structure have similar properties to the minimum-cost network flow model. So long as the arc capacities are integral and the model is soluble, then there will be an integral optimal flow pattern. The simplex algorithm can again be specialised to exploit the structure.

It is convenient, in the example, to add together and then negate all constraints (1.127), (1.128), (1.132), (1.133) and (1.134) with the new variables replacing the constant terms. This gives

$$- x_A - x_B + x_F + x_G + x_H = 0. \qquad (1.136)$$

This new constraint would represent a "dummy node", which would be appended to the network in Figure 1.19. So x_A and x_B would represent flows out of this new node and x_F, x_G and x_H flows in. Material balance at the node indicates the necessity of total flow in equalling total flow out. This example is solved in section 3.1 by a specialised method.

Sometimes the problem is just to find a feasible flow pattern. This can again be solved by specialisation of the simplex algorithm.

Example 1.23 The Assignment Problem as a Network Flow Model
Formulate the problem of assigning each member of $I = \{A, B, C, D\}$ to exactly one member of $J = \{E, F, G, H\}$, at a minimum total cost, as a minimum-cost network flow model.
 The cost of assigning $i \in I$ to $j \in J$ is given in Table 1.2.

Practical instances of this types of problem and its variants and extensions are given in *MBMP*.
 Our purpose here is to demonstrate that this problem can be regarded as a

Table 1.2

	E	F	G	H
A	7	8	2	14
B	13	13	4	10
C	7	12	5	3
D	20	12	8	8

special case of the minimum-cost network flow model. The example is solved in section 3.2 first by a network form of the simplex algorithm and then, more efficiently, by a specialist method known as the Hungarian algorithm. Figure 1.20 gives the network model.

The cost of each assignment is marked on the associated arc. Should certain assignments be impossible, we could either leave the associated arc

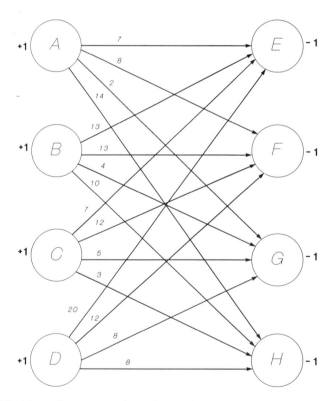

Figure 1.20 Network representation of an assignment problem

out or give it a very high cost. We have external flow in to each source node $i \in I$ and flow out of each sink node $j \in J$ of 1. Since the integrality property holds, so long as the model is soluble, there will be an optimal solution in which each unit of flow goes from a node in I to a node in J, i.e. no flow will "split" into fractional portions along different arcs. Hence this optimal solution to the LP will give a meaningful assignment.

As with the maximum-flow model example, the problem is sometimes simply to find a feasible solution. This can also be done using the specialisation of the simplex algorithm and is discussed in sections 3.1 and 3.2.

Example 1.24 The Shortest-Path Problem as a Network Flow Model
We will suppose that we want to find the shortest path in Figure 1.19 from node A to node H, where the numbers on the arcs now represent these lengths.

The model can easily be adapted to a minimum-cost network flow one by only allowing an external flow in of 1 at A and an external flow out of 1 at H. The integrality property guarantees that (so long as there is a path) there will be an optimal flow pattern in which this unit of flow takes the shortest path, i.e. does not "split" at any node.

Although the simplex algorithm can be specialised to deal with such a model, in practice it is better to use other methods. In section 3.3 we solve this model by the network form of the simplex algorithm in order to demonstrate its inefficiency, and then solve it by an efficient method known as Dijkstra's algorithm.

Economic Models

We will describe the structure that arises from a particular type of economic model known as an *input–output* model. Such models are also known as Leontief models and are discussed in *MBMP*, from which the following example is taken.

Example 1.25 An Input–Output Problem
An economy is made up of three sectors, A, B and C. To produce £1 worth of output in each sector requires inputs from the other sectors as well as labour. These requirements, in £1, are given in Table 1.3.

Notice that the value of each monetary unit of output is exactly equal to the total value of its inputs.

The economy has to cater for a certain *exogenous* consumption in each of three industries known as a *bill of goods*. It is convenient to consider a

Table 1.3

		Outputs		
		A	B	C
Inputs	A	0.1	0.5	0.4
	B	0.1	0.1	0.2
	C	0.2	0.1	0.2
	Labour	0.6	0.3	0.2

general bill of goods (measured in £millions) b_1, b_2 and b_3 in sectors A, B and C respectively.

A number of questions naturally arise concerning our economy, which a mathematical model might be used to answer.

(i) How much should each industry produce in order to satisfy a given bill of goods?
(ii) How much labour would this require?
(iii) What should the prices of each product be?

Variables x_A, x_B and x_C are introduced to represent the total output, over a period of time, in each of the sectors. This gives the following set of equations:

$$x_A = b_1 + 0.1x_A + 0.5x_B + 0 \cdot 4x_C \qquad (1.137)$$

$$x_B = b_2 + 0.1x_A + 0.1x_B + 0.2x_C \qquad (1.138)$$

$$x_C = b_3 + 0.2x_A + 0.1x_B + 0.2x_C. \qquad (1.139)$$

These equations are more conveniently written as

$$0.9x_A - 0.5x_B - 0.4x_C = b_1 \qquad (1.140)$$

$$-0.1x_A + 0.9x_B + 0.2x_C = b_2 \qquad (1.141)$$

$$-0.2x_A - 0.1x_B + 0.8x_C = b_3. \qquad (1.142)$$

In addition, outputs cannot be negative and we assume labour is limited to some level L. This gives

$$0.6x_A + 0.3x_B + 0.2x_C \leqslant L \qquad (1.143)$$

$$x_A, x_B, x_C \geqslant 0. \qquad (1.144)$$

Expressions (1.140) to (1.144) could be regarded as the constraints of an LP model. We could then investigate different optimal solutions according to different objectives. It turns out, however, that the structure of the model is such that there will be either *one* or *no* feasible solutions. Therefore, an objective function is irrelevant to solving the model.

Geometrically, the feasible region will consist of either a single point or be empty. The values of b_1, b_2, b_3 and L that correspond to each of these situations form the subjects of exercises 2.18 and 2.19.

The matrix of detached coefficients in equations (1.140) to (1.142) has a special structure. All coefficients lie between -1 and $+1$. Each variable has exactly one positive coefficient in different rows. Other coefficients are non-positive. A non-singular matrix with this structure is known as a *Leontief matrix*. It has certain properties. In particular:

(i) There is always a unique solution for any right-hand side.
(ii) The solution is non-negative so long as the coefficients b_i on the right-hand side are non-negative.

Therefore the unique solution to the equations either does or does not satisfy inequality (1.143).

In practice, there may be extra conditions that apply to such a problem, making optimisation relevant. This is discussed more fully in *MBMP*. In particular, the model may be applied over a number of time periods, leading to a dynamic structured model similar to those discussed below.

Structured Models

As discussed in *MBMP* practical models frequently arise through the combining of simpler models. For example, models for single products, produced in single plants during single time periods, may be combined into multiproduct, multiplant and multiperiod models. Such models have a very recognisable structure, as illustrated by the following example taken from *MBMP*.

Example 1.26 A Structured Model

$$\text{Maximise} \quad 10x_1 + 15x_2 + 10x_3 + 15x_4 \tag{1.145}$$

subject to

$$4x_1 + 4x_2 + 4x_3 + 4x_4 \leqslant 120 \tag{1.146}$$

$$4x_1 + 2x_2 \qquad\qquad \leqslant 80 \tag{1.147}$$

$$2x_1 + 5x_2 \qquad\qquad \leqslant 60 \tag{1.148}$$

$$5x_3 + 3x_4 \leqslant 60 \tag{1.149}$$

$$5x_3 + 6x_4 \leqslant 75 \tag{1.150}$$

$$x_1, x_2, x_3, x_4 \geqslant 0. \tag{1.151}$$

This model represents a factory with two plants. One resource represented by constraint (1.146) is shared, but the others are confined to the individual plants. The example can be solved by a specialist method known as decomposition.

Example 1.26 is an instance of a *block angular* structure. The general structure is illustrated in Figure 1.21.

Non-zero coefficients are confined to the blocks shown. $A_0, A_1, ..., A_n$ represent *common rows* including the objective function. $B_1, B_2, ..., B_n$ represent *blocks* independent of the rest of the model. The block angular structure is a special case of the *staircase* structure illustrated in Figure 1.22.

This type of structure typically arises in multiperiod models where production from one period may "feed in" to the inventory held for the next period. Specialist methods of solution are possible.

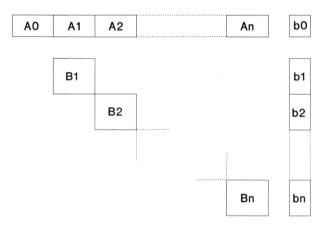

Figure 1.21 A block angular structure

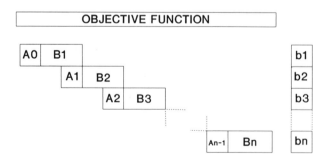

Figure 1.22 A staircase structure

Game Theory Models

We will consider *two-person zero-sum* games. These are "games" involving two opponents. When each of the opponents makes a play, they each receive a payoff that depends on which of a number of "strategies" each plays. These games are "zero sum" in the sense that one player's gains will be equal to the other's loss. The following example illustrates a typical situation.

Example 1.27 A Two-Person Zero-Sum Game
A can play a number of "pure strategies" 1, 2 or 3 against B. In turn, B can play a number of pure strategies 1, 2 or 3 against A. For each pair of pure strategies played by A and B respectively, A receives a payoff given by Table 1.4, known as a payoff matrix.

B's payoff will be the negative of A's. A and B both have full information about the possible payoffs, but have no knowledge of the choice of the opponent when making their own choice.

The problem is to determine, over a number of plays, how A should mix his pure strategies. Similarly B has a problem as to how to mix her pure strategies. While the purpose of this example is to demonstrate the structure of the resulting LP model, and not the application, it is worth mentioning the origin of this numerical example. It is known as the *eluding game*. A and B each choose a number out of 1, 2 or 3. If their choices are equal, A pays B an amount of money equal to the number. Otherwise B pays A an amount of money equal to A's chosen number.

A's problem can be formulated as an LP by introducing variables x_1, x_2 and x_3 to represent the proportion of times he should use each of his pure strategies. A wishes to make sure that whatever mixture of strategies B adopts, he maximises his minimum possible payoff. The full formulation of such "maximin" objectives is discussed in *MBMP*.

Table 1.4

		B's strategies		
		1	2	3
A's strategies	1	-1	1	1
	2	2	-2	2
	3	3	3	-3

In this example A's model becomes

$$\text{Maximise} \quad u \qquad (1.152)$$

such that

$$x_1 - 2x_2 - 3x_3 + u \leqslant 0 \tag{1.153}$$

$$- x_1 + 2x_2 - 3x_3 + u \leqslant 0 \tag{1.154}$$

$$- x_1 - 2x_2 + 3x_3 + u \leqslant 0 \tag{1.155}$$

$$x_1 + x_2 + x_3 = 1 \tag{1.156}$$

$$x_1, x_2, x_3 \geqslant 0. \tag{1.157}$$

Notice that u (the maximin payoff) is a free variable.

It is of interest also to model B's problem as an LP. B's payoff matrix is the negation of A's. The resultant model will have a similar structure to A's model. This is the subject of exercises 1.12 and 2.17.

1.6 COMPUTER DATA STRUCTURES

The manner in which an MP model is stored in a computer system is of fundamental importance for the algorithms that are used to solve it. Mathematical treatments of algorithms often neglect this consideration. A complete treatment of the subject would take us beyond the scope of this book. Nevertheless, we feel it necessary to describe the most important data structures that are used. Much fuller treatment is given in some of the references in section 1.8.

Also of relevance to the algorithms used is the *computer architecture*. We have deliberately not discussed this, leaving it to referenced texts. It should, however, be pointed out that an important distinction should be made between *serial* and *parallel* processing. Traditionally, the solution of MP models has relied on serial machines, which carry out operations strictly in a sequence. Some MP algorithms allow some operations to be carried out in parallel, with a consequent increase in speed. This is particularly true with some vector operations and tree searches. The exploitation of parallel processing in MP is still at a comparatively early stage. Considerable ingenuity can often be exercised in creating or adapting algorithms to suit parallel architectures. Some references are given in section 1.8.

Sparse Matrices and Vectors

A major feature of practical MP models is that the matrices of coefficients are *sparse*. For a model with 1000 constraints, one would expect little more than 0.1% of the coefficients to be non-zero. For larger models this percentage would be even smaller. The observation of practical LP models suggests that rarely more than 10 of the coefficients in a column are non-zero. It would clearly be inefficient, explicitly, to store all the zero coefficients.

Another sparse structure that arises in MP models is a graph or network. They are sparse in the sense that most pairs of nodes are *not* connected by an arc. Such graphs could be represented by (sparse) matrices as discussed in section 1.5. Then the data structures described here would be appropriate. It is, however, normally better to preserve the graph structure and use the approaches described below in relation to trees.

There are a number of alternative methods of storing sparse matrices. The obvious method of storing all coefficients, zero and non-zero, sequentially according to matrix position will be ignored as it is only relevant to small dense models.

A simple method of storage is to associate each non-zero coefficient with its row and column number in a matrix as shown:

ROW NO.	COL. NO.	VALUE

Most computers, to date, store integers in *words* of 32 bits (or sometimes half-words of 16 bits) and real numbers (in double precision) in double words of 64 bits. Therefore the above storage scheme would require four words (128 bits) for each non-zero coefficient. Should the coefficients be restricted to be integer, then this could be reduced to three words.

It is, however, unlikely that these non-zero coefficients will be processed independently. Frequently the coefficients in a column (a *vector*) will be processed together. Therefore, a more common method is to store such coefficients in contiguous storage positions (as a *record*) with appropriate row indices, i.e.

ROW NO.	VALUE
ROW NO.	VALUE
ROW NO.	VALUE

Such a stored vector would be said to be *packed*. A marker (occupying 16 bits) or column number can be used to indicate the start of each column. Alternatively the positions of the beginnings of columns can be stored in another array. Yet another alternative is to store the length of each record so that the column to which coefficients belong can be ascertained before they are processed. Each coefficient will now require three words (if real), together with an overhead for column markers.

Besides the columns of coefficients of the matrix of an MP, other vectors will need to be stored, e.g. the right-hand side coefficients, the objective coefficients, sets of lower and upper bounds for variables, etc. They can all be stored in the above manner. In addition to the above data, there will be vectors that are used in the course of calculation. Such vectors will be described in Chapter 4. They can also be packed in the above manner (with appropriate markers) to save storage space since they will frequently be sparse. There are, however, circumstances in which we may wish to "unpack" them. This happens when they are transformed as a result of calculations creating non-zero coefficients (known as "fill-in") in rows where there were hitherto zeros. Should such vectors be few in number, and frequently so transformed, it may be more efficient to maintain them in an unpacked form.

A totally different approach to dealing with sparse MP matrices is to create an *element pool* of coefficients. Then, although the same (non-zero) coefficient may occur more than once in a model, it need only be stored once. A suitable indexing system must be used to point to these *unique values*. This proves to be a very economical way of storing huge MP models. The economy rests on the fact that the great majority of coefficients in a practical model are repeated many times. The most common coefficients (apart from zero) will generally be ± 1, followed in frequency by the small integers. It is reported that one would usually expect to find only about 500 distinct values in a large model.

With this method of storage a column will be represented by:

ROW NO.	POINTER
ROW NO.	POINTER
ROW NO.	POINTER

The "pointers" will be the addresses of the storage positions of the unique elements. Each coefficient will now require two words of storage together with the shared overhead of the storage required for the element pool (and, of course, that for column markers). In fact, it may even be worth listing the rows of a column with entries ± 1 separately and not even pointing to these unique values.

The use of an element pool to store coefficients is often referred to as *super-sparsity*. It enables quite large models to be stored in the memory of a computer and the data therefore accessed quickly. This is in contrast to having to store data on peripheral devices, e.g. disks, where access is much slower. There is, however, a price to be paid for any of the above methods of storing sparse matrices. Computation with such matrices becomes more complex, requiring more computer instructions. This in turn requires extra storage as well as making the calculations slower. Nevertheless, MP matrices are usually so sparse that these considerations are greatly outweighed by the advantages.

Sparsity can also be exploited to advantage in alternative mathematical representations of some matrices. For example, representing matrices as products of other matrices rather than explicitly can result in the number of coefficients to be stored being less. These possibilities are described in Chapter 4.

Linked Lists and Pointers

In dealing with sparse matrices it was pointed out that we usually wish to deal with all the coefficients in a column at the same time. Therefore, they are stored consecutively to avoid the time of searching for the next coefficient in the same column. This, of course, does not allow for the possibility of looking for coefficients in the same *row*. Sometimes it is necessary to do this. Another way of allowing quick reference to coefficients that are related to each other in the structure of the model (e.g. same row or column) is to use *linked lists* with pointers. With each coefficient reference we would associate pointers to references to neighbouring coefficients. For example, each coefficient could be represented by:

ROW NO.	COL. NO.	VALUE	POINTER 1	POINTER 2

In addition to its row number, column number and value, the first pointer would be to the address of the next coefficient in the same row of the matrix and the second pointer to the address of the next coefficient in the same column of the matrix.

Such a storage scheme would generally be inefficient. It is more likely that one would still store column coefficients contiguously but associate with each coefficient a single pointer to the next coefficient in the same row of the matrix.

Other variants and additions to the above scheme are possible. If an element pool is used, the next row and/or column pointers would obviously be associated with the pointers to the elements rather than the elements themselves. Sometimes it is convenient to use *doubly linked lists* in which there are pointers backwards to previous coefficients as well as forwards.

It is not possible to be definitive about which storage scheme is best. This will depend on the type of model, computer and algorithm to be used. Nevertheless, it is important to be aware of the different possibilities in case one of them can be exploited to advantage.

Another important consideration regarding linked lists is the ease with which elements can be inserted or deleted from such lists.

Trees

These are structures that occur in a number of contexts in MP models. In particular, they will be used in the network form of the simplex algorithm and in the branch-and-bound algorithm for integer programming.

Figure 1.23 gives an example of a tree. It is a connected subset of a graph in which there are no loops.

Specialisations of this structure exist. In particular, arcs may be *directed* and the nodes may have an ordering. An important example of this is when nodes are all descendants (given the arc directions) of a particular node known as the *root* node. In such circumstances the tree is often *binary* with each node having at most two descendants. Figure 1.24 is an example. The root node has been numbered 0 and all descendants have numbers higher than their predecessors.

Different data structures can be used for storing trees. For directed binary trees, it is convenient to store the nodes as entities in the order of the numbering. Pointers can be used to indicate the structure. A typical node would be represented (in 128 bits) by:

NODE NO.	POINTER 1	POINTER 2	POINTER 3

Pointer 1 would be the address of the immediate predecessor ("father"). Pointer 2 would be the address of the left-hand immediate successor ("son"). Pointer 3 would be the address of the right-hand immediate successor ("daughter").

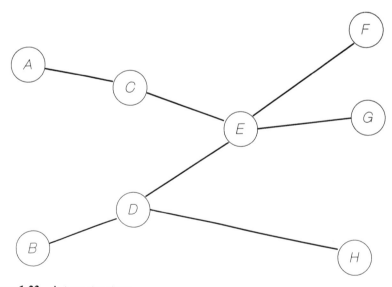

Figure 1.23   A tree structure

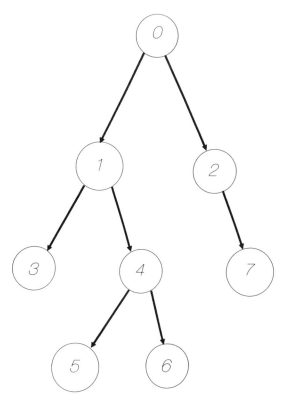

Figure 1.24 A binary tree

This is clearly an example of a doubly linked list in which it is possible to move forwards and backwards. In addition, extra information ("attributes") might be associated with each node.

If it is desired to store all the information about a binary tree contiguously, then we could avoid pointer 2 and (say) store the corresponding node immediately after it. When the last node on a "branch" is reached (e.g. node 3) we could store its sister (node 4), repeating the procedure working backwards up the tree if necessary. Pointers would be used to indicate the relationship of consecutive nodes. The resultant order in this example would be

$$0 \quad 1 \quad 3 \quad 4 \quad 5 \quad 6 \quad 2 \quad 7.$$

Such an order is known as a *preorder*. The corresponding "path" through the nodes is known as a *traversal*. Other traversals are possible. If an algorithm needs to traverse a tree in a particular order, then appropriate pointers should be included in the data structure.

For more general trees such as that illustrated in Figure 1.23, it is still often convenient to number one node arbitrarily as a root node with number 0 and then number successors with higher numbers in relation to their predecessors. For example, we might number the following nodes successively starting with O:

$$A \quad C \quad E \quad D \quad B \quad H \quad F \quad G.$$

Pointers, numbers and/or consecutive storage positions would be used to indicate relations and numbers of successors.

With some algorithms, considerable attention must be paid to the addition and deletion of arcs. In the network form of the simplex algorithm, for example, we will at stages add an arc, creating a loop, and then delete another arc in the loop created. We will only want to alter some of the node attributes in the new tree created. The data structure should facilitate an efficient implementation of this. This topic is discussed in section 4.6.

A description of all the data structures associated with trees is beyond the scope of this book. They are an example of an important structure known as a *heap*. Again the recognition of some of the possibilities for storing trees is all that is intended here. References are given in section 1.8.

Bit Maps

It has already been pointed out that practical MP models are very sparse. The relative positions of the non-zero elements are often of importance. A compact way of keeping track of the non-zero elements is a *bit map*. Each non-zero element is associated with the corresponding bit of computer storage taking the value 1. Otherwise it takes the value 0. Such a representation is, for example, valuable in the matrix inversion procedure discussed in section 4.2. Here one wishes to reorder the rows and columns of the matrix in order, as far as possible, to put the non-zero elements in a triangular submatrix. Another use of bit maps is to store compactly certain information about variables. For example, we sometimes wish to distinguish whether certain variables are at their lower or upper bounds. This is conveniently done by associating a bit with each variable.

The disadvantage of bit maps is that it is normally not possible to address computer storage at the bit level. We have to resort to the comparison of larger units of storage using Boolean operations such as "OR" and "AND" in order to distinguish settings at the bit level.

1.7 MEASURING THE NUMBER OF COMPUTATIONAL STEPS

Clearly some algorithms take longer to solve a particular type of model than other algorithms. Also, some types of model appear more difficult to solve with any algorithm. Rather than continue to talk about "efficient" algorithms and "difficult" models, it has become necessary to be more precise about these notions. This presents difficulties since one would like to remain independent, as far as possible, of the computer systems being used. Some computer systems are more efficient at solving some types of model than other systems. It turns out that it is possible to make fairly crude distinctions between algorithmic efficiency and model difficulty in a way that is largely independent of the computer system being used.

In order to make these distinctions we consider all "elementary" computer operations (addition, subtraction, multiplication, division, comparison, etc.) as of equal value. It can be shown that for most formal definitions of a computer (e.g. a Turing machine) such distinctions are "drowned" by other aspects of our definitions. If n, in some sense, represents the size of our model, we wish to know the maximum number of operations needed to solve it as a function $f(n)$. Then we can be sure that for any instance of a model of size n the "time" to solve it will not be greater than $f(n)$. This *worst-case* analysis of computational complexity is sometimes regarded as unsatisfactory. "Average-case" analysis is, however, generally much more difficult and requires assumptions about average models. We are also restricting attention to *time complexity* as opposed to *space complexity*. The latter concept can also be analysed and is an important consideration in solving many models. It is, however, related to time complexity since the generation and reading of more information leads to increases in time as well as space.

An *algorithm* is said to be *polynomial*, in time complexity, if for any model of size n the number of operations $f(n) \leqslant cn^r$ where c and r are constants. In shorthand we write $f(n) = O(n^r)$. Little attention is usually paid to the value of c. What is of more interest is how fast $f(n)$ *grows*. The value of r is far more significant in this respect. By contrast, an algorithm is said to be *exponential* if it grows faster than any polynomial function of n, but $f(n) \leqslant ca^n$ where $a > 1$ is a constant. In shorthand we say $f(n) = O(a^n)$. The distinction between polynomial and exponential growth rates is dramatic. In order to illustrate this we suppose that one computer takes n^2 (a polynomial) microseconds to solve a model and another takes 2^n (an exponential) microseconds. The resulting times for different values of n are given in Table 1.5. Whatever the values of c, a and r in the expressions above, sooner or later the explosive growth of any exponential function of n will cause it to exceed a polynomial function.

It is possible to define complexity classes between polynomial and exponential, e.g. $n^{\log n}$. We choose, however, not to be so discriminating and class anything in between as exponential.

A *model* is said to be in the P-class (polynomial) if there exists a polynomial algorithm that solves it. For example, Gaussian elimination, for solving a set of n simultaneous equations in n variables, which is discussed in section 2.1,

Table 1.5

n	n^2	2^n
1	0.000001 s	0.000002 s
10	0.0001 s	0.001 s
20	0.0004 s	1 s
30	0.0009 s	17.9 min
40	0.0016 s	12.7 days
50	0.0025 s	35.7 years
60	0.0036 s	366 centuries

is $O(n^3)$. There is, in fact, a "better algorithm" due to Strassen, which is $O(n^{\sqrt{7}})$. The main point, however, is that there exist polynomial algorithms putting the model in the P-class. Certain other types of model mentioned in this book are in this class. In particular, matching, on a graph with n nodes, defined and discussed in section 8.3, has an $O(n^3)$ algorithm, and the minimum-cost spanning tree problem on a graph with n nodes, discussed in section 8.3, has an $O(n^2)$ algorithm.

For many years it was not known if LP lay in the P-class. We show, in section 2.3, that for an LP model with n variables the simplex algorithm (using normal pivot selection rules) can take 2^n iterations, showing it to be exponential. Within these iterations the pivoting operation itself will involve a (polynomial) number of multiplications, divisions and additions, which, of course, are drowned within the 2^n complexity classification. Therefore the simplex algorithm (in its present form) is exponential. Nevertheless, *practical* LP models tend to be fairly easy to solve by the simplex algorithm, in contrast to artificially constructed worst cases. This fact suggested (perhaps rather tenuously) that there might be a polynomial algorithm for LP. In fact, no such algorithm has yet been found that is a polynomial function of n (the number of variables). It is rather unrealistic to use n as representative of the size of an LP model. If, instead, we include m (the number of constraints), we might seek a polynomial function $f(m, n)$ giving the number of operations for an algorithm (in the worst case). A function $f(mn)$ would be a special case of this. Again no such algorithm has been found, although one is still being sought. If such an algorithm were to be found, it would be known as *strongly polynomial*, for reasons explained below.

To be less ambitious we could seek an algorithm that takes into account the size of the coefficients in the matrix, as well as m and n. At this stage we must be more precise about what we mean by the "size" of a model. In previous examples we have assumed that n is proportional to the number of computer storage positions needed to state the model. Each of these storage positions will hold numbers. If the sizes of these numbers differ radically, then it may be necessary to take their size into account. In order to do this we must be careful about how we encode the data. The amount of computer storage taken up by a coefficient a would be no more than $1 + \lceil \log_2(|a| + 1) \rceil$ bits (where "$\lceil \ \rceil$" represents rounding up to an integer). In fact we can, more crudely, assume that storage is proportional to $\log |a|$ (to any base). This will be a satisfactory assumption for any "reasonable" encoding scheme. Note that simply representing a by a storage positions is not reasonable in this context and can result in some exponential algorithms appearing polynomial. Technically these algorithms are known as *pseudo-polynomial*. The dynamic programming algorithm applied to the knapsack problem in section 8.3 is pseudo-polynomial. Showing this is the subject of exercise 8.17.

To obtain an algorithm for LP polynomially bounded by $f(m, n)$, and therefore working as fast for models with large coefficients as with small, would be a major achievement and therefore somewhat unlikely. It is more reasonable to characterise the size of an LP model in terms of m, n and $\log \max |a_{ij}|$ where a_{ij} are the coefficients (including RHS and objective). Other parameters are possible, replacing, for example, the last parameter by $\Sigma_{i,j} \log |a_{ij}|$. It turns out, however, not to matter which is used. A polynomial function in terms of one set of parameters will remain a polynomial function in terms of the others. Similarly this will be the case for exponential functions. In terms of these parameters, polynomial algorithms have been found for LP placing it in the P-class. The first such algorithm is known as the ellipsoid algorithm. It is not discussed further in this book as practical experience has shown it to be inefficient. References are given in section 1.8. It has complexity $O(mn^3 \log \max_{i,j} |a_{ij}|)$. A more successful practical polynomial LP algorithm is the method of projective transformations, which is described in section 2.8. In fact, the versions usually implemented are not polynomially bounded, but there is a theoretical version that has complexity $O(mn^2 \log \max_{i,j} |a_{ij}|)$. Neither of these two complexity measures should be taken too literally. Different variants of the algorithms, with different data structures, can produce alterations. The important point is that they are *polynomial* functions of the size of the LP model. This in itself is regarded as sufficient to classify LP as a relatively easy type of model to solve. It is also worth remarking that all the known polynomial algorithms for any types of model are very low-order polynomials. Nowhere have we found $O(n^{10})$ algorithms, for example.

In contrast to models in the P-class, many models in MP so far admit no polynomial algorithms. The major type of model in this class is IP. Many of the special types of IP model discussed in Chapter 8 also have, to date, no polynomial algorithm for solving them optimally. It is, however, very difficult to prove that there can be no polynomial algorithm for problems in this class. This remains one of the major challenges of contemporary mathematics.

It is certainly true that there are (soluble) problems that can be *proved* not to be soluble in less than exponential time, but most of the problems lie outside MP. One easily understood problem is that of the tower of Hanoi. A set of n annuar discs are threaded on a spike in order of decreasing radius. Two other spikes are provided on to which discs can be transferred one at a time, never putting a larger disc on top of a smaller. It is very easy to show (exercise 1.13) by an inductive argument that $2^n - 1$ operations are needed to transfer all the discs to another spike in the same order as before. This algorithm is exponential and there can be no better algorithm. Since no "data" are involved apart from n, it might be more honest to regard the size of the problem as log n. In this case the algorithm is $O(2^{2^{\log n}} - 1)$, which is worse than exponential.

For IP models all the known algorithms are of exponential or greater complexity. The most widely used general method is branch-and-bound, which is discussed in section 6.2. This can be shown to have exponential complexity (exercise 6.16). It is, however, possible to *check* if a given solution to an IP model is optimal in polynomial time (exercise 6.7). This does not help us find such an optimal solution. To do this we need a fictional and non-realisable computational device known as a *non-deterministic Turing machine*, which produces as many general solutions as needed in polynomial time. The fact that there exist algorithms for checking solutions in polynomial time causes such models to be placed in the NP-class (NP standing for "non-deterministic polynomial"). Trivially all the P-class of models are a subset of the NP-class since not only can their solutions be checked in polynomial time, but they can be found as well. However, it is strongly suspected that the NP-class is larger than the P-class.

For many of the MP models in the NP-class it is possible to transform one type of model into another by a *polynomial transformation*. In such a transformation, a number of operations are carried out on one model in order to transform it into another. The number of such operations is a polynomial function of the size of the first model. If such a transformation exists, the first type of model is said to be *polynomially reducible* to the second. Then if a polynomial algorithm exists for solving the second type of model, it could be combined with the polynomial reduction in order to produce a polynomial algorithm for the first. Hence if the second type of model were in the P-class, so would be the first. It turns out that there are a large number of models in the NP-class to which *any* model in the NP-class can be polynomially reduced. Such models are known as *NP-complete*. (The term "complete" has a technical meaning in logic.) These models represent the most difficult models in the NP-class. The emphasis on them arises because, if a polynomial algorithm could be found for *any* one of them, then there would be a polynomial algorithm for all models in the NP-class. This would cause the NP-class to become identical with the P-class and the whole edifice for trying to distinguish between easy and difficult models would collapse. It is thought rather unlikely that this will happen since the difficult problems of MP are all known to be NP-complete. In particular, the IP class of models is NP-complete, as are many difficult combinatorial problems (some are discussed in section 8.3), such as the travelling salesman problem and the knapsack problem. It is shown in Chapter 8 that these problems can be formulated as IP models. We have, however, already pointed out that certain other specialist IP models such as matching and minimum-cost spanning trees admit polynomial algorithms.

The fact that a large number of models fall into the NP-complete class does not necessarily mean that they bear much relation to each other since polynomial reducibility is a very crude tool, which can do much violence to the structure of a model. Such a crude tool is, however, needed to override fine distinctions between different modes of computing and computer operations. The fact that it preserves an apparent chasm between the (easy) models in the P-class and the (difficult) models in the NP-complete class is intuitive evidence of the significance of this distinction.

There are algorithms that are worse than exponential and models for which even checkability is not known to be possible in polynomial time. Such models appear to be even more difficult than NP-complete models. The total class of such models as well as NP-complete models are known as NP-hard. Long before it was attempted to distinguish between models solvable in polynomial time and models requiring exponential time or worse, it was known that there are models that are not solvable by *any* algorithm. Such models arise from *undecidable* problems that grew out of Gödel's work in mathematical logic. Fortunately, few practical models arising in MP admit no algorithm. One example is, however, that of optimising a linear expression over quadratic constraints where all variables are restricted to integer values.

The suspicion that $P \neq NP$ leads to the investigation of non-optimal methods (heuristics) for obtaining "good" solutions to NP-complete models. Such heuristics are expected to involve only a low-order polynomial number of operations. They are discussed in section 8.5.

1.8 HISTORY, REFERENCES AND FUTURE DEVELOPMENTS

Linear Programming

As explained, the term "linear programming" arose from the use of the word "programming" for "planning" in a military context after the Second World War. This is discussed by Dantzig (1963), together with other applications arising at this time. Before this the term had not been used.

The special type of LP model later known as the transportation problem was initially studied independently of LP by Kantorovitch (1942) and Koopmans and Reiter (1951).

The first real study of linear inequality systems began with Fourier (1826). Descartes (1637) is credited with having originated the idea of representing algebraic problems through the coordinates of points in space.

A thorough treatment of polyhedra and polytopes from an LP point of view is given in Schrijver (1986).

Non-Linear Programming

A good description of non-linear programming models within the context of MP is Beale (1968). Powell (1981) and Fletcher (1987) are substantial tests on the subject, describing the calculus-based approaches. Rockafellar (1970) is a standard test on convexity.

Integer Programming

A very comprehensive text is Nemhauser and Wolsey (1988). *MBMP* gives extensive coverage to the modelling of IPs and the way in which they arise in practice. Disjunctive programming is treated as a subject by Sherali and Shetty (1980). The idea of special ordered sets is due to Beale and Tomlin (1970).

Application Areas

These are thoroughly discussed in *MBMP*, where many references to particular applications are given. In addition, many applications can be found in journals in operational research, management science and applied computing.

Special Types of Model

Network models were considered in the context of MP by Ford and Fulkerson (1962). Other discussions can be found in Glover and Klingman (1974) and Bradley (1975). The relationship between graph theoretical problems and MP is described in Nemhauser and Wolsey (1988) and Christofides (1975a). The economic input–output model is due to Leontief (1951). It is discussed in Dorfman, Samuelson and Solow (1958). A discussion of the relationship to LP is given by Shapiro (1979). Structured models and how they arise is described in *MBMP* and Dantzig (1974).

A standard text on game theory is Von Neumann and Morgenstern (1947).

Computer Data Structures

This subject has grown in importance and become worthy of study in its own right as the use of digital computers has grown. It is considered at a practical level in the systems manuals associated with computer packages. Such packages often have facilities for the user to write interfaces and subroutines within the structures used.

At a more theoretical (although still practically very important) level, the subject is discussed thoroughly in a number of texts. One of the best and most comprehensive is the section on information structures in Knuth (1979). A text that discusses data structures required for networks is Tarjan (1983). Brayton, Gustavson and Willoughby (1969) treats the subject of sparse matrices. The idea of element pools of coefficients is due to Kalan (1971).

Measuring the Number of Computational Steps

The analysis of the computational complexity of MP models arose from the work by Edmonds (1965), Karp (1972) and others. Cook (1971) produced the conjecture that P ≠ NP and showed that certain models are polynomially reducible to a logic problem known as the satisfiability problem. A full coverage of the subject is contained in Garey and Johnson (1979), who catalogue many NP-complete models. The non-existence of algorithms for certain classes of problem is due to Gödel (1931). Jeroslow (1972) showed that integer programming with quadratic constraints is unsolvable.

Despite this analysis there is some misgiving about the significance of this way of looking at computational complexity. This arises, in part, because the concentration has been on worst-case analysis. Smale (1983) has, however, analysed the average-case behaviour of the simplex algorithm, and Shamir (1987) surveys the area.

1.9 EXERCISES

1.1 Express Example 1.4 in standard form.

1.2 Represent the following model geometrically:

$$\text{Minimise} \quad 2x_1 + 3x_2$$

subject to

$$x_1 + x_2 \geqslant 2$$
$$2x_1 + x_2 \geqslant 3$$
$$4x_1 + 10x_2 \geqslant 11$$

$$x_1 - x_2 \leqslant 1$$
$$4x_1 + 2x_2 \leqslant 8$$
$$x_1, x_2 \geqslant 0.$$

1.3 Represent the following model in a space of two dimensions:

$$\text{Maximise} \quad -4x_1 + 5x_2 + 3x_3$$

subject to

$$-x_1 + x_2 - x_3 = 2$$
$$x_1 + x_2 + 2x_3 \leqslant 3$$
$$x_1, x_2, x_3 \geqslant 0.$$

1.4 Is the feasible region corresponding to the following constraints convex?

$$x_1^2 + x_2^2 \leqslant 4$$
$$x_1^2 + x_2^2 \geqslant 1.$$

1.5 Is the following function convex?

$$f(x) = \frac{1}{1 + x}.$$

1.6 Which of the following statements is true?
(a) If an IP is feasible then its LP relaxation is feasible.
(b) If the LP relaxation is feasible then the IP is feasible.
(c) If an IP is unbounded then its LP relaxation is unbounded.
(d) If the LP relaxation is unbounded then the IP is unbounded.

1.7 Consider the following two sets of constraints:
(a)
$$\delta_1 + \delta_2 + 2\delta_3 \leqslant 2$$
$$\delta_1, \delta_2, \delta_3 \in \{0, 1\}.$$
(b)
$$\delta_1 + \delta_3 \leqslant 1$$
$$\delta_2 + \delta_3 \leqslant 1$$
$$\delta_1, \delta_2, \delta_3 \in \{0, 1\}.$$

Represent the solutions in three-dimensional space. Have the two IPs the same solution set? Have the two LP relaxations the same solution set?

1.8 If, in Example 1.2, x_1 and x_2 were restricted to integer values, draw the convex hull of feasible solutions. Represent this convex hull by linear constraints. Give the optimal integer solution.

1.9 Represent the following LP model as a minimum-cost network flow model:

$$\text{Minimise} \quad 2x_1 + x_2 + 3x_3 + x_4 + 2x_5$$

subject to:

$$x_1 + x_2 - x_3 = 4$$
$$-x_1 + x_4 + x_5 = 1$$
$$-x_2 - x_4 = -3$$
$$x_3 - x_5 = -2$$
$$x_1, x_2, x_3, x_4, x_5 \geqslant 0.$$

1.10 In Example 1.25, take $b_1 = 20$, $b_2 = 5$ and $b_3 = 25$, and draw a picture of the three-dimensional feasible region associated with constraints (1.140) to (1.142).

What would the feasible region look like if these constraints were relaxed to be "$\leqslant$"? What would be the optimal solution to any objective with the "$\leqslant$" constraints?

1.11 If, in Example 1.26, constraint (1.146) is ignored, obtain geometrically the optimal solution to each of the subproblems. Do these provide an optimal solution to the total problem (a) without constraint (1.146) and (b) with constraint (1.146)?

1.12 For Example 1.27, represent B's model as an LP.

1.13 Show that the tower of Hanoi problem must take at least $2^n - 1$ operations.

Chapter 2
General Methods for Linear Programming

In this chapter we describe the main general method of solving LPs known as the *simplex algorithm*. The method involves successively solving simultaneous equations. Therefore, before describing the simplex algorithm, we describe how to solve a set of simultaneous equations by a method known as *Gaussian elimination*. The problem of solving a set of inequalities by an analogous approach due to Fourier, known as *Fourier–Motzkin elimination*, is then described. This is shown to be inefficient for problems of optimisation, although it gives considerable insight into the nature of LP. In particular, it helps us to explain a concept in LP, which can be exploited in solution methods, known as *duality*.

It also provides a method of finding *all* the solutions to a set of constraints. These can be characterised in terms of the extreme solutions.

Duality, applied to an LP model, gives rise to another model known as the *dual* model. The operations of the simplex algorithm, if carried out on this model, give rise to a set of operations on the original model known as the *dual simplex algorithm*, which is described in section 2.6.

Finally we describe a much more recent method of solving LP models based on projective transformations. This method is the result of a successful attempt to produce an LP algorithm of lower (polynomial) computational complexity than the simplex algorithm. Unlike the earlier attempt of the ellipsoid method, this method appears to work efficiently on large models.

2.1 SOLVING SYSTEMS OF LINEAR EQUATIONS

In section 1.1 it was emphasised that LP is concerned with *inequality* systems, although some constraints may be equations and some variables may be unconstrained (free). It is still, however, instructive first to consider systems where *all* constraints are equations and *all* variables are free. Solving such a set of equations repeatedly is central to the simplex algorithm.

Example 2.1 Solving Simultaneous Equations
Solve the following equations:

$$-x_1 + x_2 - x_3 = b_1 \qquad (2.1)$$

$$x_1 + x_2 + 2x_3 = b_2 \qquad (2.2)$$

$$x_2 + x_3 = b_3. \qquad (2.3)$$

We will use a method known as *Gaussian elimination* since this (and its variant, Gauss–Jordan elimination) is the method most widely used within LP solution methods. It is just as easy and more illustrative to solve for general coefficients on the right-hand side (RHS).

Step 1 Choose a variable (known as the *pivot variable*) to eliminate.

In this example, we will begin with x_1.

Step 2 Choose an equation in which the above variable occurs and use this equation (known as the *pivot equation*) to eliminate the pivot variable from the other equations. The coefficient of the pivot variable in the pivot equation is known as the *pivot element*.

In this example, we choose equation (2.1) to substitute x_1 out of the other equations. This gives

$$2x_2 + x_3 = b_1 + b_2 \qquad (2.4)$$

$$x_2 + x_3 = b_3. \qquad (2.5)$$

Steps 1 and 2 are then repeated until all variables have been dealt with. In this example, the system then becomes (after eliminating x_2):

$$\tfrac{1}{2}x_3 = b_3 - \tfrac{1}{2}b_1 - \tfrac{1}{2}b_2. \qquad (2.6)$$

Step 3 Solve the last resultant equation to give the value of the last variable. Substitute the value into the preceding equation and repeat the procedure taking variables in reverse order of elimination. This process is known as *back-substitution*.

In this example, this successively gives

$$x_3 = 2b_3 - b_1 - b_2$$
$$x_2 = b_1 + b_2 - b_3$$
$$x_1 = b_1 + 2b_2 - 3b_3.$$

The central operation in this method is *pivoting*, i.e. choosing a variable and an equation with which to substitute the variable out of the other equations.

This example gives us a *unique* solution for any values of the b_i. If we took, for example, $b_1 = 2$, $b_2 = 3$ and $b_3 = 3$, then equations (2.1) and (2.2) would give the constraints of Example 1.4 treated as equations. This gives rise to corresponding hyperplanes, which intersect along line CD in Figure 1.4. Equation (2.3) would correspond to points on another hyperplane intersecting CD at the point $x_1 = -1$, $x_2 = 2$, $x_3 = 1$.

We should be aware of complications that can arise. These are illustrated by a further example.

Example 2.2 Linearly Dependent Equations
Solve the following equations:

$$-x_1 + x_2 - x_3 = b_1 \tag{2.7}$$

$$x_1 + x_2 + 2x_3 = b_2 \tag{2.8}$$

$$x_1 + 3x_2 + 3x_3 = b_3. \tag{2.9}$$

Step 1 We choose x_1 as pivot variable.
Step 2 We choose (2.7) as pivot equation, reducing the system to

$$2x_2 + x_3 = b_1 + b_2 \tag{2.10}$$

$$4x_2 + 2x_3 = b_1 + b_3. \tag{2.11}$$

Steps 1 and 2 are now repeated to eliminate x_2 and x_3, giving

$$0 = b_3 - b_1 - 2b_2. \tag{2.12}$$

Two cases must now be distinguished:

(i) If the value of $b_3 - b_1 - 2b_2$ is not zero, then equation (2.12) is false, indicating that the original system is self-contradictory (infeasible), i.e. there are *no solutions*.
(ii) If, however, the value of $b_3 - b_1 - 2b_2$ is zero, then (2.12) does not provide us with an equation from which we can deduce the value of x_3. In fact x_3 can be set to any value indicating an infinite number of solutions. It can be seen that equations (2.10) and (2.11) are equivalent. We may therefore take this arbitrary value of x_3 and proceed to back-substitute using either (2.10) or (2.11) followed by (2.7).

Step 3 This gives

$$x_3 = x_3 \quad \text{(any value)}$$
$$x_2 = \tfrac{1}{2}b_1 + \tfrac{1}{2}b_3 - \tfrac{1}{2}x_3$$
$$x_1 = -\tfrac{1}{2}b_1 + \tfrac{1}{2}b_2 - \tfrac{3}{2}x_3.$$

The situation illustrated by this example arises because the expression on the left-hand side (LHS) of equation (2.9) is *linearly dependent* on the expressions in (2.7) and (2.8). In this case

$$(x_1 + 3x_2 + 3x_3) \equiv (-x_1 + x_2 - x_3) + 2(x_1 + x_2 + 2x_3). \qquad (2.13)$$

Hence equation (2.9) either *contradicts* (2.7) and (2.8) (case (i)) or is *redundant* (case (ii)). Geometrically, in Figure 1.4, the hyperplane corresponding to (2.9) is either parallel to CD and does not intersect it, or CD lies in the hyperplane. Which case occurs depends on whether the values of b_1, b_2 and b_3 satisfy equation (2.12).

In the latter case (ii) we could have ignored equation (2.9), giving us an *underdetermined system of equations* (which frequently arises in LP, together with inequalities). Such a system will have an infinite set of solutions. In LP, of course, we will be concerned with optimising an objective, as well as satisfying constraints, which will normally provide us with a further restriction. The maximum number of linearly independent expressions on the left-hand sides of a set of equations is known as the *row rank* of the system. If this is equal to the number of equations, then we are said to have a system of full row rank, leading to a unique solution above.

Notice that, if the system of equations has a unique solution, then an objective function is irrelevant since we cannot improve on this solution. If a system of equations has no solution, then an objective is again irrelevant (an infeasible model). If a system of equations has an infinite number of solutions, then either the objective can be optimised without limit (on an unbounded model) or all solutions are equally good (alternative solutions). Hence in all cases an objective function is inappropriate in determining solutions unless we also have inequalities present.

For computational accuracy and efficiency, the order in which we choose pivot variables and pivot equations is important. Such questions of computational efficiency are considered, in relation to the simplex algorithm, in Chapter 4.

2.2 SOLVING SYSTEMS OF LINEAR INEQUALITIES AND EQUATIONS

Since LP systems must involve *some* inequality constraints, if optimisation is relevant, we will consider how we might solve such systems analogously to Gaussian elimination for equations. We will illustrate this by an example. The method we adopt is known as *Fourier–Motzkin elimination*.

Example 2.3 Solving Simultaneous Inequalities
Solve the following equations and inequalities to maximise z:

$$4x_1 - 5x_2 - 3x_3 + z = 0 \tag{2.14}$$

$$-x_1 + x_2 - x_3 \leqslant b_1 \tag{2.15}$$

$$x_1 + x_2 + 2x_3 \leqslant b_2 \tag{2.16}$$

$$-x_1 \leqslant 0 \tag{2.17}$$

$$-x_2 \leqslant 0 \tag{2.18}$$

$$-x_3 \leqslant 0. \tag{2.19}$$

We have deliberately adapted Example 1.2 for our purpose. A new variable has been introduced into the model and set equal to the objective function by means of equation (2.14). The reason for doing this will become apparent when we examine the solution. As in section 2.1, it is just as easy to deal with general RHS coefficients b_i. In order to maintain the resemblance of the model to Example 1.2, we only introduce general RHS coefficients for inequalities (2.15) and (2.16). It is procedurally convenient to treat all inequalities in the "$\leqslant$" form.

Step 1   Choose a variable to eliminate (known as the *pivot variable*).

In this example we will begin with x_1.

Step 2   (a) If the pivot variable occurs in any equations, use one of them as *pivot equation* to substitute the pivot variable out of the other equations and inequalities.

In this case we have such an equation (2.14). This results in the system (after multiplying through to avoid fractions)

$$-x_2 - 7x_3 + z \leqslant 4b_1 \tag{2.20}$$

$$9x_2 + 11x_3 - z \leqslant 4b_2 \tag{2.21}$$

$$-5x_2 - 3x_3 + z \leqslant 0 \tag{2.22}$$

$$-x_2 \leqslant 0 \tag{2.23}$$

$$-x_3 \leqslant 0. \tag{2.24}$$

(b) If the pivot variable does not occur in any equations we must eliminate it between inequalities. This is illustrated for the next variable elimination.

Step 1 is repeated and we choose x_2. Since x_2 does not occur in any equations, we cannot use an equation to substitute it out. The inequalities (2.20) to (2.23) in which it occurs can be written, for illustrative purposes, as

$$\left.\begin{array}{l} -7x_3 + z - 4b_1 \\ \frac{1}{5}(-3x_3 + z) \\ 0 \end{array}\right\} \leqslant x_2 \leqslant \frac{1}{9}(4b_2 - 11x_3 + z).$$

A *consequence* of the above inequalities is that each of the three LHS expressions must be less than or equal to the RHS expression. What is more, if this is the case then *there exists* a value of x_2 satisfying the above inequalities (e.g. the maximum value of the LHS expressions or the minimum value of the RHS expressions). Hence the above inequalities are true *if and only if*

$$-7x_3 + z - 4b_1 \leqslant \frac{1}{9}(4b_2 - 11x_3 + z)$$
$$\frac{1}{5}(-3x_3 + z) \leqslant \frac{1}{9}(4b_2 - 11x_3 + z)$$
$$0 \leqslant \frac{1}{9}(4b_2 - 11x_3 + z).$$

Rewriting these resultant inequalities in a simpler form (and including (2.24)) gives the result of step 2(b) applied to eliminate x_2:

$$-13x_3 + 2z \leqslant 9b_1 + b_2 \tag{2.25}$$

$$7x_3 + z \leqslant 5b_2 \tag{2.26}$$

$$11x_3 - z \leqslant 4b_2 \tag{2.27}$$

$$-x_3 \leqslant 0. \tag{2.28}$$

Notice that the effect of the above elimination has been to take *each pair* of inequalities from (2.20) to (2.24) in which x_2 has *opposite signs* and add them in suitable multiples to eliminate x_2.

We now repeat step 1, choosing x_3 and then applying step 2(b) to give

$$3z \leqslant 7b_1 + 8b_2 \tag{2.29}$$

$$z \leqslant 11b_1 + 7b_2 \tag{2.30}$$

$$z \leqslant 5b_2 \tag{2.31}$$

$$-z \leqslant 4b_2. \tag{2.32}$$

Hence

$$-4b_2 \leqslant z \leqslant \text{Min}(\tfrac{7}{3}b_1 + \tfrac{8}{3}b_2, 11b_1 + 7b_2, 5b_2). \tag{2.33}$$

Two cases must now be distinguished:

(i) If

$$-4b_2 > \text{Min}(\tfrac{7}{3}b_1 + \tfrac{8}{3}b_2, 11b_1 + 7b_2, 5b_2)$$

i.e.

$$\text{Min}(\tfrac{7}{3}b_1 + \tfrac{20}{3}b_2, 11b_1 + 11b_2, 9b_2) < 0 \tag{2.34}$$

then there are *no solutions*, i.e. this model is infeasible.

(ii) If

$$\text{Min}(\tfrac{7}{3}b_1 + \tfrac{20}{3}b_2, 11b_1 + 11b_2, 9b_2) \geqslant 0 \tag{2.35}$$

then there are one or more solutions. Implicit in the inequalities (2.29) to (2.32) are both the maximum and minimum possible values of z and therefore any values in between. We could therefore set z to any such feasible value and, in step 3, backtrack to find all of the (generally infinite) set of solutions x_3, x_2, x_1. We have deliberately posed our problem as one of *maximising z* in order to restrict the set of the solutions to be considered. We can choose the unique value for z in step 3 below.

Step 3 Choose the maximum value of z and substitute this value into preceding inequalities. This enables us to choose values of the variables satisfying the inequalities or equations in reverse order of elimination:

$$z = \text{Min}(\tfrac{7}{3}b_1 + \tfrac{8}{3}b_2, 11b_1 + 7b_2, 5b_2) \tag{2.36}$$

$$x_3 = \text{Min}(\tfrac{1}{7}(5b_2 - z), \tfrac{1}{11}(4b_2 + z)) \tag{2.37}$$

$$x_2 = \tfrac{1}{9}(4b_2 - 11x_3 + z) \tag{2.38}$$

$$x_1 = \tfrac{1}{4}(5x_2 + 3x_3 - z). \tag{2.39}$$

In Example 1.2, $b_1 = 2$ and $b_2 = 3$, giving $z = 38/3$, $x_3 = 1/3$, $x_2 = 7/3$, $x_1 = 0$, the solution demonstrated in Figure 1.2. Expression (2.36) is known as the *value function* for the LP. It gives the optimal objective value as a function of the RHS coefficients. It can be shown that for an LP model, in standard form, the value function takes this form, i.e. is the minimum of a number of non-negative linear combinations of the RHS coefficients. Also it can be shown that the expression such as (2.35) in the feasibility condition takes the same form. This is sometimes known as the *consistency tester*.

These expressions will be returned to in section 2.7, as they illustrate an aspect of the duality result for LP.

It should be clear that eliminating a variable between *inequalities* could produce a very large increase in the size of the system. Each inequality in which the variable has a negative coefficient must be combined with each one in which it has a positive coefficient. When this is repeated for each variable, the number of inequalities resulting in the system corresponding to (2.29)–(2.32) can be astronomic. This is what makes the method impracticable as a computational tool. Some restriction on the build-up of inequalities is possible. If, after eliminating r variables, an inequality results from more than $r + 1$ of the original inequalities, it can shown to be redundant and may therefore be deleted. This does not happen in the above example. There may also be virtue in choosing the variables for elimination in a special order to minimise build-up in inequalities. When all variables have been eliminated, however, the total number of resultant inequalities will be the same. This will become apparent from the discussion in section 2.7.

For particular values of the b_i all but one of the inequalities in the final system such as (2.29) to (2.32) will turn out to be redundant. A very clear interpretation of the meaning of all these final inequalities results from considering the *dual model* and the concept of duality. This is discussed in sections 2.5, 2.6 and 2.7.

2.3 THE SIMPLEX ALGORITHM I: FINDING AN OPTIMAL SOLUTION

Basic Solutions

We begin by considering the (usual) case were all variables are non-negative. Therefore, the polytope representing the feasible region will be pointed. Other cases can be treated quite easily by the simplex algorithm and will be discussed later and in section 2.4. In that section we also give a full unified mathematical definition of the steps necessary to cover every type of situation. Before that we give a more intuitive description by means of examples.

The simplex algorithm (unlike Fourier–Motzkin elimination) requires the conversion of all the inequalities (apart from non-negativity conditions) to equations by means of the addition of extra (non-negative) variables. We will again take Example 1.2 to demonstrate this. The constraints become

$$- x_1 + x_2 - x_3 + x_4 = 2 \qquad (2.40)$$

$$x_1 + x_2 + 2x_3 + x_5 = 3 \qquad (2.41)$$

$$x_1, x_2, x_3, x_4, x_5 \geqslant 0. \qquad (2.42)$$

Notice that inequalities are still an inherent part of the system. The original "$\leqslant$" inequalities have only been converted to equations at the expense of extra, non-negativity inequalities, involving x_4 and x_5.

Variables such as x_4 and x_5 are known as *slack variables*. In contrast, the original variables such as x_1, x_2 and x_3 are known as *structural variables*.

Since we can restrict our attention, in this example, to *vertex solutions*, we will interpret them algebraically in terms of values for the variables x_1 to x_5. Figure 2.1 (in the three-dimensional space of x_1, x_2, x_3) gives the feasible region.

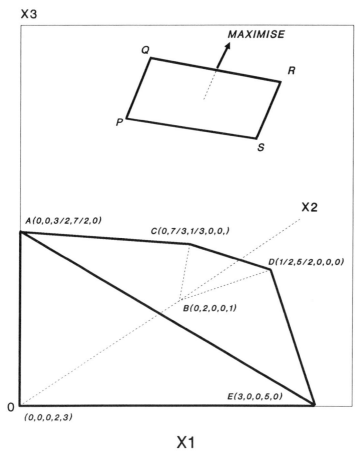

Figure 2.1   The vertices of a linear programming polytope

At each vertex we have marked the values of all the variables x_1 to x_5. Notice that, at each vertex, three of the variables are zero. This must always happen when we have a three-dimensional polytope. A vertex will arise from the junction of *at least* three facets. These facets arise from constraints, which may be non-negativity constraints, on the structural variables, such as at vertex O. In this case these variables will be zero. Alternatively, they may be a combination of non-negativity constraints and other constraints, in which case the corresponding slack variables in the other constraints will also be zero.

Notice that we could have a three-dimensional polytope in which more than three constraints intersected at a vertex. If, in this example, we also had a (redundant) constraint

$$-2x_1 + x_2 - 3x_3 \leqslant 2 \tag{2.43}$$

then this would also pass through vertex B. The slack variable corresponding to this constraint would therefore also be zero at B. This possibility does happen in practice and gives rise to a phenomenon known as *degeneracy*, which is discussed later.

Since, in this example, at least three of the variables (structurals and slacks) are zero at a vertex, then *at most* two can be non-zero. Therefore, we need only look at subsets of two of the five variables if we are considering vertex solutions. If we choose two variables and set the other three to zero, (2.40) and (2.41) give us two equations involving these two variables. So long as these equations have row rank of 2, they have a unique solution. For example, choosing x_1 and x_2 (setting $x_3 = x_4 = x_5 = 0$) gives

$$-x_1 + x_2 = 2 \tag{2.44}$$

$$x_1 + x_2 = 3 \tag{2.45}$$

leading to the unique solution $x_1 = 1/2$, $x_2 = 5/2$ corresponding to vertex D.

Choosing pairs (x_4, x_5), (x_3, x_4), (x_2, x_5), (x_2, x_3) and (x_1, x_4) leads, respectively, to vertices O, A, B, C and E. It should be noted, however, that not every pair of variables leads to a vertex solution in this way. For example, choosing x_1 and x_3 gives

$$-x_1 - x_3 = 2 \tag{2.46}$$

$$x_1 + 2x_3 = 3 \tag{2.47}$$

leading to the solution $x_1 = -7$, $x_3 = 5$. This solution corresponds to a point outside the polytope, giving an *infeasible solution*. Geometrically this infeasible solution arises from the intersection of the (extended) facets BCD, ACDE and OAE.

Another possible outcome (which does not occur in this example) is that the resultant equations, in the two chosen variables, have row rank less than 2 and do not provide a vertex solution. This would happen if two or more of the facets of the polytope were parallel and did not therefore intersect at a vertex. Exercise 2.6 illustrates this.

In general, for a model with n structural variables and m constraints (apart from non-negativity constraints), the above result generalises. Therefore, at most m of the variables can be non-zero at a vertex. A set of m variables is known as a *basis* as long as the resultant equations involving these variables have full row rank. Therefore the simplex algorithm restricts attention to *basic solutions*, i.e. the solutions derived from solving the equations in a set of basic variables.

The main problem of solving an LP model is therefore that of choosing a basis. Once this has been done, we simply have to solve a set of simultaneous equations of full row rank. The number of possible bases will, in practice, be astronomic. For a model with m equations and $m + n$ (structural and slack) variables, we have to choose a set of m out of the $m + n$ variables. The number of ways of doing this is usually written as

$$\binom{m + n}{m} = \frac{(m + n)(m + n - 1)\dots(n + 1)}{m(m - 1)\dots 1} = \frac{(m + n)!}{n!m!}.$$

In practice, the number of bases will be less than this as some subsets of variables will give a set of linearly dependent equations and not therefore provide a basis. From this reduced number of bases only some will correspond to feasible vertices. Hence, for Example 1.2, where $m = 2$ and $n = 3$, we have, from the above formula, at most 10 bases. Figure 1.2 (and Figure 2.1) demonstrates that only six of these correspond to vertices.

In a sense LP is a *combinatorial* problem, since we are searching from the *discrete* set of bases.

There is an improved upper bound on the number of vertices. This is

$$\binom{m + n - \lfloor (n + 1)/2 \rfloor}{m} + \binom{m + n - \lfloor (n + 2)/2 \rfloor}{m}$$

where $\lfloor p \rfloor$ indicates the next integer below, or equal to, p. For Example 1.2 this gives the maximum of six vertices.

It is convenient, in applying the simplex algorithm, as in Fourier–Motzkin elimination, to use another variable z to represent the value of the objective function. This is set equal to the objective function by means of an equation. In our example this gives

$$4x_1 - 5x_2 - 3x_3 + z = 0. \tag{2.48}$$

The slack variables and the z variable are known collectively as *logical variables*. When considering bases it will be convenient always to regard z as one of the basic variables. For an m constraint model we will therefore always have $m + 1$ equations, including that resulting from the objective (e.g. (2.48)), and therefore $m + 1$ basic variables. This representation of a model as a set of equations with a logical variable in each equation is known as the *canonical form* of the model. In the example, in addition, all variables apart from z (a free variable) will be constrained to be non-negative.

The Steps of the Simplex Algorithm

We now apply the simplex algorithm to the above example in canonical form.

Example 2.4 The Simplex Algorithm

Maximise z

such that

$$z + 4x_1 - 5x_2 - 3x_3 = 0 \qquad (2.49)$$

$$-x_1 + x_2 - x_3 + x_4 = 2 \qquad (2.50)$$

$$x_1 + x_2 + 2x_3 + x_5 = 3 \qquad (2.51)$$

$$x_1, x_2, x_3, x_4, x_5 \geqslant 0. \qquad (2.52)$$

Step 0 Choose a *starting basis*. It is convenient (but not necessary) to take the *all-logical* starting basis. This will consist of the requisite number of variables since there is one logical variable corresponding to each equation. Also the resulting equations will be of full row rank since each logical variable is unique in each equation. The other variables are known as *non-basic*.

Therefore in this example we choose z, x_4 and x_5.

Step 1 We express the basic variables in terms of the non-basic variables.

Another definition, sometimes used, is to refer to the basic variables as *dependent* variables and the non-basic variables as *independent variables*. We are therefore rewriting the equations in a form in which we can freely set values for the independent (non-basic) variables. This then determines the values for the dependent (basic) variables.

It is important to realise that this simply corresponds to a rearrangement of the original equations. All that the simplex algorithm does is systematically to rearrange the equations until they are in a form from which an optimal solution becomes obvious. At each stage of the calculation the current set of equations contains all the information of the original model.

In the example the rearrangement gives

$$z = 0 - 4x_1 + 5x_2 + 3x_3 \qquad (2.53)$$

$$x_4 = 2 + x_1 - x_2 + x_3 \qquad (2.54)$$

$$x_5 = 3 - x_1 - x_2 - 2x_3. \qquad (2.55)$$

The corresponding *basic solution* is obtained by setting the non-basic variables to zero. We currently consider the case in which this gives a feasible solution, i.e. no variables take negative values. What to do when this does not happen is the subject of section 2.4.

In this example we have $z = 0$, $x_4 = 2$, $x_5 = 3$. Geometrically we have the solution corresponding to vertex 0 in Figure 2.1.

Step 2   We seek a non-basic variable (currently at value zero) that could beneficially be increased in value (i.e. *enter the basis*). This is indicated (for a maximisation model) by a variable having a positive coefficient in the objective row. Any such variable would have the desired effect but it seems best to choose that with the largest positive coefficient. This choice is not, in fact, always best, but this consideration is postponed until later. From the correspondence with Gaussian elimination, this will be known as the *pivot variable*.

In the example we therefore choose x_2 as pivot variable.

Step 3   If the pivot variable is increased in value then the values of some, or all, of the current basic variables will change. We do not allow any, non-negatively constrained, variable to become negative (infeasible). This may restrict the amount by which the pivot variable may be increased. If it does not, then this is an indication that the model is *unbounded*. Such an eventuality is illustrated later in Example 2.8.

For the example x_2 can be increased to 2 when the value of x_4 drops to 0. Therefore we will regard x_4 as leaving the basis.

Here, in this step, we choose the variable to *leave the basis* as the first basic variable to decrease to zero when the pivot variable is increased.

The equation, of which the leaving basic variable is the subject, is known as the *pivot equation*. The coefficient of the pivot variable in the pivot equation is known as the *pivot element*. This equation is used to substitute the new basic variable (pivot variable) out of the other equations. The procedure that we have adopted is strictly known as Gauss–Jordan elimination rather than Gaussian elimination. Here we eliminate the pivot variable from *all* other equations, and retain the pivot equation with the pivot variable having a coefficient of 1. In fact, Gaussian elimination is more efficient although its use in the simplex algorithm is more involved. Its use is discussed in section 4.2.

In this example equation (2.54) is the pivot equation. Eliminating x_2 from the other equations gives

$$z + 5x_4 = 10 + x_1 + 8x_3 \tag{2.56}$$

$$x_2 = 2 + x_1 - x_4 + x_3 \tag{2.57}$$

$$x_5 - x_4 = 1 - 2x_1 - 3x_3. \tag{2.58}$$

We now proceed to step 1 using the new basic variables.

Notice that we could always obtain the results of step 1 by performing Gauss–Jordan elimination on the original equation set to eliminate basic variables. This is, however, unnecessary. We can achieve the same result by eliminating the new pivot variable from the current set of equations.

In the example the result of step 1 is to transform the above equations to the form

$$z = 10 + x_1 - 5x_4 + 8x_3 \tag{2.59}$$

$$x_2 = 2 + x_1 - x_4 + x_3 \tag{2.60}$$

$$x_5 = 1 - 2x_1 + x_4 - 3x_3. \tag{2.61}$$

The corresponding basic solution is $z = 10$, $x_2 = 2$, $x_5 = 1$. Geometrically we have the solution corresponding to vertex B in Figure 2.1. By bringing x_2 into the basis we moved along edge OB until we reached facet BCD, i.e. until this corresponding constraint becomes *binding* demonstrated by its slack variable x_4 leaving the basis.

The cycle that we have performed of exchanging one basic variable for another and making the new basic variable the subject of the equations is known as an *iteration*.

We now repeat steps 2 and 3 until, in step 2, there is no eligible variable (i.e. no one having a positive coefficient in the current objective equation) to enter the basis. This indicates that we have reached an *optimal solution*.

In the example, on the second iteration, steps 2 and 3 bring x_3 into the basis and take x_5 out. Step 1 then results in the representation of the equations as

$$z = \tfrac{38}{3} - \tfrac{13}{3} x_1 - \tfrac{7}{3} x_4 - \tfrac{8}{3} x_5 \tag{2.62}$$

$$x_2 = \tfrac{7}{3} + \tfrac{1}{3} x_1 - \tfrac{2}{3} x_4 - \tfrac{1}{3} x_5 \tag{2.63}$$

$$x_3 = \tfrac{1}{3} - \tfrac{2}{3} x_1 + \tfrac{1}{3} x_4 - \tfrac{1}{3} x_5. \tag{2.64}$$

This gives the basic solution $z = 38/3$, $x_2 = 7/3$, $x_3 = 1/3$. Geometrically we have moved up edge BC to the vertex at C. No further improvement in the value of z is possible since the non-basic variables all have negative coefficients in equation (2.62).

Hence this example has been solved by two iterations of the simplex algorithm.

The updated coefficients of the non-basic variables in the objective row are known as *reduced costs*. It is slightly unfortunate that the term "reduced costs" has become standard usage. For a maximisation model (the standard form in which we are considering models) the term "reduced profit" might be better. These figures will be *positive* for variables that are worth entering the basis and negative or zero for variables not worth entering (i.e. "not profitable"). In some treatments of the simplex algorithm (e.g. the revised simplex algorithm in Chapter 4), reduced costs are given opposite signs, i.e. negative before optimality and positive or zero after. The reduced costs appearing in the final set of equations have an important economic interpretation in many applications. This is discussed in *MBMP*. Also they are discussed in sections 2.5, 2.6 and 4.6.

Alternative Pivot Selection Rules

It is not necessary to choose the pivot variable as that having largest coefficient in the current objective equation

The coefficient of variable x_j in the current objective row is commonly represented by the symbol d_j. The value of d_j gives the *rate of increase* of the objective function with respect to increasing the pivot variable. It does not indicate by *how much* the variable can be increased. This latter quantity is indicated by the absolute value of the ratio between the current solution value of the outgoing basic variable in the pivot equation and the (negative) pivot element. This ratio is usually represented by θ_j. The improvement in the objective is therefore $\theta_j d_j$.

In the example on the first iteration we chose x_2 to enter the basis ($d_2 = 5$). This forced us to choose row (2.54) as pivot equation, giving $\theta_2 = 2$. The resultant improvement on the first iteration is $2 \times 5 = 10$. If, on the other hand, we had chosen x_3 to enter the basis ($d_3 = 3$), this would have forced us to choose row (2.55) as pivot equation, giving $\theta_3 = 3/2$. The resultant improvement on the first iteration would have been $(3/2) \times 3 = 9/2$. Therefore it would seem that, in this case, we made a good choice. In general the value of the coefficient d_j is only an indication of how desirable a choice of pivot variable is. It could happen that a variable with large d_j has small θ_j, causing the product $\theta_j d_j$ to be smaller than that for another variable.

Choosing the variable with *maximum* d_j is one possible criterion for choice of pivot variable. A better criterion might be to evaluate the product $\theta_j d_j$ for all variables with d_j positive and choose as pivot variable that making this product largest. This is the *maximum improvement* criterion, which requires more calculation but tends to result in less iterations.

Geometrically our different choices lead to different paths around the edges of the polytope in Figure 2.1. A large d_j indicates an edge pointing more directly towards the objective plane PQRS than one corresponding to a smaller d_j. On the other hand, the corresponding edges for the smaller d_j could be much longer (have larger values of θ_j). Different choices of variable to enter

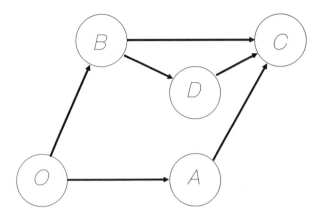

Figure 2.2 Different paths to optimality in the simplex algorithm

the basis at each iteration lead to the different paths from O to C shown in Figure 2.2.

The maximum updated objective coefficient (d_j) rule depends on the scaling of the matrix. A change in, for example, units of measurement to create a model could lead to different solution paths when solving it. This seems somewhat unsatisfactory. On the other hand, the maximum improvement ratio is independent of scaling, i.e. the solution path will be the same however the units of measurement are chosen.

There may be a choice of variables to leave the basis

This possibility may not seem serious. If, however, the choice is not made in a particular way, it can result in the simplex algorithm *circling*, i.e. going round the same calculation again and again and never terminating. We are deliberately avoiding the term "cycling", which is sometimes used, since it is also used in other contexts. Less seriously, and sometimes unavoidably, such a choice can result in *degeneracy*, i.e. the objective function not improving on a number of iterations. Hence we consider these two possibilities together.

Degeneracy and Circling

The simplex algorithm can circle unless special pivot selection rules are used to resolve choices

In practice, circling is rare. We describe how to guarantee its avoidance below. Before doing this, however, we describe the phenomenon of degeneracy by means of the extension to Example 2.2 caused by adding constraint (2.43). In Figure 2.1 this gives another hyperplane intersecting the polytope at B.

Example 2.5 A Degenerate LP

$$\text{Maximise} \quad z$$

such that

$$4x_1 - 5x_2 - 3x_3 + z = 0 \tag{2.65}$$

$$-x_1 + x_2 - x_3 + x_4 = 2 \tag{2.66}$$

$$x_1 + x_2 + 2x_3 + x_5 = 3 \tag{2.67}$$

$$-2x_1 + x_2 - 3x_3 + x_6 = 2 \tag{2.68}$$

$$x_1, x_2, x_3, x_4, x_5, x_6 \geqslant 0. \tag{2.69}$$

Step 0   We choose z, x_4, x_5 and x_6 as starting basis corresponding to vertex O in Figure 2.1.

Step 1   The equations are written as

$$z = 0 - 4x_1 + 5x_2 + 3x_3 \tag{2.70}$$

$$x_4 = 2 + x_1 - x_2 + x_3 \tag{2.71}$$

$$x_5 = 3 - x_1 - x_2 - 2x_3 \tag{2.72}$$

$$x_6 = 2 + 2x_1 - x_2 + 3x_3. \tag{2.73}$$

Step 2 x_2 enters the basis.

Step 3 x_4 or x_6 can be chosen to leave the basis since both reach the value zero simultaneously when x_2 is increased to 2. Hence either (2.71) or (2.73) can be used as pivot equation. We will (arbitrarily) choose x_6 to leave the basis with (2.73) as pivot equation.

Step 1   The equations are rewritten as

$$z = 10 + 6x_1 - 5x_6 + 18x_3 \tag{2.74}$$

$$x_4 = 0 - x_1 + x_6 - 2x_3 \tag{2.75}$$

$$x_5 = 1 - 3x_1 + x_6 - 5x_3 \tag{2.76}$$

$$x_2 = 2 + 2x_1 - x_6 + 3x_3. \tag{2.77}$$

This basis corresponds to vertex B in Figure 2.1. When, as here, there is a choice of variable to leave the basis, we choose one of them and the others will remain in the basis but their values will become zero.

Step 2 x_3 enters the basis.

Step 3 x_4 must be chosen to leave the basis with (2.75) as pivot equation. Therefore x_3 can only be "increased" to value 0. The value of θ_3 is zero, giving an improvement in the objective function of $0 \times 18 = 0$.

Notice that this example of *degeneracy* is very likely to happen after a tie in choice of pivot equations. If the pivot variable in the next iteration has a negative coefficient in the row corresponding to a basic variable that has zero value, then this row must be chosen as pivot equation. This leads to a degenerate iteration.

Step 1 The equations are rewritten as

$$z = 10 - 3x_1 + 4x_6 - 9x_4 \tag{2.78}$$

$$x_3 = 0 - \tfrac{1}{2}x_1 + \tfrac{1}{2}x_6 - \tfrac{1}{2}x_4 \tag{2.79}$$

$$x_5 = 1 - \tfrac{1}{2}x_1 - \tfrac{3}{2}x_6 + \tfrac{5}{2}x_4 \tag{2.80}$$

$$x_2 = 2 + \tfrac{1}{2}x_1 + \tfrac{1}{2}x_6 - \tfrac{3}{2}x_4. \tag{2.81}$$

This still corresponds to vertex B in Figure 2.1. We have performed an iteration with no change in the objective value. There is a danger that this phenomenon may persist since we will still have a basic variable with zero value (x_3).

Step 2 x_6 enters the basis.
Step 3 x_5 leaves the basis with (2.80) as pivot equation. Notice that, since the pivot variable x_6 has a positive entry in the row (2.79) in which a basic variable has zero value, we do not choose this row as pivot equation. Hence we "break out" of our degenerate cycle.
Step 1 The equations are rewritten as

$$z = \tfrac{33}{3} - \tfrac{13}{3}x_1 - \tfrac{8}{3}x_5 - \tfrac{7}{3}x_4 \tag{2.82}$$

$$x_3 = \tfrac{1}{3} - \tfrac{2}{3}x_1 - \tfrac{1}{3}x_5 + \tfrac{1}{3}x_4 \tag{2.83}$$

$$x_6 = \tfrac{2}{3} - \tfrac{1}{3}x_1 - \tfrac{2}{3}x_5 + \tfrac{5}{3}x_4 \tag{2.84}$$

$$x_2 = \tfrac{7}{3} + \tfrac{1}{3}x_1 - \tfrac{1}{3}x_5 - \tfrac{2}{3}x_4. \tag{2.85}$$

This corresponds to the optimal solution $z = 38/3$, $x_2 = 7/3$, $x_3 = 1/3$ at vertex C in Figure 2.1.

Vertex B can be regarded as the coincidence of two vertices. The first is the vertex arising from the interesection of hyperplanes corresponding to the non-negativity conditions on x_1 and x_3 and constraint (2.68). The second is the vertex arising from the intersection of hyperplanes corresponding to the non-negativity condition on x_1 and constraints (2.66) and (2.68). A degenerate iteration, such as the second iteration in the above example, simply moves between these coincident vertices.

The (rare) possibility of "total degeneracy" (circling) is demonstrated by the following example.

Example 2.6 An LP that Circles

Maximise z

such that

$$-\tfrac{3}{4}x_1 + 150x_2 - \tfrac{1}{50}x_3 + 6x_4 + 2 = 0 \tag{2.86}$$

$$\tfrac{1}{4}x_1 - 60x_2 - \tfrac{1}{25}x_3 + 9x_4 + x_5 = 0 \tag{2.87}$$

$$\tfrac{1}{2}x_1 - 90x_2 - \tfrac{1}{50}x_3 + 3x_4 + x_6 = 0 \tag{2.88}$$

$$x_3 + x_7 = 1 \tag{2.89}$$

$$x_1, x_2, x_3, x_4, x_5, x_6, x_7 \geqslant 0. \tag{2.90}$$

We choose the all-logical starting basis z, x_5, x_6 and x_7. Variables are then brought into the basis on the criterion of maximum d_j. When there is a tie in the possible pivot rows, we choose the first row. This leads to the following succession of bases given in row order. All give an objective value of zero.

Basis 1: z, x_5, x_6, x_7
Basis 2: z, x_1, x_6, x_7
Basis 3: z, x_1, x_2, x_7
Basis 4: z, x_3, x_2, x_7
Basis 5: z, x_3, x_4, x_7
Basis 6: z, x_5, x_4, x_7
Basis 7: z, x_5, x_6, x_7

Clearly basis 7 is the same as basis 1, causing the calculations to circle indefinitely.

For bases 1, 3 and 5 there is a choice of avoiding both degeneracy and circling. Below we give a fool-proof method that can be guaranteed to avoid circling. This method, however, does not use either the maximum d_j or maximum improvement criterion and is not therefore efficient in practice. It is simply a theoretical device for showing that circling can always be avoided if necessary. Using this method, the simplex algorithm becomes a "true algorithm", i.e. it always converges to a solution or demonstrates a model to be infeasible or unbounded.

In practice, it is assumed that circling will not occur. Cruder devices are used to try to prevent (or reduce) degeneracy. The usual method, known as ε-*perturbation*, is to replace zero solution values for basic variables by a small positive number ε. This obviously "distorts" the model from its original form. Once an optimal solution is found to this perturbed model, ε is set to zero and the optimisation continued on the true model.

ε-Perturbation is a simplified form of another technique that can also be used to guarantee the avoidance of circling. Again the full form of this technique would not be used in practice.

A Rule for Avoiding Circling

Circling can be shown to be impossible if we adopt the following pivot selection rule known as the *smallest subscript rule*.

1. Choose the pivot variable as that with smallest index from among those eligible (having positive updated objective coefficients d_j).
2. Choose the pivot equation from among those eligible (in the case of a tie) as that in which the basic variable has smallest index.

We do not prove that this is guaranteed to avoid circling. Proofs can be found from references in section 2.9.

For Example 2.6 the application of this rule would lead to the following bases.

Basis 1: z, x_5, x_6, x_7, objective = 0
Basis 2: z, x_1, x_6, x_7, objective = 0
Basis 3: z, x_1, x_2, x_7, objective = 0
Basis 4: z, x_3, x_4, x_7, objective = 0
Basis 5: z, x_3, x_4, x_7, objective = 0
Basis 6: z, x_3, x_4, x_1, objective = 1/125
Basis 7: z, x_3, x_5, x_1, objective = 1/20

Notice that, with basis 5 we now choose x_1 to enter the basis since it has the smallest subscript. In fact x_5 is also eligible (and better according to the maximum d_j criterion). Having chosen x_1 to enter, it turns out that the fourth row is the only eligible pivot now. Therefore x_7 leaves the basis, allowing us to increase x_1 by a positive amount. This takes us out of the cycle of degeneracy, ultimately leading to the optimal solution at basis 7. The full details of the calculations are left as exercise 2.20.

Notice that when using the smallest subscript rule the solution path will depend on the way in which the variables of the matrix are ordered.

The Worst-Case Performance of the Simplex Algorithm

The smallest subscript rule guarantees that the simplex algorithm will terminate after a finite number of steps. Even with this rule the algorithm could take a very large number of steps in the *worst case*. In practice, this rule would not be used exclusively. It could, however, be used in a limited form with another pivot selection rule to guarantee the prevention of circling as mentioned above. Two variable selection rules for pivoting are those of *maximum d_j* and *maximum improvement* already mentioned. In the event of a tie for choice of *pivot equation*, we will resort to the smallest subscript rule until there is a non-degenerate iteration.

Even with these modified pivot selection rules it is *possible* that the simplex algorithm will take a long time. In practice this rarely happens. We will, however, demonstrate its possibility by an example.

Example 2.7 An LP Needing Many Iterations

$$\text{Maximise} \quad z$$

subject to

$$-4x_1 - 2x_2 - x_3 + z = 0 \tag{2.91}$$

$$x_1 \qquad + x_4 = 5 \tag{2.92}$$

$$4x_1 + x_2 \qquad + x_5 = 25 \tag{2.93}$$

$$8x_1 + 4x_2 + x_3 + x_6 = 125 \tag{2.94}$$

$$x_1, x_2, x_3, x_4, x_5, x_6 \geqslant 0. \tag{2.95}$$

The polyhedron for this model is illustrated in Figure 2.3 in the space of (the structural variables) x_1, x_2 and x_3.

Using the maximum d_j rule leads to the following succession of bases.

Basis 1: z, x_4, x_5, x_6, objective = 0
Basis 2: z, x_1, x_5, x_6, objective = 20
Basis 3: z, x_1, x_2, x_6, objective = 30
Basis 4: z, x_4, x_2, x_6, objective = 50
Basis 5: z, x_4, x_2, x_3, objective = 75
Basis 6: z, x_1, x_2, x_3, objective = 95
Basis 7: z, x_1, x_5, x_3, objective = 105
Basis 8: z, x_4, x_5, x_3, objective = 125

Basis 8 is optimal. Geometrically we have followed bases corresponding to vertices O, A, B, C, D, E, F and G. Regarding this polyhedron as a (very) distorted cube, we have been around all eight vertices.

Example 2.7 can be generalised to a model with n structural variables. This is done in section 2.9. The associated polyhedron is a distorted n-dimensional hypercube with 2^n vertices. The maximum d_j rule leads to a solution path passing through every vertex. There will therefore be $2^n - 1$ iterations. For this class of model the amount of computation, using this pivot rule, will therefore be an *exponential* function of the size of the model. Such a fast growth in computational requirement is usually regarded as indication of a "slow" algorithm.

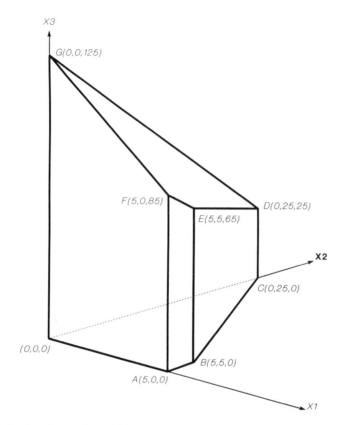

Figure 2.3 A polytope for which the simplex algorithm takes many iterations

In the case of the simplex algorithm this is misleading, since in the "average case" it behaves well. Nevertheless, the non-existence of any "fast" algorithm for a class of models is taken to demonstrate the class's inherent difficulty. In the case of LP there does turn out to be an algorithm that is fast even in the worst case. This is described in section 2.8.

In Example 2.7 if we were to use the maximum improvement rule then one iteration would take us from vertex O to G. Unfortunately, examples can also be created to demonstrate an exponential number of steps with this pivot rule. Such examples are more difficult to construct.

Example 2.7 and its generalisation to n dimensions can also easily be adapted to demonstrate that the smallest subscript rule can require an exponential number of steps. These variables can be rearranged in the model into the order in which they entered the basis in the above calculation. There are no choices of pivot equation possible in the above calculation. Hence this rearranged model would follow the same long solution path as that above.

No pivot selection rule has yet been found for the simplex algorithm that can be guaranteed, in all cases, to take less than an exponential number of iterations, as a function of the size of the model.

It is worth noticing that scaling the matrix columns differently would lead the maximum d_j rule to take a different path. If, for example, we set

$$8x_1 = x_1' \qquad 4x_2 = x_2' \qquad x_3 = x_3'$$

then with the new model, in terms of x_1', x_2' and x_3', this rule would produce the optimal solution in one iteration.

Unbounded Solutions

It was pointed out, in the solution to Example 2.4, how an unbounded solution to a model manifests itself in the simplex algorithm. We now, by means of another example, demonstrate again how this happens and how the unboundedness may be characterised by an extreme ray. We use Example 1.3, illustrated in Figure 1.3, but with the new objective (1.16). In that example we have converted the "$\geqslant$" constraint (1.13) to the "$\leqslant$" form before adding a slack variable. This gives the following example.

Example 2.8 The Simplex Algorithm With an Unbounded Model

Maximise z

subject to

$$-3x_1 + x_2 + 2 = 0 \tag{2.96}$$

$$-x_1 - 2x_2 + x_3 = -5 \tag{2.97}$$

$$2x_1 - x_2 + x_4 = 2 \tag{2.98}$$

$$x_1, x_2, x_3, x_4 \geqslant 0. \tag{2.99}$$

In this example the all-logical starting basis of z, x_3 and x_4 would be infeasible since x_3 would take the value -5. A method of dealing with this situation is given in section 2.4. In the meantime if we can select a feasible basis then we can obtain the corresponding basic solution by Gaussian elimination. From Figure 1.3 we can see that vertex B arises from the constraints (2.97) and (2.98) being binding (slack variables being non-basic) and therefore provides the feasible basis z, x_1, x_2.

Eliminating x_1 from (2.97) and (2.98) using (2.96) as pivot equation gives

$$-\tfrac{7}{3}x_2 + x_3 - \tfrac{1}{3}z = -5 \tag{2.100}$$

$$-\tfrac{1}{3}x_2 + x_4 + \tfrac{2}{3}z = 2. \tag{2.101}$$

Eliminating x_2 from (2.98) using (2.100) as pivot equation gives

$$-\tfrac{1}{7}x_3 + x_4 + \tfrac{5}{7}z = \tfrac{19}{7}. \tag{2.101a}$$

Making z the subject of this equation and back-substituting to give x_2 and x_1 we obtain

$$z = \tfrac{19}{5} + \tfrac{1}{5}x_3 - \tfrac{7}{5}x_4 \tag{2.102}$$

$$x_2 = \tfrac{8}{5} + \tfrac{2}{5}x_3 + \tfrac{1}{5}x_4 \tag{2.103}$$

$$x_1 = \tfrac{9}{5} + \tfrac{1}{5}x_3 - \tfrac{2}{5}x_4. \tag{2.104}$$

We can now attempt to apply the steps of the simplex algorithm. x_3 is the only possible pivot variable. If x_3 is increased, then neither x_1 nor x_2 decrease. Hence the objective can be increased without limit, demonstrating the model to be unbounded.

This unboundedness is characterised by the extreme ray BC in Figure 1.3, i.e. by this basic solution at B

$$z = 19/5 \qquad x_2 = 8/5 \qquad x_1 = 9/5$$

and the unbounded value of variable x_3. Keeping the other non-basic variable x_4 at zero restricts us to solutions on BC.

Alternative Solutions

The possibility of alternative solutions has already been demonstrated geometrically. For Example 1.2 we considered objective (1.11) instead of that shown in Figure 1.2 (and Figure 2.1). This yields alternative vertex solutions at B, C and D. We now demonstrate, by means of the same example, how this situation manifests itself algebraically.

Example 2.9 The Simplex Algorithm on a Model With Alternative Solutions

$$\text{Maximise} \quad z$$

subject to

$$4x_1 - 4x_2 + 4x_3 + z = 0 \tag{2.105}$$

$$-x_1 + x_2 - x_3 + x_4 = 2 \tag{2.106}$$

$$x_1 + x_2 + 2x_3 + x_5 = 3 \tag{2.107}$$

$$x_1, x_2, x_3, x_4, x_5 \geqslant 0. \tag{2.108}$$

Step 0 We choose the all-logical starting basis z, x_4, x_5.

Step 1   This gives

$$z = 0 - 4x_1 + 4x_2 - 4x_3 \tag{2.109}$$

$$x_4 = 2 + x_1 - x_2 + x_3 \tag{2.110}$$

$$x_5 = 3 - x_1 - x_2 - 2x_3. \tag{2.111}$$

Step 2 x_2 enters the basis.
Step 3 x_4 leaves the basis using (2.110) as pivot equation.
Step 1   This gives

$$z = 8 + 0x_1 - 4x_4 + 0x_3 \tag{2.112}$$

$$x_2 = 2 + x_1 - x_4 + x_3 \tag{2.113}$$

$$x_5 = 1 - 2x_1 + x_4 - 3x_3. \tag{2.114}$$

Since no reduced costs are positive this gives a basic optimal solution:

$$z = 8 \qquad x_2 = 2 \qquad x_5 = 1.$$

This corresponds to vertex B in Figure 2.1. Notice, however, that x_1 and x_3 have zero reduced costs. Although bringing either of them into the basis would not improve the objective, it would not adversely affect it either. Therefore bringing x_1 into the basis and pivoting out x_5 would give us an alternative optimal basic solution:

$$z = 8 \qquad x_2 = 5/2 \qquad x_1 = 1/2.$$

This corresponds to vertex D in Figure 2.1.

Bringing x_3 into the basis and pivoting out x_5 gives another alternative optimal basic solution:

$$z = 8 \qquad x_2 = 7/3 \qquad x_3 = 1/3.$$

This corresponds to vertex C in Figure 2.1.

The clue to these being alternative optimal solutions is the presence of non-basic variables with *zero reduced costs*. When this happens we can bring such variables into the solution, giving alternative solutions. In this example, since facet BCD in Figure 2.1 is a triangle, the two neighbouring optimal vertices to B give all basic optimal solutions. The *convex hull* of these vertices gives all the optimal solutions. In a general model, of course, there will be other optimal basic solutions, which are not neighbours of the one that is first found (there may also be extreme rays, which provide alternative optimal solutions). Finding *all* these solutions is a non-trivial task. For many applications it is sufficient to find one such basic solution and know that there are others. If it is desired to find all basic (and extreme ray) optimal solutions, then one approach is to use Fourier–Motzkin elimination. This is described in section 2.7.

Free Variables

Although it is always possible to replace free variables by the difference of non-negative variables, this is neither necessary nor efficient. Once a free variable has entered the basis, it is allowed to remain in the basis whatever its value. An example demonstrates the general treatment of free variables.

Example 2.10 The Simplex Algorithm With Free Variables

$$\text{Maximise } z$$

subject to

$$-x_1 - x_2 + z = 0 \tag{2.115}$$

$$2x_1 + x_2 + x_3 = 4 \tag{2.116}$$

$$x_1 - x_2 + x_4 = 1 \tag{2.117}$$

$$-3x_1 - x_2 + x_5 = 2 \tag{2.118}$$

$$x_2, x_3, x_4, x_5 \geqslant 0. \tag{2.119}$$

Here x_1 and z are free variables.

Step 0 We choose the all-logical starting basis z, x_3, x_4, x_5.
Step 1 The equations are written

$$z = 0 + x_1 + x_2 \tag{2.120}$$

$$x_3 = 4 - 2x_1 - x_2 \tag{2.121}$$

$$x_4 = 1 - x_1 + x_2 \tag{2.122}$$

$$x_5 = 2 + 3x_1 + x_2. \tag{2.123}$$

Step 2 x_1 enters the basis.
Step 3 x_4 leaves the basis with (2.122) as pivot equation.
Step 1 (repeated)   The equations are rewritten as

$$z = 1 - x_4 + 2x_2 \tag{2.124}$$

$$x_3 = 2 + 2x_4 - 3x_2 \tag{2.125}$$

$$x_1 = 1 - x_4 + x_2 \tag{2.126}$$

$$x_5 = 5 - 3x_4 + 4x_2. \tag{2.127}$$

Step 2 (repeated) x_2 enters the basis.
Step 3 (repeated) x_3 leaves the basis with (2.125) as pivot equation.

Step 1 (repeated) The equations are rewritten as

$$z = \tfrac{7}{3} + \tfrac{1}{3}x_4 - \tfrac{2}{3}x_3 \tag{2.128}$$

$$x_2 = \tfrac{2}{3} + \tfrac{2}{3}x_4 - \tfrac{1}{3}x_3 \tag{2.129}$$

$$x_1 = \tfrac{5}{3} - \tfrac{1}{3}x_4 - \tfrac{1}{3}x_3 \tag{2.130}$$

$$x_5 = \tfrac{23}{3} - \tfrac{1}{3}x_4 - \tfrac{4}{3}x_3. \tag{2.131}$$

Step 2 (repeated) x_4 enters the basis.

Step 3 (repeated) When x_4 is increased, the first variable to drop to zero is x_1. Since x_1 is free, it does not leave the basis and we can allow it to become negative. Therefore we continue increasing x_4 until x_5 becomes zero. Hence x_5 leaves the basis with (2.131) as pivot equation.

In general, we do not consider equations in which the corresponding basic variable is free as eligible pivot rows. This reduces the amount of calculation.

Step 1 (repeated) The equations are rewritten as

$$z = 10 - x_5 - 2x_3 \tag{2.132}$$

$$x_2 = 16 - 2x_5 - 3x_3 \tag{2.133}$$

$$x_1 = -6 + x_5 + x_3 \tag{2.134}$$

$$x_4 = 23 - 3x_5 - 4x_3. \tag{2.135}$$

This gives the optimal solution

$$z = 10 \qquad x_2 = 16 \qquad x_1 = -6.$$

Once a free variable has entered the basis, then the equation to which it corresponds is essentially redundant. It could therefore be ignored and only used to provide the value of this variable when the optimal solution has been obtained.

Figure 2.4 illustrates Example 2.10. Notice that our initial basic solution does not correspond to a vertex and is represented by O. We then move progressively through vertices A and B to the optimal solution at D. Alternatively we could have begun by bringing x_2 (instead of x_1) into the basis, taking us to the (non-vertex) solution at C.

It is important also to recognise that a free variable can be brought into the basis at a *negative level*. Therefore non-basic free variables are eligible for entry into the basis (at a negative level) if they have negative updated objective coefficients.

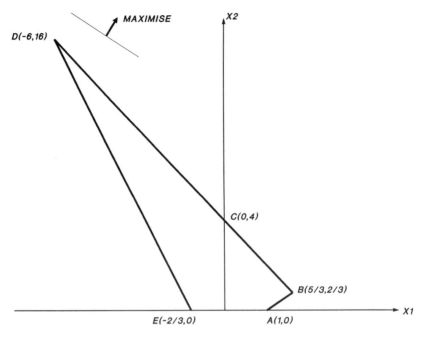

Figure 2.4 A linear programme with a non-vertex basis

This example also demonstrates that, although a vertex solution corresponds to a basic solution, the reverse need not necessarily be so. A basic solution can be a non-vertex solution if it contains free variables.

The Simplex Algorithm With Non-Pointed Polytopes

Example 2.10 demonstrated that a basic solution need not be a vertex solution. If, however, the model is not unbounded then the simplex algorithm will, for a pointed polytope, ultimately produce an optimal solution at a vertex. Should the polytope not be pointed, then this obviously cannot happen. This does not provide a difficulty but will lead to a situation that demonstrates either unboundedness or alternative solutions.

In order to demonstrate this, we consider Example 1.4, which produces the non-pointed polytope in Figure 1.4. This example is the same as Example 2.4 if we allow x_1, x_2 and x_3 to be free variables. The optimal solution to Example 2.4 is given by equations (2.62), (2.63) and (2.64). If, however, x_1 is a free variable, it can be brought into the basis at a negative level to improve the objective. When this is done, the basic variable x_2 can decrease without limit, also being a free variable. The only other basic variable x_3 increases in value. Hence

x_1 can be decreased without limit to improve the objective, demonstrating an *unbounded* model.

The only way in which such a model would not produce an unbounded solution would be if, for example, x_1 had an updated objective coefficient of 0. This would indicate alternative solutions. Such a situation would result if, for example, the objective were (1.20) as discussed in section 1.1.

2.4 THE SIMPLEX ALGORITHM II: FINDING A FEASIBLE SOLUTION WITH BOUNDED VARIABLES

In the examples in section 2.3 we obtained a feasible starting basis and then examined successive feasible bases until we either obtained an optimal basic solution or showed the model to be unbounded. Generally, we started with the all-logical basis. In practice, it will usually be the case that the all-logical basis is *not feasible*, i.e. some of the logical variables will start with non-permitted (e.g. negative) values. Example 1.1 is an instance of this and is discussed below through Example 2.11.

Usually, in a practical model, finding a feasible solution is as difficult as finding an optimal solution. Historically, finding satisfactory methods of doing this caused difficulties for algorithm designers and software producers. There are a number of possible ways of tackling the problem, some of which are mentioned in section 2.9.

We present a method here which involves driving variables from their non-permitted (often negative) values to permitted values as a first phase of the algorithm. This process is usually called *phase I* of the simplex algorithm. In order to do this, we create a new objective function known as a *pseudo-objective function*. This function represents the *sum of infeasibilities*. In practice, we usually let it be the negated sum of infeasibilities. Therefore, by maximising this function, we try to reduce the infeasibilities, hopefully to zero. Then we have a feasible basis from which we can proceed in the usual way. Full details are described below.

Instead of only regarding variables as infeasible if they are negative (excepting free variables), it is easy to generalise the concept. We therefore regard each variable as having a permitted range of values (l, u), indicating, for a variable x,

$$l \leqslant x \leqslant u.$$

If l and u are both finite, x is said to be a *bounded variable*. If x is less than its lower bound of l or greater than its upper bound of u, it is regarded as infeasible. For conventional non-negative variables we have $l = 0$ and $u = \infty$. For free variables we have $l = -\infty$ and $u = \infty$. This generalisation allows us to avoid having *explicitly* to specify constraints such as

$$x \geqslant l \qquad \text{and} \qquad x \leqslant u.$$

Instead, we deal with the restrictions implicitly through the *bounded-variable version of the simplex algorithm*. Before doing this, we demonstrate the general approach to phase I of the simplex algorithm by solving Example 1.1. In that example we have a "$\geqslant$" constraint, which causes the all-logical basis to be infeasible.

Example 2.11 An LP With a Non-Feasible Starting Basis

$$\text{Maximise} \quad 3x_1 + 2x_2 \tag{2.136}$$

subject to

$$x_1 + x_2 \leqslant 4 \tag{2.137}$$

$$2x_1 + x_2 \geqslant 5 \tag{2.138}$$

$$-x_1 + 4x_2 \geqslant 2 \tag{2.139}$$

$$x_1, x_2 \geqslant 0. \tag{2.140}$$

When using the simplex algorithm we convert constraints (2.137) and (2.138) to equations by (non-negative) slack variables x_3 and x_4. For the "$\geqslant$" constraint (2.139) we could convert it to the "$\leqslant$" form and append a slack variable x_5 giving

$$x_1 - 4x_2 + x_5 = -2. \tag{2.141}$$

For the all-logical basis x_5 would start with the non-permitted value of -2. Hence the basis would be infeasible. Geometrically this corresponds to the point O in Figure 1.1, which is clearly not on the boundary of the feasible region ABCD.

Instead of converting (2.139) to the "$\leqslant$" form, it is conceptually simpler to append x_5 by subtracting it as a *surplus variable* giving

$$-x_1 + 4x_2 - x_5 = 2. \tag{2.142}$$

x_5 will still, however, start with the infeasible value of -2. Surplus variables (together with slack variables and free variables representing objectives) are also known as logical variables.

A "$\geqslant$" constraint will always give rise to an initially infeasible, logical variable if the RHS value is positive.

Our model now takes the form

$$\text{Maximise} \quad z$$

subject to

$$z - 3x_1 - 2x_2 = 0 \quad (2.143)$$

$$x_1 + x_2 + x_3 = 4 \quad (2.144)$$

$$2x_1 + x_2 + x_4 = 5 \quad (2.145)$$

$$-x_1 + 4x_2 - x_5 = 2 \quad (2.146)$$

$$z \in (-\infty, \infty) \qquad x_1, x_2, x_3, x_4, x_5 \in [0, \infty). \quad (2.147)$$

Notice that each variable has a permitted range.

We now carry out the steps of the simplex alogithm, amending them to deal with the infeasibility.

Step 0   We choose the all-logical starting basis z, x_3, x_4, x_5.

Step 1   The equations are written as

$$z = 0 + 3x_1 + 2x_2 \quad (2.148)$$

$$x_3 = 4 - x_1 - x_2 \quad (2.149)$$

$$x_4 = 5 - 2x_1 - x_2 \quad (2.150)$$

$$x_5 = -2 - x_1 + 4x_2. \quad (2.151)$$

Since the corresponding basic solution is infeasible, we create a pseudo-objective function representing the negated sum of infeasibilities. In this example, in order to do this, we wish to

$$\text{Maximise} \quad x_5. \quad (2.152)$$

Since, however, x_5 is currently a basic variable, we wish to have it absent from all the other expressions in the model, in particular the pseudo-objective. Therefore we express x_5 in terms of the non-basic variables by means of equation (2.151). This gives us the pseudo-objective in the form

$$\text{Maximise} \quad -2 - x_1 + 4x_2. \quad (2.153)$$

The constant in this equation does not affect the procedure but simply represents the total negated infeasibility (which we wish to drive to zero). In general, we would add together all expressions on the right of equations, such as (2.151), corresponding to infeasible variables in order to give us a pseudo-objective such as (2.153).

It is again convenient to represent the pseudo-objective by a (free) logical variable, which we call s. This gives the equations as

$$s = -2 - x_1 + 4x_2 \tag{2.154}$$

$$z = 0 + 3x_1 + 2x_2 \tag{2.155}$$

$$x_3 = 4 - x_1 - x_2 \tag{2.156}$$

$$x_4 = 5 - 2x_1 - x_2 \tag{2.157}$$

$$x_5 = -2 - x_1 + 4x_2. \tag{2.158}$$

Our starting basis will now be s, z, x_3, x_4 and x_5. Since we have added an equation to our model, we have one more variable in the basis.

It is convenient to retain the true objective equation (2.155) in order to allow us to obtain the value of z when we obtain a feasible solution. It does not, however, impose a constraint since z is a free variable, as discussed in the last section.

Step 2 x_2 enters the basis since it has the (only) most positive coefficient in the pseudo-objective row (2.154).

Step 3 x_5 leaves the basis using (2.158) as a pivot equation, since it is the first to reach its lower bound (from below). Notice that the only eligible pivot rows are those in which the basic variable is not free.

Step 1   (repeated)   The equations are rewritten as

$$s = 0 + 0x_1 + x_5 \tag{2.159}$$

$$z = 1 + \tfrac{7}{2}x_1 + \tfrac{1}{2}x_5 \tag{2.160}$$

$$x_3 = \tfrac{7}{2} - \tfrac{5}{4}x_1 - \tfrac{1}{4}x_5 \tag{2.161}$$

$$x_4 = \tfrac{9}{2} - \tfrac{9}{4}x_1 - \tfrac{1}{4}x_5 \tag{2.162}$$

$$x_2 = \tfrac{1}{2} + \tfrac{1}{4}x_1 + \tfrac{1}{4}x_5 \tag{2.163}$$

The corresponding basic solution $s = 0$, $z = 1$, $x_3 = 7/2$, $x_4 = 9/2$, $x_2 = 1/2$ is now feasible.

In this example, since we now have a feasible basic solution, we can ignore the pseudo-objective and proceed using the true objective (2.160) (phase II of the simplex algorithm).

Geometrically we have moved to the point D in Figure 1.1, which lies on the boundary of this feasible region.

Step 2   (repeated) x_1 enters the basis.

Step 3   (repeated) x_4 leaves the basis using (2.162) as pivot equation.

Step 1   The equations (dropping the pseudo-objective) are rewritten as

$$z = 8 - \tfrac{14}{9}x_4 + \tfrac{1}{9}x_5 \tag{2.164}$$

$$x_3 = 1 + \tfrac{5}{9}x_4 - \tfrac{1}{9}x_5 \tag{2.165}$$

$$x_1 = 2 - \tfrac{4}{9}x_4 - \tfrac{1}{9}x_5 \tag{2.166}$$

$$x_2 = 1 - \tfrac{1}{9}x_4 + \tfrac{2}{9}x_5. \tag{2.167}$$

Step 2 (repeated) x_5 enters the basis.
Step 3 (repeated) x_3 leaves the basis using (2.165) as pivot equation.
Step 1 (repeated) The equations are rewritten as

$$z = 9 - x_4 - x_3 \tag{2.168}$$

$$x_5 = 9 + 5x_4 - 9x_3 \tag{2.169}$$

$$x_1 = 1 - x_4 + x_3 \tag{2.170}$$

$$x_2 = 3 + x_4 - 2x_3. \tag{2.171}$$

The corresponding basic solution is now optimal and is $z = 9$, $x_5 = 9$, $x_1 = 1$, $x_2 = 3$. Geometrically this is represented by point B in Figure 1.1.

Bounded Variables

We will demonstrate by means of another example how bounds on variables may be treated implicitly through phase I of the simplex algorithm.

It will now be possible for a variable to be non-basic at one of its finite bounds. Previously variables (apart from free variables) were only non-basic if they were at their lower bound of zero. The way in which this happens is demonstrated through the following example.

Example 2.12 The Bounded-Variable Simplex Algorithm

$$\text{Maximise} \quad x_1 + 2x_2 \tag{2.172}$$

subject to

$$3 \leqslant x_1 + x_2 \leqslant 4 \tag{2.173}$$

$$2x_1 + 3x_2 \geqslant 7 \tag{2.174}$$

$$z \in (-\infty, \infty), \quad x_1 \in [1, 2], \quad x_2 \in [\tfrac{3}{2}, 2]. \tag{2.175}$$

Besides restricting the two structural variables to lie within finite ranges, we have also imposed a "double constraint" in (2.173). Such a condition could, of course, be modelled as two separate constraints. Instead, we will deal with it by imposing a *range* of 1 on one of the constraints. Such a range implies an upper bound of 1 on the corresponding logical variable. The use of ranges in modelling LPs is mentioned in *MBMP*. If we are using the bounded-variable version of the simplex algorithm, it seems better to use ranges, where possible, rather than explicit extra constraints.

The example can now be written in the form

$$\text{Maximise} \quad z \tag{2.176}$$

subject to

$$x_1 + 2x_2 - z = 0 \tag{2.177}$$

$$x_1 + x_2 + x_3 = 4 \tag{2.178}$$

$$2x_1 + 3x_2 - x_4 = 7 \tag{2.179}$$

$$z \in (-\infty, \infty), \quad x_1 \in [1, 2], \quad x_2 \in [\tfrac{3}{2}, 2], \quad x_3 \in [0, 1], \quad x_4 \in [0, \infty). \tag{2.180}$$

Step 0 We choose the all-logical starting basis z, x_3, x_4.
Step 1 The equations are written as

$$z = 0 + x_1 + 2x_2 \tag{2.181}$$

$$x_3 = 4 - x_1 - x_2 \tag{2.182}$$

$$x_4 = -7 + 2x_1 + 3x_2. \tag{2.183}$$

In order to obtain a basic solution, we set the non-basic variables to one of their bounds. If we set them each to their lower bounds, we obtain the basic solution

$$z = 4 \qquad x_3 = 3/2 \qquad x_4 = -1/2.$$

This solution is infeasible since some of the variables lie outside these permitted limits. In particular, x_3 is *above* its permitted upper bound of 1 and x_4 is *below* its permitted lower bound of 0.

Our pseudo-objective will therefore be taken as

$$\text{Maximise} \quad -x_3 + x_4. \tag{2.184}$$

Notice that we give x_3 a negative sign since we wish to make it smaller, but give x_4 a positive sign since we wish to make it larger.

Expressed in terms of the non-basis variables, (2.184) is written as

$$\text{Maximise} \quad -11 + 3x_1 + 4x_2. \tag{2.185}$$

Representing this expression by a new logical variable s we have

$$s = -11 + 3x_1 + 4x_2 \tag{2.186}$$

$$z = 0 + x_1 + 2x_2 \tag{2.187}$$

$$x_3 = 4 - x_1 - x_2 \tag{2.188}$$

$$x_4 = -7 + 2x_1 + 3x_2. \tag{2.189}$$

Notice that the pseudo-objective row is formed by *subtracting* rows (e.g. (2.182)) in which the basic variable is above its permitted upper limit and *adding* rows (e.g. (2.183)) in which the basic variable is below its permitted lower limit.

Step 2   Both non-basic variables are at their lower bounds and can therefore be increased. x_2 enters the basis (from its lower bound of 3/2).

Step 3 x_2 can only be increased by at most 1/2 since it would then reach its upper bound of 2. The effect of increasing x_2 on x_3 and x_4 is as follows: x_3 decreases from its infeasible value of 3/2; x_4 increases from its infeasible value of $-1/2$. The first variable (basic or non-basic) to reach a bound is x_4. Therefore x_4 leaves the basis at its lower value of 0 using (2.189) as pivot equation.

If the incoming variable could have been switched to its opposite bound without a basic variable reaching a bound, then no variable would have entered the basis. We would simply switch the non-basic variable to its opposite bound.

Step 1   (repeated)   The equations are now rewritten as

$$s = -\tfrac{5}{3} + \tfrac{1}{3}x_1 + \tfrac{4}{3}x_4 \tag{2.190}$$

$$z = \tfrac{14}{3} - \tfrac{1}{3}x_1 + \tfrac{2}{3}x_4 \tag{2.191}$$

$$x_3 = \tfrac{5}{3} - \tfrac{1}{3}x_1 - \tfrac{1}{3}x_4 \tag{2.192}$$

$$x_2 = \tfrac{7}{3} - \tfrac{2}{3}x_1 + \tfrac{1}{3}x_4. \tag{2.193}$$

The non-basic variables are now $x_1 = 1$, $x_4 = 0$, i.e. at their lower bounds. This gives the basic solution $s = -4/3$, $z = 13/3$, $x_3 = 4/3$, $x_2 = 5/3$. The solution is infeasible since x_3 is above its upper bound of 1. The pseudo-objective remains the same, representing the negated row (2.192).

Step 2   (repeated) x_1 enters the basis.

Step 3   (repeated) x_1 can be increased (from its lower bound of 1) by at most 1 (when it reaches its upper bound). The effect of increasing x_1 on x_3 and x_2 is as follows: x_3 decreases from its infeasible value of 4/3; x_2 decreases from its feasible value of 5/3. When x_1 is increased by 1/4, x_2 falls to its lower bound of 3/2 while x_1 remains within its bounds and x_3 remains infeasible. Therefore x_2 leaves the basis with (2.193) as pivot equation.

Step 1   (repeated)   The equations are rewritten as

$$s = -\tfrac{1}{2} - \tfrac{1}{2}x_2 + \tfrac{3}{2}x_4 \tag{2.194}$$

$$z = \tfrac{7}{2} + \tfrac{1}{2}x_2 + \tfrac{1}{2}x_4 \tag{2.195}$$

$$x_3 = \tfrac{1}{2} + \tfrac{1}{2}x_2 - \tfrac{1}{2}x_4 \tag{2.196}$$

$$x_1 = \tfrac{7}{2} - \tfrac{3}{2}x_2 + \tfrac{1}{2}x_4. \tag{2.197}$$

The non-basic variables are now $x_2 = 3/2$, $x_4 = 0$, i.e. at their lower bounds. This gives the basic solution $s = -5/4$, $z = 17/4$, $x_3 = 5/4$, $x_1 = 5/4$. The solution is still infeasible since x_3 is above its upper bound of 1. The reformed pseudo-objective remains the same, representing the negated row (2.196).

In this particular case (as a result of no variable becoming feasible on the last iteration) the same updated pseudo-objective row (2.194) can be used.

Step 2 (repeated) x_4 enters the basis.

Step 3 (repeated) x_4 does not possess a finite upper bound. The limitation on increasing it therefore results from limits on x_3 and x_1: x_3 decreases from its infeasible value of $5/4$; x_1 increases from its feasible value of $5/4$. When x_4 is increased by $1/2$, x_3 falls to the feasible value of 1 (its upper bound). x_1 remains within its bounds. Therefore x_3 leaves the basis (at its upper bound) with (2.196) as pivot equation.

Step 1 (repeated) The equations are rewritten as

$$s = 0 + 0x_2 - x_3 \qquad (2.198)$$

$$z = 4 + x_2 - x_3 \qquad (2.199)$$

$$x_4 = 1 + x_2 - 2x_3 \qquad (2.200)$$

$$x_1 = 4 - x_2 - x_3. \qquad (2.201)$$

The non-basic variables are now $x_2 = 3/2$, $x_3 = 1$, i.e. at their lower and upper bounds respectively, giving the basic solution $s = -1$, $z = 9/2$, $x_4 = 1/2$, $x_1 = 3/2$. This solution is now feasible. The pseudo-objective may therefore be dropped.

Step 2 (repeated) Using the true objective row (2.199) we see that either x_2 can be increased from its lower bound or x_3 can be decreased from its upper bound. Both have the same rate of improvement on the value of z. We will choose to bring x_2 into the basis.

Step 3 (repeated) x_2 can be increased by at most $1/2$ (taking it to its upper bound). Increasing x_2 also increases x_4 but decreases x_1. When x_2 is increased to $1/2$ then x_1 (just) falls to its lower bound of 1. We therefore have a tie. Either we can switch x_2 to its upper bound and keep it out of the basis, or we can bring it into the basis to replace x_1. We will avoid the use of a systematic tie-breaking procedure and simply do the former. Therefore it is not necessary to perform an iteration. We simply switch the non-basic variable x_2 to its upper bound.

The non-basic variables are therefore $x_2 = 2$ and $x_3 = 1$, i.e. both at their upper bound, giving the basic solution $z = 5$, $x_4 = 1$, $x_1 = 1$.

Step 1 (repeated) The equations remain as in (2.198) to (2.201).

Step 2 (repeated) x_2 cannot be increased since it is at its upper bound. x_3 can however be decreased from its upper bound to good effect. Therefore x_3 enters the basis (by decreasing it from its upper bound).

Step 3 (repeated) x_3 can be decreased by at most 1 (when it reaches its lower bound). The effect of decreasing x_3 is to increase x_4 and x_1. These variables do not, however, reach their bounds before x_3. Therefore x_3 switches to its lower bound of 0. The equations remain unchanged.

The non-basic variables remain but take the values $x_2 = 2$ and $x_3 = 0$, giving the basic solution $z = 6$, $x_4 = 3$, $x_1 = 2$.

Notice that following the tie in the previous application of step 2 we have a basic variable at one of its bounds. Degeneracy could result at the next interation (if there is one).

Since both x_2 and x_1 are at their upper bounds there can be no further improvement in the objective. Therefore we have obtained the optimal solution.

With the bounded-variable version of the simplex algorithm it is arbitrary whether one starts with the non-basic variables set to their lower or upper bounds. For illustrative purposes we started by setting x_1 and x_2 to their lower bounds. If, instead, we had set them to their upper bounds, we would have obtained the optimal solution immediately.

While the bounded-variable version of the algorithm involves more complicated tests, less arithmetic is involved in rewriting the equations. For large practical models this results in considerable saving.

If the bounds on variables were to be formulated as explicit constraints, then we would have more constraints and hence more basic variables. In the bounded-variable algorithm some of these variables will be regarded as non-basic but at their non-zero bounds.

Equality Constraints

In all models, to which we have so far applied the simplex algorithm, the original constraints have been of the " $\leqslant$ " or " $\geqslant$ " form. After appending slack or surplus variables respectively, we have produced a canonical form in which each equation contains exactly one logical variable. These logical variables provided a convenient starting basis.

If, however, some of the original constraints were *equations*, then it is not clear what the corresponding basic variables should be. The usual way of dealing with such equality constraints is also to append a logical variable to each. In order that the resulting equation still be valid, this appended variable can only be allowed to take the value *zero* in a feasible solution. Such a variable is known as an *artificial variable*. It must have lower and upper bounds of zero. Clearly the name "artificial" is appropriate since it is just a computational device with no useful interpretation in terms of the model. Indeed, once it leaves the basis it could be dropped from the model.

The use of artificial variables is demonstrated by an example.

Example 2.13 The Simplex Algorithm With Artificial Variables

$$\text{Maximise} \quad x_1 - 9x_2 \tag{2.202}$$

subject to

$$x_1 + 3x_2 + 2x_3 \leq 12 \tag{2.203}$$

$$2x_1 + 2x_3 = 14 \tag{2.204}$$

$$5x_1 + 3x_2 + 8x_3 = 50 \tag{2.205}$$

$$x_1, x_2, x_3 \geq 0. \tag{2.206}$$

We introduce the following logical variables: z (a free variable) represents the objective, a slack variable x_4 is introduced into (2.203), and artificial variables x_5 and x_6 are introduced into (2.204) and (2.205). The model now takes the form

$$\text{Maximise} \quad z \tag{2.207}$$

subject to

$$-x_1 + 9x_2 + 2 = 0 \tag{2.208}$$

$$x_1 + 3x_2 + 2x_3 + x_4 = 12 \tag{2.209}$$

$$2x_1 + 2x_3 + x_5 = 14 \tag{2.210}$$

$$5x_1 + 3x_2 + 8x_3 + x_6 = 50 \tag{2.211}$$

$$z \in (-\infty, \infty) \qquad x_1, x_2, x_3, x_4 \in [0, \infty) \qquad x_5, x_6 \in [0, 0]. \tag{2.212}$$

Step 0 The starting basis is taken as z, x_4, x_5, x_6.
Step 1 The equations are written as

$$z = 0 + x_1 - 9x_2 \tag{2.213}$$

$$x_4 = 12 - x_1 - 3x_2 - 2x_3 \tag{2.214}$$

$$x_5 = 14 - 2x_1 - 2x_3 \tag{2.215}$$

$$x_6 = 50 - 5x_1 - 3x_2 - 8x_3. \tag{2.216}$$

If the non-basic variables are set to their lower bounds of 0, we have the basic solution

$$z = 0, \quad x_4 = 12, \quad x_5 = 14, \quad x_6 = 50.$$

This is infeasible since x_5 and x_6 are above their upper bounds of 0. We therefore append a pseudo-objective row to be maximised consisting of the negated sum of the two expressions on the right of (2.215) and (2.216). This gives the equation

$$s = -64 + 7x_1 + 3x_2 + 10x_3. \tag{2.217}$$

Step 2 Using (2.217) as objective x_3 enters the basis.
Step 3 x_4 leaves the basis with (2.214) as pivot equation.
Step 1 The equations are rewritten as

$$s = -4 + 2x_1 - 12x_2 - 5x_4 \tag{2.218}$$

$$z = 0 + x_1 - 9x_2 \tag{2.219}$$

$$x_3 = 6 - \tfrac{1}{2}x_1 - \tfrac{3}{2}x_2 - \tfrac{1}{2}x_4 \tag{2.220}$$

$$x_5 = 2 - x_1 + 3x_2 + x_4 \tag{2.221}$$

$$x_6 = 2 - x_1 + 9x_2 + 4x_4. \tag{2.222}$$

The corresponding basic solution is

$$s = -4, \quad z = 0, \quad x_3 = 6, \quad x_5 = 2, \quad x_6 = 2.$$

This is still infeasible. The reformed pseudo-objective is still (2.218).

Step 2 x_1 enters the basis.
Step 3 x_5 leaves the basis (note there is a tie) using (2.221) as pivot equation.
Step 1 The equations are rewritten as

$$s = 0 - 2x_5 - 6x_2 - 3x_4 \tag{2.223}$$

$$z = 2 - x_5 - 6x_2 + x_4 \tag{2.224}$$

$$x_3 = 5 + \tfrac{1}{2}x_5 - 3x_2 - x_4 \tag{2.225}$$

$$x_1 = 2 - x_5 + 3x_2 + x_4 \tag{2.226}$$

$$x_6 = 0 + x_5 + 6x_2 + 3x_4. \tag{2.227}$$

The corresponding basic solution is

$$s = 0, \quad z = 2, \quad x_3 = 5, \quad x_1 = 2, \quad x_6 = 0.$$

This is now feasible since each variable lies within its permitted ranges. We therefore drop the pseudo-objective row. Also we can drop the artificial variable x_5, which has left the basis.

Step 2   Using the true objective (2.224) x_4 enters the basis.

Step 3   If x_4 is increased x_3 decreases and x_1 and x_6 increases. But x_6 cannot be allowed to increase above its upper bound of 0. Therefore x_4 can only be "increased" by 0 when x_6 reaches its upper bound of 0. Hence x_6 leaves the basis using (2.227) as pivot equation.

Notice that we therefore perform a degenerate iteration.

Step 1   The equations are rewritten as

$$z = 2 - 8x_2 + \tfrac{1}{3}x_6 \tag{2.228}$$

$$x_3 = 5 - x_2 - \tfrac{1}{3}x_6 \tag{2.229}$$

$$x_1 = 2 + x_2 + \tfrac{1}{3}x_6 \tag{2.230}$$

$$x_4 = 0 - 2x_2 + \tfrac{1}{3}x_6. \tag{2.231}$$

This gives the optimal basic solution

$$z = 2, \quad x_3 = 5, \quad x_1 = 2, \quad x_4 = 0.$$

The bounded-variable version of the simplex algorithm deals with this model satisfactorily by preventing the artificial, but still basic, variable rising above its upper bound of 0 on the last iteration. It is worth pointing out that any version of the algorithm must guard against this possibility. If an artificial variable leaves the basis, then we can either drop it or stop it entering again. On the other hand, if it remains in the basis at the feasible value of 0, it could "rise again" to create an infeasibility unless we guard against this. In fact, some commercial LP codes exhibit this feature as a "bug".

Infeasible Models

We demonstrate by means of Example 1.7 how the simplex algorithm recognises an infeasible model. After appending logical variables we have the following example.

Example 2.14 The Simplex Algorithm With an Infeasible Model

$$x_1 + 2x_2 + x_3 = 3 \tag{2.232}$$

$$x_1 + x_2 - x_4 = 4 \tag{2.233}$$

$$x_1, x_2, x_3, x_4 \in [0, \infty). \tag{2.234}$$

An objective function is irrelevant here if we are simply trying to obtain a feasible solution.

Step 0 The all-logical basis is x_3, x_4.

Step 1 The equations are written as

$$x_3 = 3 - x_1 - 2x_2 \tag{2.235}$$

$$x_4 = -4 + x_1 + x_2. \tag{2.236}$$

The corresponding basic solution (with the non-basic variables set to their lower bounds) is

$$x_3 = 3, \quad x_4 = -4.$$

This is infeasible and we form the pseudo-objective equation

$$s = -4 + x_1 + x_2. \tag{2.237}$$

Step 2 x_1 enters the basis.

Step 3 x_3 leaves the basis using (2.235) as pivot equation.

Step 1 (repeated) The equations are rewritten as

$$x_1 = 3 - x_3 - 2x_2 \tag{2.238}$$

$$x_4 = -1 - x_3 - x_2. \tag{2.239}$$

The corresponding basic solution is

$$x_1 = 3, \quad x_4 = -1$$

which is still infeasible. We reform the pseudo-objective equation as

$$s = -1 - x_3 - x_2. \tag{2.240}$$

Step 2 Neither of the non-basic variables x_2 or x_3 will improve the pseudo-objective (reduce the total infeasibility) if brought into the basis. Therefore it is not possible to remove all infeasibilities, demonstrating that the model, itself, is infeasible.

It can be argued that one should guard against building infeasible models by converting the contraints to "goal" forms. This is done by explicitly introducing slack or surplus variables (or both) into constraints that allow them to be violated. These are given objective coefficients of a suitable magnitude so that the optimal solution will satisfy the original constraints if possible.

A rather more economical version of the method is to introduce one extra variable into the model with a unit coefficient in each constraint and a suitably sized objective coefficient. On the first iteration this variable is brought into the basis by pivoting in the row where the basic variable has largest infeasibility. This results in a "feasible" basic solution, apart from the presence of the new variable. Phase II of the simplex algorithm is then performed. If the new variable eventually leaves this basis we have achieved a truly feasible solution. Otherwise the model is infeasible.

The Complete Simplex Algorithm

In section 2.3 and this section we have developed the simplex algorithm by solving progressively more complicated numerical examples. To complete the section, we now present the total algorithm in symbolic form.

We begin by introducing logical variables. A free variable z is introduced to represent the objective. Slack variables are appended to "$\leqslant$" constraints, surplus variables to "$\geqslant$" constraints and artificial variables to "$=$" constraints. We will suppose that the original model had m constraints, apart from simple bounds on variables, and structural variables. Therefore we will have appended $m + 1$ logical variables.

At each stage of the algorithm we will have a set of $m + 1$ basic variables (including z) and n non-basic variables. We will denote the basic variables by

$$z, x_{i_1}, x_{i_2}, ..., x_{i_m}$$

and the non-basic variables by

$$x_{j_1}, x_{j_2}, ..., x_{j_n}.$$

Notice that we have avoided labelling the variables x_1, x_2, etc., in order to emphasise that they may appear in any order at an intermediate state in the calculation.

Each variable will have lower and upper bounds:

$$z \in (-\infty, \infty)$$
$$x_{i_k} \in [l_{i_k}, u_{i_k}] \qquad \text{for } k = 1, 2, ..., m$$
$$x_{j_k} \in [l_{j_k}, u_{j_k}] \qquad \text{for } k = 1, 2, ..., n.$$

The non-basic variables (apart from any that are free) will currently be set to one of their bounds. We will denote the current values of the non-basic variables by $\bar{x}_{j_k}$.

Step 1   We express the basic variables in terms of the non-basic variables by equations. At any stage in the calculation these will take the form

$$z = b_0 + c_1 x_{j_1} + c_2 x_{j_2} + \cdots + c_n x_{j_n} \qquad (2.241)$$

$$x_{i_1} = b_1 - a_{11} x_{j_1} - a_{12} x_{j_2} - \cdots - a_{1n} x_{j_n} \qquad (2.242)$$

$$x_{i_2} = b_2 - a_{21}x_{j_1} - a_{22}x_{j_2} - \cdots - a_{2n}x_{j_n} \qquad (2.243)$$
$$\vdots$$
$$x_{i_m} = b_m - a_{m1}x_{j_1} - a_{m2}x_{j_2} - \cdots - a_{mn}x_{j_n}. \qquad (2.244)$$

By substituting $\bar{x}_{j_k}$ for x_{j_k} in the above equations we can obtain current values for the basic variables z, x_{i_k} and will denote these values by $\bar{z}$, $\bar{x}_{i_k}$.

We will denote the following sets of indices of basic variables:

S_0 = set of indices, k, of basic variables x_{i_k}
within their bounds, i.e. feasible

S_1 = set of indices, k, of basic variables x_{i_k}
above their bounds

S_{-1} = set of indices, k, of basic variables x_{i_k}
below their bounds

and the following sets of indices of non-basic variables:

L = set of indices, k, of non-basic variables x_{j_k}
at their lower bounds

U = set of indices, k, of non-basic variables x_{j_k}
at their upper bound.

If S_1 and S_{-1} are both empty we will have a feasible solution. We are then in phase II and can proceed to step 2 using the objective (2.241).

If S_1 and S_{-1} are not both empty we have an infeasible solution and must create a pseudo-objective equation. This is written as

$$s = e_0 + f_1 x_{j_1} + f_2 x_{j_2} + \cdots + f_n x_{j_n} \qquad (2.245)$$

where s is a new (free) logical variable to be maximised.
The coefficients are calculated as

$$e_0 = -\sum_{k \in S_1} b_k + \sum_{k \in S_{-1}} b_k$$

$$f_h = \sum_{k \in S_1} a_{kh} - \sum_{k \in S_{-1}} a_{kh}$$

i.e. the pseudo-objective is formed by subtracting those rows in which the basic variable is above its upper bound and adding those rows in which the basic variable is below its lower bound.

We are in phase I and proceed to step 2 using the objective (2.245). To save excessive pedantry we will refer to the current objective coefficients as b_0, c_1, c_2, etc., whether this be (2.241) or (2.245).

Step 2 x_{j_k} is eligible to enter the basis if

(i) $k \in L$ and $c_k > 0$, i.e. it can be increased from its lower bound, causing an increase in the objective;

(ii) $k \in U$ and $c_k < 0$, i.e. it can be decreased from its upper bound, causing an increase in the objective;

(iii) x_{j_k} is a free variable and $c_k > 0$, i.e. it can be increased, causing an increase in the objective;

(iv) x_{j_k} is a free variable and $c_k < 0$, i.e. it can be decreased, causing an increase in the objective.

If there are no variables eligible to enter the basis we have optimised either the pseudo-objective, if in phase I, or the true objective, if in phase II. In the former case the model is infeasible if the solution is infeasible. In the latter case we have obtained the optimal solution. Otherwise (using the maximum updated objective coefficient criterion) we choose that eligible variable with maximum $|c_k|$ to enter the basis and denote the variables as x_q.

Step 3   In cases (i) and (iii) above we evaluate the following:

$$
\theta_q = \min_k
\begin{cases}
(\bar{x}_{i_k} - l_{i_k})/a_{kq} & \text{for } a_{kq} > 0,\ k \in S_0 & (2.246)\\[4pt]
(u_{i_k} - \bar{x}_{i_k})/|a_{kq}| & \text{for } a_{kq} < 0,\ k \in S_0 & (2.247)\\[4pt]
(\bar{x}_{i_k} - u_{i_k})/a_{kq} & \text{for } a_{kq} > 0,\ k \in S_1 & (2.248)\\[4pt]
(l_{i_k} - \bar{x}_{i_k})/|a_{kq}| & \text{for } a_{kq} < 0,\ k \in S_{-1} & (2.249)\\[4pt]
u_q - l_q. & & (2.250)
\end{cases}
$$

In cases (ii) and (iv) above we evaluate the following:

$$
\theta_q = \min_k
\begin{cases}
(\bar{x}_{i_k} - l_{i_k})/|a_{kq}| & \text{for } a_{kq} < 0,\ k \in S_0 & (2.251)\\[4pt]
(u_{i_k} - \bar{x}_{i_k})/a_{kq} & \text{for } a_{kq} > 0,\ k \in S_0 & (2.252)\\[4pt]
(\bar{x}_{i_k} - u_{i_k})/|a_{kq}| & \text{for } a_{kq} < 0,\ k \in S_1 & (2.253)\\[4pt]
(l_{i_k} - \bar{x}_{i_k})/a_{kq} & \text{for } a_{kq} > 0,\ k \in S_{-1} & (2.254)\\[4pt]
u_q - l_q. & & (2.255)
\end{cases}
$$

If θ_q is given by (2.246), (2.249), (2.251) or (2.254) then the appropriate x_{i_k} leaves the basis at its lower bound, and $\bar{x}_{i_k}$ is set to l_{i_k}.

If θ_q is given by (2.247), (2.248), (2.252) or (2.253) then the appropriate x_{i_k} leaves the basis at its upper bound, and $\bar{x}_{i_k}$ is set to u_{i_k}.

If θ_q is given by (2.250) or (2.255) there is no basis change and x_q switches to its opposite bound. We therefore alter the value of $\bar{x}_q$ to the alternative of l_q or u_q.

If there is no minimum of the above ratio, then the model is unbounded since the objective can be increased without limit.

If there is a basis change we denote the index i_k of the leaving variable x_{i_k} by p. x_p and x_q are interchanged.

Step 1 (repeated) If there was no basis change equations (2.241) to (2.244) remain unchanged. Otherwise we convert the pivot equation

$$x_p = b_k - a_{k1}x_{j_1} - \cdots - a_{kh}x_q - \cdots - a_{kn}x_{j_n} \qquad (2.256)$$

to

$$x_q = \frac{b_k}{a_{kh}} - \frac{a_{k1}}{a_{kh}}x_{j1} - \cdots - \frac{1}{a_{kh}}x_p - \cdots - \frac{a_{kn}}{a_{kh}}x_{j_n} \qquad (2.257)$$

by interchanging x_p and x_q. x_p becomes renamed x_{j_h} and x_q becomes renamed x_{i_k} for the appropriate h and k. It is convenient to denote these h and k by $h(q)$ and $k(p)$. We then substitute x_q out of the other equations (2.241) to (2.244) using (2.257). This results in the equations

$$z = b_0' + c_1'x_{j_1} + c_2'x_{j_2} + \cdots + c_n'x_{j_n} \qquad (2.258)$$

$$x_{i_1} = b_1' - a_{11}'x_{j_1} - a_{12}'x_{j_2} - \cdots - a_{1n}'x_{j_n} \qquad (2.259)$$

$$x_{i_2} = b_2' - a_{21}'x_{j_1} - a_{22}'x_{j_2} - \cdots - a_{2n}'x_{j_n} \qquad (2.260)$$

$$\vdots$$

$$x_{i_m} = b_m' - a_{m1}'x_{j_1} - a_{m2}'x_{j_2} - \cdots - a_{mn}'x_{j_n} \qquad (2.261)$$

where

$$b_0' = b_0 + c_q(b_{k(p)}/a_{pq})$$
$$b_i' = b_i - a_{iq}(b_{k(p)}/a_{pq}) \qquad \text{for } i = 1, 2, \ldots, m, i \neq k(p)$$
$$b_p' = b_p/a_{pq}$$
$$c_j' = c_j - c_q(a_{pj}/a_{pq}) \qquad \text{for } j = 1, 2, \ldots, n, j \neq h(p)$$
$$c_q' = -c_q/a_{pq}$$
$$a_{ij}' = a_{ij} - a_{iq}(a_{pj}/a_{pq}) \qquad \text{for } i = 1, 2, \ldots, m, i \neq k(p)$$
$$\qquad\qquad\qquad\qquad\qquad j = 1, 2, \ldots, n, j \neq h(q)$$
$$a_{pj}' = a_{pj}/a_{pq} \qquad \text{for } j = 1, 2, \ldots, n, j \neq h(q)$$
$$a_{iq}' = -a_{iq}/a_{pq} \qquad \text{for } i = 1, 2, \ldots, m, i \neq k(p)$$
$$a_{pq}' = 1/a_{pq}$$

We now have a set of equations of the same form as (2.241) to (2.244) and can proceed as before.

In the above description we have not incorporated an anti-circling procedure. This can be done, if necessary, in a similar manner to that described in section 2.3.

2.5 THE DUAL OF A LINEAR PROGRAMME

If we consider an LP model as a maximisation, then it is possible to derive an *upper bound* on the optimal objective value without solving the model directly. Finding the *least* such upper bound turns out itself to give an LP model known as the *dual* model. The optimal solutions to this model, and the original (usually known as the *primal*) model, are intimately linked. Similarly, for a minimisation model the dual model involves finding the greatest lower bound on the optimal objective value.

Besides giving much insight into the structure of LPs and their solutions, duality is of computational importance. In addition, it provides important economic information. This last aspect is beyond the scope of this book, but is discussed at length in *MBMP*.

We will take an LP model in the standard form discussed in section 1.1:

$$\text{Maximise} \quad c_1 x_1 + c_2 x_2 + \cdots + c_n x_n \tag{2.262}$$

subject to

$$a_{11} x_1 + a_{12} x_2 + \cdots + a_{1n} x_n \leqslant b_1 \tag{2.263}$$

$$a_{21} x_1 + a_{22} x_2 + \cdots + a_{2n} x_n \leqslant b_2 \tag{2.264}$$

$$\vdots$$

$$a_{m1} x_1 + a_{m2} x_2 + \cdots + a_{mn} x_n \leqslant b_m \tag{2.265}$$

$$- x_1 \leqslant 0 \tag{2.266}$$

$$- x_2 \leqslant 0 \tag{2.267}$$

$$\vdots$$

$$- x_n \leqslant 0. \tag{2.268}$$

The non-negativity conditions (2.266) to (2.268) have deliberately been written as "$\leqslant$" constraints to clarify the argument below.

This model will be referred to as the PRIMAL model.

We will add together the constraints (2.263) to (2.268) in non-negative multiples $y_1, y_2, ..., y_m, {}_{m+1}, y_{m+2}, ..., y_{m+n}$ so as to give (if possible) a "$\leqslant$" inequality whose left-hand side is expression (2.258). This will give

$$c_1 x_1 + c_2 x_2 + \cdots + c_n x_n \leqslant b_1 y_1 + b_2 y_2 + \cdots + b_n y_n \tag{2.269}$$

where

$$a_{11} y_1 + a_{21} y_2 + \cdots + a_{m1} y_m - y_{m+1} = c_1 \tag{2.270}$$

$$a_{12}y_1 + a_{22}y_2 + \cdots + a_{m2}y_m - y_{m+2} = c_2 \qquad (2.271)$$
$$\vdots$$
$$a_{1n}y_1 + a_{2n}y_2 + \cdots + a_{mn}y_m - y_{m+n} = c_n. \qquad (2.272)$$

The expression on the right of inequality (2.269) clearly gives an upper bound for the maximum objective value of the PRIMAL model. By minimising this expression, we can obtain as *tight* an upper bound as possible. Therefore we treat the y_i quantities as (non-negative) variables, observing that $y_{m+1}, y_{m+2}, \ldots, y_{m+n}$ are equivalent to surplus variables. This gives the model:

$$\text{Minimise} \quad b_1 y_1 + b_2 y_2 + \cdots + b_m y_m \qquad (2.273)$$

subject to

$$a_{11}y_1 + a_{21}y_2 + \cdots + a_{m1}y_m \geqslant c_1 \qquad (2.274)$$
$$a_{12}y_1 + a_{22}y_2 + \cdots + a_{m2}y_m \geqslant c_2 \qquad (2.275)$$
$$\vdots$$
$$a_{1n}y_1 + a_{2n}y_2 + \cdots + a_{mn}y_m \geqslant c_n \qquad (2.276)$$
$$y_1, y_2, \ldots, y_m \geqslant 0. \qquad (2.277)$$

This model is known as the DUAL model.

The Duality Theorem

The major result of the *duality theorem* of LP is that, so long as the PRIMAL model is not unbounded or infeasible, then not only does (2.273) provide an upper bound for (2.262), this upper bound *equals* (2.262).

Why this strong result should hold will become apparent from the discussion in section 2.7.

The duality theorem implies that, in order to find the maximum objective value of the PRIMAL, we could equally well find the minimum objective value of the DUAL. In some circumstances this might be easier. If we only wanted to find an upper bound for the maximum value of the PRIMAL, we could simply find the objective value associated with a feasible solution to the DUAL. Figure 2.5 illustrates the situation.

Should the PRIMAL model be *unbounded*, it must be impossible to devise an upper bound for (2.262) in this way. Hence the DUAL model must be *infeasible*.

If the PRIMAL model itself is *infeasible*, then there is no attainable upper bound for (2.262), i.e. the DUAL model might also be *infeasible* or (2.273) could be made as small as we like, i.e. the DUAL might be *unbounded*.

It is straightforward to show that the dual of the DUAL gives the PRIMAL

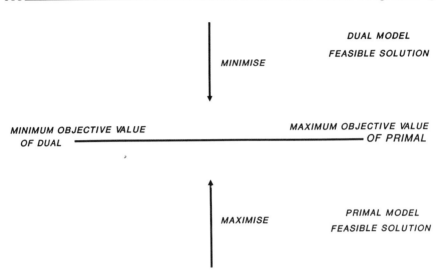

Figure 2.5   The relation between dual solutions

model. This may be demonstrated by

 (i) Converting the DUAL to a maximisation subject to "$\leqslant$" constraints:
 (ii) Taking the dual of the result.
 (iii) Converting this to a maximisation subject to "$\leqslant$" constraints.

   Besides the equality of the optimal objective values of the PRIMAL and DUAL (if solvable), there is also a relationship between the solution values of both, which we explain below.

Orthogonality

In an optimal solution to an LP model, generally only some of the constraints will be binding. The other constraints are (with hindsight) redundant. Therefore we need only consider non-negative multiples of the binding constraints to give the least upper bound for the objective. Multipliers for the other constraints can be taken as zero.

   A PRIMAL constraint is either a non-negativity constraint

$$x_j \geqslant 0 \tag{2.278}$$

or, after appending a slack variable x_{n+i}, of the form

$$a_{i1}x_1 + a_{i2}x_2 + \cdots + a_{in}x_n + x_{n+i} = b_i. \tag{2.279}$$

If (2.278) is binding, $x_j = 0$, and if the inequality corresponding to (2.279) is binding, $x_{n+i} = 0$. On the other hand if (2.278) is non-binding (redundant), the associated multiplier (dual variable) $y_{m+j} = 0$, and if the inequality corresponding to (2.279) is non-binding (redundant), $y_i = 0$.

This aspect of the duality theorem is usually known as *orthogonality* or *complementarity*. We associate the PRIMAL and DUAL variables with each other in the following order:

PRIMAL structural variable $\leftrightarrow$ DUAL surplus variable

(x_j) $\qquad\qquad\qquad\qquad\quad (y_{m+j})$

PRIMAL slack variable $\leftrightarrow$ DUAL structural variable.

(x_{m+i}) $\qquad\qquad\qquad\qquad (y_i)$

For each such pair, therefore, at least one must be zero. Again this has important economic consequences discussed in *MBMP*.

This relationship can also be summarised by the equation

$$x_1 y_{m+1} + x_2 y_{m+2} + \cdots + x_n y_{m+n} + x_{n+1} y_1 + x_{n+2} y_2 + \cdots + x_{n+m} y_m = 0.$$

$$(2.280)$$

The correspondence between solutions in primal and dual models extends to one between non-optimal solutions. For a non-optimal, but feasible, solution to the primal, an orthogonal dual solution will be infeasible. The following are both necessary and sufficient conditions for optimality of both primal and dual solutions:

(i) Orthogonal feasible solutions.
(ii) Feasible solutions of equal objective value.

The above relationships are illustrated by considering Example 1.2 from section 1.1, which we state again.

Example 2.15 The Relationship Between Solutions of Duals
The primal model (P) is

$$\text{Maximise} \quad -4x_1 + 5x_2 + 3x_3 \qquad (2.281)$$

subject to

$$-x_1 + x_2 - x_3 \leqslant 2 \qquad (2.282)$$

$$x_1 + x_2 + 2x_3 \leqslant 3 \qquad (2.283)$$

$$x_1, x_2, x_3 \geqslant 0. \qquad (2.284)$$

The dual model (D) is

$$\text{Minimise} \quad 2y_1 + 3y_2 \qquad (2.285)$$

subject to

$$-y_1 + y_2 \geqslant -4 \tag{2.286}$$

$$y_1 + y_2 \geqslant 5 \tag{2.287}$$

$$-y_1 + 2y_2 \geqslant 3 \tag{2.288}$$

$$y_1, y_2 \geqslant 0. \tag{2.289}$$

The optimal solution to P (including the slack variables), derived by a variety of methods in previous sections, is

$$x_1 = 0, \quad x_2 = 7/3, \quad x_3 = 1/3, \quad x_4 = x_5 = 0, \quad \text{objective} = 38/3. \tag{2.290}$$

We will consider a feasible (but non-optimal) solution to D (including surplus variables)

$$y_1 = 0, \quad y_2 = 5, \quad y_3 = 9, \quad y_4 = 0, \quad y_5 = 7. \tag{2.291}$$

Adding the constraints of P in these multiples gives

$$5 \times (x_1 + x_2 + 2x_3 \leqslant 3)$$
$$+9 \times (-x_1 \leqslant 0)$$
$$+7 \times (-x_3 \leqslant 0)$$

implying

$$-4x_1 + 5x_2 + 3x_3 \leqslant 15$$

i.e. we have an upper bound of 15 for the maximum objective value of P. If, however, we were to take the *optimal solution* to D

$$y_1 = 7/3, \quad y_2 = 8/3, \quad y_3 = 13/3 \tag{2.292}$$

this gives

$$\tfrac{7}{3} \times (-x_1 + x_2 - x_3 \leqslant 2)$$
$$+\tfrac{8}{3} \times (x_1 + x_2 + 2x_3 \leqslant 3)$$
$$+\tfrac{13}{3} \times (-x_1 \leqslant 0)$$

implying

$$-4x_1 + 5x_2 + 3x_3 \leqslant 38/3$$

i.e. we have a *tight* upper bound giving the maximum value for the objective of P.

Comparing corresponding solution values for the optimal solutions of P and D we have

$$x_1 = 0 \qquad y_3 = 13/3$$
$$x_2 = 7/3 \qquad y_4 = 0$$
$$x_3 = 1/3 \qquad y_5 = 0$$
$$x_4 = 0 \qquad y_1 = 7/3$$
$$x_5 = 0 \qquad y_2 = 8/3$$

i.e. one of each pair is always zero, giving

$$x_1 y_3 + x_2 y_4 + x_3 y_5 + x_4 y_1 + x_5 y_2 = 0.$$

There is a geometrical way of interpreting duality that is helpful and can be explained in relation to this example. In Figure 1.2 it is seen that, at the optimal solution C, the objective plane parallel to PQRS, which goes through C, does not intersect any other point of the feasible region. This is only possible if the expression representing this plane can be expressed as a nonnegative combination of the expressions in the constraints that are binding at C, i.e. giving rise to the planes OACB, BCD and ACDE. The multipliers in the combination are the optimal dual values. This concept extends to nonlinear programming if the constraint and objective surfaces are replaced by their tangents at the optimal solution, and gives rise to an analogous duality result, which is discussed in section 5.4.

Deriving the Optimal Primal Solution From That of the Dual

Suppose, in Example 2.15, that we had been given the optimal solution (2.292) to D but not that to P. We can use it to deduce the optimal solution of P as follows.

(i) Since y_1 and y_2 are positive, (2.282) and (2.283) must be binding. Therefore

$$- x_1 + x_2 - x_3 = 2$$
$$x_1 + x_2 + 2x_3 = 3.$$

(ii) Since y_3 is positive, $x_1 = 0$. Therefore

$$x_2 - x_3 = 2$$
$$x_2 + 2x_3 = 3.$$

These equations have the unique (optimal) solution

$$x_2 = 7/3 \qquad x_3 = 1/3.$$

The objective value can be checked to be 38/3.

It was pointed out in section 2.3 that the main problem of LP is that of determining a set of *basic variables*. Once these have been chosen, and the non-basic variables set to zero, then we will have a uniquely solvable set of equations. In the above example we have used the orthogonality result, and the optimal basis of the dual, to deduce the optimal basis of the primal. From this, the solution follows by simply solving, uniquely, a set of equations.

Equally we could use the optimal solution of the primal to deduce that of the dual.

If, however, the primal model were to have *alternative solutions*, then the above procedure presents a difficulty, as shown by taking Example 1.1 from section 1.1 (illustrated in Figure 1.1) with objective (1.10).

Example 2.16 Degeneracy and Alternative Solutions

$$\text{Maximise} \quad 4x_1 + 2x_2 \tag{2.293}$$

subject to

$$x_1 + x_2 \leqslant 4 \tag{2.294}$$

$$2x_1 + x_2 \leqslant 5 \tag{2.295}$$

$$x_1 - 4x_2 \leqslant -2 \tag{2.296}$$

$$x_1, x_2 \geqslant 0. \tag{2.297}$$

The dual model is

$$\text{Minimise} \quad 4y_1 + 5y_2 - 2y_3 \tag{2.298}$$

subject to

$$y_1 + 2y_2 + y_3 \geqslant 4 \tag{2.299}$$

$$y_1 + y_2 - 4y_3 \geqslant 2 \tag{2.300}$$

$$y_1, y_2, y_3 \geqslant 0. \tag{2.301}$$

This has optimal solution

$$y_1 = 0, \quad y_2 = 2, \quad y_3 = y_4 = y_5 = 0 \quad \text{objective} = 10. \tag{2.302}$$

If we apply a similar argument to that above, to try to deduce the optimal solution to the primal model, we deduce only that (2.295) is binding, giving

$$2x_1 + x_2 = 5.$$

This equation does not have a unique solution.

The difficulty arises from the fact that (2.302) is a *degenerate* solution to the dual. We could have, in addition to the basic variable y_2, either

(a) y_1 in the basis at zero value and y_3 non-basic (and therefore zero),

or
(b) y_3 in the basis at zero value and y_1 non-basic (and therefore zero).

From the practical point of view, for the dual solution, these two solutions would be indistinguishable.

If, however, we were to take the case (a), then we would regard (2.294), in the primal model, as binding, leading to

$$x_1 + x_2 = 4$$
$$2x_1 + x_2 = 5$$

and the solution

$$x_1 = 1 \qquad x_2 = 3. \qquad (2.303)$$

In case (b) we would regard (2.296), in the primal model, as binding, leading to

$$2x_1 + x_2 = 5$$
$$x_1 - 4x_2 = -2$$

and the solution

$$x_1 = 2 \qquad x_2 = 1. \qquad (2.304)$$

These are the two alternative basic solutions represented by vertices B and C in Figure 1.1. Both correspond to objective values of 10.

It is worth noting that *degeneracy* and *alternative solutions* are dual phenomena.

An important result of the dual relationship between optimal solutions is that it provides a *proof of optimality*. If, for example, we were to be given the solution (2.303) to P, then it is straightforward to check its *feasibility* by substituting into the constraints. In order to prove the additional property of *optimality*, we can deduce the corresponding dual solution (2.302). So long as this solution is feasible within the dual, then optimality of the original primal solution follows.

The need to obtain (implicitly) a feasible solution to the dual, as well as the primal, suggests another algorithm known as the *dual simplex algorithm*, which is the subject of section 2.6.

Unbounded and Infeasible Models

It has already been pointed out that, if an LP model is unbounded, the dual must be infeasible. We demonstrate this by reconsidering Example 1.3 with objective (1.16) in standard form.

Example 2.17 Unboundedness, Infeasibility and Duality

$$\text{Maximise} \quad 3x_1 - x_2 \tag{2.305}$$

subject to

$$-x_1 - 2x_2 \leqslant -5 \tag{2.306}$$

$$2x_1 - x_2 \leqslant 2 \tag{2.307}$$

$$x_1, x_2 \geqslant 0. \tag{2.308}$$

This model is unbounded, as illustrated by Figure 1.3 and Example 2.9. The dual model is

$$\text{Minimise} \quad -5y_1 + 2y_2 \tag{2.309}$$

subject to

$$-y_1 + 2y_2 \geqslant 3 \tag{2.310}$$

$$-2y_1 - y_2 \geqslant -1 \tag{2.311}$$

$$y_1, y_2 \geqslant 0. \tag{2.312}$$

It is easy to see that this is infeasible either graphically or by observing that twice constraint (2.311) added to constraint (2.310) yields $-5y_1 \geqslant 1$, which contradicts the non-negativity constraint on y_1.

This dual model is clearly itself an example of a model that is infeasible whose own dual (the original primal) is unbounded.

The possibility of both the primal and dual being infeasible is demonstrated by a further example

Example 2.18 Infeasible Duals

$$\text{Maximise} \quad x_1 + x_2 \tag{2.313}$$

subject to

$$-2x_1 - x_2 \leqslant -1 \tag{2.314}$$

$$x_1 \leqslant -1 \tag{2.315}$$

$$x_1, x_2 \geqslant 0. \tag{2.316}$$

This is infeasible since constraint (2.315) contradicts the non-negativity of x_1.

The dual model is

$$\text{Minimise} \quad -y_1 - y_2 \tag{2.317}$$

subject to

$$-2y_1 + y_2 \geqslant 1 \tag{2.318}$$

$$-y_1 \geqslant 1 \tag{2.319}$$

$$y_1, y_2 \geqslant 0. \tag{2.320}$$

This is also infeasible since constraint (2.319) contradicts the non-negativity of y_1.

Dual Multipliers for Greater-Than and Equality Constraints

The dual has been defined for any LP model in standard form. When in this standard form, *non-negative* dual values provide constraint multipliers to give an upper bound on the objective value. If there are also " $\geqslant$ " and " $=$ " constraints, these may be translated into " $\leqslant$ " constraints as described in section 1.1.

For a " $\geqslant$ " constraint, we negate both sides and convert it to the " $\leqslant$ " form. Alternatively, we could keep it in the " $\geqslant$ " form and restrict the multipliers (dual variables) to *non-positive* values. For an " $=$ " constraint, we could express it as two constraints, one of the " $\leqslant$ " form and one of the " $\geqslant$ " form. The two dual multipliers would be non-negative and non-positive respectively. When combined, they would produce a *free variable* (i.e. unconstrained in sign).

To summarise, we have the following correspondence between primal constraints and dual variables:

> primal " $\leqslant$ " constraint $\leftrightarrow$ non-negative dual variable
>
> primal " $\geqslant$ " constraint $\leftrightarrow$ non-positive dual variable
>
> primal " $=$ " constraint $\leftrightarrow$ free dual variable.

This correspondence is obviously reflexive, i.e. the dual of a model with non-positive or free variables has " $\geqslant$ " or " $=$ " constraints respectively.

Shadow Prices and Reduced Costs

The optimal dual values for an LP model arise automatically out of the solution from the simplex algorithm. In order to illustrate this, we return again to Example 1.2. This was solved using Fourier–Motzkin elimination as Example 2.3, by the simplex algorithm as Example 2.4 and illustrated the duality theorem as Example 2.15. We present the example again.

Example 2.19 Shadow Prices, Dual Values and Reduced Costs

$$\text{Maximise} \quad -4x_1 + 5x_2 + 3x_3 \tag{2.321}$$

subject to

$$-x_1 + x_2 - x_3 \leqslant 2 \qquad (2.322)$$

$$x_1 + x_2 + 2x_3 \leqslant 3 \qquad (2.323)$$

$$-x_1 \leqslant 0 \qquad (2.324)$$

$$-x_2 \leqslant 0 \qquad (2.325)$$

$$-x_3 \leqslant 0. \qquad (2.326)$$

The dual solution allows us to express the objective (2.321) as a linear combination of the expressions on the left-hand sides of (2.322) to (2.326). In the final set of equations, resulting from the simplex algorithm in Example 2.4, this updated objective equation is

$$z = \tfrac{38}{3} - \tfrac{13}{3}x_1 - \tfrac{7}{3}x_4 - \tfrac{8}{3}x_5. \qquad (2.327)$$

Since x_4 and x_5 are the logical variables, appended uniquely to constraints (2.322) and (2.323), their coefficients (changed in sign) provide the dual multipliers for these constraints. This gives $y_1 = 7/3$, $y_2 = 8/3$. The (negated) coefficient of x_1 provides the dual multiplier for the constraint (2.324). Hence $y_3 = 13/3$.

Therefore the optimal dual solution, given as (2.292) in Example 2.15, can also be obtained from these *reduced costs* of the primal model.

Notice that only non-basic variables, e.g. x_1, x_4 and x_5, will have non-zero reduced costs. This is consistent with dual multipliers being applied only to binding constraints, e.g. (2.322), (2.323) and (2.324). Other constraints will be redundant and have zero multipliers.

The optimal reduced costs have considerable economic significance, which is discussed in *MBMP*. They also have importance for *sensitivity analysis*, which is discussed in section 4.5. We do, however, demonstrate how they also arise in Fourier–Motzkin elimination in order to illustrate this point.

The dual values $y_1 = 7/3$, $y_2 = 8/3$ arose in Example 2.3 as the multipliers of b_1 and b_2 in expression (2.36). If $b_2 = 2$ and $b_3 = 3$, giving our current example, then the expression $7/3b_1 + 8/3b_2$ gives the optimal objective value. This again demonstrates that the tightest upper bound for the objective can be obtained by taking suitable multipliers applied to the constraints. The expression $7/3b_1 + 8/3b_2$ continues to give the optimal objective value if b_1 and b_2 are changed by small amounts. Therefore, the coefficient 7/3 gives the *rate of change* of the objective value with respect to a change in the RHS coefficient b_1 of the first constraint. Similarly, the coefficient 8/3 gives the rate of change with respect to a change in the RHS coefficient b_2 of the second constraint. Such quantities, representing the effect of marginal changes in the RHS

Table 2.1

	Structural			Logical	
PRIMAL variables	x_1	x_2	x_3	x_4	x_5
Solution values	$-$	7/3	1/3	$-$	$-$
Reduced costs	13/3	$-$	$-$	7/3	8/3
	Logical			Structural	
DUAL variables	y_3	y_4	y_5	y_1	y_2
Solution values	13/3	$-$	$-$	7/3	8/3
Reduced costs	$-$	7/3	1/3	$-$	$-$

coefficients on the optimal objective values, are known as *shadow prices* or *marginal values* on the corresponding constraints.

The optimal dual values will often be the same as the shadow prices, as happens in the above example. Indeed, some commercial packages refer to reduced costs on logical variables as "shadow prices" for the corresponding constraints. Strictly speaking they are dual values. If the optimal solution is degenerate, they may be different. The reason why this can happen is explained in section 2.7.

As would also be expected, since the dual of the dual is the primal, the reduced costs of the dual model provide us with the solution to the primal. This full relationship is illustrated for Example 2.19 in Table 2.1.

The variables are ordered in the table so as to reflect the natural correspondence between primal and dual variables described before. Non-basic variables have zero solution values indicated by " $-$ " and basic variables have zero reduced costs also indicated by " $-$ ". It can be seen that, if a variable is basic in one model, then its corresponding variable is non-basic in the other, with a reduced cost equal to the solution value in the former.

2.6 THE DUAL SIMPLEX ALGORITHM

In section 2.5 it was shown that the following situation holds for the optimal solution to an LP model. There is:

(i) a feasible solution to the *primal* model;
(ii) a feasible solution to the *dual* model; and
(iii) these solutions are orthogonal.

At each stage of the simplex algorithm we have a set of solution values and reduced costs for the variables. These values are orthogonal, i.e. we maintain condition (iii). Phase I of the simplex algorithm tries also to satisfy condition (i). Then in phase II we seek optimality by trying to find a solution in which the reduced costs take the appropriate sign (while maintaining conditions (i) and (iii)). Since reduced costs are dual solution values, this amounts to trying to satisfy (ii).

An alternative approach to trying successively to satisfy these conditions in the order (iii), (i) and (ii) is to try to satisfy them in the order (iii), (ii) and (i). This effectively amounts to applying the simplex algorithm to the dual model but the corresponding operations are conveniently carried out on the primal model. The resultant method is known as the *dual simplex algorithm* and is described below.

We describe the dual simplex algorithm by reconsidering Example 2.11.

Example 2.20 The Dual Simplex Algorithm
Solve the following model by the dual simplex algorithm:

$$\text{Maximise} \quad 3x_1 + 2x_2 \tag{2.328}$$

subject to

$$x_1 + x_2 \leqslant 4 \tag{2.329}$$

$$2x_1 + x_2 \leqslant 5 \tag{2.330}$$

$$x_1 - 4x_2 \leqslant -2 \tag{2.331}$$

$$x_1, x_2 \geqslant 0. \tag{2.332}$$

It is instructive also to view the method in relation to the dual model, which is:

$$\text{Minimise} \quad 4y_1 + 5y_2 - 2y_3 \tag{2.333}$$

subject to

$$y_1 + 2y_2 + y_3 \geqslant 3 \tag{2.334}$$

$$y_1 + y_2 - 4y_3 \geqslant 2 \tag{2.335}$$

$$y_1, y_2, y_3 \geqslant 0. \tag{2.336}$$

Step 0 We choose the all-logical basis x_3, x_4, x_5 for the primal model, as in Example 2.11, with the same interpretation of variables. As in Example 2.11 the resulting equations are written

$$z = 0 + 3x_1 + 2x_2 \tag{2.337}$$

$$x_3 = 4 - x_1 - x_2 \tag{2.338}$$

$$x_4 = 5 - 2x_1 - x_2 \tag{2.339}$$

$$x_5 = -2 - x_1 + 4x_2. \tag{2.340}$$

The corresponding primal solution is

$$x_1 = 0, \quad x_2 = 0, \quad x_3 = 4, \quad x_4 = 5, \quad x_5 = -2, \quad \text{objective} = 0. \tag{2.341}$$

The corresponding dual solution is

$$y_4 = -3, \quad y_5 = -2, \quad y_1 = 0, \quad y_2 = 0, \quad y_3 = 0, \quad \text{objective} = 0 \tag{2.342}$$

where y_4 and y_5 are the surplus variables in (2.334) and (2.335) and the solution has been written in the order of correspondence of variables described in section 2.5.

Notice that these solutions are orthogonal but both infeasible. The values of y_4 and y_5 correspond to the negated objective coefficients in (2.328). Ultimately we want these (updated) objective coefficients to be non-positive for optimality, i.e. the corresponding dual variables to take non-negative values.

Step 1   Instead of beginning by trying to find a (primal) feasible solution (phase I), we seek a dual feasible solution. In order to do this, we wish to make the coefficients of the non-basic variables in (2.337) non-positive. There is a convenient device for doing this. It is, in fact, the dual of the device mentioned at the end of section 2.4 for finding a "feasible" basis. So long as the model is not unbounded, we can specify an upper bound for the sum of the non-basic variables. For the example we already have such a constraint in the form (2.329). In general, we could introduce such a new constraint if necessary. The basic (slack) variable associated with this constraint is then made to leave the basis by pivoting, being replaced by the non-basic variable with largest objective coefficient (x_1 in the example). This will always result in a dual feasible solution. This results, for the example, in the set of equations

$$z = 12 - 3x_3 - x_2 \tag{2.343}$$

$$x_1 = 4 - x_3 - x_2 \tag{2.344}$$

$$x_4 = -3 + 2x_3 + x_2 \tag{2.345}$$

$$x_5 = -6 + x_3 + 5x_2. \tag{2.346}$$

The corresponding (infeasible) primal solution is

$$x_1 = 4, \quad x_2 = 0, \quad x_3 = 0, \quad x_4 = -3, \quad x_5 = -6, \quad \text{objective} = 12. \tag{2.347}$$

The corresponding (feasible) dual solution is

$$y_4 = 0, \quad y_5 = 1, \quad y_1 = 3, \quad y_2 = 0, \quad y_3 = 0, \quad \text{objective} = 12. \quad (2.348)$$

Notice that these solutions are still orthogonal (with the same objective value) but that also (2.348) is now feasible.

Geometrically, in Figure 1.1, we have managed to express the objective function (a line parallel to RS) as a positive combination of " $-x_2 \leqslant 0$ " (the x_1 axis) and (2.329) (line AB). These two lines intersect at $x_1 = 4$, $x_2 = 0$, giving the solution (2.347), which violates constraints (2.330) and (2.331). If it were not for these constraints, we would have an optimal solution. Instead, we have an upper bound on the optimal objective value.

We now seek a primal feasible solution, while maintaining orthogonality and dual feasibility. In order to do this we seek a basic variable with a negative value to *leave* the basis (this corresponds, in the dual model, to seeking a *non-basic* variable with a positive d_j to *enter* the basis). It is convenient to choose the most negative one. This determines the pivot row. In the example the variable is x_5 and the pivot row is (2.346).

Step 2   We seek a variable to enter the basis. In order to maintain dual feasibility we must choose that variable whose ratio of (negated) updated objective coefficient to positive coefficient in the pivot row is least (in the dual model this corresponds to finding the variable to *leave* the basis by the ratio test between the updated objective coefficient and entries in the pivot row). In the example x_2 is therefore chosen to leave the basis.

Step 3   We perform the pivot step, as in the normal simplex algorithm, to produce the following set of equations:

$$z = \tfrac{54}{5} - \tfrac{14}{5} x_3 - \tfrac{1}{5} x_5 \qquad (2.349)$$

$$x_1 = \tfrac{14}{5} - \tfrac{4}{5} x_3 - \tfrac{1}{5} x_5 \qquad (2.350)$$

$$x_4 = -\tfrac{9}{5} + \tfrac{9}{5} x_3 + \tfrac{1}{5} x_5 \qquad (2.351)$$

$$x_2 = \tfrac{6}{5} - \tfrac{1}{5} x_3 + \tfrac{1}{5} x_5. \qquad (2.352)$$

The corresponding (infeasible) primal solution is

$$x_1 = 14/5, \quad x_2 = 6/5, \quad x_3 = 0, \quad x_4 = -9/5, \quad x_5 = 0, \quad \text{objective} = 54/5.$$
$$(2.353)$$

The corresponding (feasible) dual solution is

$$y_4 = 0, \quad y_5 = 0, \quad y_1 = 14/5, \quad y_2 = 0, \quad y_3 = 1/5, \quad \text{objective} = 54/5.$$
$$(2.354)$$

Again these solutions are orthogonal. They correspond to the intersection of the extension of lines AB and DC in Figure 1.1.

Step 1 x_4 leaves the basis.
Step 2 x_5 enters the basis.
Step 3   The new set of equations is

$$z = 9 - x_3 - x_4 \tag{2.355}$$

$$x_1 = 1 + x_3 - x_4 \tag{2.356}$$

$$x_5 = 9 - 9x_3 + 5x_4 \tag{2.357}$$

$$x_2 = 3 - 2x_3 + x_4. \tag{2.358}$$

The solution is now primal feasible and therefore optimal. For comparison the primal solution is

$$x_1 = 1, \quad x_2 = 3, \quad x_3 = 0, \quad x_4 = 0, \quad x_5 = 9, \quad \text{objective} = 9. \tag{2.359}$$

and the corresponding dual solution is

$$y_4 = 0, \quad y_5 = 0, \quad y_1 = 1, \quad y_2 = 1, \quad y_3 = 0, \quad \text{objective} = 9. \tag{2.360}$$

These are both feasible and orthogonal and therefore optimal. They correspond to the intersection of lines AB and BC in Figure 1.1.

The set of equations (2.355) to (2.358) is the same as that obtained when the same model was solved by the normal simplex algorithm as Example 2.11, but they have been obtained by a different process.

In order to give the general rules (for bounded variables) we refer to the symbolic description of the primal simplex algorithm given in section 2.4. For the dual simplex algorithm we begin by choosing a *basic* variable that is outside its bounds. As with the primal simplex algorithm, different pivoting rules exist. One is simply to choose the most infeasible of these basic variables. We are assuming that the solution is already dual feasible. If the chosen basic variable x_p is *above* its upper bound, in order to decrease it, we choose the non-basic variable x_q such that

$$|c_q/a_{pq}| = \underset{a'_{pj} < 0}{\text{Min}} \begin{cases} c_j/a_{pj}, x_j & \text{at lower bound} \\ -c_j/a_{pj}, x_j & \text{at upper bound.} \end{cases} \tag{2.361}$$

If the chosen basic variable is *below* its lower bound, we choose the non-basic variable x_q such that

$$|c_q/a_{pq}| = \underset{a'_{pj} > 0}{\text{Min}} \begin{cases} -c_j/a_{pq}, x_j & \text{at lower bound} \\ c_j/a_{pq}, x_j & \text{at upper bound.} \end{cases} \tag{2.362}$$

The normal updating rules are then used to take variable x_p out of the basis at its upper or lower bound respectively by bringing x_q into the basis.

Exercise 2.21 involves solving the dual model to this example by the normal simplex algorithm. It should be observed how the steps mirror those of the example above to produce successively solutions (2.342), (2.348), (2.354) and (2.360).

In the dual simplex algorithm, the objective function starts at an unattainable value and progressively gets worse (smaller for a maximisation, and larger for a minimisation) until a feasible solution is obtained.

This makes it like the cutting planes approach to integer programming described in section 6.4. At each step (by moving towards primal feasibility) extra constraints are effectively enforced. Indeed, the most effective way of incorporating cutting planes for integer programming, in the course of optimisation, is to use the dual simplex algorithm.

2.7 GENERATING ALL VERTICES AND EXTREME RAYS

It was demonstrated in section 1.1 that, for solvable LP models, represented by pointed polyhedra, we can restrict our search for an optimal solution to vertices of the polyhedron. Should the model be unbounded, this can be characterised by an extreme ray.

In some applications there is interest in enumerating all vertices and extreme rays. We are then in a position to give an optimal solution for *any* objective function. We will show that Fourier–Motzkin elimination, as described in section 2.2, when applied to the dual model, provides a way of doing this. It also illustrates, very clearly, duality concepts arising in section 2.5. In order to illustrate this, we will deduce all the vertices and extreme rays for the following LP model.

Vertices and Extreme Rays of an LP

Example 2.21 Obtaining All Vertices and Extreme Rays of an LP

$$\text{Minimise} \quad b_1 y_1 + b_2 y_2 \tag{2.363}$$

subject to

$$-y_1 + y_2 \geqslant -4 \tag{2.364}$$

$$y_1 + y_2 \geqslant 5 \tag{2.365}$$

$$-y_1 + 2y_2 \geqslant 3 \tag{2.366}$$

$$y_1, y_2 \geqslant 0. \tag{2.367}$$

An objective function is irrelevant if we are concerned with all vertices and extreme rays. Therefore, we have deliberately taken a *general* objective function so as to find the optimal value for *all possible* coefficients b_1 and b_2.

If $b_1 = 2$ and $b_3 = 3$, this model is the dual of Example 1.2 considered in section 2.5. Therefore, we refer to the variables as y_1 and y_2 and, when necessary, the surplus variables as y_3, y_4 and y_5.

A two-variable model has deliberately been chosen so that it can be represented geometrically in Figure 2.6. For general b_1 and b_2 it is the dual of Example 2.3 in section 2.2.

When we applied Fourier–Motzkin elimination to that example, the optimal objective value arose from one of the inequalities

$$z \leqslant \tfrac{7}{3} b_1 + \tfrac{8}{3} b_2 \tag{2.368}$$

$$z \leqslant 11 b_1 + 7 b_2 \tag{2.369}$$

$$z \leqslant 5 b_2. \tag{2.370}$$

Each of these inequalities arises as a non-negative combination of some of the original inequalities (2.15) to (2.19) added to the objective equation (2.14).

It can be verified, by recording the multiples in which constraints are combined to eliminate variables, that

(i) (2.368) arises as $(2.14) + \tfrac{7}{3}(2.15) + \tfrac{8}{3}(2.16) + \tfrac{13}{3}(2.17)$
(ii) (2.369) arises as $(2.14) + 11(2.15) + 7(2.16) + 13(2.18)$
(iii) (2.370) arises as $(2.14) + 5(2.16) + 9(2.17) + 7(2.19)$.

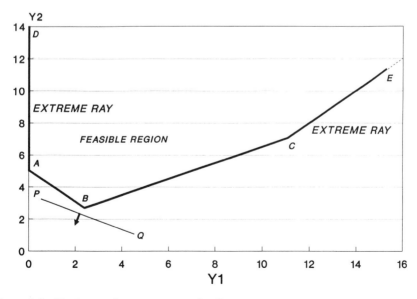

Figure 2.6 Vertices and extreme rays of a linear programme

The multipliers above therefore provide dual multipliers for Example 2.3 relative to different RHS coefficients b_1 and b_2. Hence they provide different solutions for Example 2.21 (the dual of Example 2.3), i.e.

(i) $y_1 = 7/3$, $\quad y_2 = 8/3$, $\quad y_3 = 13/3$, $\quad$ objective $= \frac{7}{3}b_1 + \frac{8}{3}b_2$

(ii) $y_1 = 11$, $\quad y_2 = 7$, $\quad y_4 = 13$, $\quad$ objective $= 11b_1 + 7b_2$

(iii) $y_2 = 5$, $\quad y_3 = 9$, $\quad y_5 = 7$, $\quad$ objective $= 5b_2$.

From Figure 2.6 it can be seen that these solutions correspond respectively to vertices B, C and A. Since objective (2.363) is a minimisation, we choose (i), (ii) or (iii) according to

$$\text{Min}(\tfrac{7}{3}b_1 + \tfrac{8}{3}b_2, 11b_1 + 7b_2, 5b_2). \tag{2.371}$$

Expression (2.371), known as the value function, also appeared in section 2.2 as (2.36), giving the optimal objective value for Example 2.3. This demonstrates the equality of the optimal objective values of Example 2.3, and its dual Example 2.21.

We have therefore shown that each of the vertex solutions for Example 2.21 illustrated in Figure 2.6 gives rise to a non-negative linear combination of the constraints to its dual model (Example 2.3) derivable by Fourier–Motzkin elimination. Hence solving the dual model for general RHS coefficients, which is possible using this algorithm, gives multipliers that provide all the vertex solutions for the original primal model.

If $b_2 = 2$ and $b_3 = 3$ the objective (2.363) has orientation PQ in Figure 2.6, demonstrating the optimal solution $y_1 = 7/3$, $y_2 = 8/3$. Other values of b_1 and b_2 give objectives with different orientations, giving rise to different vertices.

In section 2.2 it was shown that Example 2.3 was only feasible for certain values of b_1 and b_2. If z is eliminated from (2.29) to (2.32) we obtain the inequalities

$$0 \leqslant \tfrac{7}{3}b_1 + \tfrac{20}{3}b_2 \tag{2.372}$$

$$0 \leqslant 11b_1 + 11b_2 \tag{2.373}$$

$$0 \leqslant 9b_2 \tag{2.374}$$

which gives rise to the inequality (2.35).

Inequality (2.372) can be shown to depend on more than four of the original inequalities and is therefore redundant by the criterion mentioned in section 2.2. Dividing (2.373) through by 11 and (2.374) through by 9, we obtain a simplification of condition (2.35) for feasibility, namely

$$\text{Min}(b_1 + b_2, b_2) \geqslant 0. \tag{2.375}$$

Each of inequalties (2.373) and (2.374) (after dividing through by 11 and

9 respectively) arises from a non-negative combination of some of the original inequalities (2.15) to (2.19).

It can be verified that

(iv) (2.373) arises as (2.15) + (2.16) + 2(2.18) + (2.19)
(v) (2.374) arises as (2.16) + (2.17) + (2.18) + 2(2.19).

The multipliers above correspond to *homogeneous* solutions to Example 2.21, i.e.

(iv) $y_1 = y_2 = 1,\quad y_4 = 2,\quad y_5 = 1,\quad$ objective $= b_1 + b_2$
(v) $y_2 = y_3 = y_4 = 1,\quad y_5 = 2,\quad$ objective $= b_2$.

By "homogeneous" solutions we mean solutions for the model in which the RHS coefficients are zero. It can be seen that, after appending the logical variables y_3, y_4 and y_5, each of the above solutions satisfies the constraints of Example 2.21 if made homogeneous. Therefore if either of the terms $b_1 + b_2$ or b_2 were negative, then the corresponding homogeneous solution (iv) or (v) above could be added in an unlimited positive multiple to a feasible solution of Example 2.21 to improve the objective. Therefore the example would be *unbounded*. Hence a set of values for b_1 and b_2 that makes Example 2.3 infeasible makes Example 2.21 unbounded, demonstrating the dual relationship between infeasibility and unboundedness mentioned in section 2.5.

Geometrically, in Figure 2.6, each of the homogeneous solutions (iv) and (v) corresponds to an *extreme ray*. The values of y_1 and y_2 give the *directions* of these rays, i.e. (iv) corresponds to CE and (v) to AD. The extreme rays of a polytope can therefore also be obtained when the dual model is solved by Fourier–Motzkin elimination. These are provided by the multipliers of the original constraints giving rise to the feasibility conditions.

Should an LP model have a non-pointed polytope, the interpretation of the result of applying Fourier–Motzkin elimination to the dual is provided by exercise 2.16.

Alternative Dual Solutions and Shadow Prices

It has already been demonstrated, in section 2.5, that shadow prices are not necessarily synonymous with dual values. In order to demonstrate this, we consider the following example.

Example 2.22 Alternative Dual Values
Find the shadow prices for the following model:

$$\text{Minimise} \quad 2y_1 + 3y_2 \tag{2.376}$$

subject to

$$-y_1 + y_2 \geqslant b_1 \tag{2.377}$$

$$y_1 + y_2 \geqslant b_2 \tag{2.378}$$

$$-y_1 + 2y_2 \geqslant b_3 \tag{2.379}$$

$$y_1, y_2 \geqslant 0. \tag{2.380}$$

This model has already been considered for the case $b_1 = -4$, $b_2 = 5$, $b_3 = 3$ as the dual of Example 1.2. Therefore we refer to the variables as y_1 and y_2.
We consider the situation for general b_1, b_2 and b_3.
The dual of the above model is

$$\text{Maximise} \quad b_1 x_1 + b_2 x_2 + b_3 x_3 \tag{2.381}$$

subject to

$$-x_1 + x_2 - x_3 \leqslant 2 \tag{2.382}$$

$$x_1 + x_2 + 2x_3 \leqslant 3 \tag{2.383}$$

$$x_1, x_2, x_3 \geqslant 0. \tag{2.384}$$

The common optimal value of the objective function is therefore given by the maximum value of (2.381) arising from a vertex of the polytope defined by (2.382) and (2.383). This polytope is illustrated in Figure 1.2. Since it is closed, no LP associated with it can be unbounded. Therefore there is no feasibility condition for Example 2.22, i.e. the model is feasible for all values of b_1, b_2 and b_3. Taking the coordinates of the vertices marked in Figure 1.2 gives the value function for Example 2.22:

$$\text{Max}(0, \tfrac{3}{2} b_3, 2b_2, \tfrac{7}{3} b_2 + \tfrac{1}{3} b_3, \tfrac{1}{2} b_1 + \tfrac{5}{2} b_2, 3b_1). \tag{2.385}$$

We will deduce the shadow prices for the case $b_1 = -4$, $b_2 = 4$, $b_3 = -4$. This corresponds to the dual model having objective (1.11) resulting in the three alternative solutions given in section 1.1.
Substituting these values for b_i in (2.385) gives

$$\text{Max}(0, -6, 8, 8, 8, -12) = 8. \tag{2.386}$$

Notice that the three expressions corresponding to the three alternative dual solutions are

$$2b_2 \tag{2.387}$$

$$\tfrac{7}{3} b_2 + \tfrac{1}{3} b_3 \tag{2.388}$$

$$\tfrac{1}{2} b_1 + \tfrac{5}{2} b_2. \tag{2.389}$$

All produce this same optimal objective value.

Table 2.2

Constraint	Lower shadow price	Upper shadow price
(2.377)	0	1/2
(2.378)	2	5/2
(2.379)	0	1/3

If any of b_1, b_2 or b_3 is marginally *increased*, then the value of expression (2.386) will change at a rate given by the *maximum* corresponding coeffcient in the three expressions (2.387), (2.388) and (2.389). If, however, any one of them is marginally *decreased*, then the value will change at a rate given by the *minimum* corresponding coefficient. This results in *two-valued shadow prices* as given in Table 2.2.

In the case of alternative dual solutions, the shadow prices are therefore obtainable from *some* of the dual values. Nonetheless, it is necessary to generate *all* alternative dual solutions in order to deduce the shadow prices. This might induce a prohibitive amount of computation. Only if the dual solution is unique can we equate it with the shadow prices.

It has already been pointed out that alternative dual solutions correspond to a degenerate primal solution. Hence this difficulty of calculating shadow prices arises when a model has a degenerate optimal solution.

2.8 THE METHOD OF PROJECTIVE TRANSFORMATIONS

It was pointed out in section 2.3 that, in the worst case, the simplex algorithm can take an exponential number of computational steps, in relation to the size of a model. Experience, however, indicates that LP models are relatively "easy" to solve in comparison with some other models (e.g. integer programming models). Therefore, it was suspected that there were algorithms for LP where the number of computational steps only increased as a polynomial function of the size of the model. The first such method, reported in 1980, is known as the ellipsoid method. References to this method are given in section 2.9. Although the number of steps will not increase explosively with the size of the model, for practical models that method has proved inefficient. We do not therefore discuss if further in this book.

In 1984 another method was discovered. This relies on *projectively* transforming the solution space of the model at each step and is therefore referred to as the method of *projective transformations*. It is also commonly referred to as Karmarkar's algorithm, after its discoverer. This method has proved efficient for solving large models, although the simplex algorithm can still prove more efficient for small and medium-sized models. The method is, however, in its infancy and still subject to an evolution of variants and modifications. Also many computational refinements involving data structures and numerical calculations are being developed in a manner analogous to the development for the simplex algorithm over the last 40 years.

The version of the projective method described here is not actually "polynomially bounded". As with the simplex algorithm, refinements to improve convergence in the "worst case" often do not prove worth while in practice. References to the method and some of its variants are given in section 2.9. We demonstrate the method by deliberately employing the same numerical example used for Fourier–Motzkin elimination (Example 2.3) and the simplex algorithm (Example 2.4). For convenience, we have included slack variables. The comparative inefficiency of the projective method for such a (trivially) small example should be apparent.

Example 2.23 The Method of Projective Transformations
Solve the following LP model:

$$\text{Maximise} \quad -4x_1 + 5x_2 + 3x_3 \tag{2.390}$$

subject to

$$-x_1 + x_2 - x_3 + x_4 = 2 \tag{2.391}$$

$$x_1 + x_2 + 2x_3 + x_5 = 3 \tag{2.392}$$

$$x_1, x_2, x_3, x_4, x_5 \geqslant 0. \tag{2.393}$$

The method is an "interior" method in the sense that successive solutions lie in the interior of the feasible region. By scaling the variables, these interior solutions can be made to correspond to setting all (including slack and surplus) variables to 1. In order to find an initial interior solution, we are faced with a similar problem to that tackled through phase I of the simplex algorithm and discussed in section 2.4. The problem here could be dealt with in a similar manner through a pseudo-objective function.

Rather than obscure our description by the extra phase I calculations, we will begin with a known feasible interior solution, $x_1 = 1/2$, $x_2 = 1$, $x_3 = 1/2$, $x_4 = 2$, $x_5 = 1/2$. Since it is convenient that the interior solution have all variables of value unity, this is achieved by rescaling the non-unit-valued variables to give the model in the form:

$$\text{Maximise} \quad -2x_1^{(1)} + 5x_2^{(1)} + \tfrac{3}{2}x_3^{(1)} \tag{2.394}$$

subject to

$$-\tfrac{1}{2}x_1^{(1)} + x_2^{(1)} - \tfrac{1}{2}x_3^{(1)} + 2x_4^{(1)} = 2 \tag{2.395}$$

$$\tfrac{1}{2}x_1^{(1)} + x_2^{(1)} + x_3^{(1)} + \tfrac{1}{2}x_5^{(1)} = 3 \tag{2.396}$$

$$x_1^{(1)}, x_2^{(1)}, x_3^{(1)}, x_4^{(1)}, x_5^{(1)} \geqslant 0 \tag{2.397}$$

where

$$x_1^{(1)} = 2x_1, \quad x_2^{(1)} = x_2, \quad x_3^{(1)} = 2x_3, \quad x_4^{(1)} = \tfrac{1}{2}x_4, \quad x_5^{(1)} = 2x_5. \tag{2.398}$$

A number of transformations are now necessary in order to convert the model into the form in which the method is best understood.

The first transformation is to make all, except one, constraints *homogeneous* (i.e. to have RHS coefficients of 0). This is achieved by introducing another variable $x_6^{(1)}$, constrained to be 1, to represent the RHS. The resultant model is

$$\text{Maximise} \quad -2x_1^{(1)} + 5x_2^{(1)} + \tfrac{3}{2}x_3^{(1)} \tag{2.399}$$

subject to

$$-\tfrac{1}{2}x_1^{(1)} + x_2^{(1)} - \tfrac{1}{2}x_3^{(1)} + 2x_4^{(1)} - 2x_6^{(1)} = 0 \tag{2.400}$$

$$\tfrac{1}{2}x_1^{(1)} + x_2^{(1)} + x_3^{(1)} + \tfrac{1}{2}x_5^{(1)} - 3x_6^{(1)} = 0 \tag{2.401}$$

$$x_6^{(1)} = 1 \tag{2.402}$$

$$x_1^{(1)}, x_2^{(1)}, x_3^{(1)}, x_4^{(1)}, x_5^{(1)} \geqslant 0. \tag{2.403}$$

The next transformation is to make the non-homogeneous constraint the sum of all variables. In order for the method to converge, it is necessary that the model not be unbounded. Therefore, we can impose a constraint on the sum of the variables in such a way as not to restrict the optimal solution. Our knowledge of the example allows us to stipulate that

$$x_1^{(1)} + x_2^{(1)} + x_3^{(1)} + x_4^{(1)} + x_5^{(1)} \leqslant 6. \tag{2.404}$$

Introducing a slack variable $x_7^{(1)}$ gives the equation

$$x_1^{(1)} + x_2^{(1)} + x_3^{(1)} + x_4^{(1)} + x_5^{(1)} + x_7^{(1)} = 6. \tag{2.405}$$

We have deliberately chosen an upper bound that allows the solution, with all variables unity, to be feasible. Another bound could be imposed and the variables refined by scaling to achieve the same result. Constraints (2.402) and (2.405) can now be replaced by subtracting and adding them in suitable multiples to give

$$x_1^{(1)} + x_2^{(1)} + x_3^{(1)} + x_4^{(1)} + x_5^{(1)} - 6x_6^{(1)} + x_7^{(1)} = 0 \tag{2.406}$$

$$x_1^{(1)} + x_2^{(1)} + x_3^{(1)} + x_4^{(1)} + x_5^{(1)} + x_6^{(1)} + x_7^{(1)} = 7 \tag{2.407}$$

i.e. a homogeneous constraint and a constraint forcing the sum of variables to be equal to their number.

The model is now in the "standard" form in which the method can be explained. For completeness, we restate the transformed model using floating-point numbers. Subsequent calculations will be done in floating-point arithmetic. Results will be given to two decimal places although the underlying calculations are of greater precision.

$$\text{Maximise} \quad -2x_1^{(1)} + 5x_2^{(1)} + 1.5x_3^{(1)} \tag{2.408}$$

subject to

$$-0.5x_1^{(1)} + x_2^{(1)} - 0.5x_3^{(1)} + 2x_4^{(1)} - 2x_6^{(1)} = 0 \tag{2.409}$$

$$0.5x_1^{(1)} + x_2^{(1)} + x_3^{(1)} + 0.5x_5^{(1)} - 3x_6^{(1)} = 0 \tag{2.410}$$

$$x_1^{(1)} + x_2^{(1)} + x_3^{(1)} + x_4^{(1)} + x_5^{(1)} - 6x_6^{(1)} + x_7^{(1)} = 0 \tag{2.411}$$

$$x_1^{(1)} + x_2^{(1)} + x_3^{(1)} + x_4^{(1)} + x_5^{(1)} + x_6^{(1)} + x_7^{(1)} = 7 \tag{2.412}$$

$$x_1^{(1)}, x_2^{(1)}, x_3^{(1)}, x_4^{(1)}, x_5^{(1)}, x_6^{(1)}, x_7^{(1)} \geqslant 0. \tag{2.413}$$

By design, the solution

$$x_1^{(1)} = x_2^{(1)} = x_3^{(1)} = x_4^{(1)} = x_5^{(1)} = x_6^{(1)} = x_7^{(1)} = 1, \quad \text{objective} = 4.5$$

satisfies all the constraints.

Constraints (2.412) and (2.413) force the variables to represent points on a geometric object known as a *simplex*. A simplex (not to be confused with the simplex algorithm) in two dimensions is a triangle and in three dimensions is a tetrahedron. It is worth visualising how a model, of the form above, would look if there were only three variables. The equivalent of constraint (2.412) would be

$$x_1 + x_2 + x_3 = 3. \tag{2.414}$$

Assuming all variables to be non-negative, this would constrain the solution to lie in the simplex (equilateral triangle) PQR in Figure 2.7.

The other, homogeneous, constraints would define a plane through the origin O. This would intersect PQR along a line such as ST. Since it would have been arranged that the solution $x_1 = x_2 = x_3 = 1$ was feasible, ST would pass through this point lying at the centre of the simplex PQR.

The homogeneous constraint defines a subspace, and a line such as ST is a *projection* of this subspace on to the simplex. For general models we will be working in more dimensions.

For our example, (2.412) and (2.413) represent a six-dimensional simplex and the subspace, represented by the homogeneous constraints (2.409) to (2.411), projects on to this simplex. We wish to move from our current solution, in the centre of the simplex, through this section, in a direction in

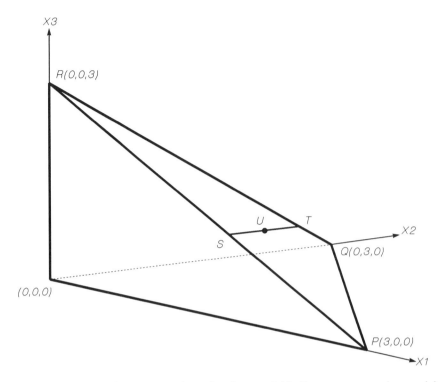

Figure 2.7 Geometric representation of a three-variable linear programming model

which the objective function increases. Since the projection needed, in order to find the direction of greatest objective improvement, is most clearly explained using vectors and matrices, we resort to this notation. The matrix associated with the transformed model is

$$A = \begin{bmatrix} -0.5 & 1 & -0.5 & 2 & 0 & -2 & 0 \\ 0.5 & 1 & 1 & 0 & 0.5 & -3 & 0 \\ 1 & 1 & 1 & 1 & 1 & -6 & 1 \\ 1 & 1 & 1 & 1 & 1 & 1 & 1 \end{bmatrix} \qquad (2.415)$$

and the vector of objective coefficients is

$$c = [-2, 5, 1.5, 0, 0, 0, 0]^{\mathrm{T}}. \qquad (2.416)$$

This vector can be interpreted, in our seven-dimensional solution space, as the direction of maximum improvement in the objective. We do not, however, wish to move out of the section of the simplex defined by constraints (2.409) to (2.413). Therefore we project vector c into the corresponding section the simplex. The set of vectors x that satisfy the equation $Ax = 0$ form what is known as the *null space* of A. Therefore the set of vectors satisfying constraints (2.409) to (2.413) consist of the vector $(1, 1, 1, 1, 1, 1, 1)$ (our current solution) added to vectors in the null space of A. We begin by projecting c into the null space of A. This is a standard operation in linear algebra. Rather than derive the result, we simple state it. It can be verified that the matrix

$$P = I - A^T(AA^T)^{-1}A \tag{2.417}$$

projects any vector into the null space of A. We therefore calculate Pc. This can be done indirectly by solving the equations

$$(AA^T)y = Ac \tag{2.418}$$

$$Pc = c - A^Ty. \tag{2.419}$$

The vector y provides a set of multipliers, analogous to shadow prices, with which to transform the objective coefficients to "reduced costs".

In the subsequent calculations the results are reported to two decimal places only but the underlying calculations are to a greater precision.

For our example we can calculate

$$y = [1.45, 4.34, -2.54, 0.64]^T \tag{2.420}$$

giving

$$Pc = [-1.54, 1.12, -0.21, -1, -0.27, 0, 1.9]^T. \tag{2.421}$$

It is easy to verify that this vector lies in the null space of A. In order to improve the objective value, we add a multiple of the vector to the current solution vector, giving

$$x^{(1)} = [1, 1, 1, 1, 1, 1, 1]^T + \theta[-1.54, 1.12, -0.21, -1, -0.27, 0, 1.9]^T. \tag{2.422}$$

In order to remain feasible (satisfy constraints (2.413)), we must keep θ no larger than

$$\text{Min}\left(\frac{1}{1.54}, \frac{1}{0.21}, \frac{1}{1}, \frac{1}{0.27}\right) = 0.65. \tag{2.423}$$

If θ were set to this value x_1 would become zero and we would have reached one of the boundaries of the simplex.

Instead of doing this we restrict θ to a *fraction* of this value. In the theoretical version of the algorithm, it is necessary to make this fraction depend on the number of variables in the model, in order to prove polynomial boundedness. For practical applications, experiment has suggested a, generally larger, fraction of about 0.9. Therefore we set

$$\theta = 0.9 \times 0.65 = 0.58. \tag{2.424}$$

This produces the solution

$$x_1^{(1)} = [0.1, 1.65, 0.88, 0.42, 0.84, 1, 2.1]^T \qquad (2.425)$$

with an objective value of 9.3.

The restricting of the change in the solution, in order to maintain an *interior* solution, was deliberate. Clearly the solution still lies inside the simplex given by constraints (2.412) and (2.413). By means of a projective transformation, it is now possible to transform the simplex into itself in such a way that the solution just obtained becomes the centre point, with all variables unity. This is done by means of the transformation

$$x^{(r+1)} = \frac{nD^{-1}x^{(r)}}{e^T D^{-1}x^{(r)}} \qquad (2.426)$$

where n is the number of variables in the transformed model (in this case 7) and e is a vector of "1"s. D is a diagonal matrix whose entries are given by the current solution values. In this case

$$D = \begin{bmatrix} 0.1 & & & & & & \\ & 1.65 & & & & & \\ & & 0.88 & & & & \\ & & & 0.42 & & & \\ & & & & 0.84 & & \\ & & & & & 1 & \\ & & & & & & 2.1 \end{bmatrix}. \qquad (2.427)$$

It can be checked that this transformation leaves all points on the boundary of the simplex unchanged. All points within the simplex are transformed to other points within the simplex, and in particular the current solution becomes

$$x_1^{(2)} = x_2^{(2)} = x_3^{(2)} = x_4^{(2)} = x_5^{(2)} = x_6^{(2)} = x_7^{(2)} = 1.$$

From (2.426) we obtain

$$x^{(r)} = \frac{nDx^{(r+1)}}{e^T Dx^{(r+1)}}. \qquad (2.428)$$

Substituting this expression for $x^{(r)}$ into the objective (2.408) and constraints (2.409) to (2.413) gives a new transformed model:

Maximise

$$\frac{-1.41x_1^{(2)} + 57.65x_2^{(2)} + 9.21x_3^{(2)}}{0.1x_1^{(2)} + 1.65x_2^{(2)} + 0.88x_3^{(2)} + 0.42x_4^{(2)} + 0.84x_5^{(2)} + x_6^{(2)} + 2.1x_7^{(2)}} \qquad (2.429)$$

subject to

$$-0.35x_1^{(2)} + 11.53x_2^{(2)} - 3.07x_3^{(2)} + 5.91x_4^{(2)} - 14x_6^{(2)} = 0 \quad (2.430)$$

$$0.35x_1^{(2)} + 11.53x_2^{(2)} + 6.14x_3^{(2)} + 2.96x_5^{(2)} - 21x_6^{(2)} = 0 \quad (2.431)$$

$$0.71x_1^{(2)} + 11.53x_2^{(2)} + 6.14x_3^{(2)} + 2.95x_4^{(2)}$$
$$+ 5.92x_5^{(2)} - 42x_6^{(2)} + 14.72x_7^{(2)} = 0 \quad (2.432)$$

$$x_1^{(2)} + x_2^{(2)} + x_3^{(2)} + x_4^{(2)} + x_5^{(2)} + x_6^{(2)} + x_7^{(2)} = 7 \quad (2.433)$$

$$x_1^{(2)}, x_2^{(2)}, x_3^{(2)}, x_4^{(2)}, x_5^{(2)}, x_6^{(2)}, x_7^{(2)} \geqslant 0. \quad (2.434)$$

It is straightforward to transform this fractional programming model into an LP (by a method given in *MBMP*). However, an objective improvement can be obtained by maximising the numerator of (2.429), since the denominator will always be positive.

We now have a model in the same form as before where

$$A = \begin{bmatrix} -0.35 & 11.53 & -3.07 & 5.91 & 0 & -14 & 0 \\ 0.35 & 11.53 & 6.14 & 0 & 2.96 & -21 & 0 \\ 0.71 & 11.53 & 6.14 & 2.95 & 5.92 & -42 & 14.72 \\ 1 & 1 & 1 & 1 & 1 & 1 & 1 \end{bmatrix}$$

$$(2.435)$$

and

$$c = [-1.41, 57.65, 9.21, 0, 0, 0, 0]^{\mathrm{T}}. \quad (2.436)$$

Calculating P as in (2.417) we can project (2.436) into the null space of (2.435) to give

$$Pc = [-9.97, 14.69, -1.63, -15.21, -8.04, 6.29, 13.88]^{\mathrm{T}}. \quad (2.437)$$

We can now create a new solution

$$x^{(2)} = [1, 1, 1, 1, 1, 1, 1]^{\mathrm{T}}$$
$$+ \theta[-9.97, 14.69, -1.63, -15.21, -8.04, 6.29, 13.88]^{\mathrm{T}} \quad (2.438)$$

setting

$$\theta = 0.9 \times \frac{1}{15.21} = 0.06 \quad (2.439)$$

to give

$$x^{(2)} = [0.4, 1.88, 0.9, 0.09, 0.52, 1.38, 1.83]^{\mathrm{T}}. \quad (2.440)$$

Using (2.428) to transform this solution back into the space of the model expressed in terms of $x^{(1)}$, we obtain the solution

$$x^{(1)} = [0.03, 2.25, 0.58, 0.03, 0.32, 1, 2.8]^T \qquad (2.441)$$

with an objective value of 12.06.

We repeat the process using a diagonal matrix constructed from (2.440) to transform the model projectively into a space expressed in terms of new variables $x^{(3)}$. The solution (2.440) becomes the centre of the new simplex. When improved, in the direction of the objective projected into the new null space, we obtain

$$x^{(3)} = [0.24, 1.54, 1.66, 0.1, 0.39, 1.49, 1.58]^T. \qquad (2.442)$$

Transforming $x^{(3)}$ back into the space of the model, expressed in terms of $x^{(1)}$, we obtain the solution

$$x^{(1)} = [0, 2.32, 0.64, 0, 0.1, 1, 2.9]^T \qquad (2.443)$$

with an objective value of 12.56.

Once this solution has become sufficiently "close" to a vertex solution, we can be sure that the corresponding vertex is optimal. The theoretical test for when the condition is reached is not used in practice. Instead, a cruder test is usually applied. Although we would normally carry on iterating further, for our example we assume we have reached this state with the variables $x_2^{(1)}$, $x_3^{(1)}$, $x_6^{(1)}$ and $x_7^{(1)}$ providing a basis. The corresponding basic solution can be obtained by a matrix inversion to give

$$x^{(1)} = [0, 2.33, 0.67, 0, 0, 1, 3]^T \qquad (2.444)$$

with an objective value of 12.67. In terms of the original variables, which were transformed by (2.398), we have $x_1 = 0$, $x_2 = 2.33$, $x_3 = 0.33$, $x_4 = x_5 = 0$ with the objective value of 12.67.

It must again be emphasised that on small examples, such as that above, the method of projective transformation appears lengthy. Also the resultant matrices tend to be less sparse than those in the simplex algorithm. Many refinements are possible as the development of this method is at an early stage.

2.9 HISTORY, REFERENCES AND FUTURE DEVELOPMENTS

Solving Systems of Linear Equations

The idea of solving linear equations by successive elimination of variables goes back to Legendre (1805) and Gauss (1809.)

This topic forms the subject of *linear algebra*. A clear exposition of this and

Gaussian elimination is given by Cohn (1958). The calculations are usually expressed in terms of *matrices*, as will be the case in Chapter 4. Many computational refinements are possible to improve efficiency. These are also discussed there.

The number of operations in Gaussian elimination can be shown to be $O(n^3)$. The better method, due to Strassen (1969), is $O(n^{2.8})$, but it is not obviously possible to exploit the *sparsity* (i.e. most coefficients are zero) of LP matrices to advantage with this method.

Solving Systems of Linear Inequalities and Equations

The method described here is essentially due to Fourier (1826), although Motzkin (1936) applied what is essentially the same method to game theory. A full discussion and set of references can be found in Williams (1986), who also discusses a link with logic.

The method can be streamlined and also presented in the form of matrices. This has not, however, been done, in view of the inherent computational complexity of the method. It can be shown to require an exponential number of steps. The method does, however, enable one to understand aspects of LP in a very clear manner.

The Simplex Algorithm I: Finding an Optimal Solution

This method was invented by Dantzig and is fully described in Dantzig (1963). There are many variants and refinements possible, some of which are described there. He also explains the reason for using the word "simplex". The use of the word "basis" derives from abstract linear algebra. If, for a set of m equations, we regard the columns of coefficients as m-tuples in an m-dimensional vector space, then we are seeking a linearly independent set of columns that span the space. This is a basis for the space.

The bound on the number of vertices is due to McMullen (1970).

A very full theoretical discussion of the method (and LP in general) is given by Schrijver (1986). This includes discussion of the computational complexity of the method. Another, very good, reference is Chvátal (1983).

The circling example (Example 2.6) is due to Beale (1955), who shows that it is the smallest possible such model for which this can happen. The ε-perturbation technique for avoiding circling is due to Wolfe (1963). The method given of the smallest subscript rule is due to Bland (1977). Example 2.7, demonstrating exponential growth in the simplex algorithm, is a special case of the general model due to Klee and Minty (1972). The general model is

$$\text{Maximise} \quad 2^{n-1}x_1 + 2^{n-2}x_2 + \cdots + 2x_{n-1} + x_n$$

subject to

$$x_1 \leqslant 5$$
$$4x_1 + x_2 \leqslant 25$$
$$8x_1 + 4x_2 + x_3 \leqslant 125$$
$$\vdots$$
$$2^n x_1 + 2^{n-1} x_2 + 2^{n-2} x_3 + \cdots + 4x_{n-1} + x_n \leqslant 5^n$$
$$x_1, x_2, \ldots, x_n \geqslant 0.$$

This can be shown to take $2^n - 1$ iterations to solve using the maximum reduced cost (d_j) criterion. Jeroslow (1973) has shown that models exist requiring an exponential number of steps with the maximum improvement criterion.

There are a number of unresolved questions concerning the simplex algorithm. One such is the Hirsch conjecture. This is that, for an LP model with m constraints (apart from non-negativity constraints) which is represented by a (bounded) polytope, an optimal vertex is connected to any other vertex by at most m edges. Hence it should be possible to optimise, from a feasible starting basis, in at most m iterations using suitable pivot selections. It is unlikely that any uniform rule could be devised for these pivot selections even if the conjecture is true. It is still possible that there could be devised a pivot selection rule that bounds the number of operations in the simplex algorithm by a polynomial function of the size of the data.

Given that the "worst-case" behaviour of the simplex algorithm is rare in practice, analysis has been made of the average-case behaviour by, in particular, Smale (1983).

The whole subject of computational complexity is described fully by Garey and Johnson (1979).

The Simplex Algorithm II: Finding a Feasible Solution With Bounded Variables

The problem of finding a feasible starting basis for the simplex algorithm presented some difficulty in the early days. Two alternative approaches to that developed here are as follows:

(i) Pivot out the infeasible variables one at a time.
(ii) Give the infeasible variables large objective coefficients of appropriate sign so that optimisation will drive them out of the basis (if the model is feasible). This is usually known as the "big-M" approach. An economical variant of this method is mentioned at the end of section 2.4.

It should be pointed out that some treatments of the simplex algorithm involve introducing artificial variables (as well as surplus variables) into " $\geqslant$ "

constraints. Phase I of the simplex algorithm then only involves removing artificial variables. There seems little merit in doing this.

The idea of dealing with bounded variables by the modification of the simplex algorithm described here is due to Dantzig (1955).

The Dual of a Linear Programme

The recognition of the dual of an LP is due to von Neumann and to Dantzig, and is explained in von Neumann and Morgenstern (1947). It was formally stated and the relationships proved by Gale, Kuhn and Tucker (1951). The economic significance of the concept can be found in Dorfman, Samuelson and Solow (1958).

The Dual Simplex Algorithm

This algorithm is due to Lemke (1954).

Generating All Vertices and Extreme Rays

A number of methods have been proposed for finding all vertices of a polytope. In particular, see Dyer and Proll (1977) and Mattheiss and Schmidt (1980). The method given here can be implemented by mirroring, on the primal model, the operations of Fourier–Motzkin elimination applied to the dual model. This is described in Williams (1986). It involves successively eliminating the *constraints* of an LP model by a transformation of variables. As with Fourier–Motzkin elimination, it can result in an enormous build-up of storage requirements. It can, however, be applied in a limited form to generate a starting basis for the simplex algorithm as described by Williams (1984).

The Method of Projective Transformations

This method was discovered by Karmarkar (1984) although it has subsequently been shown to be equivalent to a non-linear programming method in which the constraints are incorporated into the objective function by a "logarithmic barrier function". This connection is described by Gill et al. (1986). A good theoretical description of the algorithm is given by Todd (1989). The method of converting an LP model into the nearly homogeneous form is due to Tomlin (1987), who gives some computational experience.

2.10 EXERCISES

2.1 Solve the following set of equations by Gaussian elimination:

$$-x_1 + x_2 = b_1$$
$$x_1 + x_2 + x_3 = b_2$$
$$-x_1 + 2x_2 + x_3 = b_3.$$

2.2 Solve the following set of equations by Gaussian elimination, eliminating the variables in the order x_1, x_2, x_3 by (i) attempting to use the first equation at each stage as pivot equation and (ii) using another pivot order:

$$x_1 - x_2 + x_3 = b_1$$
$$-x_1 + x_2 = b_2$$
$$2x_1 - 2x_2 - 3x_3 = b_3.$$

2.3 Solve Example 1.2 with objective (1.1) using Fourier–Motzkin elimination.

2.4 Attempt to solve Example 1.3 with objective (1.16) using Fourier–Motzkin elimination.

2.5 Construct the value function and feasibility condition for Example 1.1 with general RHS coefficients using Fourier–Motzkin elimination.

2.6 After appending slack and surplus variables in exercise 1.2, list all pairs of variables that correspond to (i) basic solutions and (ii) vertex solutions. Remark on the significance of parallel constraints.

2.7 Solve the following model by the simplex algorithm:

$$\text{Maximise} \quad 2x_1 + x_2 - x_3$$

subject to

$$x_1 + x_3 \leqslant 3$$
$$2x_1 + 3x_2 + x_3 \leqslant 7$$
$$x_1 - x_3 \leqslant 1$$
$$x_1, x_2, x_3 \geqslant 0.$$

2.8 Solve the model in exercise 1.2 by the simplex algorithm, making reference to exercise 2.6.

2.9 Compare the results of the three pivoting rules discussed in section 2.3 on exercise 2.7.

2.10 Show, using the simplex algorithm, that the dual of Example 1.3 with objective (1.16) is unbounded.

2.11 Show, using the simplex algorithm, that the dual of Example 2.17 is infeasible.

2.12 Write the dual of Example 1.1 in standard form and create its dual, showing that it is equivalent to the original model.

2.13 Write the dual of the model in exercise 1.2 and deduce its optimal solution from that derived in exercise 2.8.

2.14 Show that the model created in exercise 1.12 is the dual of that created for Example 1.27.

2.15 Find, for exercise 1.10 with the constraints relaxed to "$\leqslant$", the vertices and extreme rays using the method of section 2.6.

2.16 Apply the method of section 2.7 to try to find the vertices and extreme rays for Example 1.4.

2.17 Solve the model resulting from the game theory example (Example 1.27) by the simplex algorithm. Use the solution to deduce the optimal solution to the dual model (the other player's model) described in exercise 1.12.

2.18 Solve the Leontief model in Example 1.25 by means of Fourier–Motzkin elimination for general b_1, b_2, b_3 and L. Show that there is either no solution or a unique solution.

2.19 For a feasible set of b_1, b_2, b_3 and L derived from exercise 2.18, formulate the dual of the model in exercise 2.18. Solve the model by Fourier–Motzkin elimination. Hence show that the model in exercise 2.18 has only one solution.

2.20 Solve Example 2.6 using the rule for avoiding circling.

2.21 Solve the dual of Example 1.1 by the simplex algorithm, mirroring the steps of Example 2.20.

2.22 Solve Example 1.1 by the dual simplex algorithm.

2.23 Solve Example 1.1 by the method of projective transformations, choosing a suitable feasible starting solution.

2.24 Show that Gaussian elimination requires $O(n^3)$ computational steps.

2.25 Calculate the number of computational steps required in Fourier–Motzkin elimination, as a function of m and n.

Chapter 3
─────── Methods for Specialist Linear Programming Models

Although the simplex algorithm is a very powerful method of solving a wide range of, often very large, LP models, there are circumstances in which it can be specialised to advantage. This is particularly true for the two types of network model discussed in section 3.1.

For even more specialised (and simple) types of model, such as the assignment and shortest-path problems, the simplex algorithm is inefficient because it exhibits degeneracy. Nevertheless, it is instructive first to apply the specialised form of the simplex algorithm to them in order to illustrate that these models are special cases as well as to show why the method is inefficient. This and more efficient algorithms will be given in sections 3.2 and 3.3.

3.1 MINIMUM-COST AND MAXIMUM FLOW THROUGH A NETWORK

It has already been shown in section 1.5 that the minimum-cost network flow (MCNF) model can be formulated as an LP with a special structure. When applying the simplex algorithm to such a model, it is very instructive to interpret the steps in terms of the original network. Besides giving insight, this also allows one to specialise some of the steps. It also allows a computer implementation to use compact data structures as discussed in sections 1.6 and 4.6.

The Interpretation of a Basis

We will interpret basic solutions for Example 1.21 in terms of the network given in Figure 1.19. Before doing this it is important to realise that the equations defining the constraints for a MCNF model will not have full row rank. In order for the model to be feasible, the sum of external flows in must equal the sum of external flows out. Therefore, if we add together the equations for a model such as (1.127) to (1.134) they will cancel out, since each variable has one $+1$ and one -1 entry in the constraints. This implies that any one constraint equation is implied by the others. For example, adding together equations (1.127) to (1.133) gives

$$-x_{DH} + x_{HG} = -6. \tag{3.1}$$

This is clearly the constraint (1.134) with coefficients all negated. *Any* one constraint (such as (3.1)) can be regarded as redundant in the presence of the others. For the purposes of the LP model it could be removed. This demonstrates that, for an m-constraint model, at most $m-1$ variables would be non-zero in a basic solution, i.e. there would always be degeneracy.

Hence the concept of a basis for a MCNF model with m constraints is amended to involve just $m-1$ variables. In this, particularly simple, type of LP model we do not need to introduce logical variables in constraints or the objective. Therefore such a basis will consist of choosing $m-1$ of the original variables (arcs) so long as, after leaving out any one constraint, the resulting matrix of coefficients has full row rank. This will be illustrated in relation to the LP model and network for Example 1.21.

One such basis for the eight-constraint model consists of the seven variables x_{AC}, x_{BD}, x_{CE}, x_{DE}, x_{DH}, x_{EF} and x_{HG}. These arcs associated with these variables are shown in Figure 3.1.

The form of this subnetwork is known as a *spanning tree*. A spanning tree is a set of (undirected) arcs that connect together all the nodes but contain no loops. It can be shown that, for a connected network (i.e. no unconnected components), with n nodes, a spanning tree must consist of exactly $n-1$ arcs.

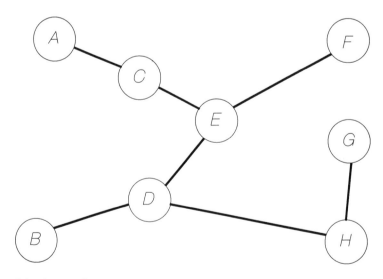

Figure 3.1 A spanning tree

Our amended concept of a basis for a MCNF model can be interpreted as a spanning tree for the associated network. We therefore have the following correspondence between a network associated with a MCNF model and the LP in the form of equations:

$$\text{Arc} \leftrightarrow \text{Variable}$$
$$\text{Node} \leftrightarrow \text{Constraint}$$
$$\text{Spanning tree} \leftrightarrow \text{Basis}$$

If, for an n-node connected network, we were to consider any subset of arcs that did not form a spanning tree, then it could not correspond to a basis. In order to demonstrate this, consider, for example, the sets of arcs AC, BD, CE, DE, DH, EG and HG. This does not form a spanning tree since node F is not connected. We consider the equations (1.127) to (1.134) involving those variables from Example 1.21. These are

$$- x_{AC} = - 10 \tag{3.2}$$

$$- x_{BD} = - 15 \tag{3.3}$$

$$x_{AC} - x_{CE} = 0 \tag{3.4}$$

$$x_{BD} - x_{DE} - x_{DH} = 0 \tag{3.5}$$

$$x_{CE} + x_{DE} - x_{EG} = 0 \tag{3.6}$$

$$x_{EG} + x_{HG} = 10 \tag{3.7}$$

$$x_{DH} - x_{HG} = 6. \tag{3.8}$$

Notice that equation (1.132) of Example 1.21, corresponding to node F, is not present. Leaving out any one equation results in a linearly dependent set of expressions. This situation will always occur if a set of $m - 1$ arcs do not form a spanning tree since, by definition, at least one node must be disconnected. Therefore the associated variables will not satisfy the condition for a basis stipulated in section 2.3.

We can now apply the steps of the simplex algorithm to Example 1.21, which we restate below.

Minimum-Cost Flow

Example 3.1 A Minimum-Cost Network Flow Problem Solved by the Network Form of the Simplex Algorithm

Find the minimum-cost flow through the network shown in Figure 3.2.

Unit costs are marked on the arcs and external flows in and out at the source and sink nodes are given in square boxes.

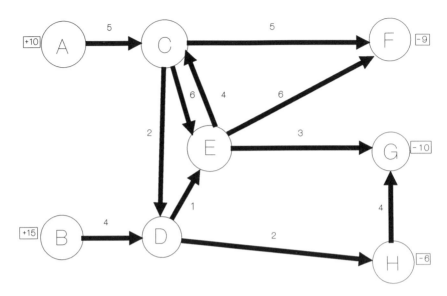

Figure 3.2 A minimum-cost network flow problem

Step 0 We choose a *starting spanning tree*. As we are no longer using logical variables, we must seek a set of $m - 1$ of the arcs. Although any spanning tree will suffice, it is advantageous to find one corresponding to a *feasible basis*. This is one in which flow patterns will be possible in the allowed directions. If it is difficult to find such a feasible spanning tree, then phase I of the simplex algorithm can be applied to move from an infeasible spanning tree to a feasible one (if it exists). This is the case in exercise 3.1.

A reasonable "heuristic" approach is to choose arcs pointing *away* from the source and *into* the sinks and then progressively add more arcs with the appropriate directions. At no time must a loop be created. When $m - 1$ arcs have been chosen we have a spanning tree.

For this example we choose the following arcs in order AC, BD, EF, EG, DH, CE and DE, giving the spanning tree illustrated in Figure 3.3.

Step 1 From the current spanning tree we can determine the associated flow pattern uniquely. This is done by calculating the flow in arcs at the "tips" of the tree first, maintaining material balance at each node.

In this example this results in the *flow pattern* shown in Figure 3.3, with flows in square boxes. It can be verified that the flow pattern illustrated, corresponding to a basic solution of the LP model, has a total cost of 275.

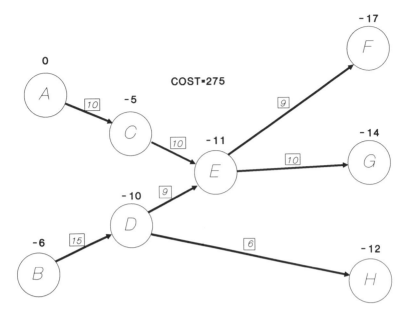

Figure 3.3 Initial flow pattern

Step 2 Seeking a non-basic variable to make basic corresponds to seeking an arc not in the current spanning tree to introduce. In order to do this, we first calculate the *dual values* for the corresponding LP model.

Since the constraints of the LP model, given in Example 1.21, are all equalities, the corresponding dual variables will be free (unrestricted in sign). These dual variables will be associated with the nodes corresponding to the LP constraints. It has already been pointed out that any one constraint of the LP model can be regarded as redundant in the presence of the others. This constraint (node) will then have a dual value of zero. The arbitrariness of which constraint (node) is so chosen corresponds to the alternative dual solutions resulting from degeneracy in the primal model, as remarked on in section 2.5. We therefore conveniently associate a dual value of zero with one of the nodes, which will be known as the *root node*.

For the example we will arbitrarily choose node A as root node, marking the dual value of 0 at the node in Figure 3.3.

Those arcs in the current spanning tree correspond to variables that are currently basic in the LP model. Following the discussion of section 2.5, the associated constraints of the dual model will currently be binding. This allows us to calculate all the dual values. In particular, when the model of

Example 1.21 is converted to a maximisation (by negating the objective function), the dual constraint corresponding to basic arc AC is

$$-y_A + y_C \geqslant -5 \tag{3.9}$$

where y_A and y_C are the dual values associated with nodes A and C and -5 is the negated unit cost associated with arc AC. Since $y_A = 0$ and (3.9) is binding (satisfied as an equation), we have $y_C = -5$. Similarly we can calculate the dual values for all other nodes using the unit costs of arcs in the current spanning tree. These values are marked at the nodes in Figure 3.3.

It is sometimes useful to regard the dual values as analogous to pressures for fluid flow or potentials for electrical flows. References for these analogues are given in *MBMP*. With this interpretation the "pressure drop" down each arc of the spanning tree must equal the unit cost of that arc.

Again using the duality results discussed in section 2.5, for non-included arcs (non-basic variables), the (negated) reduced cost has the same value as the corresponding surplus variable in the dual solution. For example, for the non-included arc CF, we have the corresponding dual constraint

$$-y_C + y_F \geqslant -5. \tag{3.10}$$

Since $y_C = -5$ and $y_F = -17$ it is not satisfied by the current dual solution and the surplus is -7. Therefore, arc (non-basic variable) CF has a reduced cost of -7, indicating that it can, with benefit, be brought into the spanning tree (basis). Similarly reduced costs can be calculated for all other non-included arcs. Arcs that are worth bringing into the tree will have negative reduced costs (i.e. positive "reduced profits"). The formula resulting from this method of calculating the reduced costs is:

Reduced cost of arc = Unit cost of arc
$\qquad\qquad\qquad\quad$ − Dual value of predecessor node
$\qquad\qquad\qquad\quad$ + Dual value of successor node.

The full set of reduced costs is as follows:

Arc	Reduced cost
CF	−7
CD	−3
EC	10
HG	2

This demonstrates that CF is worth bringing into the spanning tree. Hence *CF enters the spanning tree* (basis).

The mechanical analogy is that the "pressure drop" of 12 along CF exceeds the unit cost of 5 by 7, making it worth diverting flow along CF.

Step 3   By introducing an extra arc into a spanning tree, a loop must be created.

In the example, by introducing arc CF into the tree in Figure 3.3 we create the loop shown in Figure 3.4.

If a flow of θ is sent along CF, then to compensate we must reduce the flows in CE and EF by θ as shown. No flow can be allowed to be negative. Therefore, in this example, we set θ to its maximum possible value of 9. Hence flow in arc EF drops to zero, i.e. arc *EF leaves the spanning tree* (basis).

Step 1   (repeated)   Flow in arcs CF and CE is suitably adjusted, giving the spanning tree and associated flow pattern shown in Figure 3.5.

The associated cost of the flow can be verified to be 212. As would be expected, the cost of the flow in Figure 3.3 has been reduced by 9×7, i.e. the product of the flow change θ and the reduced cost of CF. The quantity θ corresponds to the ratio used in the simplex algorithm and discussed in section 2.3.

Step 2   (repeated)   The dual values are recalculated again using (arbitrarily) A as root node with a dual value of 0. This results in the new set of dual values associated with the nodes in Figure 3.5. Notice that many of the dual values are unchanged. In practice, it is unnecessary to update them all. This computational refinement is described in section 4.6.

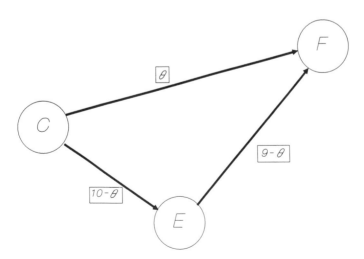

Figure 3.4   A cost-reducing circuit

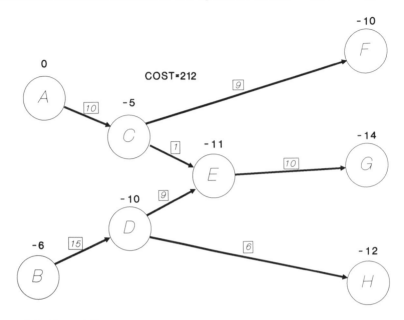

Figure 3.5 Second flow pattern

The reduced costs for the non-included arcs resulting from these dual values are:

Arc	Reduced cost
CD	− 3
EC	10
EF	7
HG	2

CD has a negative reduced cost and should therefore be introduced into the spanning tree.

Step 3 (repeated)   We create the loop shown in Figure 3.6.

The flow θ in CD can be increased to 1 when CE leaves the tree.

Step 1 (repeated)   The new tree and flow pattern are shown in Figure 3.7.

The cost of this flow pattern is 209.

Step 2 (repeated)   The new dual values are calculated and marked in Figure 3.7.

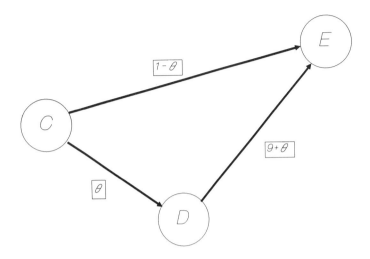

Figure 3.6 A cost-reducing circuit

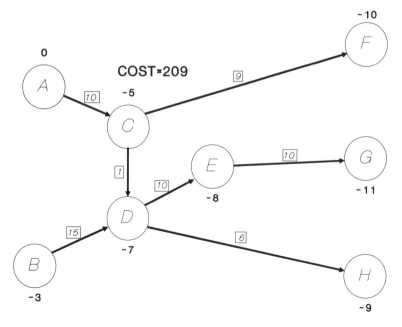

Figure 3.7 Third flow pattern

They result in the following reduced costs for non-included arcs:

Arc	Reduced cost
EC	7
EF	4
HG	2
CE	3

Since these are all non-negative, no arc is worth bringing into the spanning tree. Therefore the flow pattern in Figure 3.7 is optimal.

The above version of the simplex algorithm can be executed in all-integer arithmetic. Therefore the optimal solution found will be integral.

There is considerable scope for improving efficiency in computer implementations of this method. This is described in section 4.6.

A Rule for Avoiding Circling

One particular concern should be mentioned here. As with the more general simplex algorithm, circling can theoretically occur unless methods are taken to prevent it. In practice this seldom happens. Therefore, such a method need only be used when circling (or degeneracy) manifests itself. A rule that guarantees that circling cannot happen is given below:

> *If, from a choice of arcs to enter the tree, there will be a degenerate iteration (i.e. the arc will enter with a zero flow), then choose an arc to enter that is directed away from the root node in the new tree created.*

Maximum Flow

In order to find the maximum flow through a network (MNF) we can also adapt the bounded-variable version of the simplex algorithm, which was discussed in section 2.4.

Exercise 3.2 involves solving Example 1.22 in this way.

There is, however, a specialised method of solving this problem known as the Ford–Fulkerson algorithm, which we describe through the same example.

Example 3.2 A Maximum-Flow Problem Solved by the Ford–Fulkerson Algorithm

Find the maximum flow through the network in Figure 3.8, where A and B are sources and F, G and H are sinks.

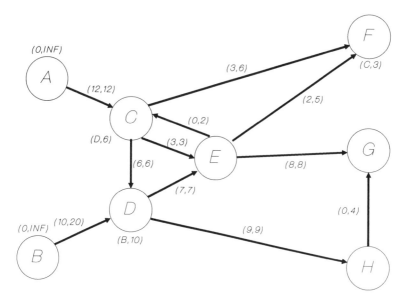

Figure 3.8 A maximum-flow problem with first labelling

The second figures in parentheses on the arcs represent upper bounds on flow (capacities). Lower bounds are taken as zero (for this example).

Step 1 We begin by seeking a feasible (but generally non-basic) flow pattern. This may be done by setting all flows to zero. Alternatively we can seek a "better" initial flow pattern heuristically. In the example we mark such a flow pattern by the first figure in brackets on each arc.

Step 2 We seek a *flow augmenting path* from a source to a sink. That is, a path where flow can be increased along forward arcs and decreased along backward arcs to increase the flow from source to sink. In order to do this we start at a source and scan a successor node to which flow can be increased. The successor node is labelled with its predecessor's name and amount by which flow can be increased. At each stage (apart from the beginning) we also scan predecessor nodes to see if "backwards flow" can be sent to them by decreasing flow from them to the current node. If so, the predecessor node is labelled by the current node and the amount of "backwards flow". We proceed in this way, attempting to reach a sink.

In the example we start at node A. It is labelled $(0, \infty)$ in Figure 3.8, i.e.

it has no predecessor and as yet no limit to the flow in it. No further nodes can be labelled from A. Starting at node B, it is labelled $(0, \infty)$. D is labelled (B, 10) since 10 more units could flow along BD. C is labelled (D,6) since a backwards flow of 6 could be sent along DC. F (a sink) is labelled (C, 3) since 3 more units could be sent from C to F. We have now reached sink F, giving us the flow augmenting path marked in Figure 3.9.

The flow increases or decreases possible are found by working backwards from node F and are marked in Figure 3.9.

Step 2 (repeated)   The new flow pattern is marked in Figure 3.10.

We seek another augmenting path. In the example we do this by the labelling shown starting at nodes A and B. We cannot reach a sink. Therefore the flow pattern is optimal.

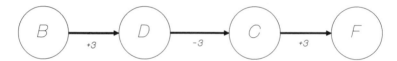

Figure 3.9   A flow augmenting path

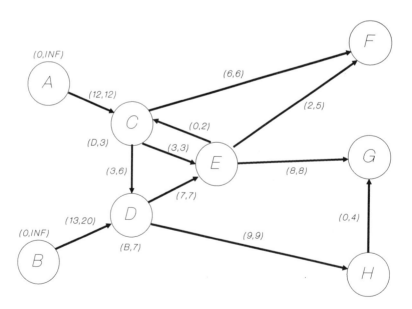

Figure 3.10   Flow pattern with second labelling

The proof that this method produces the optimal flow pattern can be shown by the duality theorem of linear programming. We do not do this rigorously but can demonstrate it intuitively for this example. The demonstration can be generalised into a proof.

The total flow that we have produced from the source nodes A and B is 25 units. Nodes A, B, C and D only have been given final labellings. Therefore all arcs directed out of these nodes, towards the sinks, must be "saturated". These are arcs CF, CE, DE and DH, which "cut-off" the sources from the sinks and have a total capacity of 25. This "maximum flow equals minimum cut" result is a special case of the LP duality theorem and is a sufficient condition for optimality.

3.2 THE ASSIGNMENT PROBLEM

We begin by solving Example 1.23 by the network form of the simplex algorithm in order to demonstrate its inefficiency.

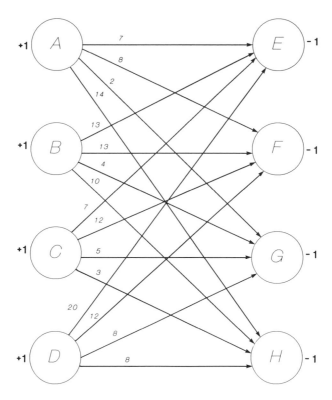

Figure 3.11 An assignment problem

Example 3.3 The Assignment Problem Solved by the Network Simplex Algorithm (Inefficient)

Solve example 1.23 using the network form of the simplex algorithm.

For convenience we redraw the network in Figure 3.11. Costs are marked on each arc.

Step 0   We choose a starting spanning tree for the network. This is given in Figure 3.12. The tree has been chosen arbitrarily.

Step 1   The associated flows are given and seen to be feasible. Should it be difficult to find such a feasible flow pattern (if some arcs are excluded), then phase I of the simplex algorithm can be involved.

It should be noted that an assignment of m items to m items will involve exactly m arcs with flows of 1. But a spanning tree will consist of $2m - 1$ arcs. Therefore $m - 1$ arcs will have flows of 0, leading to degeneracy. It is this feature which makes the method inefficient.

Step 2   We calculate dual values for the nodes using A as root node and the costs given in Figure 3.11. These dual values are marked in

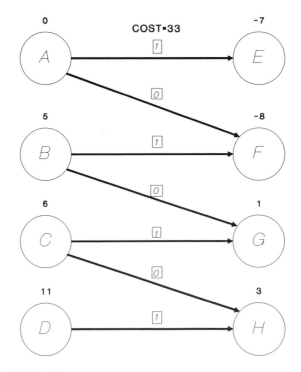

Figure 3.12   Initial assignment

Figure 3.12 and lead to the following reduced costs for non-included arcs:

Arc	Reduced cost
AG	3
AH	17
BE	1
BH	8
CE	− 6
CF	− 2
DE	2
DF	− 7
DG	− 2

Therefore DF is introduced into the tree, creating the loop shown in Figure 3.13.

Step 3 If the flow in DF is increased by θ then θ can be made as large as 1. BF (or an alternative) leaves the tree.

Step 1 (repeated) The new tree is given in Figure 3.14 with flows in the arcs.

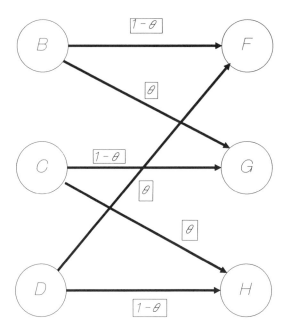

Figure 3.13 A cost-reducing circuit

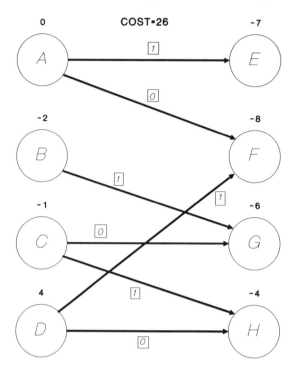

Figure 3.14 Second assignment

Step 2 (repeated) The new dual values are marked and result in the following reduced costs for non-included arcs:

Arc	Reduced cost
AG	− 4
AH	10
BE	8
BH	8
CE	1
CF	5
DE	9
DG	− 2
BF	7

Therefore AG is introduced into the tree, creating the loop shown in Figure 3.15.

Step 3 (repeated) The most flow that can be introduced into AG is 0 when AF (or an alternative) leaves the tree. This is a degenerate iteration.

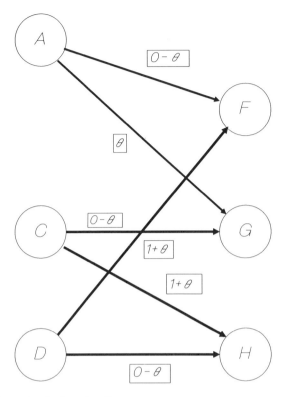

Figure 3.15 A cost-reducing circuit

Step 1 (repeated) The new tree is shown in Figure 3.16 with flow patterns.

Step 2 (repeated) The dual values are marked in Figure 3.16 and result in the following reduced costs for non-included arcs:

Arc	Reduced cost
AH	14
BE	4
BH	8
CE	− 3
CF	5
DE	5
DG	− 2
BF	7
AF	4

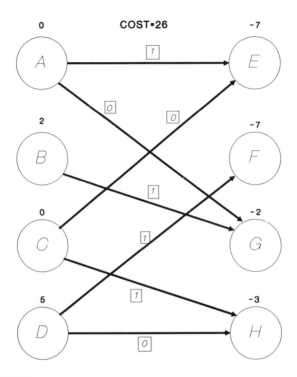

Figure 3.16   Third assignment

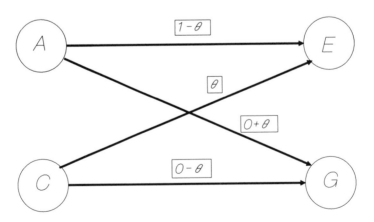

Figure 3.17   A cost-reducing circuit

Therefore CE is introduced into the tree, creating the loop shown in Figure 3.17.

Step 3 (repeated)   The most flow that can be introduced into CE is 0 when CG (or AE) leaves the tree. This is again a degenerate iteration.

Step 1 (repeated)   The new tree is shown in Figure 3.18.

Step 2 (repeated)   The dual values are marked in Figure 3.18 and result in the following reduced costs for non-included arcs:

Arc	Reduced cost
AH	11
BE	4
BH	5
CF	5
DE	8
DG	1
BF	4
AF	1
CG	3

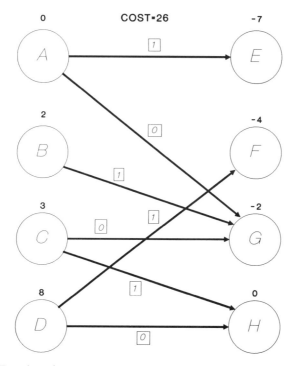

Figure 3.18   Fourth assignment

Since the reduced costs are all non-negative, we have *proved* that the assignment given in Figure 3.18 is optimal.

Notice, however, that we did in fact obtain this assignment after one iteration in Figure 3.14. It was not, however, possible to be sure that it was optimal. A further three *degenerate* iterations were needed to do this.

We will now resolve the example by a specialist means known as the Hungarian algorithm. This algorithm is known as a primal–dual method since it works by simultaneously seeking feasible solutions to both the primal and dual models. It then seeks to adjust these solutions until the orthogonality relation (2.280) of section 2.5 is obtained. The resultant solution is optimal by virtue of the results in that section.

The LP form of the assignment problem can be written as:

$$\text{Minimise} \quad \sum_{i,j} w_{ij} x_{ij}$$

subject to

$$\sum_j x_{ij} \geqslant 1 \qquad \text{all } i \tag{3.11}$$

$$\sum_i x_{ij} \geqslant 1 \qquad \text{all } j \tag{3.12}$$

$$x_{ij} \geqslant 0 \qquad \text{all } i, j. \tag{3.13}$$

We assume that all w_{ij} are positive. There is no loss of generality in this assumption since a constant value can be added to each coefficient, if necessary, without changing the optimal assignment.

The dual model is

$$\text{Maximise} \quad \sum_i u_i + \sum_j v_j$$

subject to

$$u_i + v_j \leqslant w_{ij} \qquad \text{all } i, j \tag{3.14}$$

$$u_i, v_j \geqslant 0 \qquad \text{all } i, j. \tag{3.15}$$

In order for a pair of solutions x_{ij}^* together with u_i^* and v_j^* to be optimal, they must, following the discussion of section 2.5, satisfy the following conditions:

(i) x_{ij}^* must be feasible, i.e. satisfy (3.11), (3.12) and (3.13).
(ii) u_i^* and v_j^* must be feasible, i.e. satisfy (3.14) and (3.15).

Also x_{ij}^* and u_i^*, v_j^* must be orthogonal, i.e. the following hold:

(iii) $x_{ij}^* > 0$ $\Rightarrow$ $u_i^* + v_j^* = w_{ij}$.

(iv) $u_i^* > 0$ $\Rightarrow$ $\Sigma_j x_{ij}^* = 1$.

(v) $v_j^* > 0$ $\Rightarrow$ $\Sigma_i x_{ij}^* = 1$.

Example 3.4 The Assignment Problem Solved by the Hungarian Algorithm
Solve Example 1.23 by the Hungarian algorithm.

It is convenient to present the example again as a cost matrix in tabular form; see Table 3.1.

Step 1   Obtain a feasible solution to the dual model. This may be done by subtracting the minimum element in each row to give u_i and then subtracting the minimum element from each column to give v_j.

For the example the resultant u_i, v_j and reduced cost matrix are given in Table 3.2.

Step 2   We now consider a subnetwork consisting of those arcs corresponding to cells of the reduced cost matrix that have become zero. A maximum-flow problem will be considered on this subnetwork, allowing at most unit flow into each node of U and out of each node of V in Figure 3.19. In order to formulate this restriction on node capacities, we introduce a source node S and a sink node T with arcs of unit capacities joining S to nodes in U and nodes in V to T.

Table 3.1

	E	F	G	H
A	7	8	2	14
B	13	13	4	10
C	7	12	5	3
D	20	12	8	8

Table 3.2

v_j u_i		E 4	F 4	G 0	H 0
A	2	1	2	0	12
B	4	5	5	0	6
C	3	0	5	2	0
D	8	8	0	0	0

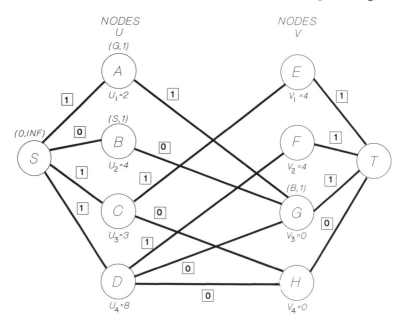

Figure 3.19   First maximum-flow model arising from assignment problem

For the example, the resultant maximum-flow problem is shown in Figure 3.19.

Step 3   We solve the maximum-flow problem formulated in step 2 by the Ford–Fulkerson algorithm of section 3.1. This results in a flow pattern and a final labelling of the nodes. If this flow pattern involves a flow of 1 into each node of U and a flow of 1 out of each node of V, then we have a feasible solution to the primal model. What is more, it is easy to see that all the conditions (i) to (v) above are satisfied, demonstrating optimality.

   If the flow pattern does not involve a flow of 1 into or out of each node of U and V respectively, then we proceed to step 4.

In the example the resultant flow pattern together with the final labelling is shown in Figure 3.19. Notice that we do not yet have a feasible solution to the primal model.

Step 4   The final labellings allow us to deduce a change in the dual solution. We examine the reduced costs $(w_{ij} - u_i - v_j)$ of arcs of the original network that go from a labelled node of U to an unlabelled node of V. Such reduced costs must be strictly positive. Otherwise the corresponding arcs would have been included in the subnetwork and their successor nodes would have been labelled. The smallest such reduced cost δ is selected and this quantity is *subtracted* from the dual values associated with the unlabelled nodes in U and *added* to the dual values associated with labelled nodes in V. As a result, dual feasibility is preserved but at least one new arc now has a reduced cost of 0 and may be added to the subnetwork. (Some arcs may no longer have zero reduced costs and must be removed. Such arcs must currently have zero flow since only their predecessor node can be unlabelled (having its dual value reduced). Therefore total flow cannot be reduced by their removal.)

Step 3 can now be repeated, labelling more nodes and increasing the total flow.

For the example the smallest reduced cost of an arc from a labelled to an unlabelled node is 1, being that of the arc AE. Therefore 1 is subtracted from u_3 and u_4 and added to v_1, v_2 and v_4. The new dual values and reduced costs are given in Table 3.3.

Therefore we add arc AE to the subnetwork and delete arc DG. The new subnetwork and maximum-flow problem is shown in Figure 3.20.

Step 1 (repeated)   For the example, the solution to the new maximum-flow problem is shown in Figure 3.20. In this case all nodes in U and V have unit flows in and out respectively. Therefore this flow pattern gives the optimal assignment:

A to E
B to G
C to H
D to F

of cost 26.

This method is frequently described by drawing row lines on the reduced cost matrix (corresponding to *unlabelled* nodes of U) and column lines (corresponding to *labelled* nodes of V) in such a way as to cover all cells with 0

Table 3.3

u_i \ v_j	E 5	F 5	G 0	H 1
A 2	0	1	0	11
B 4	4	4	0	5
C 2	0	5	3	0
D 7	8	0	1	0

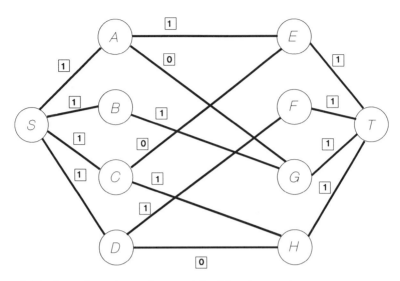

Figure 3.20 Second maximum-flow model arising from assignment problem

by the minimum number of lines. Then the smallest entry in an uncovered cell is subtracted from all uncovered cells and added to cells covered by two lines. This gives the new reduced cost matrix. While this is a convenient intuitive method, it is important to realise that the drawing of the lines corresponds to the labelling procedure.

The primal–dual method given above can be generalised to solve any MCNF model. Although such a method is worth while for the specialised assignment problem, it is questionable whether such a generalisation is worth while.

3.3 THE SHORTEST-PATH PROBLEM AND DYNAMIC PROGRAMMING

We begin by solving Example 1.24 by the simplex algorithm in order to illustrate its inefficiency.

Example 3.5 The Shortest-Path Problem Solved by the Simplex Algorithm (Inefficient)
Find the shortest path from A to H in Figure 3.21 where arc lengths are marked.

Step 0 We choose a starting spanning tree.

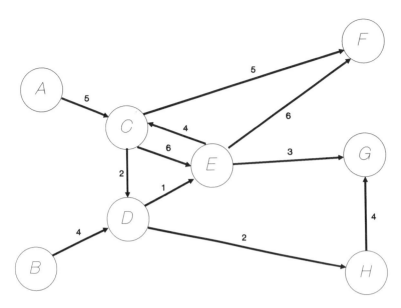

Figure 3.21   The shortest-path problem

In the example, for convenience, we use the same initial spanning tree as for Example 3.1. This is given in Figure 3.22.

Step 1   We determine the flow pattern.

For the example, this is marked on Figure 3.22. Notice that this flow is infeasible as well as degenerate.

Step 2   In order to reduce the infeasibility, we give arcs with infeasible flows costs of 1 in reverse of that direction and other arcs costs of 0.

For this example, arc ED (DE reversed) has a cost of 1 and other arcs costs of 0. This results in the dual values shown in Figure 3.22 with A as root node. The reduced costs of the non-included arcs are:

Arc	Reduced cost
CF	0
CD	−1
EC	0
HG	1

We choose CD to enter the tree.

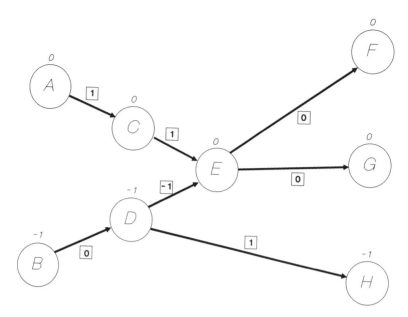

Figure 3.22 Initial spanning tree for the shortest-path problem

Step 3 An extra arc is introduced into the tree, creating a loop around which flow can be adjusted.

For the example the loop created is shown in Figure 3.23. Flow is increased to 1 in CD, and DE (the infeasible flow) leaves the tree. The resultant tree is shown in Figure 3.24.

Step 1 (repeated) The flow in the tree is redetermined.

For the example this is shown in Figure 3.24. The flow is now feasible.

Step 2 (repeated) Using the costs of arcs, which are marked for the example in Figure 3.24, dual values are calculated for the model.

Reduced costs of non-included arcs are:

Arc	Reduced cost
CF	− 7
EC	10
HG	− 1
DE	− 3

Arc CF enters the tree.

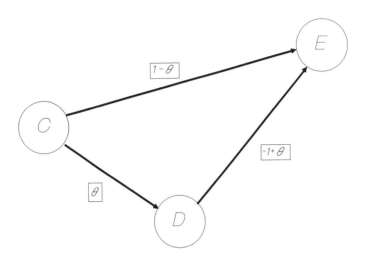

Figure 3.23   A cost-reducing circuit

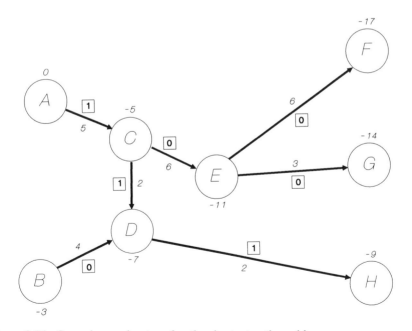

Figure 3.24   Second spanning tree for the shortest-path problem

Step 3 (repeated)   A loop is created as shown in Figure 3.25.

Flow can only be "increased" by 0 when arc CE (arbitrarily) leaves the tree. The new tree, resulting from the degenerate iteration, is shown in Figure 3.26.

Step 1 (repeated)   The flow in the new tree is determined and marked in Figure 3.26.

Step 2 (repeated)   New dual values are marked, resulting in the reduced costs of non-included arcs:

Arc	Reduced cost
EC	3
HG	6
DE	4
CE	7

Since these are all positive, the flow pattern in Figure 3.26 is optimal, giving the minimum path from A to H of length 9 along arcs AC, CD and DH.

Notice, however, that although this flow pattern was also found in Figure 3.24 an extra degenerate iteration was needed to prove it optimal.

It can be seen that the dual values associated with the nodes each give the (negated) shortest distance from that node to the origin A (counting any backword arcs needed negatively).

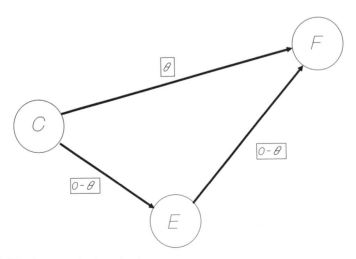

Figure 3.25   A cost-reducing circuit

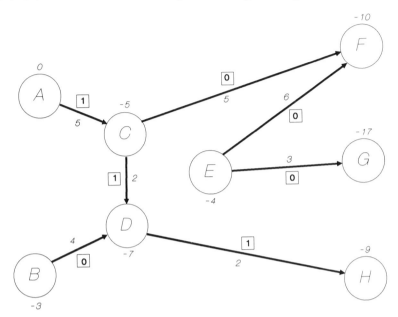

Figure 3.26   Third spanning tree for the shortest-path problem

Degeneracy is very likely to arise, as with the assignment problem, since a spanning tree may contain many arcs not on a path from source to sink. Such arcs must have "flows" of 0.

We now resolve Example 3.5 by a more efficient method due to Dijkstra. This method assumes that the lengths of all arcs are positive. It proceeds by finding the closest node to the origin, the next closest and so on until the destination is found. If continued until completion, the shortest paths to *all* nodes are found. An informative way of viewing the algorithm is to consider a "frontier" progressively moving out from the origin sweeping up nodes once the frontier reaches them (in the shortest possible way).

Example 3.6 The Shortest-Path Problem Solved by Dijkstra's Algorithm
Solve Example 3.5 by Dijkstra's algorithm.

Step 0   The origin node is *permanently* labelled (0, 0) (its distance from the origin). Other nodes are temporarily labelled (A, ∞).

In the example shown in Figure 3.27, we begin with only A permanently labelled.

Step 1   Each non-permanently labelled node is relabelled with the minimum of its currently labelled distance and sum of distances

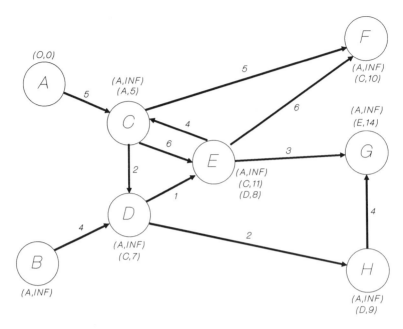

Figure 3.27 A shortest-path problem with labellings from Dijkstra's algorithm

from each direct predecessor added to the predecessor's labelled distance. Should the minimum result from adding to a permanently labelled predecessor's distance, then the current node's label becomes permanent. Otherwise it remains temporary.

The step is repeated until the destination node becomes permanently labelled. Then the labelled distance is the length of the shortest path. This path can be found by backtracking through the labels of precedessor nodes.

In this example the successive labels are marked at the nodes, demonstrating the shortest path ACDH of length 9.

Example 3.6 above contains a number of *cycles*, e.g. CDEC. Since all arc lengths are positive, we can be sure that it would be non-optimal to go round this cycle. Were this not the case and cycles were to exist with a total negative length, then we might be able to go round the cycle indefinitely producing shorter and shorter paths, showing the problem to be unbounded. Dijkstra's algorithm can be guaranteed to work if we make the assumption that all arc lengths are positive. Exercise 3.5 shows what can go wrong if this is not the case.

If we make an even stronger assumption that a network has no cycles, then an even more efficient procedure can be applied. The algorithm that we will demonstrate for such *acyclic networks* is due to Bellman. We explain it, since many practical problems result in acyclic networks, and this method underlies the important principle of dynamic programming.

Dynamic Programming

If we know that a network has no cycles then it is possible to number the nodes in such a way that there is an arc from node i to node j only if $i < j$. Then, the shortest path from the origin (node 0) to a given node can be found once the shortest paths to *preceding* nodes in the numbering have been found. If $d(i)$ represents the shortest path from the origin to node i we have the recursive relations

$$d(0) = 0 \tag{3.16}$$

$$d(j) = \underset{i < j}{\text{Min}} \, (c_{ij} + d(i)) \tag{3.17}$$

where c_{ij} is the length of arc ij. If arc ij does not exist, $c_{ij} = \infty$.

Relation (3.17) is the well known *principle of optimality*. When it applies, the result is that, if the shortest path from node 0 to j passes through node i, then that portion of the shortest path up to node i is also the shortest path from node 0 to node i. Therefore the calculation of the shortest path to node j can be carried out sequentially as demonstrated in the next example.

Example 3.7 The Shortest Path Through an Acyclic Network Solved by Dynamic Programming
Find the shortest path from node 0 to node 8 in Figure 3.28 using dynamic programming.

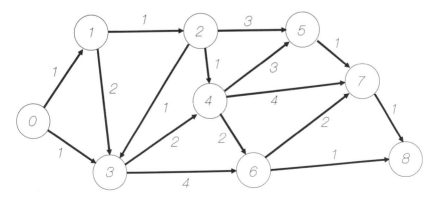

Figure 3.28 An acyclic network

Table 3.4

i	0	1	2	3	4	5	6	7	8
$d(i)$	0	1	2	1	3	5	5	6	6

Table 3.5

i	0	1	2	3	4	5	6	7	8
$p(i)$	–	0	1	0	2	2	4	5	6

The nodes have been numbered in such a way that if ij is an arc then $i < j$. This is possible only because the network is acyclic. For each node in turn we calculate $d(i)$ and $p(i)$ representing the predecessor node of i on the shortest path. In order to do this we use equation (3.17), filling in Tables 3.4 and 3.5 simultaneously for each in turn.

The steps are straightforward. A typical illustrative step is for $i = 3$ having calculated $d(j)$ and $p(j)$ for $j = 0, 1, 2$:

$$d(3) = \text{Min} \begin{Bmatrix} d(0) + 1 \\ d(1) + 2 \\ d(2) + 1 \end{Bmatrix} = \text{Min} \begin{Bmatrix} 1 \\ 3 \\ 3 \end{Bmatrix} = 1.$$

Since the minimum arises from $d(0) + 1$, the predecessor of node 3 on the shortest path is 0. Therefore $p(3) = 0$.

Dynamic programming is often explained in contexts other than that of the shortest path through an acyclic network. Any deterministic dynamic programming problem can, however, be so viewed, and the above algorithm applied. Further illustrations of dynamic programming and their relation to the above method are given when it is applied to the knapsack problem in section 8.3.

Another important application that is viewed in terms of networks is that of finding the *critical path* through a planning network. In this case one wishes to find the *longest* path through a network. This problem is very difficult in general but planning networks are by their nature acyclic. The longest-path problem then reduces to the shortest-path problem with negated arc lengths.

3.4 HISTORY, REFERENCES AND FUTURE DEVELOPMENTS

Minimum-Cost and Maximum Flow Through a Network

This way of viewing models is considered by Ford and Fulkerson (1962), although the special case of the transportation problem was considered originally by Kantorovitch (1942) and Koopmans and Reiter (1951). Its treatment by the simplex algorithm is discussed by Dantzig (1963) and Glover and Klingman (1974), together with many others.

The special algorithm described for the maximum-flow problem is also described in Ford and Fulkerson (1962).

The Assignment Problem

The Hungarian algorithm is due to Kuhn (1955). Its name arises from connections with the work of the Hungarian mathematician Egervary. The method can be generalised to deal with the minimum-cost network flow problem. This is explained in Ford and Fulkerson (1962). Another generalisation is to the matching problem. This problem is explained in section 8.3 as it gives an integer programming model. It is described by Edmonds (1965). The problem is that of "pairing" nodes of a graph together using connecting edges in an optimal way. If the graph is bipartite (i.e. splits into two parts as in the assignment problem) then this matching problem becomes particularly simple. The integrality property then applies, allowing non-integer programming methods to be used.

The Shortest-Path Problem and Dynamic Programming

Dijkstra (1959) presents his algorithm and Bellman (1958) gives his method for acyclic networks. The latter wrote the first book (Bellman, 1957) on dynamic programming.

3.5 EXERCISES

3.1 Solve the minimum-cost network flow problem of Example 3.1 starting with the spanning tree given in Figure 3.1.

3.2 Adapt the bounded-variable form of the simplex algorithm, as described in section 2.4, to a network form and solve the maximum-flow problem in Example 3.2 in this way.

3.3 Find a feasible assignment to the problem given in Table 3.4. Only assignments corresponding to cells with a " ● " are allowed. Use (i) the Hungarian algorithm, and (ii) the network form of the simplex algorithm.

Table 3.4

	G	H	I	J	K	L
A		●			●	
B	●		●			
C				●		●
D	●		●			
E		●				●
F				●		●

3.4 Solve the shortest-path problem of Example 3.7 using Dijkstra's algorithm.

3.5 In Figure 3.21 give arc CE a length of -5. Show why Dijkstra's algorithm fails.

3.6 Demonstrate why dynamic programming is inapplicable to solving the shortest-path problem of Example 3.6.

3.7 Find the number of computer operations needed by Dijkstra's algorithm to find the shortest path through a network with m nodes and n arcs.

3.8 Find the number of computer operations needed by applying dynamic programming to find the shortest path through an acyclic network with m nodes and n arcs.

Chapter 4
____ Computational Implementation of the Simplex Algorithm

The simplex algorithm, as described in sections 2.3 and 2.4, has undergone a major evolution since its discovery, resulting in sophisticated refinements. These refinements have been intimately linked to its implementation on computers. Therefore, we will describe them in relation to computing considerations, including, where necessary, the relevant data structures. This resultant evolved algorithm is known as the *revised simplex algorithm*. It is best explained in terms of matrices, and this notation will be used in this chapter.

The calculation of additional information relating to the optimal solution of an LP model is best described in relation to the revised simplex algorithm. This is done in section 4.5 and is usually known as post-optimal analysis.

The specialist network form of the simplex algorithm as described in section 3.1 can also be adapted very efficiently for computation. This is described in section 4.6.

4.1 THE REVISED SIMPLEX ALGORITHM AND PRODUCT FORM OF THE INVERSE

It would clearly be inefficient (although possible) to carry out the steps of the simplex algorithm as described in Chapter 2 in symbolic form (using equations) on a computer. Instead, we will work on the numerical data in *detached coefficient* form with suitable indexing to name the parts of the model to which they belong. In order to illustrate this, we will reconsider Example 2.4. This can be written as

	z	x_1	x_2	x_3	x_4	x_5	RHS
OBJ	1.0	4.0	-5.0	-3.0	0	0	0
C1	0	-1.0	1.0	-1.0	1.0	0	2.0
C2	0	1.0	1.0	2.0	0	1.0	3.0

$$(4.1)$$

LB	$-\infty$	0	0	0	0	0
UB	$+\infty$	∞	∞	∞	∞	∞

.

Floating-point numbers will be represented as such in order to emphasise their form. The columns and rows of coefficients would be stored using one of the data structures described in section 1.6, exploiting the fact that, in a real-life example, the data would be sparse (most coefficients would be zero and not stored). In practice, columns and rows would be given meaningful names by the user (not z, x_1, etc.), although internally they would probably be numbered with a dictionary relating numbers to names. We have chosen to define rows of lower and upper bounds (LB and UB) explicitly. In this simple case they are 0 and ∞ (apart from the free variable z), but in general they could take other values.

Mathematically we could write the above model as

$$Ax = b \tag{4.2}$$

$$l \leqslant x \leqslant u \tag{4.3}$$

where A is the $m \times n$ matrix of detached coefficients, b the RHS vector of length m, l and u the vectors of lower and upper bounds and x the solution vector, all of length n.

At each stage of the calculation we need to record which variables are in the basis. This will be done by a list of the m basis vectors (by name or number). For the example, the all-logical starting basis will be

$$\boxed{z \quad x_4 \quad x_5} . \tag{4.4}$$

Notice that we need this alternative way of specifying the basic variables rather than making them the subjects of the equations as in Chapter 2. We also need to record which of the non-basic variables are at their lower bounds and which at their upper bounds. This is conveniently done by means of a bit map (see section 1.6). In this example the situation does not arise, since all variables have upper bounds of ∞.

The Pivot Step

For each iteration we need to choose a non-basic variable to enter the basis, and a basic variable to leave. Before describing how this is done, we describe how the process of rearranging the equations is represented in the revised simplex algorithm. This process is known as *pivoting*. We again use Example 2.4, illustrated in detached coefficient form above.

If, as was the case, we wish to bring x_2 (whose column of coefficients is known as the *pivot column*) into the basis in place of x_4, then we would have:

(i)   made x_2 the subject of equation C1 (the row for which x_4 was the subject); and

(ii) used this row (the *pivot row*) to substitute x_2 out of the other equations.

In our new format these steps would become:

(i)   divide through row C1 by the coefficient of x_2 (the *pivot element*);

(ii) subtract or add suitable multiples of this row to the other rows to eliminate x_2 from them; and

(iii) update the basis list by replacing x_4 by x_2 (in the same position).

Steps (i) and (ii) are well known operations in the linear algebra of solving systems of equations (see section 2.1) known as *elementary row operations*. As an alternative to carrying them out *explicitly* on the matrix of detached coefficients (the classical simplex algorithm), we can carry them out *implicitly* by representing the operations themselves by *elementary matrices*. For the example, the pivoting operations just described could be performed by (pre)multiplying by the matrix

$$\begin{bmatrix} 1.0 & 5.0 & 0 \\ 0 & 1.0 & 0 \\ 0 & -1.0 & 1.0 \end{bmatrix}. \tag{4.5}$$

The reader should verify that this has the effect of carrying out the operations (i) and (ii) above. These matrices are particularly simple. They are identity matrices apart from one column known as an *eta vector* (η). Hence they can be defined by specifying only this vector together with the index of the column of the identity matrix that it replaces. In this case, we would have

$$\begin{array}{|c|} \hline 2 \\ \hline 5.0 \\ 1.0 \\ -1.0 \\ \hline \end{array}. \tag{4.6}$$

In general, if the updated column (numbered q) of detached coefficients of the incoming variable (the pivot column) is

$$\begin{array}{|c|} \hline a_{1q} \\ a_{2q} \\ \vdots \\ a_{pq} \\ \vdots \\ a_{mq} \\ \hline \end{array} \tag{4.7}$$

and the leaving variable is the basic variable corresponding to row p (the pivot row), it can be verified easily that the resulting eta vector is

$$
\begin{array}{|c|}
\hline
p \\
\hline
-a_{1q}/a_{pq} \\
-a_{2q}/a_{pq} \\
\vdots \\
1/a_{pq} \\
\vdots \\
-a_{mq}/a_{pq} \\
\hline
\end{array}
\tag{4.8}
$$

The reason for defining eta vectors rather than updating the "tableau" of detached coefficients explicitly is twofold. First, we will only subsequently be interested in those columns of A whose associated variables are candidates to enter the basis. Therefore, it is wasteful to transform all of A. Secondly, it turns out that it is generally more compact to store the necessary information in the form of eta vectors. These vectors will generally be sparse and therefore stored using one of the sparse data structures described in section 1.6.

The step that we are carrying out implicitly (eliminated a variable from *all* other equations) is Gauss–Jordan elimination. As mentioned in section 2.1, a better procedure in solving simultaneous equations is to use Gaussian elimination followed by back-substitution. This modification is possible and is described separately in section 4.3, as it is more involved.

At each iteration we will produce an eta vector. Therefore these will be accumulated as a file (known as the *eta file*) of (sparse) vectors. It is convenient to represent this file as

$$
\eta_r \eta_{r-1} \dots \eta_3 \eta_2 \eta_1
\tag{4.9}
$$

where the indices represent the order of generation. Taking the elementary matrices corresponding to these vectors and denoting them by E_1, E_2, etc., if we wanted to update the tableau A we would perform the matrix multiplications

$$
E_r E_{r-1} \dots E_3 E_2 E_1 A
\tag{4.10}
$$

$$
E_r E_{r-1} \dots E_3 E_2 E_1 b.
\tag{4.11}
$$

This demonstrates the reason for listing them backwards. It is consistent with the convention for ordering matrix multiplication.

Updating the Reduced Costs

Our new treatment of the simplex algorithm results in two modifications concerning reduced costs. First, the coefficients of all variables (basic and non-basic) are incorporated in the matrix A on the opposite side of the equation in (4.2) to b. Therefore, candidates to enter the basis will be either non-basic variables at their lower bounds with *negative* entries in the updated objective row or non-basic variables at their upper bounds with *positive* entries in the updated objective row, i.e. the signs of the reduced costs have been reversed. It is convenient now to refer to these negated figures as reduced costs. Secondly, the reduced costs of the variables will not be readily available since we are not explicitly updating the tableau of detached coefficients. In order to obtain them, we will need to update some of the tableau A. It would, however, be wasteful to update it all. If, as in the example, the objective row is the first row of A, then we need only update this. In general, we may wish to update a *linear combination of the rows*. The most obvious case for this is in phase I of the simplex algorithm (see section 2.4). In this case we wish to form (implicitly) a pseudo-objective row by *adding* together (the non-basic portion of) rows in which the basic variable is below its lower bound and *subtracting* (the non-basic portion of) rows in which the basic variable is above its upper bound. Another circumstance in which we wish to add together rows to form an objective is when the user specifies his or her objective as a linear combination of other objectives, e.g. if there are "multiple objectives".

In order to allow the possibility of forming the objective out of other rows, we form an *initial pricing vector*. This will be a row vector with m entries. Each entry will be

$+1$ if we wish to add the corresponding row

-1 if we wish to subtract the corresponding row

0 otherwise.

For the simple case considered here, we simply want the first row of the detached coefficient matrix, giving an initial pricing vector

$$\boxed{1.0 \quad 0 \quad 0}^{\text{T}}. \tag{4.12}$$

In general, we will denote the initial pricing vector by p_0^{T}. The row of reduced costs will then be given by

$$p_0^{\text{T}} E_r E_{r-1} \dots E_3 E_2 E_1 A. \tag{4.13}$$

The above matrix multiplication is more conveniently done *backwards* by successively evaluating $p_0^{\text{T}} \eta_r, (p_0^{\text{T}} \eta_r) \eta_{r-1}$, etc. This recursive operation is known technically as BTRAN, standing for "backward transformation". Let us define

$$p_1^{\text{T}} = p_0^{\text{T}} E_r \tag{4.14}$$

$$p_2^{\text{T}} = p_0^{\text{T}} E_r E_{r-1} = p_1^{\text{T}} E_{r-1} \tag{4.15}$$

etc. In general, let

$$\boldsymbol{p}_k = (p_{k1}, p_{k2}, ..., p_{km}) \tag{4.16}$$

and

$$E_{r-k+1} = \begin{bmatrix} 1 & & & \eta_1 & & \\ & 1 & & \eta_2 & & \\ & & \ddots & \vdots & & \\ & & & \eta_p & 1 & \\ & & & \vdots & & \ddots \\ & & & \eta_m & & & 1 \end{bmatrix} \tag{4.17}$$

then it can be verified that

$$\boldsymbol{p}_{k+1} = (p_{k1}, p_{k2}, ..., p_{k,p-1}, p_{k1}\eta_1 + p_{k2}\eta_2 + \cdots + p_{km}\eta_m, p_{k,p+1}, ..., p_{km}) \tag{4.18}$$

i.e. $\boldsymbol{p}_{k+1}$ is obtained from $\boldsymbol{p}_k$ by replacing its pth entry by its scalar product with the next eta vector in the multiplication.

It is important to note that the vectors $\boldsymbol{p}_k$ are updated "on top of themselves" and must therefore be in expanded ("unpacked") form, i.e. not stored as sparse vectors.

At the end of the successive BTRAN operations on a particular iteration, we will have created a *pricing vector*. This row vector, when multiplied by A, gives the required reduced costs. It is usually denoted by $\boldsymbol{\pi}$. Hence, in our previous notation,

$$\boldsymbol{\pi}^{\mathrm{T}} = \boldsymbol{p}_r^{\mathrm{T}}. \tag{4.19}$$

If the row vector of reduced costs (the updated objective row of A) is denoted by $\boldsymbol{d}^{\mathrm{T}}$, we have

$$\boldsymbol{d}^{\mathrm{T}} = \boldsymbol{\pi}^{\mathrm{T}}A. \tag{4.20}$$

In order to calculate the reduced cost for a particular variable, we therefore calculate the scalar product of $\boldsymbol{\pi}$ with the corresponding vector of coefficients from A. This operation is known as *pricing*. In practice, we might only "price" certain of the vectors of A until we found one with a reduced cost of suitable sign. This might not be "best" from the criterion of *maximum (negated) d_j* as discussed in section 2.3, but, as pointed out there, such a criterion gives no guarantee of being the most efficient anyway. It therefore does not seem worth the extra work of pricing all vectors and choosing that with the best reduced cost. In practice, a certain number will be priced, based on the storage and speed considerations of the system with the model being solved.

In order to demonstrate the full process, we calculate the reduced costs for the example after two iterations. The current eta file at this stage is (using a precision of only three decimal places for illustration)

$$
\begin{array}{|c|}
\hline 3 \\
\hline 2.667 \\
0.333 \\
0.333 \\
\hline
\end{array}
\qquad
\begin{array}{|c|}
\hline 2 \\
\hline 5.0 \\
1.0 \\
-1.0 \\
\hline
\end{array}
\tag{4.21}
$$

The initial pricing vector is

$$
p_0^T = \boxed{1.0 \ | \ 0 \ | \ 0} . \tag{4.22}
$$

Hence (by the BTRAN operation)

$$
p_0^T = \boxed{1.0 \ | \ 0 \ | \ 2.667} \tag{4.23}
$$

$$
\pi^T = p_2^T = \boxed{1.0 \ | \ 2.333 \ | \ 2.667} . \tag{4.24}
$$

This enables us to calculate the row of reduced costs as

$$
\boxed{1.0 \ | \ 4.333 \ | \ 0 \ | \ 0 \ | \ 2.333 \ | \ 2.667} . \tag{4.25}
$$

It can be verified that this is the (negated) row of reduced costs given by equation (2.62) in section 2.3. Notice that the current basic variables (apart from z) have zero reduced costs, as one would expect. In practice, these figures will not be exactly zero through rounding errors. Such deviations from zero can be used to test for numerical accuracy as discussed in section 4.4.

Updating the Pivot Column

Once it has been decided, as a result of the reduced costs, which variable should enter the basis, it is necessary to update the corresponding column of coefficients (the pivot column) in the A matrix. If the pivot column is denoted by a_q we must evaluate

$$
E_r E_{r-1} \ldots E_3 E_2 E_1 a_q . \tag{4.26}
$$

This is most efficiently done by successively evaluating $E_1 a_q$, $E_2(E_1 a_q)$, etc. At each stage of this recursion we transform a partially updated vector by the next eta matrix. In this case we process a_q by the eta matrices taken in their order of generation. This process is known as FTRAN (standing for "forward transformation"), in contrast to BTRAN. The need to do FTRAN as well as BTRAN operations on each iteration suggests data structures that allow the vectors to be processed in reverse as well as forward orders. Let us define

$$a_q^{(1)} = E_1 a_q \tag{4.27}$$

$$a_q^{(2)} = E_2 E_1 a_q = E_2 a_q^{(1)} \tag{4.28}$$

etc. In general let

$$a_q^{(k)} = \begin{bmatrix} a_{1q}^{(k)} \\ a_{2q}^{(k)} \\ \vdots \\ a_{pq}^{(k)} \\ \vdots \\ a_{mq}^{(k)} \end{bmatrix} \tag{4.29}$$

and

$$E_k = \begin{bmatrix} 1 & & & \eta_1 & & \\ & 1 & & \eta_2 & & \\ & & \ddots & \vdots & & \\ & & & \eta_p & 1 & \\ & & & \vdots & & \ddots \\ & & & \eta_m & & 1 \end{bmatrix} \tag{4.30}$$

then it can be verified that

$$a_q^{(k+1)} = \begin{bmatrix} a_{1q}^{(k)} + \eta_1 a_{pq}^{(k)} \\ a_{2q}^{(k)} + \eta_2 a_{pq}^{(k)} \\ \vdots \\ \eta_p a_{pq}^{(k)} \\ \vdots \\ a_{mq}^{(k)} + \eta_m a_{pq}^{(k)} \end{bmatrix}. \tag{4.31}$$

As with BTRAN the vectors $a_p^{(k)}$ are updated on top of themselves and must therefore be in expanded form. Therefore the pivot column selected from A for updating must be unpacked before processing.

For our example if, after two iterations, we had obtained the row of reduced costs given above, we would conclude that we had reached optimality and that no variable was worth bringing into the basis. For illustrative purposes, however, we can still update a column using FTRAN. The column corresponding to x_1 is

$$a_1^{(0)} = \begin{array}{|c|} \hline 4.0 \\ \hline -1.0 \\ \hline 1.0 \\ \hline \end{array} \tag{4.32}$$

and the current eta file is

3	2
2.667	5.0
0.333	1.0
0.333	−1.0

$$\qquad (4.33)$$

Performing FTRAN gives

$$a_1^{(1)} = \begin{array}{|c|} \hline -1.0 \\ \hline -1.0 \\ \hline 2.0 \\ \hline \end{array} \qquad (4.34)$$

$$a_2^{(1)} = \begin{array}{|c|} \hline 4.333 \\ \hline -0.333 \\ \hline 0.677 \\ \hline \end{array} . \qquad (4.35)$$

It should again be verified that this (negated) column corresponds to that given in equations (2.62) to (2.64) of section 2.3.

Once the updated pivot column has been obtained, the ratio test can be applied in exactly the same way as described in section 2.3 to decide the variable to leave the basis. The updated pivot column is then used for calculating a new eta vector.

In the ratio test it is necessary to use the updated solution vector. Since this vector will be needed on each iteration, it is convenient to maintain it in an unpacked form and to update it on each iteration.

The Complete Revised Simplex Algorithm

We will solve the above example completely by the revised simplex algorithm.

Example 4.1 The Revised Simplex Algorithm

$$\text{Maximise} \quad z = -4x_1 + 5x_2 + 3x_3 \qquad (4.36)$$

subject to

$$-x_1 + x_2 - x_3 \leqslant 2 \qquad (4.37)$$

$$x_1 + x_2 + 2x_3 \leqslant 3 \qquad (4.38)$$

$$x_1, x_2, x_3 \geqslant 0. \qquad (4.39)$$

We define the model by means of the matrix and vectors given in (4.1).

Step 1   We choose the all-logical starting basis expressed as the row (4.4). Notice that in this case the logical vectors form an identity matrix and that the RHS vector forms the initial solution vector. If some of the constraints had been of the "$\geqslant$" form, the coefficients of the corresponding surplus variables would have been -1. In order that these variables be basic, it is necessary to multiply explicitly or implicitly the corresponding row through by -1. This is conveniently done by creating eta vectors with -1 in the appropriate (index) position and zeros elsewhere. At the same time the RHS vector is updated by negating the entries in the appropriate rows.

Step 2   We examine which basic variables are outside their bounds and create an initial pricing vector as described above. In the example, since the all-logical basis is feasible, our initial pricing vector is

$$\boxed{1.0 \quad 0 \quad 0}. \tag{4.40}$$

Since the eta file is empty, the pricing vector is the same. When used with (4.1) to create the row of reduced costs, we obtain

$$\boxed{1.0. \quad 4.0 \quad -5.0 \quad -3.0 \quad 0 \quad 0} \tag{4.41}$$

which is, of course, at this initial stage, the objective row of the original tableau.

This indicates that x_2 should enter the basis. Therefore the corresponding column of (4.1) corresponding to x_2 is updated. Again this is trivial, since there are no initial era vectors, so the "updated" column is

$$\boxed{\begin{matrix} -5.0 \\ 1.0 \\ 1.0 \end{matrix}}. \tag{4.42}$$

Step 3   The ratio test compared with the initial solution vector demonstrates that the basic variable in the second row (x_4) should leave. We use column (4.42) to create the first eta vector

$$\boxed{\begin{matrix} 2 \\ \hline 5.0 \\ 1.0 \\ -1.0 \end{matrix}} \tag{4.43}$$

and update the solution vector to

$$\begin{array}{|c|} \hline 10.0 \\ 2.0 \\ 1.0 \\ \hline \end{array}$$ (4.44)

and the basis list to

$$\begin{array}{|c|c|c|} \hline z & x_2 & x_5 \\ \hline \end{array}.$$ (4.45)

Step 2 (repeated)   We again form an initial pricing vector similar to (4.40) and update this using the BTRAN operation with the current eta file (4.43) to give the pricing vector

$$\begin{array}{|c c c|} \hline 1.0 & 5.0 & 0 \\ \hline \end{array}.$$ (4.46)

This is used with (4.1) to give the vector of reduced costs

$$\begin{array}{|c|c|c|c|c|c|} \hline 1.0 & -1.0 & 0 & -8.0 & 5.0 & 0 \\ \hline \end{array}$$ (4.47)

demonstrating that x_3 is a candidate to enter the basis.

The column for x_3 from (4.1) is updated using the FTRAN operation with the current eta file (4.43) to give

$$\begin{array}{|c|} \hline -8.0 \\ -1.0 \\ 3.0 \\ \hline \end{array}.$$ (4.48)

Step 3 (repeated)   The updated column (4.48) is compared with the updated solution vector (4.44) using the ratio test to demonstrate that the third variable in the basis list (4.45), i.e. x_5, should leave the basis. Column (4.48) is therefore used to create a new eta vector, which when appended to (4.43) gives an eta file

$$\begin{array}{|c|c|} \hline 3 & 2 \\ \hline 2.667 & 5.0 \\ 0.333 & 1.0 \\ 0.333 & -1.0 \\ \hline \end{array}.$$ (4.49)

The solution vector (4.44) is updated to

$$\begin{array}{|c|} \hline 12.667 \\ 2.333 \\ 0.333 \\ \hline \end{array}$$ (4.50)

and the basis list to

$$\boxed{z \mid x_2 \mid x_3}.$$ (4.51)

Step 2 (repeated) We must update the initial pricing vector using BTRAN with (4.49) to give the pricing vector

$$\boxed{1.0 \quad 2.333 \quad 2.667}.$$ (4.52)

This is used with (4.1) to give the vector of reduced costs

$$\boxed{1.0 \quad 4.333 \quad 0 \quad 0 \quad 2.333 \quad 2.667}.$$ (4.53)

Since none of these is negative (and no non-basic variables are at upper bounds), the optimal solution has been achieved. This solution can be obtained by reading the basis list (4.51) in conjunction with the solution vector (4.50) to give

$$z = 12.667, \quad x_2 = 2.333, \quad x_3 = 0.333.$$

Other variables are non-basic and at one of their bounds (in this case 0).

4.2 REINVERTING THE BASIS MATRIX

The eta file, at any stage of the calculation, has an important interpretation. It gives a representation of the *inverse* of the current basis matrix. This inverse is, of course, expressed as a product of elementary matrices. Hence the name given to this form of the revised simplex algorithm is the *product form of the inverse*. In order to illustrate this fact, we consider the final basis of Example 4.1 given by the basis list (4.51). The corresponding columns from (4.1) give the matrix

$$\begin{bmatrix} 1 & -5.0 & -3.0 \\ 0 & 1.0 & -1.0 \\ 0 & 1.0 & 2.0 \end{bmatrix}.$$ (4.54)

Multiplying this by the eta file (4.49) gives

$$\begin{bmatrix} 1.0 & 0 & 2.667 \\ 0 & 1.0 & 0.333 \\ 0 & 0 & 0.333 \end{bmatrix} \begin{bmatrix} 1.0 & 5.0 & 0 \\ 0 & 1.0 & 0 \\ 0 & -1.0 & 1.0 \end{bmatrix} \begin{bmatrix} 1 & -5.0 & -3.0 \\ 0 & 1.0 & -1.0 \\ 0 & 1.0 & 2.0 \end{bmatrix}$$

$$= \begin{bmatrix} 1.0 & 0 & 0 \\ 0 & 1.0 & 0 \\ 0 & 0 & 1.0 \end{bmatrix}$$ (4.55)

i.e. produces the identity matrix, demonstrating that (4.49) represents the inverse of (4.54). In general, the product of the eta matrices will give the inverse of the current basis matrix *permuted* according to the basis list.

It is important to recognise that this representation of the inverse of a matrix by the product of elementary matrices is not unique. For example, it can be verified easily that the following eta file

$$
\begin{array}{|c|c|c|}
\hline
2 & & 3 \\
\hline
-1.333 & & 1.5 \\
0.667 & & 0.5 \\
-0.333 & & 0.5 \\
\hline
\end{array}
\tag{4.56}
$$

would have exactly the same effect as (4.49). In this case (4.56) has no virtue over (4.49). Both involve the storage of six floating-point numbers as well as two indices. For larger models, some representations will be much sparser than others.

After each iteration a new eta vector is created and the eta file gets larger. In consequence, through the BTRAN and FTRAN operations, each iteration takes longer. Sooner or later it may be worth while incurring the computational cost of reinverting the current basis and expressing it as a product of eta matrices with comparatively fewer non-zero entries. As a result each subsequent iteration will be quicker and more accurate. When this should be done depends on characteristics of the computer system being used, e.g. storage schemes and numerical precision. Another situation in which it is necessary to invert the basis is when an optimisation is restarted from an intermediate stage or uses a basis for a slightly changed form of a model. It is not necessary to store the (large) old eta files.

We will describe a method of reinverting this basis in order to give a relatively sparse representation. Before doing this we introduce more matrix notation. The basis columns of the matrix A (permuted according to the basis list) can be represented by a square matrix B. It is convenient to imagine the columns of A reordered so that the columns making up B come first. The non-basic columns will be represented by N. Therefore

$$A = (B \mid N). \tag{4.57}$$

Our eta file gives a representation of B^{-1}. We therefore have

$$B^{-1}A = B^{-1}(B \mid N) = (I \mid B^{-1}N). \tag{4.58}$$

As expected, the basic portion of the *updated* matrix is the identity matrix (after a possible permutation).

The original form of the revised simplex algorithm consisted of maintaining and updating the *explicit inverse* B^{-1} after each iteration, i.e. it was not a product form. Not only does this involve more operations, more seriously, experimental results demonstrate that such a representation involves more non-zero coefficients than the product form. Therefore, we confine our discussion to the product form of the inverse.

The possibility of representing the inverse of a current basis in a more economical manner, as a product of eta matrices, than that generated by the iterations of the simplex algorithm arises for two reasons. First, some variables will probably have entered and then left the basis again. The two eta vectors corresponding to these iterations could (with hindsight) be replaced by one eta vector. Secondly, by altering the order and rows in which variables are pivoted into the basis, it may be possible to create a more economical representation. An extreme form of this possibility is illustrated by a matrix that can be triangularised, i.e. a matrix for which the rows and columns can be permuted so that all non-zero coefficients lie on, or below, the main diagonal. This is illustrated by an example.

Triangularising the Basis

Example 4.2 Triangularising and Reinverting a Matrix
We will consider the following basis matrix

$$\begin{array}{ccc} & A & B & C \\ B = & \begin{bmatrix} -1.0 & -1.0 & 3.0 \\ 2.0 & 0 & 0 \\ 1.0 & 0 & 1.0 \end{bmatrix} & \begin{matrix} 1 \\ 2. \\ 3 \end{matrix} \end{array} \qquad (4.59)$$

It is convenient to number the rows and letter the columns, as indicated.
It can be verified that the following eta file is a representation of B^{-1}:

$$\begin{array}{|c|c|c|} \hline 3 & 2 & 1 \\ \hline 1.0 & 0.5 & -1.0 \\ 2.0 & -0.5 & 2.0 \\ 1.0 & -0.5 & 1.0 \\ \hline \end{array} \qquad (4.60)$$

This might have been obtained by pivoting the variables into the basis in the order A, B, C using pivot rows 1, 2 and 3 respectively. The resulting basis list would be

$$\boxed{\text{A} \quad \text{B} \quad \text{C}}. \qquad (4.61)$$

The disadvantage of this procedure is illustrated by the pivoting of variable A, creating non-zero coefficients (known as "fill-in") in rows 2 and 3 of columns B and C. This is likely to result in non-zero coefficients in the eta vectors corresponding to the subsequent pivoting of those variables. Indeed, the final eta file (4.60) is completely dense.

If instead the variables are pivoted into the basis in a *different order* using *different pivot rows*, then it might be possible to obtain a sparser representation. In order to make this clear, we can *implicitly* reorder the rows and columns. It is important to emphasise that this reordering need only be done implicitly to achieve the desired effect. In order to describe it, however, it is convenient to reorder explicitly.

The matrix B in the above example can be reordered as

$$B = \begin{matrix} & A & C & B \\ & \begin{bmatrix} 2.0 & 0 & 0 \\ 1.0 & 1.0 & 0 \\ -1.0 & 3.0 & -1.0 \end{bmatrix} & \begin{matrix} 2 \\ 3 \\ 1 \end{matrix} \end{matrix} \qquad (4.62)$$

by permuting rows and columns in the manner demonstrated by the row numbers and column letters. This reordered matrix is *triangular*. If we were to perform the first pivoting operation on column A, with row 2 as pivot row, then because this row has *zero coefficients in all other columns* no extra non-zero elements will be created. Nor will the coefficients in columns B and C be changed. The corresponding eta vector is (with original row order).

$$\begin{array}{|c|} \hline 2 \\ \hline 0.5 \\ 0.5 \\ -0.5 \\ \hline \end{array} \qquad (4.63)$$

It can be verified that the only effect this has on the original matrix B is to transform column A to have a 1 in row 2 and zeros elsewhere. Columns B and C are unchanged. The next pivoting operation is performed on column C using row 3 as pivot row. The corresponding eta vector is (with original row order)

$$\begin{array}{|c|} \hline 3 \\ \hline -3.0 \\ 0 \\ 1.0 \\ \hline \end{array} \qquad (4.64)$$

Again the rest of the matrix (column B) is unchanged. Finally a pivoting operation is carried out on column B using row 1 as pivot row to produce the eta vector

$$
\begin{array}{|c|}
\hline
1 \\
\hline
-1.0 \\
0 \\
0 \\
\hline
\end{array}\ .
\tag{4.65}
$$

The full alternative eta file to (4.60) is therefore

$$
\begin{array}{|c|}
\hline
1 \\
\hline
-1.0 \\
0 \\
0 \\
\hline
\end{array}
\quad
\begin{array}{|c|}
\hline
3 \\
\hline
-3.0 \\
0 \\
1.0 \\
\hline
\end{array}
\quad
\begin{array}{|c|}
\hline
2 \\
\hline
0.5 \\
0.5 \\
-0.5 \\
\hline
\end{array}\ .
\tag{4.66}
$$

It should be verified that multiplying this into the matrix B of (4.59) gives the permuted identity matrix

$$
\begin{array}{ccc}
\text{A} & \text{B} & \text{C} \\
\end{array}
$$
$$
\begin{bmatrix}
0 & 1.0 & 0 \\
1.0 & 0 & 0 \\
0 & 0 & 1.0
\end{bmatrix}\ .
\tag{4.67}
$$

This would be an identity matrix if the columns were taken in the order of a basis list

$$
\boxed{\text{B}\quad\text{A}\quad\text{C}}\ .
\tag{4.68}
$$

Such a basis list order is given by listing the columns in the order of their pivot rows. Notice that the reordered matrix (4.62) defines the pivot elements as those on the main diagonal. These must all be non-zero (for a triangular matrix) otherwise the "basis" would be singular (and not a basis).

We summarise the advantages of triangularising the basis matrix before inverting:

(i) No updating of columns is necessary as a result of taking pivots in rows where all remaining columns have zero entries. Hence the inversion will be quicker and can be carried out in packed form.

(ii) No new non-zero elements will be created, hence the representation can be expected to be sparser. In the example (4.66) has six floating-point numbers but (4.60) has nine.

Exercises 4.5 and 4.6 give a larger example of a matrix that can be triangularised, demonstrating even more dramatically the advantage of doing this.

There are some special types of model where complete triangularisation is possible. In particular, bases associated with network flow models will always be triangular. Now, however, we will consider the general case where, although complete triangularisation is not possible, the sparsity of practical models causes one to expect that partial triangularisation may be possible.

Partial Triangularisation and Block Triangular Form

We (implicitly) reorder the basis matrix into the form of Figure 4.1, where the non-zero elements are confined to the submatrices A1, A2, A3, B1, B2 and C1. The matrix form illustrated in Figure 4.1 is known as *block triangular* form. Submatrices A1 and C1 must have non-zero elements on the main diagonal. Reordering in this way is straightforward. We first search for *singleton* rows, i.e. rows in which there is only one non-zero element. Such a row is placed as the first row with the column corresponding to the non-zero element as the first column. Then, ignoring this row and column, the process is repeated until no more singleton rows can be found. This gives us A1. Secondly, we search for *singleton* columns in an analogous manner. Such a column is placed as the last column with the corresponding row as the last row. Then this column and row are ignored and the procedure repeated until we have found C1.

When we come to create eta vectors from the A and C portions, this will not create fill-in or cause updating. The eta vectors created from the B portion will, however, cause fill-in and updating. Submatrix B1 is known as the *nucleus*. The larger it is, the more time-consuming will be the inversion and

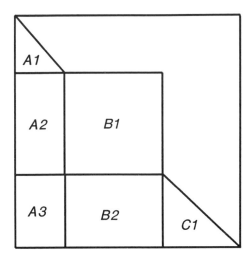

Figure 4.1   A partially triangularised matrix

denser the resulting eta file. Even within the nucleus there is merit in (implicitly) reordering the rows and columns in order to reduce fill-in and updating. Finding that reordering which minimises this is a known difficult combinatorial problem, and it is not generally worth the computational effort of finding the "best" order. However, it is well worth while adopting a *heuristic* approach to the reordering. A number of schemes exist. We outline one approach and give references to others in section 4.7.

Suppose we were to pivot on a non-zero element in column q of the matrix shown in Figure 4.2 using row p as pivot row. Also suppose this row and column to have non-zero entries in the positions marked "x". If there are (as is very likely in a sparse matrix) zero elements in the positions marked "o", the pivoting will "fill in" those positions with non-zero elements. This will be undesirable for two reasons. First, it will create extra calculation. Secondly, the matrix will become denser, causing extra calculation later and a denser eta file. Therefore we seek pivot positions (p, q) where the fill-in will be minimised. For each such position we can calculate a "merit number". This is defined as

$$\left[\left(\begin{array}{c}\text{Number of non-zero}\\ \text{elements in row } p\end{array}\right) - 1\right] \times \left[\left(\begin{array}{c}\text{Number of non-zero}\\ \text{elements in column } q\end{array}\right) - 1\right]$$

i.e. it is the number of new elements that will be created by fill-in (if there are initially zero elements in these positions). For the example in Figure 4.2 the merit number of pivot (p, q) is $3 \times 4 = 12$. Pivots with small merit numbers will be desirable.

A practical procedure is to reorder the rows and columns of B1 with non-zero elements down the main diagonal in order of increasing merit number. We do this by seeking the (non-zero) pivot with smallest merit number and placing it in the top left position. Then we seek the next best pivot in the remaining rows and columns of B1, continuing in this manner. Of course, those elements already positioned on the row diagonal in A1 and C1 have merit numbers of 0. This procedure is not a fool-proof way of minimising

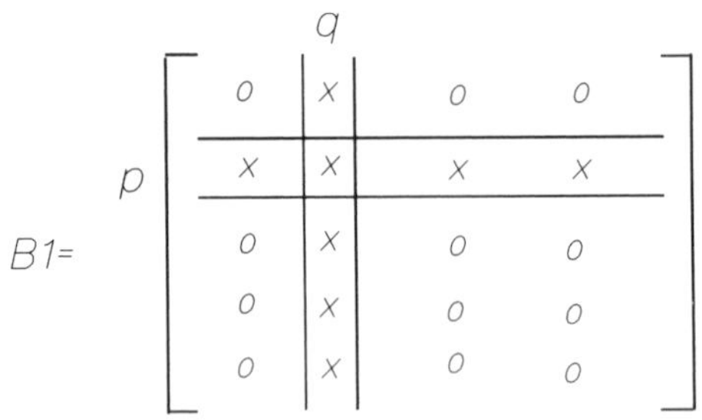

$$B1 = \begin{array}{c} \\ \\ p \\ \\ \\ \end{array}\begin{bmatrix} o & x & o & o \\ x & x & x & x \\ o & x & o & o \\ o & x & o & o \\ o & x & o & o \end{bmatrix}$$

Figure 4.2 Fill-in from pivoting in a sparse matrix

fill-in, since in the course of pivoting the resultant fill-in will alter the merit numbers of future possible pivots. Also zeros may be created, ruling out previously planned pivots. A possible improvement is to recalculate merit numbers after performing each pivot. This is generally not considered worth the extra computational cost. A faster compromise that is sometimes done is to update a bit map of the non-zero elements of the nucleus using Boolean operations, i.e. assuming any operations done in non-zero elements give non-zero elements (i.e. no cancellation takes place) as well as non-zero elements being created by fill-in. Should a planned pivot become zero, then an adjustment must be made. Usually such columns are then left to the end, and row pivots chosen (irrespective of merit numbers) from the remaining eligible rows. Hopefully this will be a rare occurrence, although it can happen frequently with some structures.

Having decided the potential pivot sequences and positions by (implicitly) ordering the rows and columns so that they lie on the main diagonal in Figure 4.1, we can carry out the pivoting to create eta vectors. This can be done by creating an eta vector for each column taken from left to right using pivots on the main diagonal. An alternative approach has however been shown to lead to even sparser representations and is therefore described.

L\U Decomposition of a Matrix Inverse

This approach is based on Gaussian elimination as opposed to Gauss–Jordan elimination. Instead of creating eta vectors to eliminate a variable from *all* rows, apart from the pivot row, in the B section of Figure 4.1 we eliminate below the main diagonal only, by means of an eta vector. Later the necessary back-substitution is performed by another eta vector. An example demonstrates the procedure.

Example 4.3 Inverting a Matrix by L\U Decomposition
Invert the following matrix in product form:

$$B = \begin{bmatrix} A & B & C & D & E & F & G \\ 1.0 & 0 & 0 & 0 & 0 & 0 & 0 \\ 2.0 & 2.0 & 0 & 0 & 0 & 0 & 0 \\ 0 & 1.0 & 1.0 & 2.0 & 0 & 0 & 0 \\ -1.0 & 0 & 2.0 & -1.0 & 1.0 & 1.0 & 0 \\ 3.0 & 1.0 & 0 & 2.0 & 1.0 & -1.0 & 0 \\ 1.0 & -1.0 & 1.0 & 0 & 3.0 & -2.0 & 0 \\ 1.0 & 0 & -2.0 & 1.0 & 1.0 & 0 & 2.0 \end{bmatrix} \begin{matrix} 1 \\ 2 \\ 3 \\ 4. \\ 5 \\ 6 \\ 7 \end{matrix} \qquad (4.69)$$

This has deliberately and explicitly been ordered into block triangular form, with potential pivots on the main diagonal, for illustrative purposes.

The eta vectors associated with columns A, B and C are straightforward. Since elimination below the diagonal is all that is necessary, we have single eta vectors representing Gaussian elimination. No back-substitution is necessary here. This gives eta vectors (corresponding respectively to C, B and A):

3
0
0
1.0
-2.0
0
-1.0
2.0

2
0
0.5
-0.5
0
-0.5
0.5
0

1
1.0
-2.0
0
1.0
-3.0
-1.0
1.0

$$ (4.70) $$

The eta vector corresponding to column C (part of the nucleus) causes D to be updated to

D
0
0
2.0
-5.0
2.0
-2.0
5.0

$$ (4.71) $$

Instead of eliminating all entries in D, apart from the pivot in row 4, we initially only eliminate the entries below the diagonal (the "L" portion) as well as converting the pivot entry to 1. This is achieved by the eta vector

4
0
0
0
-0.2
0.4
-0.4
1.0

$$ (4.72) $$

Column E, as part of the nucleus, also needs to be updated. Notice that the eta vector corresponding to C does not affect E since E has a zero in its pivot row (row 3). Therefore E only needs to be updated by (4.72), giving

$$
\text{E} \quad
\begin{bmatrix}
0 \\
0 \\
0 \\
-0.2 \\
1.4 \\
2.6 \\
2.0
\end{bmatrix} . \qquad (4.73)
$$

The eta vector that eliminates entries below row 5 (the pivot row) of E is

$$
\begin{bmatrix}
5 \\
\hline
0 \\
0 \\
0 \\
0 \\
0.714 \\
-1.857 \\
-1.429
\end{bmatrix} . \qquad (4.74)
$$

Column F, as part of the nucleus, needs to be updated by the eta vectors arising from columns D and E (since F has a non-zero entry in their pivot rows). The updating produces

$$
\text{F} \quad
\begin{bmatrix}
0 \\
0 \\
0 \\
-0.2 \\
-0.429 \\
-1.286 \\
1.857
\end{bmatrix} \qquad (4.75)
$$

and the corresponding eta vector to eliminate entries below row 6 is

$$
\begin{array}{|c|}
\hline
6 \\
\hline
0 \\
0 \\
0 \\
0 \\
0 \\
-0.778 \\
1.444 \\
\hline
\end{array}
. \tag{4.76}
$$

The eta vector for G (outside the nucleus) is

$$
\begin{array}{|c|}
\hline
7 \\
\hline
0 \\
0 \\
0 \\
0 \\
0 \\
0 \\
0.5 \\
\hline
\end{array}
. \tag{4.77}
$$

Readers should check that the eta vectors in (4.70), (4.72), (4.74), (4.76) and (4.77) would transform B to the following upper unit triangular matrix:

$$
U = \begin{bmatrix}
1.0 & 0 & 0 & 0 & 0 & 0 & 0 \\
0 & 1.0 & 0 & 0 & 0 & 0 & 0 \\
0 & 0 & 1.0 & 2.0 & 0 & 0 & 0 \\
0 & 0 & 0 & 1.0 & -0.2 & -0.2 & 0 \\
0 & 0 & 0 & 0 & 1.0 & -0.429 & 0 \\
0 & 0 & 0 & 0 & 0 & 1.0 & 0 \\
0 & 0 & 0 & 0 & 0 & 0 & 1
\end{bmatrix}
. \tag{4.78}
$$

The remaining eta vectors (the "U" portion), which eliminate the elements above the main diagonal, can be obtained at the same time as the eta vectors for eliminating those below the diagonal. They will have the same pivot positions as the corresponding eta vectors for the "L" portion but are applied in reverse order. This gives (for the upper portions of

D, E and F)

4	5	6
0	0	0
0	0	0
− 2.0	0	0
1.0	0.2	0.2
0	1.0	0.429
0	0	1.0
0	0	0

$$. \qquad (4.79)$$

The full eta file is therefore

4	5	6	7	6	5	4	3	2	1
0	0	0	0	0	0	0	0	0	1.0
0	0	0	0	0	0	0	0	0.5	− 2.0
− 2.0	0	0	0	0	0	0	1.0	− 0.5	0
1.0	0.2	0.2	0	0	0	− 0.2	− 2.0	0	1.0
0	1.0	0.429	0	0	0.714	0.4	0	− 0.5	− 3.0
0	0	1.0	0	− 0.778	− 1.857	− 0.4	− 1.0	0.5	− 1.0
0	0	0	0.5	1.444	− 1.429	1.0	2.0	0	− 1.0

$\underbrace{\hspace{5em}}_{\text{"U" file}}$ $\underbrace{\hspace{12em}}_{\text{"L" file}}$

$$(4.80)$$

In general, the matrices corresponding to such eta vectors are conveniently written as

$$U_1^{-1}U_2^{-1} \ldots U_{m-1}^{-1}U_m^{-1}L_m^{-1}L_{m-1}^{-1} \ldots L_2^{-1}L_1^{-1} \qquad (4.81)$$

emphasising the fact that we simultaneously calculate L_r^{-1} and U_r^{-1} but process them in the order shown. Usually, for a reason that will become apparent in section 4.3, we store the "L" and "U" portions on separate files. The "U" portion corresponding to the triangular portions of the block tri-angular form do not, of course, arise. They would simply be identity matrices and can be ignored. Hence for the example we do not need to specify $U_1^{-1}, U_2^{-1}, U_3^{-1}$ and U_7^{-1}.

The basis list corresponding to (4.80) is determined by the order of the pivot rows and is

A	B	C	D	E	F	G

$\qquad (4.82)$

Storing only the non-zero entries in the eta file and recognising that the pivot row entries of 1.0 in the "U" portion can always be assumed allows us to store, for the example, only 28 floating-point numbers (and 10 indices). If L\U decomposition had not been used and full eta vectors specified to eliminate entries above and below the main diagonal at the same time for each column, the following eta file would result:

7	6	5	4	3	2	1
0	0	0	0	0	0	1.0
0	0	0	0	0	0.5	-2.0
0	0.444	-0.286	0.4	1.0	-0.5	0
0	-0.222	0.143	-0.2	-2.0	0	1.0
0	-0.333	0.714	0.4	0	-0.5	-3.0
0	-0.778	-1.857	-0.4	-1.0	0.5	-1.0
0.5	1.444	-1.429	1.0	2.0	0	-1.0

$$. \quad (4.83)$$

This involves the storage of 30 floating-point numbers (and seven indices).

The reason for the increase in floating-point numbers is that, if a full eta vector is used for column D (instead of the bottom half), non-zero entries are created in row 3 of columns E and F when updated. This causes the full eta vectors for columns E and F to contain more non-zero entries than would otherwise be the case. In a larger example this fill-in would in turn cause further fill-in when updating, leading to a progressive increase in density. On the other hand, with L\U decomposition the eta vectors associated with the "U" portion only depend on the original columns updated by the "L" portion only.

While the increase in floating-point numbers without L\U decomposition is modest for such a small example, it will generally be much greater for large matrices. In practice, sparse LP models seem much more likely to exhibit fill-in than cancellation, making L\U decomposition universally preferable.

Exercises 4.9 and 4.10 involve finding the eta files for both methods applied to a permutation of the rows and columns of B, so losing the block triangular form, leading to denser eta files yet again.

For interest the explicit inverse of B is

$$B^{-1} = \begin{bmatrix} 1 & 0 & 0 & 0 & 0 & 0 & \\ -1 & 0.5 & 0 & 0 & 0 & 0 & 0 \\ 2.111 & 0.278 & 1 & -0.222 & -1.111 & 0.444 & 0 \\ -0.556 & -0.389 & 0 & 0.111 & 0.556 & -0.222 & 0 \\ -2.333 & -0.333 & -1 & 0.667 & 1.333 & -0.333 & 0 \\ -1.444 & -0.611 & -1 & 0.889 & 1.444 & -0.778 & 0 \\ 3.056 & 0.639 & 1.5 & 0.611 & -2.056 & 0.722 & 0.5 \end{bmatrix} .$$

$$(4.84)$$

As expected, this is denser and would involve storing 33 floating-point numbers.

4.3 MAINTAINING AN L\U INVERSE BETWEEN ITERATIONS

Although the inverse of a partially triangularised basis matrix using L\U decomposition usually delivers a sparse representation, the advantages of this will gradually be lost if normal simplex iterations are then performed. These result in basic variables being eliminated from all rows apart from the pivot (Gauss–Jordan as opposed to Gaussian elimination), so losing triangularity. It is, however, possible to overcome this undesirable feature by a method that we now describe.

Suppose we wished to replace column D of matrix B by the following column H as a result of a simplex iteration (with row 4 as pivot row):

$$
\begin{array}{c}
\text{H} \\
\begin{bmatrix}
2.0 \\
1.0 \\
-1.0 \\
1.0 \\
-1.0 \\
3.0 \\
-2.0
\end{bmatrix}
\end{array}. \qquad (4.85)
$$

Multiplying B by the "L" portion of the eta file (4.80) would no longer produce an upper unit triangular matrix. The reader should verify that it produces the matrix

$$
\bar{U} = -
\begin{bmatrix}
1.0 & 0 & 0 & 2.0 & 0 & 0 & 0 \\
0 & 1.0 & 0 & -1.5 & 0 & 0 & 0 \\
0 & 0 & 1.0 & 0.5 & 0 & 0 & 0 \\
0 & 0 & 0 & -0.4 & -0.2 & -0.2 & 0 \\
0 & 0 & 0 & -3.357 & 1.0 & -0.429 & 0 \\
0 & 0 & 0 & -5.389 & 0 & 1.0 & 0 \\
0 & 0 & 0 & 7.861 & 0 & 0 & 1
\end{bmatrix}. \qquad (4.86)
$$

Clearly this matrix is the upper unit triangular matrix U apart from a single column, which is the column H updated by the "L" eta file. This will be the general pattern that results.

It would be possible to transform this matrix into upper unit triangular form by the following transformations:

(i) The new column is (in practice implicitly) placed last, giving

$$\begin{bmatrix} 1.0 & 0 & 0 & 0 & 0 & 0 & 2.0 \\ 0 & 1.0 & 0 & 0 & 0 & 0 & -1.5 \\ 0 & 0 & 1.0 & 0 & 0 & 0 & 0.5 \\ 0 & 0 & 0 & -0.2 & -0.2 & 0 & -0.4 \\ 0 & 0 & 0 & 1.0 & -0.429 & 0 & -3.357 \\ 0 & 0 & 0 & 0 & 1.0 & 0 & -5.389 \\ 0 & 0 & 0 & 0 & 0 & 1.0 & 7.861 \end{bmatrix} . \quad (4.87)$$

(ii) Elementary *column* operations are applied to eliminate all entries, apart from the last, in the pivot row corresponding to the new column. These elementary column operations can be performed by a matrix differing from the identity matrix in only one *row*. This row gives rise to a *row eta* vector, i.e. it is defined by a row vector and an index of the row of the identity matrix that it replaces. It can be verified (exercise 4.11) that the row eta that performs this operation is the row of U^{-1} corresponding to the pivot row. The pivot row of U^{-1} can be obtained by a BTRAN operation on the "U" portion of the current eta file. In fact, we can confine ourselves to those eta vectors in the "U" file corresponding to columns after that replaced since we only need to eliminate elements to the right of the diagonal in (4.87). In the example this gives

$$[0 \ 0 \ 0 \ 1.0 \ 0 \ 0 \ 0] \, U_5^{-1} U_6^{-1} = [0 \ 0 \ 0 \ 1.0 \ 0.2 \ 0.286 \ 0]. \quad (4.88)$$

The corresponding row eta would therefore be

$$\boxed{4 \mid 0 \ \ 0 \ \ 0 \ \ 1.0 \ \ 0.2 \ \ 0.286 \ \ 0} \qquad (4.89)$$

representing the 7×7 identity matrix, with this row replacing the fourth row, i.e.

$$\begin{bmatrix} 1.0 & & & & & & \\ & 1.0 & & & & & \\ & & 1.0 & & & & \\ & & & 1.0 & 0.2 & 0.286 & 0 \\ & & & & 1.0 & & \\ & & & & & 1.0 & \\ & & & & & & 1.0 \end{bmatrix} . \qquad (4.90)$$

It should be verified that multiplying this matrix into that given in (4.78) eliminates all entries in the fourth row apart from the diagonal element.

Therefore it must also eliminate all entries in the fourth row of (4.87), apart from that in the last column, transforming it to

$$
\begin{bmatrix}
1.0 & 0 & 0 & 0 & 0 & 0 & 2.0 \\
0 & 1.0 & 0 & 0 & 0 & 0 & -1.5 \\
0 & 0 & 1.0 & 0 & 0 & 0 & 0.5 \\
0 & 0 & 0 & 0 & 0 & 0 & -2.612 \\
0 & 0 & 0 & 1.0 & -0.429 & 0 & -3.357 \\
0 & 0 & 0 & 0 & 1.0 & 0 & -5.389 \\
0 & 0 & 0 & 0 & 0 & 1.0 & 7.861
\end{bmatrix} . \quad (4.91)
$$

The last element in the transformed row must be non-zero, otherwise the matrix would be singular and could not have arisen as a basis. In order that it be scaled to 1.0, the row eta can be so scaled (after calculating the scaling factor by applying the "L" eta file to the new column), giving the row eta vector

$$
\boxed{4 \mid 0 \quad 0 \quad 0 \quad -0.383 \quad -0.077 \quad -0.109 \quad 0} . \quad (4.92)
$$

The row eta is placed at the end of the "L" file. This is possible since the "L" and "U" files are stored separately.

(iii) The transformed row of U could be moved (implicitly) to the bottom of the matrix, giving the upper unit triangular matrix required.

Since the U matrix has changed by the deletion of elements in the pivot row for the new column, the corresponding elements must be deleted from the "U" file. As only deletion is involved, the file can be retained in packed form. The eta vector corresponding to the elimination of the replaced column in the "U" file is also deleted. A new eta vector must then be created and added to the end of the "U" file to eliminate the "U" portion of the new column (after updating). This is (with the original row order)

$$
\begin{array}{|c|}
\hline
4 \\
\hline
-2.0 \\
1.5 \\
-0.5 \\
1.0 \\
3.357 \\
5.389 \\
-7.861 \\
\hline
\end{array} . \quad (4.93)
$$

The new "L" and "U" files are therefore

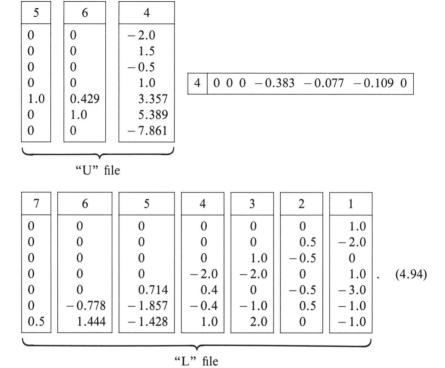

"U" file

. (4.94)

"L" file

The basis list corresponding to this eta file is

| A | B | C | H | E | F | G |

. (4.95)

Iterations between inversions will therefore amend the eta files as above, creating a series of row etas at the end of the "L" file and new column etas at the beginning of the "U" file. In addition, deletions will take place among elements and vectors in the "U" file.

4.4 NUMERICAL CONSIDERATIONS

Because the arithmetic of the revised simplex algorithm is generally done with floating-point numbers, rounding and truncation errors will result. Such errors could result in inaccuracy and slowness of the calculation. Measures must therefore be taken to mitigate the effects. It is unlikely that such errors will result in a wrong solution since this is defined by a *basis*. Once the (presumed) optimal basis has been found, the resultant solution only depends on solving the resultant set of equations (inverting the basis matrix), which can be done to a greater precision if necessary. A more likely effect of numerical error is to slow down the calculation. This can happen since it is relatively easy regularly to check for errors in the course of calculation and rectify them if necessary by, for example, reinverting the current basis to obtain a sparser eta file. Such checking usually involves *tolerance* values for the sizes of different quantities. The main tolerances are described.

Tolerances

Certain quantities can be evaluated in the course of the revised simplex algorithm that should theoretically be zero. In practice they will not be through rounding errors. However, it will be necessary to treat them as zero. This may be done either explicitly by replacing them by zero or (less satisfactorily) by treating them as zero. Numerical tolerances need to be defined. If the absolute values of the quantities fall below these values, then they will be regarded as zero. The best settings for these numerical values depend on both the model (e.g. sizes of coefficients) and the computer system (e.g. precision of the arithmetic). To some extent the first can be dealt with by scaling the model, which is discussed below. If we assume that floating-point numbers are stored as double words, then reasonable tolerance values are those given below. It should be pointed out that making the tolerance levels too small could result in spurious calculations, e.g. dividing by a zero coefficient. On the other hand, making the tolerance levels too large could result in an unintended change to the model, e.g. spuriously treating a small coefficient as zero. Therefore the correct settings are important, although it is impossible to make them entirely model-independent. Some models are notoriously ill-conditioned, making them difficult to solve through numerical error. "We pivoted on a bit of dirt" is a phrase that has sometimes been heard. We discuss the main tolerances needed, with suggested values.

Pivot tolerance (10^{-6})

Any coefficient whose absolute value is below this will be regarded as zero and cannot be a pivot element.

d_j *tolerance* (10^{-5})

As explained in section 2.3, the reduced cost of a basic variable must be zero. When the pricing operation is done in the revised simplex algorithm (section 4.1), it is convenient, however, to price basic variables (as well as non-basic ones) to test if their d_j values are below this tolerance level. If not, it is evidence that rounding errors have built up to an unacceptable level. The usual remedy is to reinvert the basis to produce a sparser eta file. This tolerance is also used to test for optimality.

RHS tolerance (10^{-8})

The values of the variables at any stage (including logical variables) should, when substituted into the rows of the model, produce total row activities equal to the RHS coefficients. If these values differ by more than the tolerance, this is again evidence of excessive rounding errors, calling for a reinversion of the basis. It could also demonstrate that infeasibilities may have crept into the solution, calling for a return to phase I of the simplex algorithm.

Feasibility tolerance (10^{-8})

In phase II of the simplex algorithm the values of the variables (basic and non-basic) must be between their lower and upper bounds. Should they fall outside these values by more than this tolerance, then the current solution must be regarded as infeasible and phase I be reinvoked until feasibility is again achieved.

Singularity tolerance (10^{-5})

It has been pointed out in section 2.3 that the matrix of coefficients associated with a basis must, by definition, be non-singular (i.e. have a non-zero determinant). If, in the course of calculation, the basis matrix does become nearly singular, then substantial errors could result. The products of the pivot elements following an inversion give the value of the determinant. Should this be less, in absolute value, than this tolerance, then a new basis should be sought. One way of doing this is to replace one or more basic variables by logical variables and reinvert the basis.

Scaling

Ideally all the non-zero coefficients in an LP model should be of roughly the same (absolute) magnitude between (say) 0.1 and 10. By a sensible choice of units of measurement it should be possible to formulate a model in this way. The possibility of unacceptable rounding errors is reduced when this is done. It is, however, possible and often necessary automatically to scale a model before solving it. After solution it must, of course, be descaled. This can be done by dividing columns and rows by different factors. Many different schemes exist. For example, one fairly successful, and simple, method is to divide the coefficients in each row by the square root of the maximum (absolute) coefficient multiplied by the minimum (absolute) non-zero coefficient in the row. The procedure is then repeated for the columns.

Such a scaling method is *static* as it is only done on the original matrix of coefficients. Alternatively, one can apply *dynamic* scaling to portions of the updated matrix of coefficients. One such method, known as the "Devex" method, has been particularly successful with some models. It is based on the observation, discussed in section 2.3, that the criterion of *maximum d_j* for choosing the pivot column is affected by the scaling of the column. It seems somewhat unsatisfactory that the solution path should depend on the units of measurement and not on the absolute underlying model. The *maximum improvement* criterion is independent of the scaling but requires updating of all columns and doing the ratio test on them all. It would therefore be prohibitively expensive. The Devex method scales the d_j values dynamically according to a scale of reference based on the updated columns at different stages. In this way the criterion is more independent of the original scaling of the matrix. It seems particularly successful on models where a lot of the activities are closely "competing", i.e. we need to discriminate among them fairly carefully to avoid the variables frequently entering, leaving and re-entering the basis. References are given in section 4.7.

The revised simplex algorithm has reached such a state of sophistication that there is virtue in "fine tuning" the algorithm to improve performance. We describe some of the more straightforward refinements here. Others can be found in the references in section 4.7.

Multiple Pricing

It has been pointed out that the value of the reduced cost for an incoming variable only represents the *rate of improvement* of the objective function with respect to this variable. In order to find that variable which gives *maximum improvement* we would need to update all columns and apply the ratio test, which would be prohibitively costly. A compromise is to update a few of the columns (typically about six) having suitably signed reduced costs. The ratio test can then be applied to all of these in order to find which yields the greatest objective improvement. This variable can then be brought into the basis. Having updated a subset in this way (a *major iteration*) it is wasteful not to complete the updating on those in the subset not brought into the basis. This can be done quickly as a result of the iteration just done. Those which still have suitably signed reduced costs are still candidates to enter the basis. The resultant *minor iterations* are very quick and can be continued until no variables in the subset still have worthwhile d_j values. This procedure is known as *sub-optimisation* since we are sub-optimising the LP consisting of this subset of the variables. The number of columns to be updated at each major iteration is influenced by the storage available within the computer memory for holding unpacked columns.

Cycling and Block Pricing

Since the reduced costs only give a partial indication of the relative desirabilities of bringing different variables into the basis, it seems wasteful to carry out the pricing operation on all columns. This is particularly true towards the beginning of the optimisation process. All that is needed is a subset of columns with suitably signed reduced costs. *Cycling* (not to be confused with circling) consists of performing the pricing operation on only a subset of the columns (say 100) on each major iteration. On the following major iteration the next set of 100 columns would be priced. In this way we "cycle" over the whole of the matrix.

A disadvantage of the above scheme is that columns within a cycle may represent rather similar activities. Searching for the "best" among them may not be as valuable as searching for the best among dissimilar activities. A way of doing this is *block pricing*, where the subset of variables with suitable reduced costs is deliberately split between blocks of the matrix. These blocks can be specified by markers placed in the matrix file.

Epsilon-Perturbation

In section 2.3 it was pointed out that the simplex algorithm could theoretically circle unless a (costly) modification was made to the pivot selection rule. More likely, the algorithm could go through many degenerate iterations, resulting in increased solution time. A fairly crude, but usually satisfactory, method of overcoming this is to replace zero solution values for basic variables by a small positive quantity (ε). This "perturbation" to the model will hopefully take the calculation off a degenerate path. Once the iterations have ceased to be degenerate, ε should be reset to zero and the optimisation continued.

Crashing

Intuitively the all-logical basis for an LP might seem to be a poor starting point for an optimisation since one would expect a reasonable number of the structural variables to be in the optimal basis. There is therefore virtue in trying to construct a good starting basis with many structural variables as quickly as possible. It is not sufficient simply to choose (for an m-row model) a set of m variables, since the corresponding (sparse) matrix would almost certainly be singular. Nevertheless, the more computationally costly steps of the simplex algorithm can be avoided.

Two particularly useful steps in a crashing procedure are as follows:

(i) Pivot out at many artificial variables as possible by finding a structural variable with a non-zero entry in the appropriate row.
(ii) Pivot in as many structural variables as possible using a "merit number" calculation (as discussed with regard to inversion). The motive for this is that, if a structural variable is pivoted into the basis in a row with few non-zero entries, then all the structural variables with zero entries in this and previous pivot rows do *not* need to be updated. Therefore we can bring more structural variables into the basis without the costly procedure of unpacking and updating.

The methods that are used in crashing procedures are essentially heuristic. Sometimes there is virtue in tailoring them to a particular model structure. Crashing is closely connected with *reducing* (presolving) a model. Reducing involves (quickly) removing redundancies from a model prior to solution. Methods of doing this are not discussed here but in *MBMP* since they are closer to the modelling process than to the solution process. Nevertheless, the distinction is blurred. Solving an LP model can be viewed as removing all redundant constraints and variables until we have a uniquely soluble set of simultaneous equations. Unfortunately this is a non-trivial process, if carried to completion, for which we need a method such as the simplex algorithm. Nonetheless, some such redundancies can often be recognised quickly. It is these which are relevant to crashing and reduction procedures.

4.5 SENSITIVITY ANALYSIS AND PARAMETRIC PROGRAMMING

The values of the variables are usually only one of the pieces of information required from the optimal solution to an LP model. In addition, the solution to the dual model will often be required. This provides very important economic information, which is discussed in *MBMP*. Such information can be used for *marginal analysis* as explained below. If the data in the model change, then it is important to be able to predict the changes in the optimal solution. This forms the subject of *sensitivity analysis*. Small changes can be predicted by calculating *ranges* for some of the coefficients. Larger changes require the carrying out of additional steps of the simplex algorithm, giving rise to *parametric programming*. These topics, which all form the subject of *post-optimal analysis*, are discussed below. Although they can be discussed theoretically, it seems more satisfactory to relate this discussion to their practical derivation, which is why the subject is contained in this chapter.

Marginal Analysis

Two very important pieces of information usually required are the *reduced costs* of structural variables not in the optimal basis and the *dual values* associated with binding constraints. These latter are, of course, the reduced costs of the associated logical variables in the corresponding constraints. This information is valuable in obtaining pricing and costing information in practical models. The interpretation depends on the model and is discussed very fully in *MBMP*. Here we confine our attention to the derivation rather than the interpretation. Although this information can be obtained from the optimal solution to the dual model, as discussed in section 2.5, it was also pointed out there that it can be obtained directly from the optimal tableau in the standard simplex algorithm. For the revised simplex algorithm we need to update the objective row of the model by means of the BTRAN operation. The values corresponding to structural variables give their reduced costs and the values corresponding to logical variables give dual values. It is important to give the correct interpretation to these values. As discussed in section 2.5, if there are alternative dual solutions then we will only obtain one of them. To calculate *shadow prices* associated with binding constraints would require evaluating all the dual solutions. This is generally computationally prohibitive. It is, however, straightforward to recognise if the dual solution is unique. This corresponds to the primal solution being non-degenerate, which is recognised by there being no basic variables at their lower or upper bounds. In this case dual values can be interpreted as shadow prices and represent the effect of marginal changes.

Another use for reduced costs and dual values is the recognition of alternative (primal) solutions. If non-basic variables have zero reduced costs then this indicates alternative solutions. Obtaining all of them is again generally prohibitively costly, although theoretically the method described in section 2.7 could be used.

The reduced costs represent the effect (subject to the proviso above) of marginal changes on the optimal *objective* value. We can also, fairly easily, obtain the effect on the solution values. This information comes from the *marginal rates of substitution* and is discussed in *MBMP*. These values are obtained from the updated columns of the corresponding variables. Their derivation is best demonstrated by an example.

Example 4.4 Calculating Marginal Rates of Substitution
Obtain the marginal rates of substitution for the optimal solution to Example 4.1.

The optimal solution to this example has been obtained, giving $z = 12.667$, $x_2 = 2.333$ and $x_3 = 0.333$. x_1 is out of the optimal basis at value 0. If we wished to find the effect on the optimal solution of bringing it (marginally) into the basis, we would need to update its column of coefficients using the FTRAN operation with the eta file (4.49). This gives the column

$$\boxed{\begin{array}{c} 4.333 \\ -0.333 \\ 0.667 \end{array}} . \qquad (4.96)$$

The positive reduced cost (4.333) represents the rate of degradation of the objective function on bringing x_1 into the basis. The entry in the second row (-0.333) represents the rate of increase in the basic variable in this row caused by bringing x_1 into the basis. This basic variable is (from the basis list (4.51)) x_2. Since the value is negative, x_2 will *increase* at a rate of 0.333 (per unit of x_1 increase). Similarly the third variable in the basis (x_3) will *decrease* at a rate of 0.667 per unit of increase in x_1. These are the rates of change of the solution values caused by *marginal* changes in x_1. It is important again to emphasise the marginal nature of these values. If x_1 is increased (or decreased) by more than some amount (which could be zero in the case of alternative solutions), they no longer apply because there is a basis change. Further investigation requires parametric programming. Finding what these limits are requires *ranging*, discussed below.

Verifying the above interpretation of the marginal rates of substitution is straightforward when the full set of simultaneous equations is considered. The reader can refer to the standard simplex algorithm applied to this same example in section 2.3, where the set of equations (2.62) to (2.64) represent the updated matrix.

The marginal rates of substitution for non-structural variables have a different interpretation, but similar derivation. The effect of, for example, bringing x_4 (the slack variable in the first constraint) into the basis can be investigated. This constraint is binding. Increasing or decreasing the value of x_4 (from 0) can be equated with decreasing or increasing the value of the RHS coefficient. The column of coefficients for x_4 must be updated by the FTRAN operative to give

$$\boxed{\begin{array}{c} 2.333 \\ 0.667 \\ -0.333 \end{array}} . \qquad (4.97)$$

These figures give the rate of decrease respectively in the values of z (the objective), x_2 and x_3 of marginally increasing the RHS coefficient of 2. Conversely they also give the rate of increase in the values of these variables of marginally decreasing the RHS coefficient of 2 (corresponding to introducing negative slack x_4). The derivation of the marginal rates of substitution associated with variable x_5 is similarly straightforward and considered as part of exercise 4.13.

All the above information is immediately available from the optimal tableau of the standard simplex algorithm, although for the revised simplex algorithm it does necessitate updating parts of the matrix of coefficients by means of the eta file.

Further information for post-optimal analysis requires extra calculation. The derivation of this information is described below.

Ranging RHS Coefficients

It has already been emphasised that reduced costs, dual values and marginal rates of substitution can only be guaranteed (or in the absence of degeneracy) to predict the effect on the optimal solution of marginal changes in the values of non-basic variables. It is, however, usually the case that these values can be applied, not just marginally, but over a *range* of changes. Within these ranges the optimal basis does not change and sometimes the solution does not change either. The interpretation of this ranging information is again given more extensive coverage in *MBMP*.

RHS ranges

We will consider an example.

Example 4.5 Calculating RHS Ranges

Obtain upper and lower ranges within which the RHS coefficients can be changed, and the effect on the solution be given by the rèduced costs and marginal rates of substitution derived in Example 4.4.

We will again consider the first constraint (which is binding in the optimal solution). The reduced cost and marginal rates of substitution for the corresponding slack variable x_4 were given by (4.97), the updated column of coefficients for x_4. In order to calculate the ranges, we consider how large or small we can make x_4 before it drives another variable out of the basis. The maximum level to which x_4 can be brought into the solution before there is a basis change is, as in the simplex algorithm, given by the minimum ratio between solution values and *positive* coefficients in the updated column of coefficients corresponding to constraint rows. In this example, there being only one such positive coefficient, this minimum ratio is, comparing the solution vector (4.50) with (4.97) $2.333/0.667 = 3.5$. Hence x_4 can be made as large as 3.5, demonstrating that the

lower range on constraint 1 is $2.0 - 3.5 = -1.5$.

Below this lower range (arising from the ratio in constraint 1) the basic variable in the second row (x_2) would *leave* the basis. Then the marginal information would no longer apply.

In order to calculate the upper range we consider bringing x_4 into the basis at a *negative* level. Although this is not strictly allowed, it is a valid way of showing how large the RHS coefficient can be made. The minimum level to which x_4 can be reduced is given by the maximum (in effect negated minimum absolute) ratio between solution values and *negative* coefficients in the updated column. Again, in the small example, there is only one such negative coefficient giving a ratio of $0.333/(-0.333) = -1.0$. Hence x_4 can be made as small as -1.0, demonstrating that the

upper range on constraint 1 is $2.0 + 1.0 = 3.0$.

Calculating ranges for the second constraint forms exercise 4.14.

Should there be no positive coefficient in the updated column being considered, the lower range will be $-\infty$, i.e. there is no lower limit to the marginal interpretation. Similarly, if there is no negative coefficient, the upper range will be ∞.

If a constraint is non-binding (which is not the case in this example) the calculation and interpretation of the corresponding RHS range is relatively trivial. The (basic) logical variable in the constraint can be moved between its bounds without affecting the optimal *solution*. Corresponding adjustments can therefore be made in the RHS coefficient without affecting the solution. Notice that in this case the interpretation of ranges is stronger. Not only will the optimal basis not change, for RHS coefficient changes within ranges, but the solution will not change either.

For completeness we give the general calculation for RHS ranges. Let the constraint under consideration have a RHS coefficient of b and let the updated (by FTRAN) column of coefficients of the corresponding logical variable be (for the constraint rows)

$$\begin{array}{c} a_{1q} \\ a_{2q} \\ \vdots \\ a_{mq} \end{array} \qquad (4.98)$$

Also, let the updated solution vector be

$$\boxed{\begin{array}{c} \bar{x}_{i_1} \\ \bar{x}_{i_2} \\ \vdots \\ \bar{x}_{i_m} \end{array}} \tag{4.99}$$

corresponding to a basis list

$$\boxed{\begin{array}{c|c|c|c} x_{i_1} & x_{i_2} & \cdots & x_{i_m} \end{array}}. \tag{4.100}$$

We will assume for simplicity that the logical variable (x_q) has an entry $+1$ in the constraint being considered. Otherwise our derivation is changed in a manner shown later. Also we will assume that the logical variable has lower and upper bounds of 0 and ∞, i.e. there are no prior ranges specified for the constraint.

Referring to the ratios given by (2.246) to (2.255) in section 2.4, the upper limit to x_q before there is a basis change is

$$\theta_q = \underset{k}{\text{Min}} \begin{cases} (\bar{x}_{i_k} - l_{i_k})/a_{kq} & \text{for } a_{kq} > 0 \\ (u_{i_k} - \bar{x}_{i_k})/|a_{kq}| & \text{for } a_{kq} < 0. \end{cases} \tag{4.101}$$

This gives the

$$\text{lower range} = b - \theta_q. \tag{4.102}$$

At the lower range the appropriate x_{i_k} *leaves* the basis at one of its bounds. If there is no valid ratio in (4.101) the lower range is $-\infty$. Similarly the lower limit to x_q before there is a basis change is

$$\theta_q' = \underset{k}{\text{Min}} \begin{cases} (\bar{x}_{i_k} - l_{i_k})/|a_{kq}| & \text{for } a_{kq} < 0 \\ (u_{i_k} - \bar{x}_{i_k})/a_{kq} & \text{for } a_{kq} > 0. \end{cases} \tag{4.103}$$

This gives the

$$\text{upper range} = b + \theta_q'. \tag{4.104}$$

At this upper range the appropriate x_{i_k} *leaves* the basis at one of its bounds. If there is no valid ratio in (4.103) the upper range is $+\infty$.

A geometrical explanation and interpretation of RHS ranges is easily given by two-dimensional examples as is done in *MBMP* and exercise 4.15.

Should the logical variable x_q have an entry -1 in the constraint being considered (i.e. if it is a "$\geqslant$" constraint), then (4.102) and (4.104) must respectively be replaced by

$$\text{lower range} = b - \theta_q' \tag{4.105}$$

and

$$\text{upper range} = b + \theta_q. \tag{4.106}$$

For Example 4.5 the RHS ranges could also be deduced, and understood, clearly from the value function given as (2.36). This is the subject of exercise 4.20.

Ranging Objective Coefficients

In the following treatment we are adopting our convention of considering only maximisation models. Minimisation models can, of course, be treated as such by negating the objective coefficients.

From the duality results discussed in section 2.5, it should be apparent that there will be a close similarity between the ranges on objective coefficients and ranges on RHS coefficients in dual models. In fact one set of values will be the same as the other set in the dual model. Nevertheless, all the information is obtainable from the solution to the primal model.

There is one important difference, which is easy to demonstrate geometrically as is done in *MBMP* and exercise 4.15. It has been pointed out that for changes (one at a time) within the RHS ranges the optimal *basis* does not change although the solution generally will change when the constraint is binding. For changes (one at a time) of objective coefficients within ranges the *solution* does not change either.

An example will again be used to demonstrate the derivation of objective ranges.

Example 4.6 Calculating Objective Ranges
Obtain upper and lower ranges within which the objective coefficients of Example 4.1 can be changed but the optimal solution values remain unchanged.

In the optimal solution, given under Example 4.4, x_1 is non-basic. The ranges on its objective coefficient of -4.0 are therefore straightforward to obtain. If the value of its coefficient is reduced, x_1 will still remain non-basic. Therefore

$$\text{lower range on objective coefficient of } x_1 = -\infty.$$

If the value of the coefficient is increased by its reduced cost (given by the objective row updated by BTRAN) of 4.333 then the penalty of marginally bringing x_1 into the basis (the reduced cost) is just offset by its contribution to the objective. Therefore

$$\text{upper range on objective coefficient of } x_1 = -4.0 + 4.333 = 0.333.$$

This straightforward case of the ranges for the objective coefficient of a non-basic (in effect redundant) variable corresponds dually to the straightforward case, already mentioned, of the RHS ranges on a non-binding (in effect redundant) constraint. The reader should recall the equality of reduced costs and solution values between dual models explained in section 2.5.

If a variable is non-basic at its upper bound then the range calculation above is, of course, applied in the opposite direction.

The ranges on the objective coefficients of basic variables require more calculation. We will consider the effect of a change of Δ in the objective coefficient of x_2, changing it to $5.0 + \Delta$. In the initial tableau (4.1) the corresponding coefficient would therefore be $-5.0 - \Delta$. If, for the sake of argument, the eta file (4.49) were to be applied to the whole of the matrix file (4.1), we would obtain the updated tableau

$$\begin{array}{|ccccc|}
1.0 & 4.333 - \Delta & 0 & 2.333 & 2.667 \\
0 & -0.333 & 1.0 & 0 & 0.667 & 0.333 \\
0 & 0.667 & 0 & 1.0 & -0.333 & 0.333
\end{array} = \begin{array}{|c|} 12.667 \\ 2.333 \\ 0.333 \end{array} . \quad (4.107)$$

In order to maintain a zero reduced cost for the basic variable x_2 we would have to perform an elementary row operation on the tableau (4.107), adding Δ times the second row (the row in which x_2 is basic) to the updated objective row. This would result in a new updated objective row

$$\boxed{1.0 \mid 4.333 - \Delta \times 0.333 \mid 0 \mid 0 \mid 2.333 + \Delta \times 0.667 \mid 2.667 + \Delta \times 0.333} .$$
$$(4.108)$$

For the current solution to remain optimal, all these reduced costs must remain non-negative. This is the case so long as

$$-\text{Min}\{2.333/0.667, 2.667/0.333\} \leqslant \Delta \leqslant 4.333/0.333. \quad (4.109)$$

Hence

$$-3.5 \leqslant \Delta \leqslant 13.0. \quad (4.110)$$

lower range on objective coefficient of $x_2 = 5.0 - 3.5 + 1.5$.

Below this lower range the reduced cost of x_1 would become negative. Therefore x_1 would *enter* the basis. Also

upper range for objective coefficient of $x_2 = 5.0 + 13.0 = 18.0$.

Above this upper range the reduced cost of x_4 would become negative. Therefore x_4 would *enter* the basis.

The upper and lower ranges on the objective coefficient of x_3 can be treated similarly and form the subject of exercise 4.16.

In general, in order to calculate ranges on the objective coefficient of a basic variable x_p we update the objective row and row p using BTRAN (ignoring entries in columns for artificial variables). Let the portion of the updated objective row corresponding to non-basic variables be

$$
\begin{array}{cccc}
x_{j_1} & x_{j_2} & \cdots & x_{j_n} \\
\hline
d_{j_1} & d_{j_2} & \cdots & d_{j_n} \\
\hline
\end{array}
\qquad (4.111)
$$

and the updated row p be

$$
\begin{array}{cccc}
\hline
a_{pj_1} & a_{pj_2} & \cdots & a_{pj_n} \\
\hline
\end{array}.
\qquad (4.112)
$$

We calculate the following ratios between elements in these two rows (contrast taking ratios between *rows* for calculating objective ranges and ratios between *columns* for RHS ranges):

$$
\gamma_p = \mathrm{Min} \begin{cases} d_{j_k} / |a_{pj_k}| & \text{for } a_{pj_k} < 0 \text{ if } x_{j_k} \text{ at lower bound} \quad (4.113) \\ |d_{j_k}| / a_{pj_k} & \text{for } a_{pj_k} > 0 \text{ if } x_{j_k} \text{ at upper bound.} \quad (4.114) \end{cases}
$$

This gives

$$
\text{upper range} = c_p + \gamma_p'.
$$

If the objective coefficient falls below this value the appropriate x_{j_k} must *enter* the basis. Also

$$
\gamma_p' = \mathrm{Min} \begin{cases} d_{j_k} / a_{pj_k} & \text{for } a_{pj_k} > 0 \text{ if } x_{j_k} \text{ at lower bound} \quad (4.115) \\ d_{j_k} / a_{pj_k} & \text{for } a_{pj_k} < 0 \text{ if } x_{j_k} \text{ at upper bound.} \quad (4.116) \end{cases}
$$

This gives

$$
\text{lower range} = c_p - \gamma_p'.
$$

If the objective coefficient rises above this value the appropriate x_{j_k} must *enter* the basis.

In either case if there are no valid ratios (4.113) or (4.114) then the ranges are $-\infty$ or ∞ respectively.

Our derivation of ranges has been confined to RHS and objective coefficients (the "rim" of a model). It is also possible to obtain ranges on individual matrix coefficients. This is not described, as such information is rarely required.

The objective ranges for Example 4.6 can also be deduced by considering the RHS ranges for the dual model illustrated in Figure 2.6. This is the subject of exercise 4.21.

Parametric Programming

Should we wish to investigate the effect on the optimal solution of simultaneously making more than one change in RHS or objective coefficients or of changes outside the ranges, extra simplex iterations are required. RHS coefficient changes are specified by a *change column* and objective coefficient changes by a *change row*. We consider the objective case first by means of an example.

Example 4.7 Parametric Programming on the Objective Function

Simultaneously increase the objective coefficients of each structural variable in Example 4.1 at the same rate up to a maximum increase of 12.0. Give the effect on the optimal objective value and basis changes necessary.

As described in *MBMP* such a requirement would be specified in the model by a change row.

An upper limit of 12.0 is specified for a parameter θ representing the multiple of the change row to be added to the objective. By other change rows any mixture of simultaneous changes to the objective could be so considered.

The change rows would normally be incorporated (as non-constraint rows) in the original matrix file and (implicitly) updated by means of the eta vectors calculated. Appending rows to a model *after* optimisation is normally cumbersome with a data structure based on columns as records.

For the example the matrix file (4.1) could be amended to

	z'	z	x_1	x_2	x_3	x_4	x_5		
OBJ	0	1.0	4.0	-5.0	-3.0	0	0		0
CNG	1.0	0	-1.0	-1.0	-1.0	0	0	$=$	0
C1	0	0	-1.0	1.0	-1.0	1.0	0		2.0
C2	0	0	1.0	1.0	2.0	0	1.0		3.0

$$(4.117)$$

	z'	z	x_1	x_2	x_3	x_4	x_5
LB	$-\infty$	$-\infty$	0	0	0	0	0
UB	∞	∞	∞	∞	∞	∞	∞

The change row is CNG (with a logical variable z'). Notice that the coefficients have been negated, consistent with the negation of the objective coefficients in the tableau form.

When this model is optimised the resultant eta file is

4	3
2.667	5.0
0.667	1.0
0.333	1.0
0.333	-1.0

$$(4.118)$$

corresponding to basis list

z	z'	x_2	x_3

$$(4.119)$$

and solution vector

$$\begin{array}{|c|} \hline 12.667 \\ 2.667 \\ 2.333 \\ 0.333 \\ \hline \end{array} \quad . \tag{4.120}$$

The objective and change rows may be updated using the BTRAN operation with initial pricing vectors of

$$[1.0 \quad 0 \quad 0 \quad 0] \tag{4.121}$$

and

$$[0 \quad 1.0 \quad 0 \quad 0] \tag{4.122}$$

respectively to produce the updated rows

$$\begin{array}{cccccccc} z' & z & x_1 & x_2 & x_3 & x_4 & x_5 \\ [0 & 1.0 & 4.333 & 0 & 0 & 2.333 & 2.667] \end{array} \tag{4.123}$$

and

$$\begin{array}{ccccccc} z' & z & x_1 & x_2 & x_3 & x_4 & x_5 \\ [1.0 & 0 & -0.667 & 0 & 0 & 0.333 & 0.667]. \end{array} \tag{4.124}$$

Therefore the new set of reduced costs will be

$$\begin{array}{cccccc} z' & z & x_1 & x_2 \; x_3 & x_4 & x_5 \\ [-\theta & 1.0 & 4.333 - \theta \times 0.667 & 0 \quad 0 & 2.333 + \theta \times 0.333 & 2.667 + \theta \times 0.667]. \end{array}$$
$$\tag{4.125}$$

These will remain non-negative so long as

$$0 \leqslant \theta \leqslant 6.5.$$

When $\theta = 6.5$, x_1 must enter the basis in order to maintain optimality. The updated column for x_1 is (by FTRAN) after setting θ to 6.5.

$$\begin{array}{|c|} \hline 0 \\ \hline -0.667 \\ -0.333 \\ 0.667 \\ \hline \end{array} \tag{4.126}$$

which, when compared with the solution vector (4.120), demonstrates that x_3 leaves the basis to be replaced by x_1, creating a new basis list

$$\begin{array}{|c|c|c|c|} \hline z & z' & x_2 & x_1 \\ \hline \end{array} \tag{4.127}$$

solution vector

$$
\begin{array}{c}
30.0 \\
2.667 \\
2.333 \\
0.333
\end{array}
\qquad (4.128)
$$

and eta file

4	4	3
0	2.667	5.0
1.0	−0.667	−1.0
0.5	0.333	1.0
−1.5	0.333	−1.0

$$(4.129)$$

The process can now be repeated, increasing the value of θ until another basis change is necessary to maintain optimality. The carrying out of the remaining calculation is left as exercise 4.17. θ can be increased until either the limit of 12.0 is reached or the model becomes unbounded.

The general steps of parametric programming on the objective function should easily be deducible from the above example. It is important to realise that variables can enter the basis from their upper as well as their lower bounds. Hence to maintain optimality, as θ is increased, we must examine non-basic variables at their upper bounds, whose reduced costs must stay non-positive, as well as those at their lower bounds with negative reduced costs.

It should be recognised that as θ is continuously increased the optimal objective value will change continuously as well (in piecewise-linear steps). Exercise 4.17 illustrates this. The optimal solution values will not, however, change continuously. At a basis change an alternative solution becomes possible, which then becomes the solution and remains the same until the next basis change. Again, exercise 4.17 illustrates this.

Example 4.8 Parametric Programming on the RHS
Simultaneously increase the RHS coefficients of Example 4.1, increasing the first coefficient at twice the rate of the second up to a maximum increase of 12.0. Give the effect on the optimal objective value and basis changes necessary.

As described in *MBMP*, such a requirement would be specified in the model by a change column

$$
\begin{array}{c}
0 \\
1.0 \\
0.5
\end{array}
\qquad (4.130)
$$

with an upper limit of 12.0 for a parameter θ representing the multiple of (4.130) to be added to the RHS. By other change columns any mixture of simultaneous changes to the RHS could be so considered.

Unlike the objective parametric case it is not usually necessary to add RHS change rows to the original matrix file. They can, with a data structure organised by columns, be updated using the eta file from the original matrix representation.

We begin with the optimal solution to the original model ($\theta = 0$). This is given by the basis list (4.51) and eta file (4.49) applied to the matrix file (4.1). In addition to maintaining the updated solution vector (4.50), we must now update (4.130) by the eta file, giving

$$\begin{vmatrix} 3.667 \\ 0.833 \\ -0.167 \end{vmatrix}. \qquad (4.131)$$

For a general value of θ the new updated solution vector will therefore be

$$\begin{bmatrix} 12.667 + \theta \times 3.667 \\ 2.333 + \theta \times 0.833 \\ 0.333 - \theta \times 0.167 \end{bmatrix}. \qquad (4.132)$$

As θ is increased, the solution values will change according to (4.132). These cannot be allowed to go outside their bounds. In the example a limit is reached when θ becomes 2.0, since the value of x_3 becomes 0. To prevent the solution becoming infeasible we must make a basis change. This is done by bringing a variable into the basis in place of x_3 using row 3 as the pivot row. The variable to be brought into the basis must be chosen so as to prevent any of the reduced costs becoming negative (for variables at lower bound) or positive (for variables at upper bound). In order to make this choice we must update both the objective row using BTRAN and the pivot row (using BTRAN with a "pricing vector" of $[0, 0, 1.0]$). These updated rows are, respectively

$$\begin{array}{cccccc} z & x_1 & x_2 & x_3 & x_4 & x_5 \\ [1.0 & 4.333 & 0 & 0 & 2.333 & 2.667] \end{array} \qquad (4.133)$$

and

$$\begin{array}{cccccc} z & x_1 & x_2 & x_3 & x_4 & x_5 \\ [0 & 0.667 & 0 & 1.0 & -0.333 & 0.333]. \end{array} \qquad (4.134)$$

When a variable is brought into the basis to replace x_3 the pivot step involves adding a multiple Δ of (4.134) to (4.133), giving

$$z \quad\quad x_1 \quad\quad x_2 \quad x_3 \quad\quad x_4 \quad\quad\quad x_5$$
$$[1.0 \quad 4.333 + \Delta \times 0.667 \quad 0 \quad \Delta \quad 2.333 - \Delta \times 0.333 \quad 2.667 + \Delta \times 0.333].$$

$$(4.135)$$

Using the same argument as for objective ranges Δ can only be made as large as $2.333/0.333 = 7.0$ in order to keep all the reduced costs non-negative. Therefore x_4 enters the basis. The new basis list is

$$\boxed{z \mid x_2 \mid x_4} \qquad\qquad (4.136)$$

and solution vector

$$\begin{array}{|c|} \hline 20.0 \\ 4.0 \\ 0 \\ \hline \end{array} .$$

Clearly the basis changes are determined by ratios between the updated pivot row (which is determined first) and the updated objective row. The procedure is the same as in the dual simplex algorithm described in section 2.6. Again, the full details are not given but should be deducible taking into account that non-basic variables may be at lower or upper bounds.

The procedure can now be repeated increasing θ beyond 7.0 until the next basis change up to the limit of 12.0 or until the model becomes infeasible. Exercise 4.18 involves completing this calculation.

In contrast to the objective case the solution (as well as the objective value) changes continuously as θ changes. Exercise 4.19 illustrates this.

4.6 COMPUTATIONAL IMPLEMENTATION OF THE NETWORK FORM OF THE SIMPLEX ALGORITHM

In section 3.1 we showed how, on a network, the simplex algorithm could be visualised in terms of graphical structures. If some of the data structures described in section 1.6 are used, then the computer implementation can be made very efficient. In addition to these considerations there is, of course, virtue in using some of the approaches described in section 4.4, such as multiple pricing. It is generally only worth considering a subset of the arcs that are worth entering the tree at a time. These considerations do not differ from those for the general revised simplex algorithm and are therefore not repeated here.

We will use Example 3.1, illustrated in Figure 3.2, in this section.

Representing a Spanning Tree

It is convenient to order the nodes of a spanning tree with the root node first (number zero). Nodes will be given higher numbers than their predecessors when tracing a path from the root node. Figure 4.3 illustrates this for the second spanning tree of Example 3.1.

Instead of naming the nodes A, B, C, etc., we have numbered them. The correspondence between the original naming and the numbering can, of course, be maintained if necessary by a dictionary.

In order to be able, efficiently, to trace paths through the tree we establish a *predecessor table* of nodes and their predecessors:

Node	0	1	2	3	4	5	6	7
Predecessor	–	0	1	2	3	3	2	1

A path from any node back to the root can then be found by successively finding predecessors.

It is also convenient, for a reason to become apparent below, to be able to know the "depth" of a node in the ordered tree; that is, the number of arcs

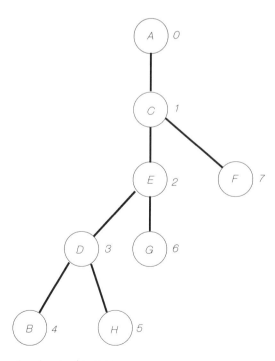

Figure 4.3 An ordered spanning tree

that must be traced from the root in order to reach it. This can also be given by a table:

Node	0	1	2	3	4	5	6	7
Depth	0	1	2	3	4	4	3	2

Finding a Loop

Once we have chosen an arc to enter a tree, using reduced costs, we need to find the loop that is created by adding it to the tree. This can be done by tracing paths from its two endpoints back to the root and finding where they intersect. For Example 3.1, on the second iteration, we added arc CD to the tree. While it is easy to see from Figure 4.3 that this creates the loop CDE, such spatial intuition is denied to the present generation of computers. Instead, we use the predecessor table to trace the (unique) paths back from C and D respectively towards the root A.

By means of the depth table we can compare nodes on these paths when they are at the same depth. To begin with we trace back the path from D (at depth 3) to E (at depth 2) to C (at depth 1) until we are at the same depth as C.

The path from C has therefore joined this path immediately at C, demonstrating the loop made up of DEC and the new arc CD.

Updating the Dual Values

In section 3.1 we updated all dual values after each iteration. In fact, it could be observed that many of the dual values remained unchanged. It is easy to see why this should be so and to reduce the updating necessary. When an arc is deleted from a tree, the tree is split into two separate trees. These are reunited by the new arc introduced. One of the separated subtrees will contain the root node. In this subtree all dual values will remain unchanged. For the other subtree all dual values will be changed by a constant amount equal to the difference between the dual values calculated through this new arc and through the old. We illustrate this again by Example 3.1. On the second iteration CE leaves the tree, creating the two subtrees illustrated in Figure 4.4.

The dual values in the top tree, containing node A, will remain unchanged as shown (comparing with Figure 3.5). Those for the bottom tree will all be increased by 3 since the second tree will now be connected to the first by arc CD (cost 2) instead of CE (cost 6), which combined with the cost of DE of 1 gives the net saving of 3.

The reader should verify that the resultant dual values marked in Figure 4.4 correspond to those of the third spanning tree shown in Figure 3.7.

The efficient identification of the subtrees is more complicated and not described. It is sometimes worth creating extra data structures to facilitate this.

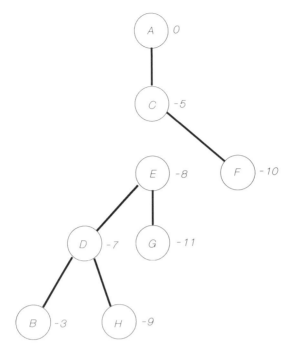

Figure 4.4 Two subtrees created after deleting an arc from a tree

Once an iteration has been completed, the predecessor and depth tables must of course be modified before the procedures are repeated.

4.7 HISTORY, REFERENCES AND FUTURE DEVELOPMENTS

The Revised Simplex Algorithm and Product Form of the Inverse

The development of the simplex algorithm into its revised form for automatic computation is due to many people. In particular, Dantzig and Orchard-Hays (1953) and Beale (1968) played large parts. The oldest book devoted just to computer implementations is Orchard-Hays (1969). A more recent book is Murtagh (1981). Some descriptions of the methods used can be found in manuals associated with commercial LP systems.

Reinverting the Basis Matrix

A vast amount of research has gone into the problem. One of the earliest recognitions of the advantage of triangularising the basis is Markowitz (1957), who suggested the idea of merit numbers for potential pivot elements. An improved method of ordering the nucleus to reduce fill-in is due to Hellerman and Rarick (1971). Duff, Erisma and Reid (1986) discuss the general problem of inverting sparse matrices.

The variant of the product form of the inverse based on Gaussian elimination (L\U decomposition) as opposed to Gauss–Jordan elimination is sometimes known as the eliminant form of the inverse (although it is still a product form) and was suggested by Markowitz (1957).

Maintaining an L\U Inverse Between Iterations

The method described here is due to Forrest and Tomlin (1972). An earlier, different, method that emphasised numerical accuracy as opposed to sparsity is due to Bartels and Golub (1969).

Numerical Considerations

Many of the considerations given here have become "folk-lore" in the industry and are not widely documented. The setting of tolerances is normally the result of experiment rather than theory, as is scaling. Devex is a method of dynamic scaling due to Harris (1973), who used it with great success on the LP models of British Petroleum.

The ideas of tactical refinements are again not widely documented outside commercial (sometimes internal) manuals. Some of them are mentioned in Orchard-Hays (1969), Murtagh (1981) and Chvátal (1983).

The method of ε-perturbation is a rudimentary implementation of the method of lexicographic ordering due to Wolfe (1983).

Crashing and reduction procedures have been considered by Brearley, Mitra and Williams (1978) and the volume edited by Karwan et al. (1983).

Sensitivity Analysis and Parametric Programming

The practical importance and interpretation of this topic is given wide coverage in *MBMP*. Many standard textbooks on LP give the mathematics of the methods.

Computational Implementation of the Network Form of the Simplex Algorithm

Many authors have considered this problem and its special case, the transportation problem. References are given in section 3.4. Dantzig (1951) was one of the first to consider specialising the simplex algorithm. Mulvey (1978) and

Bradley, Brown and Graves (1977) give descriptions of the algorithm. The method of avoiding circling is due to Cunningham and Klincewicz (1983).

4.8 EXERCISES

4.1 Solve the model in exercise 2.7 by the revised simplex algorithm.

4.2 Solve Example 2.12 (with bounded variables) using the revised simplex algorithm.

4.3 For exercises 2.1 represent the Gaussian elimination steps by elementary matrices. Do the same for Gauss–Jordan elimination.

4.4 Consider an LP representation of a minimum-cost network flow model leaving out one (redundant) constraint. Show that the basis matrix corresponding to a spanning tree can be completely triangularised.

4.5 Invert the following matrix in the product form, without triangularising, by pivoting down the main diagonal:

$$\begin{bmatrix} 1.0 & & & & 1.0 \\ 1.0 & 1.0 & & & \\ & 1.0 & 1.0 & & \\ & & 1.0 & 1.0 & \\ & & & 1.0 & 1.0 \end{bmatrix}.$$

4.6 Triangularise the matrix in exercise 4.5 and invert in the product form. Contrast the sparsity of this representation with that for exercise 4.5.

4.7 Give the explicit inverse of the matrix in Example 4.5 and compare its sparsity with the representations in 4.5 and 4.6.

*4.8 If $B = L \times U$, where B is a square non-singular matrix and L and U are triangular and upper unit triangular matrices, show that (i) the sparsity of the conventional product form depends on the sparsity of L and U^{-1} but (ii) the sparsity of the eliminant product form based on L and U depends on the sparsity of L and U.

4.9 Find the eta file corresponding to the inversion of B in Example 4.3 using pivots (4,A), (3,B), (6,C), (7,D), (5,E), (1,F), (2,G) in that order.

4.10 Perform exercise 4.9 using the L\U product form.

4.11 Verify that the row eta vector used to maintain triangularity in iterations between inversions is the row of U^{-1} corresponding to the pivot row.

4.12 For exercise 2.7 take x_1, x_2 and x_3 as a starting basis. Invert the basis in the L\U product form and proceed with the revised simplex algorithm to optimality.

4.13 Find the marginal rates of substitution for variable x_5 in the optimal solution to Example 4.4.

4.14 Calculate the ranges for the second constraint in Example 4.5.

4.15 For Example 1.1 illustrate the interpretation of RHS and objective ranges geometrically.

4.16 For Example 4.6, calculate lower and upper ranges for the objective coefficient of x_3.

4.17 Complete the parametric objective calculation of Example 4.7. Draw graphs to show how the objective and variable values change with θ.

4.18 Complete the parametric RHS calculation of Example 4.8. Draw graphs to show how the objective and variable values change with θ.

4.19 Solve Example 3.1 by the network form of the simplex algorithm, explaining how the predecessor and depth tables would be used and how the dual values could be updated in a computer implementation.

4.20 Calculate the RHS ranges for Example 4.5 using the value function (2.36).

4.21 Calculate the objective ranges for Example 4.6 by considering the dual model illustrated in Figure 2.6.

Chapter 5
Non-Calculus Methods for Non-Linear Programming

There is a distinction between the kinds of model to which optimisation methods based on the calculus are most applicable and those which are considered in this book. The former types of model contain, often complicated, non-linear functions that are differentiable. Then the values of derivatives provide directions for improvement. Constraints are dealt with in a variety of ways, either by incorporating them in the objective function by means of Lagrange multipliers or by restricting the search directions. References to the extensive literature on this branch of optimisation are given in section 5.5.

In contrast, in this book we are more concerned with models in which constraints play the dominant role. It was shown, in Chapter 1, that LP models are *essentially* concerned with inequality systems. As a result, optimal solutions always lie on the boundary of the feasible region. The non-linear programming (NLP) models, with which we will be concerned in this chapter, contain non-linear expressions in the objective function, or constraints, or both, but inequality constraints are still a major feature. Therefore there is virtue in using methods that can be regarded as extensions of LP. NLP models arising in operational research tend to be of this kind, whereas models arising in, say, engineering design are often of the former kind mentioned above.

Another important distinction between different types of NLP models was described in section 1.2, i.e. the distinction between *convex* and *non-convex* models. The calculus-based methods rely on moving in directions of local improvement and will only obtain local optima. These will, of course, be global optima if models are convex. The method that we describe in section 5.1 also only guarantees local optima for non-convex models. It can, however, be extended by means of *integer programming* (IP), as described in sections 5.3 and 7.3, to provide *global optima*.

Although the methods described here do not use the calculus, algorithmically it is possible to combine the classical calculus conditions for optimality with those of duality to give sufficient conditions for local optimality of an NLP. This is done in section 5.4. For general NLPs this is of little algorithmic value. The conditions can, however, be exploited to give a method (linear complementarity) for solving quadratic (and linear) programming models.

5.1 SEPARABLE MODELS

A *separable function* is a function that can be expressed as the sum of functions of *single variables*. For example, the function $5x_1^3 - 14x_1^2 + 11x_1 + 2x_2$, which appears in a constraint of Example 1.9, is separable since the non-linear terms are each functions of one variable. In contrast, the functions $x_1/(1 + x_2)$, x_1x_2 and $x_1 \sin x_2 + x_1^{x_3}$ are not separable, as the non-linear expressions each involve more than one variable. Nevertheless, it is often possible to transform non-separable functions into a separable form, by introducing new variables and constraints. This is described in *MBMP*.

A *separable model* is an NLP model in which all the non-linear expressions, occurring in the objective or constraints, or both, are separable functions.

In order to deal with these non-linearities, we carry out the following transformations:

(i) Each non-linear expression is replaced by a single variable.
(ii) The non-linear relationships between the newly introduced variables and the single variables, of which they are non-linear functions, is modelled.

The transformation (ii) involves making a *piecewise-linear* approximation to the non-linear functions. This is illustrated by reconsidering Example 1.9 from Chapter 1.

Example 5.1 *Making Piecewise-Linear Approximations to Non-Linear Functions*
Make piecewise-linear approximations to the non-linear expressions in

$$\text{Maximise} \quad 2x_1 + 3x_2 \tag{5.1}$$

subject to

$$-x_1 + 4x_2 \geqslant 2 \tag{5.2}$$

$$5x_1^3 - 14x_1^2 + 11x_1 + 2x_2 \leqslant 8 \tag{5.3}$$

$$4x_1 - 4x_2^2 + 20x_2 \leqslant 29 \tag{5.4}$$

$$x_1, x_2 \geqslant 0. \tag{5.5}$$

We could replace either the non-linear function $5x_1^3 - 14x_1^2$ by a new variable or the whole function $5x_1^3 - 14x_1^2 + 11x_1$ by a new variable. It is convenient to do the latter, replacing it by the new variable y, as this results in smaller values of y over the range of values of x_1 being considered. Since our non-linear function is of a single variable, we can represent the relationship between x_1 and y graphically, as is done in Figure 5.1.

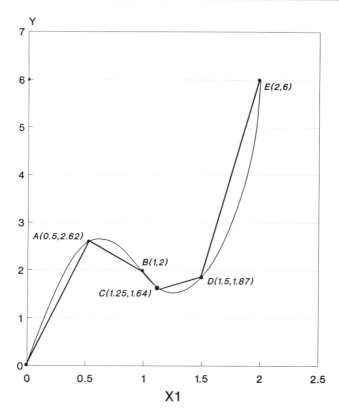

Figure 5.1 Piecewise-linear approximation to a non-linear function
$y = 5x_1^3 - 14x_1^2 + 11x_1$

We need only consider the graph for relevant values of x_1. Note that generally there is no reason why the new variable y should be non-negative. This must therefore be regarded as a free variable and allowed to take negative values if necessary.

The relationship between x_1 and y is modelled indirectly through new variables $\lambda_0, \lambda_1, \lambda_2$, etc. These can be interpreted as "weights" to be given to vertices O, A, B, C, etc., in the (very coarse) piecewise-linear approximation of the curve shown in Figure 5.1.

We model the relationships between x_1 and y, etc., by the equations

$$x_1 = 0\lambda_0 + 0.5\lambda_1 + 1\lambda_2 + 1.25\lambda_3 + 1.5\lambda_4 + 2\lambda_5 \tag{5.6}$$

$$y = 0\lambda_0 + 2.62\lambda_1 + 2\lambda_2 + 1.64\lambda_3 + 1.87\lambda_4 + 6\lambda_5 \tag{5.7}$$

$$\lambda_0 + \lambda_1 + \lambda_2 + \lambda_3 + \lambda_4 + \lambda_5 = 1 \tag{5.8}$$

$$\lambda_0, \lambda_1, \lambda_2, \lambda_3, \lambda_4, \lambda_5 \geqslant 0. \tag{5.9}$$

Notice that the λ coefficients in (5.6) are the x_1 coordinates of the vertices and the λ coefficients in (5.7) are the y coordinates of the vertices.

In addition, we must impose the following "qualitative" constraint:

at most two adjacent λ's can be non-zero. (5.10)

This last constraint was also mentioned in section 1.3 and referred to as a special ordered set of type 2 (SOS2). It calls for an extra algorithmic treatment, which is discussed in section 5.2 and section 7.3. For the present we will assume that we can deal with it. It should be apparent that constraints (5.6) to (5.10) model a piecewise-linear relationship between x_1 and y. If, for example, $x_1 = 0.25$, we would have $\lambda_0 = \lambda_1 = 0.5$, giving $y = 1.31$ (the point halfway between O and A), in contrast to the true value of $y = 5x_1^3 - 14x_1^2 + 11x_1 = 1.95$. Clearly with such a coarse grid there is great inaccuracy in the approximation.

Notice that there is no need to have a uniform grid. We have chosen to have an x_1 grid of 0.5 except between 1 and 1.5, when the curvature seems to merit a more refined grid. It is possible to refine the grid in the region of the optimum, when discovered, in order to reduce inaccuracy. In some algorithmic methods it is possible to do this automatically.

The above type of formulation is known as a "λ-formulation". There is an alternative method known as the "δ-formulation". Both of these are discussed at greater depth in *MBMP*.

Similarly we can represent the non-linear expression $-4x_2^2 + 20x_2$ by a variable w. Making a piecewise-linear approximation to the curve results in the equations

$$x_2 = 0\mu_0 + 1\mu_1 + 2\mu_2 + 3\mu_3 + 4\mu_4 \qquad (5.11)$$

$$w = 0\mu_0 + 16\mu_1 + 24\mu_2 + 24\mu_3 + 16\mu_4 \qquad (5.12)$$

$$\mu_0 + \mu_1 + \mu_2 + \mu_3 + \mu_4 = 1 \qquad (5.13)$$

and the condition:

at most two adjacent μ's can be non-zero. (5.14)

Since the original model only contained two variables (x_1 and x_2) we can draw the piecewise-linear approximation to the feasible region resulting from this formulation in Figure 5.2. It should be compared with Figure 1.7. For general models we would not, of course, be able to obtain such geometrical intuition.

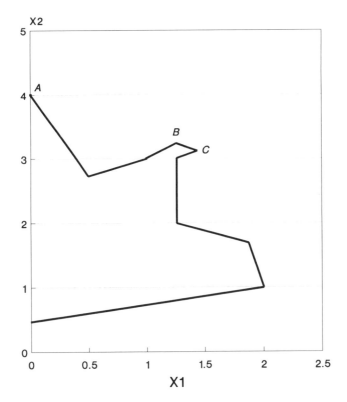

Figure 5.2   Piecewise-linear approximation to a non-convex region

5.2 SEPARABLE PROGRAMMING FOR LOCAL OPTIMA

Separable programming involves a restricted form of the simplex algorithm. In order to maintain the constraints (5.10) and (5.14), we do not allow a variable λ_i to enter the basis if it would violate this condition. Similarly we also do this for the μ_i. This is demonstrated by taking the piecewise-linear approximation to Example 5.1.

Example 5.2 Solving a Separable Programming Model
Solve the following model by the separable programming variant of the simplex algorithm:

$$\text{Maximise} \quad 2x_1 + 3x_2 \tag{5.15}$$

subject to

$$-x_1 + 4x_2 \geqslant 2 \qquad (5.16)$$

$$2x_2 + y \leqslant 8 \qquad (5.17)$$

$$4x_1 + w \leqslant 29 \qquad (5.18)$$

$$-x_1 + 0.5\lambda_1 + \lambda_2 + 1.25\lambda_3 + 1.5\lambda_4 + 2\lambda_5 = 0 \qquad (5.19)$$

$$-y + 2.62\lambda_1 + 2\lambda_2 + 1.64\lambda_3 + 1.87\lambda_4 + 6\lambda_5 = 0 \qquad (5.20)$$

$$-x_2 + \mu_1 + 2\mu_2 + 3\mu_3 + 4\mu_4 = 0 \qquad (5.21)$$

$$-w + 16\mu_1 + 24\mu_2 + 24\mu_3 + 16\mu_4 = 0 \qquad (5.22)$$

$$\lambda_0 + \lambda_1 + \lambda_2 + \lambda_3 + \lambda_4 + \lambda_5 = 1 \qquad (5.23)$$

$$\mu_0 + \mu_1 + \mu_2 + \mu_3 + \mu_4 = 1 \qquad (5.24)$$

$$x_1, x_2, \lambda_0, \lambda_1, \lambda_2, \ldots, \lambda_5, \mu_0, \mu_1, \ldots, \mu_4 \geqslant 0 \qquad (5.25)$$

$$\{\lambda_0, \lambda_1, \ldots, \lambda_5\} \quad \text{and} \quad \{\mu_0, \mu_1, \ldots, \mu_4\} \text{ are SOS2 sets.} \qquad (5.26)$$

We introduce a surplus variable x_3 into constraint (5.16), slack variables x_4 and x_5 into constraints (5.17) and (5.18), and artificial variables x_6, x_7, x_8 and x_9 into constraints (5.19) to (5.22). For simplicity, we treat λ_0 and μ_0 as the slack variables in constraints (5.23) and (5.24). z represents the objective function (5.15).

Step 0 We choose the logical starting basis

$$z, x_3, x_4, x_5, x_6, x_7, x_8, x_9, \lambda_0, \mu_0.$$

Step 1 The equations are written as

$$z = 8 - 2x_1 - 3x_2 \qquad (5.27)$$

$$x_3 = -2 - x_1 + 4x_2 \qquad (5.28)$$

$$x_4 = 8 - 2x_2 - y \qquad (5.29)$$

$$x_5 = 29 - 4x_1 - w \qquad (5.30)$$

$$x_6 = 0 + x_1 - 0.5\lambda_1 - \lambda_2 - 1.25\lambda_3 - 1.5\lambda_4 - 2\lambda_5 \qquad (5.31)$$

$$x_7 = 0 + y + 2.62\lambda_1 - 2\lambda_2 - 1.64\lambda_3 - 1.87\lambda_4 - 6\lambda_5 \qquad (5.32)$$

$$x_8 = 0 + x_2 - \mu_1 - 2\mu_2 - 3\mu_3 - 4\mu_4 \qquad (5.33)$$

$$x_9 = 0 + w - 16\mu_1 - 24\mu_2 - 24\mu_3 - 16\mu_4 \qquad (5.34)$$

$$\lambda_0 = 1 - \lambda_1 - \lambda_2 - \lambda_3 - \lambda_4 - \lambda_5 \qquad (5.35)$$

$$\mu_0 = 1 - \mu_1 - \mu_2 - \mu_3 - \mu_4. \qquad (5.36)$$

We set the non-basic variables to their finite lower bounds of 0 as well as y and w to 0, giving an infeasible basic solution ($x_3 = -2$).

We omit the detailed calculations. It can be verified that if we solved this model by the simplex algorithm ignoring conditions (5.26) we would obtain the "optimal" solution:

$$x_1 = 1.5, \quad x_2 = 3.065, \quad y = 1.87, \quad w = 12.32, \quad \lambda_4 = 0, \quad \mu_0 = 0.23,$$
$$\mu_4 = 0.77, \quad \text{objective} = 12.26 \quad (5.37)$$

This solution can be seen (by reference to Figure 5.2) to be (just) infeasible. It is because we have the non-adjacent variables μ_0 and μ_4 taking non-zero values that we have obtained a spurious representation of the non-linear function $w = -4x_2^2 + 20x_2$.

Instead, we will carry out the steps of the simplex algorithm but restrict entry of the λ and μ variables into the basis so that if one member of (say) the λ set is in the basis only a neighbouring λ will be allowed to enter. If two neighbouring λ's are in the basis, no others will be allowed in. Similar restrictions will apply to the μ set. We could relax this restriction somewhat to allow another member of a set into the basis if the outgoing basic variable is the member of the set, which results in there still being only two adjacent members in the basis. In a computational implementation of the method this would require more work and is therefore not usually done.

For our example we apply this restricted simplex algorithm and eventually obtain (leaving out artificial variables) the set of equations

$$z = 12 + 1.24\lambda_2 + 1.87\lambda_3 + 2.29\lambda_4 + 1.71\lambda_5 - 6.71\mu_1$$
$$- 4.47\mu_2 - 2.24\mu_3 - 0.38x_4 + 8.95\mu_0 \quad (5.38)$$

$$\mu_4 = 1 - \mu_1 - \mu_2 - \mu_3 - \mu_4 - \mu_0 \quad (5.39)$$

$$x_5 = 13 - 2.47\lambda_2 - 3.75\lambda_3 - 4.57\lambda_4 - 3.42\lambda_5 - 4.58\mu_1$$
$$- 11.05\mu_2 - 9.53\mu_3 + 0.76x_4 + 9.9\mu_0 \quad (5.40)$$

$$y = 0 + 6\mu_1 + 4\mu_2 + 2\mu_3 - x_4 + 8\mu_0 \quad (5.41)$$

$$x_3 = 14 + 0.62\lambda_2 - 0.94\lambda_3 - 1.14\lambda_4 - 0.85\lambda_5 - 13.14\mu_1$$
$$- 8.76\mu_2 - 4.38\mu_3 + 1.19x_4 - 17.53\mu_0 \quad (5.42)$$

$$\lambda_1 = 0 - 0.76\lambda_2 - 0.63\lambda_3 - 0.71\lambda_4 - 2.29\lambda_5 + 2.29\mu_1$$
$$+ 1.53\mu_2 + 0.76\mu_3 + 0.38\mu_4 + 3.08\mu_0 \quad (5.43)$$

$$x_1 = 0 + 0.62\lambda_2 + 0.94\lambda_3 + 1.14\lambda_4 + 0.85\lambda_5 + 1.14\mu_1$$
$$+ 0.76\mu_2 + 0.38\mu_3 + 0.19\mu_4 - 3.08\mu_0 \quad (5.44)$$

$$\lambda_0 = 1 - 0.24\lambda_2 - 0.37\lambda_3 - 0.29\lambda_4 + 1.29\lambda_5 - 2.29\mu_1$$
$$- 1.53\mu_2 - 0.76\mu_3 + 0.38\mu_4 \quad (5.45)$$

$$x_2 = 4 + 3\mu_1 + 2\mu_2 - \mu_3 - 4\mu_0 \quad (5.46)$$

$$w = 16 + 8\mu_1 + 8\mu_2 - 16\mu_0. \quad (5.47)$$

These equations correspond to the solution:

$$x_1 = 0, \quad x_2 = 4, \quad y = 0, \quad w = 16, \quad \lambda_0 = 1, \quad \mu_4 = 1, \quad \text{objective} = 12.$$
$$(5.48)$$

Notice that λ_0 and λ_1 are in the basis, as is μ_4. In the unrestricted simplex algorithm any of λ_2, λ_4, λ_5 and μ_0 are candidates to enter the basis. By our restriction, however, none is allowed to enter since conditions (5.10) or (5.14) would be broken by so doing. Therefore the algorithm terminates at this point. We have clearly obtained the solution at A in Figures 1.7 and 5.2. This is a *local optimum*. In order to move from this position (and remain feasible) we would have to bring μ_3 into the basis, but this would degrade the objective.

The *global optimum* (to the piecewise-linear approximation) is, in fact, given by the point C where

$$x_1 = 1.44, \quad x_2 = 3.09, \quad \lambda_3 = 0.25, \quad \lambda_4 = 0.75,$$
$$\mu_3 = 0.91, \quad \mu_4 = 0.09, \quad \text{objective} = 12.16. \quad (5.49)$$

This approximate optimal solution should be compared with that given in section 1.2. Inaccuracies arise because of the piecewise-linear approximation. It can be verified that this gives $y = 5x_1^3 - 14x_1^2 + 11x_1$ a value of 1.81 as opposed to its true value of 1.74 and $w = -4x_2^2 + 20x_2$ a value of 23.29 as opposed to its value of 23.62. A more refined grid could be used to reduce these errors.

The global optimum might, in practice, be found by using different starting bases to achieve different local optima, then choosing the best. This is the subject of exercise 5.6. A systematic search for the global optimum does, however, require integer programming and is discussed in section 7.3.

Another difficulty with separable programming is that a local (infeasible) "optimum" may be found in phase I of the restricted simplex algorithm, i.e. it may prove impossible to find a feasible starting basis. Such a solution will, in practice, be useless.

For convex models, none of these problems arise. It is not necessary to restrict the simplex algorithm since the conditions of the form (5.10) will be satisfied automatically. Exercises 5.1 and 5.2 illustrate this.

5.3 CONVERSION OF NON-LINEAR SEPARABLE MODELS TO INTEGER PROGRAMMES

In the previous section we dealt with the constraints (5.10) and (5.14) by restricting the basis entry in the simplex algorithm. This, however, has the disadvantage that local optima may be produced. There is an alternative algorithmic approach using the branch-and-bound algorithm that guarantees a global optimum, usually at greater computational cost. The set of variables $\lambda_0, \lambda_1, \ldots$, etc., known as an SOS2, is treated as an entity akin to an integer variable. This approach is described in section 7.3 as the method in essentially one of IP.

Constraint (5.10) can, however, be formulated explicitly by means of an IP model. This is done by

$$\lambda_0 - \delta_1 \leqslant 0 \tag{5.50}$$

$$\lambda_1 - \delta_1 - \delta_2 \leqslant 0 \tag{5.51}$$

$$\lambda_2 - \delta_2 - \delta_3 \leqslant 0 \tag{5.52}$$

$$\lambda_3 - \delta_3 - \delta_4 \leqslant 0 \tag{5.53}$$

$$\lambda_4 - \delta_4 - \delta_5 \leqslant 0 \tag{5.54}$$

$$\lambda_5 - \delta_5 \leqslant 0 \tag{5.55}$$

$$\delta_1 + \delta_2 + \delta_3 + \delta_4 + \delta_5 = 1 \tag{5.56}$$

$$0 \leqslant \delta_1, \delta_2, \delta_3, \delta_4, \delta_5 \leqslant 1 \quad \text{and integer.} \tag{5.57}$$

General methods for solving IP models as described in Chapter 6 can then be applied.

5.4 CONDITIONS FOR LOCAL OPTIMALITY

In section 2.5 it was shown that if we have feasible solutions to both a primal LP model and its dual which are orthogonal (complementary), then this is a sufficient condition for optimality. This result can be extended to NLP models if the non-linear functions are differentiable. We define a general primal NLP in the form

$$\text{Maximise} \quad f(x_1, x_2, \ldots, x_n) \tag{5.58}$$

subject to

$$g_i(x_1, x_2, \ldots, x_n) \leqslant b_i \tag{5.59}$$

$$x_1, x_2, \ldots, x_n \geqslant 0 \tag{5.60}$$

where f and g_i are functions that may be non-linear.

Clearly any NLP can be converted into this standard form in a similar fashion to LPs.

The dual model is defined as

$$\text{Minimise} \quad b_1 y_1 + b_2 y_2 + \cdots + b_m y_m \tag{5.61}$$

subject to

$$y_1 \frac{\partial g_1}{\partial x_1} + y_2 \frac{\partial g_2}{\partial x_1} + \cdots + y_m \frac{\partial g_m}{\partial x_1} \geqslant \frac{\partial f}{\partial x_1} \tag{5.62}$$

$$y_1 \frac{\partial g_1}{\partial x_2} + y_2 \frac{\partial g_2}{\partial x_2} + \cdots + y_m \frac{\partial g_m}{\partial x_2} \geqslant \frac{\partial f}{\partial x_2} \tag{5.63}$$

$$\vdots$$

$$y_1 \frac{\partial g_1}{\partial x_n} + y_2 \frac{\partial g_2}{\partial x_n} + \cdots + y_m \frac{\partial g_m}{\partial x_n} \geqslant \frac{\partial f}{\partial x_n} \tag{5.64}$$

$$y_1, y_2, \ldots, y_m \geqslant 0. \tag{5.65}$$

It is easy to verify that this reduces to the LP dual if f and g_i are all linear expressions.

As with LP there is an alternative representation of the dual with equality constraints. This arises if we consider the constraints (5.60) to be incorporated among (5.59). The multipliers associated with them (the surplus variables needed for (5.62) to (5.64)) get included in y_1 to y_m, making (5.62) to (5.64) equations. This equality representation of the dual is quite common since some of the variables may not be required to be non-negative.

The optimal solution to (5.61) provides a strict (attainable) upper bound for (5.58) in the *neighbourhood* of a *local optimum*. That is, the objective value cannot increase for small variations in the solution. We do not prove the results. Feasible solutions to both the primal and the dual which are orthogonal are sufficient conditions for local optimality. These conditions can be summarised as:

(i) $g_i(x) \leqslant b_i \qquad i = 1, 2, \ldots, m$ \qquad (5.66)

(ii) $\displaystyle\sum_{i=1}^{m} y_i \frac{\partial g_i}{\partial x_j} \geqslant \frac{\partial f}{\partial x_j} \qquad j = 1, 2, \ldots, n$ \qquad (5.67)

(iii) $\displaystyle\sum_{i=1}^{m} y_i [b_i - g_i(x)] = 0$ \qquad (5.68)

(iv) $\displaystyle\sum_{j=1}^{n} x_j \left(\sum_{i=1}^{m} y_i \frac{\partial g_i}{\partial x_j} - \frac{\partial f}{\partial x_j} \right) = 0$ \qquad (5.69)

(v) $x_j \geqslant 0 \qquad j = 1, 2, \ldots, n$ \qquad (5.70)

(vi) $y_i \geqslant 0 \qquad i = 1, 2, \ldots, m.$ \qquad (5.71)

They are known as the Kuhn–Tucker conditions and are illustrated and interpreted by reconsidering Example 1.8 in standard form.

Example 5.3 Kuhn–Tucker Conditions for Local Optimality
Find sufficient conditions for optimality of

$$\text{Maximise} \quad 2x_1 + 3x_2 \tag{5.72}$$

subject to

$$6x_1 + x_2^2 - x_2 \leqslant 12 \tag{5.73}$$

$$x_1 - 4x_2 \leqslant -2 \tag{5.74}$$

$$x_1, x_2 \geqslant 0. \tag{5.75}$$

Conditions (5.67)–(5.69) and (5.71) give

$$6y_1 + y_2 \geqslant 2 \tag{5.76}$$

$$(2x_2 - 1)y_1 - 4y_2 \geqslant 3 \tag{5.77}$$

$$y_1(12 - 6x_1 - x_2^2 + x_2) + y_2(-2 - x_1 + 4x_2) = 0 \tag{5.78}$$

$$x_1(6y_1 + y_2 - 2) + x_2[(2x_2 - 1)y_1 - 4y_2 - 3] = 0 \tag{5.79}$$

$$y_1, y_2 \geqslant 0 \tag{5.80}$$

which together with (5.73), (5.74) and (5.75) make up the sufficient conditions.

The optimal solution (by reference to Figure 1.6) is $x_1 = 0$, $x_2 = 4$, which taken with $y_1 = 3/7$, $y_2 = 0$ can be verified to satisfy (5.72) to (5.80). It is useful to name y_3 and y_4 as the surplus variables in constraints (5.76) and (5.77), which therefore take values of $4/7$ and 0 respectively. Constraints (5.72) and "$x_1 \geqslant 0$" are clearly binding at A in Figure 1.6 and have associated positive multipliers y_1 and y_3 while (5.73) and "$x_2 \geqslant 0$" are nonbinding with zero multipliers. Recalling the geometrical interpretation of duality in section 2.5, constraints (5.76) and (5.77) are equivalent to specifying that the bound on the objective function arises from a nonnegative combination of the binding tangent constraint at A and "$x_1 \geqslant 0$".

In order to illustrate that the Kuhn–Tucker conditions are sufficient for only a local optimum, we also consider Example 1.9 in standard form.

Example 5.4 Kuhn–Tucker Conditions and Local Optima
Find sufficient conditions for a local optimum of

$$\text{Maximise} \quad 2x_1 + 3x_2 \tag{5.81}$$

subject to

$$x_1 - 4x_2 \leqslant -2 \qquad (5.82)$$

$$5x_1^3 - 14x_1^2 + 11x_1 + 2x_2 \leqslant 8 \qquad (5.83)$$

$$4x_1 - 4x_2^2 + 20x_2 \leqslant 29 \qquad (5.84)$$

$$x_1, x_2, x_3 \geqslant 0. \qquad (5.85)$$

The conditions (together with (5.81) to (5.85)) are

$$y_1 + (15x_1^2 - 28x_1 + 11)y_2 + 4y_3 \geqslant 2 \qquad (5.86)$$

$$-4y_1 + 2y_2 + (-8x_2 + 20)y_3 \geqslant 3 \qquad (5.87)$$

$$y_1(-2 - x_1 + 4x_2) + y_2(8 - 5x_1^3 + 14x_1^2 - 11x_1 - 2x_2)$$
$$+ y_3(29 - 4x_1 + 4x_2^2 - 20x_2) = 0 \qquad (5.88)$$

$$x_1[y_1 + (15x_1^2 - 28x_1 + 11)y_2 + 4y_3 - 2]$$
$$+ x_2[-4y_1 + 2y_2 + (-8x_2 + 20)y_3 - 3] = 0 \qquad (5.89)$$

$$y_1, y_2, y_3 \geqslant 0. \qquad (5.90)$$

Taking $x_1 = 0$, $x_2 = 4$, $y_1 = 0$, $y_2 = 1.5$ and $y_3 = 0$, it can be verified that the solution at A in Figure 1.7 is a local optimum.

The better solution $x_1 = 1.41$, $x_2 = 3.16$, $y_1 = 0$, $y_2 = 1.5$ and $y_3 = 0$ also satisfies the conditions and is a local optimum. This solution occurs where the objective contour is tangential to the boundary at B in Figure 1.7.

Hence we cannot use these conditions to verify if a solution is globally optimal except when a model is known to be convex.

Another difficulty can arise with non-convex models, which demonstrates that while these conditions are *sufficient* for a local optimum they are not *necessary*. The situation is somewhat pathological and is illustrated by an example.

Example 5.5 Non-Necessity of the Kuhn–Tucker Conditions
Demonstrate that the Kuhn–Tucker conditions are not satisfied at the optimal solution to

$$\text{Maximise} \quad x_1 \qquad (5.91)$$

subject to

$$(x_1 - 1)^3 + x_2 \leqslant 0 \qquad (5.92)$$

$$x_1, x_2 \geqslant 0. \qquad (5.93)$$

The model is illustrated in Figure 5.3.

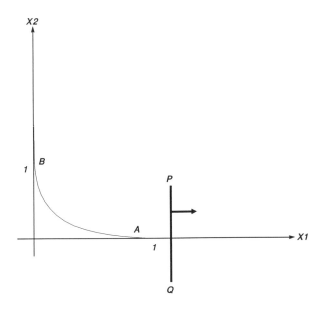

Figure 5.3 Non-necessity of Kuhn–Tucker conditions

This demonstrates that the optimal solution at A is

$$x_1 = 1, \quad x_2 = 0, \quad \text{objective} = 1. \tag{5.94}$$

If the dual variable associated with (5.92) is y, the first Kuhn–Tucker condition (5.67) gives

$$3y(x_1 - 1)^2 \geqslant 1. \tag{5.95}$$

This clearly cannot be satisfied by any value of y when $x_1 = 1$.

The difficulty arises because of the "cusp" shape of the feasible region at A. Both the tangent to the binding constraint (5.92) and the binding constraint "$x_2 \geqslant 0$" are represented by line OA, which is orthogonal to the objective lines parallel to PQ. Therefore no line parallel to PQ can be expressed as a positive combination of them and the conditions cannot be met.

This situation obviously can only arise with non-convex models when the conditions would only be sufficient for a local optimum anyway.

A *quadratic programme* is usually referred to as one in which the constraints are all linear but the objective function is quadratic. In such a case the Kuhn–Tucker conditions take an especially simple form. All the conditions give rise to linear constraints, apart from the orthogonality conditions. This is illustrated by an example. Notice that in this example the non-linear function is not separable (although it is comparatively easy so to transform it, by methods described in *MBMP* and is the subject of exercise 5.13).

Example 5.6 A Quadratic Programme
Find sufficient conditions for local optimality of

$$\text{Maximise} \quad -4x_1^2 - 2x_2^2 + 4x_1x_2 + 7x_1 \tag{5.96}$$

subject to

$$x_1 + x_2 \leqslant 4 \tag{5.97}$$

$$2x_1 + x_2 \leqslant 5 \tag{5.98}$$

$$x_1 - 4x_2 \leqslant -2 \tag{5.99}$$

$$x_1, x_2 \geqslant 0. \tag{5.100}$$

The negated objective function (which would be minimised) for this example is, in fact, convex. This can be seen by writing it in the form $(2x_1 - x_2)^2 + x_2^2 - 7x_1$ where all the "square terms" have positive coefficients. Therefore satisfaction of the Kuhn–Tucker conditions will, for this example, guarantee global optimality.

It is convenient, in this application, to specify the slack variables x_3, x_4 and x_5 in constraints (5.97) to (5.99) and to include surplus variables y_4 and y_5 together with the variables y_1, y_2 and y_3 for the dual. Conditions (5.66) to (5.71) can then be written as

$$x_1 + x_2 + x_3 = 4 \tag{5.101}$$

$$2x_1 + x_2 + x_4 = 5 \tag{5.102}$$

$$x_1 - 4x_2 + x_5 = -2 \tag{5.103}$$

$$y_1 + 2y_2 + y_3 - y_4 = -8x_1 + 4x_2 + 7 \tag{5.104}$$

$$y_1 + y_2 - 4y_3 - y_5 = 4x_1 - 4x_2 \tag{5.105}$$

$$y_1x_3 + y_2x_4 + y_3x_5 + y_4x_1 + y_5x_2 = 0 \tag{5.106}$$

$$x_1, x_2, x_3, x_4, x_5 \geqslant 0 \tag{5.107}$$

$$y_1, y_2, y_3, y_4, y_5 \geqslant 0. \tag{5.108}$$

Notice that the orthogonality conditions (5.68) and (5.69) have been combined into one equation for convenience.

This form of model, in which we have a set of linear constraints with an orthogonality condition among the variables, is known as a linear complementarity problem. There exists a special algorithm for finding a (local) solution, which is referenced in section 5.5.

5.5 HISTORY, REFERENCES AND FUTURE DEVELOPMENTS

There is an extensive literature on "traditional" methods of non-linear optimisation. Two standard books are Powell (1981) and Fletcher (1987).

Separable Models

A number of ways of converting non-linear expressions into the form required by a separable programming model are described in *MBMP*. In fact, almost any non-linear function can, in principle, be so converted with suitable ingenuity. There is a generalisation of separable functions to involve more than one variable. This is due to Beale (1980). It involves extending the idea of a grid to more dimensions and is described in *MBMP*.

Separable Programming for Local Optima

The idea of restricting the simplex algorithm to deal with separable models is due to Miller (1963). Although a "cheap" way of solving such models, the disadvantage of obtaining local optima for non-convex models has meant that it has largely been superseded by IP methods. The alternative "δ-formulation" of a separable model as described in *MBMP* is also amenable to a restricted version of the (bounded-variable) simplex algorithm.

It should be pointed out that it may be possible to model non-linear functions in more than one way using SOS2. If, for example, the two non-linear expressions in Example 5.1 could be combined, then a piecewise-linear approximation could be made with a single SOS2. Ignoring this SOS2 condition would result in a model where the piecewise-linear approximation to the feasible region in Figure 1.7 was replaced by its convex hull. Solving by the unrestricted simplex algorithm would produce the optimal solution. This forms the subject of exercise 5.9. Modelling in such a "global" fashion may be impracticable. Further discussion is beyond the scope of this book, but is discussed by Jeroslow (1989).

Conversion of Non-Linear Separable Models to Integer Programmes

The formulation of the SOS2 condition by means of 0–1 integer variables is given in Dantzig (1963). Alternative formulations are possible for this "logical" condition in both the λ and δ forms.

Conditions for Local Optimality

These are usually regarded as due to Kuhn and Tucker (1951), but were derived by Karush (1939).

The representation of linear and quadratic programmes as linear complementarity problems allows the algorithm of Lemke (1970) to be used.

5.6 EXERCISES

5.1 Formulate and solve Example 1.8 as a separable programming model. Observe that the SOS2 condition is satisfied without restricting the simplex algorithm.

5.2 Formulate and solve Example 1.11 by making a piecewise-linear approximation. Observe that it is not necessary to restrict the simplex algorithm.

5.3 Solve exercise 5.2 using the δ-formulation (see *MBMP*).

5.4 Formulate and solve Example 1.12 by making a piecewise-linear approximation. Interpret your solution geometrically in relation to Figure 1.12.

5.5 Convert the following model into a separable form (see *MBMP*) and solve it by separable programming:

$$\text{Minimise} \quad x_1 x_2 + \frac{x_2}{1 + x_1} + x_3$$

subject to

$$x_1 + x_2 + x_3 \geqslant 2$$
$$x_1 + x_2 \leqslant 1$$
$$x_1, x_2, x_3 \geqslant 0.$$

5.6 By means of a computer program, solve Example 5.2 from different starting bases in order to try to obtain a global optimum.

5.7 Refine the grid for Example 5.2 in the region of the global optimum and resolve, by means of a computer program, in order to obtain a more accurate solution.

5.8 Solve Example 1.16 by separable programming to obtain a, possibly local, optimum. Interpret your solution in relation to Figure 1.14.

5.9 Model the feasible set for Example 5.1 by *one* piecewise-linear function and solve by the (unrestricted) simplex algorithm.

5.10 Write down sufficient conditions for a local optimum for Example 1.10. Demonstrate that the local optima given in Figure 1.9 satisfy these conditions.

5.11 Convert Example 5.6 into a separable model using methods given in *MBMP*. Solve this model by the simplex algorithm. Is it necessary to restrict the simplex algorithm? Check that your answer satisfies the conditions derived for Example 5.6.

Chapter 6
General Methods for Integer Programming

The simplex algorithm has proved to be an almost universally powerful method of solving LP models irrespective of their structure or size. It and its extensions have been used for over 40 years, although recently the method of projective transformations has become a competitor. In contrast, for IP, no universally powerful method has emerged. From the considerations of computational complexity discussed in section 1.7, this may not seem surprising. Therefore, one sometimes needs to use specialist IP algorithms that exploit the structure of particular types of model. Some such methods are considered in Chapter 8. It is, however, possible to solve a large number of general mixed integer programming (MIP) models by a method known as *branch and bound*. This method is explained in section 6.2. It can be regarded as a framework (therefore we use the term "method" rather than algorithm) within which specialist and heuristic methods can sometimes be incorporated. In this chapter we will describe a specific version of the method. This version begins by solving the LP model associated with an IP model. This is known as the *LP relaxation*. It can happen that this model itself gives integral solutions, obviating the need for further investigation. Model structures where this can happen are important to recognise and are discussed in section 6.1.

Although this book is mainly concerned with algorithmic methods, rather than modelling, it is difficult entirely to distinguish the two with regard to IP. It is sometimes possible to model in order to obtain the integrality property mentioned above, or to be "closer" to a model in which this happens. This is discussed in sections 6.3 and 6.4 but at greater length in *MBMP*.

6.1 TOTAL UNIMODULARITY AND THE INTEGRALITY PROPERTY

There is an important class of practical models for which the LP relaxation will automatically produce an integer optimal solution. This class contains the minimum-cost network flow and the maximum network flow models. The specialisation of the simplex algorithm described in section 3.1 for solving these models could be implemented in all-integer arithmetic. Therefore, if all external flows and capacities are integral, there will be an integral optimal solution. (In the case of alternative solutions there will be integral optimal vertex solutions among the alternatives.) Since the assignment and shortest-path problems discussed in sections 3.2 and 3.3 can be regarded as special cases, the property also applies to them. It will also apply to models where the *dual* model takes one of these forms.

Recognising, in general, when the integrality property holds is computationally difficult and may not be worth while. It is, however, often possible to recognise a network flow model. Methods of doing this, and of attempting to convert models to this form, are given in *MBMP*. There is a larger class of models for which the integrality property holds for all integer right-hand sides (and bounds) and any objective function. The matrices associated with these models are known as *totally unimodular*. It can be shown that all square submatrices of them must have determinant 0 or ±1. Such matrices can always be "decomposed" into submatrices that are MCNF matrices and their transposes, and the following "special" matrices:

$$\begin{bmatrix} 1 & -1 & 0 & 0 & -1 \\ -1 & 1 & -1 & 0 & 0 \\ 0 & -1 & 1 & -1 & 0 \\ 0 & 0 & -1 & 1 & -1 \\ -1 & 0 & 0 & -1 & 1 \end{bmatrix} \quad \begin{bmatrix} 1 & 1 & 1 & 1 & 1 \\ 1 & 1 & 1 & 0 & 0 \\ 1 & 0 & 1 & 1 & 0 \\ 1 & 0 & 0 & 1 & 1 \\ 1 & 1 & 0 & 0 & 1 \end{bmatrix}. \quad (6.1)$$

References to these results and methods of determining total unimodularity are given in section 6.6.

It is theoretically always possible to reformulate an IP model so that the constraints define the *convex hull* of feasible integer solutions. This is discussed in *MBMP*. When this is done, the vertices of the feasible region of the LP relaxation will be integral, guaranteeing an integral optimal solution for any objective. Again, this is not normally a practicable procedure, although it is sometimes possible to derive some of the *facets* of the convex hull in the form of cutting planes as discussed in section 6.4.

6.2 THE BRANCH-AND-BOUND METHOD

The method that we describe can be used to solve any (mixed or pure) integer programming model. If the integer variables are 0–1, then the method takes an especially simple form, which is pointed out. We will demonstrate the method by an example. Although this is a pure IP (PIP) model, the procedure is obviously also applicable to mixed IP (MIP) models.

Example 6.1 The Branch-and-Bound Method

$$\text{Minimise} \quad 2x_1 + 7x_2 + 2x_3 \tag{6.2}$$

subject to

$$x_1 + 4x_2 + x_3 \geqslant 10 \tag{6.3}$$

$$4x_1 + 2x_2 + 2x_3 \geqslant 13 \tag{6.4}$$

$$x_1 + x_2 - x_3 \geqslant 0 \tag{6.5}$$

$$x_1, x_2, x_3 \geqslant 0 \quad \text{and integer.} \tag{6.6}$$

Step 0 We solve the LP relaxation.

In this example this yields

$$x_1 = 2\tfrac{2}{7}, \quad x_2 = 1\tfrac{13}{14}, \quad x_3 = 0, \quad \text{objective} = 18\tfrac{1}{14}. \tag{6.7}$$

Clearly this solution is unacceptable as the integrality condition is violated.

Step 1 We choose a variable that we wish to take an integer value but which currently takes a fractional value and impose extra constraints on it. The choice of this variable is *heuristic*. How this choice is made can have a large effect on how quickly the model is solved.

Efficient ways of making this choice are described in section 7.2. A quick and simple choice would be to choose the variable whose value is closest to an integer. We will adopt this rule for illustrating this example. The variable chosen is known as the *branching* variable for a reason that will become apparent below.

In this example we choose variable x_2. The situation is illustrated below:

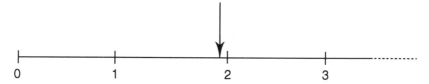

with x_2 taking the value given by the arrow. Since x_2 can only take integer values, there is no loss of generality in stipulating that

$$\text{either} \quad x_2 \leqslant 1 \quad \text{or} \quad x_2 \geqslant 2. \tag{6.8}$$

In general, if an integer variable x takes a fractional value $N + f$, where N is an integer and f is a fraction such that $0 < f < 1$, then we can stipulate

$$\text{either} \quad x \leqslant N \quad \text{or} \quad x \geqslant N + 1. \tag{6.9}$$

These conditions are appended individually to the original model to create two new *submodels* known respectively as the *son* and *daughter* models.

It is convenient to represent the situation diagrammatically using a tree structure as illustrated for the example in Figure 6.1. Each node of the tree corresponds to an IP model. Node 0 is the original model. Node 1 is this model with the first of constraints (6.8) appended and node 2 is the original model with the second of constraints (6.8) appended. The nodes are conveniently numbered in order of their generation.

Having created the IP models corresponding to the son and daughter nodes, it is convenient (but not necessary) to solve their LP relaxations immediately. This is because we can use the optimal solution of the LP relaxation of the parent IP model as a starting solution. Such computational considerations are discussed in section 7.4.

In the example, we therefore solve the LP relaxations of the models corresponding to nodes 1 and 2 to give

Node 1: $\quad x_1 = 2\frac{1}{2}, \quad x_2 = 1, \quad x_3 = 3\frac{1}{2}, \quad$ objective $= 19$ $\qquad$ (6.10)

Node 2: $\quad x_1 = 2\frac{1}{4}, \quad x_2 = 2, \quad x_3 = 0, \quad$ objective $= 18\frac{1}{2}.$ $\qquad$ (6.11)

It should be noted that the objective function values associated with these LP relaxations have got worse (larger for a minimisation or smaller for a maximisation). This would be expected to happen as we have added more constraints. Strictly speaking, we can only be sure the objective value will get no better. If there were alternative solutions to the LP relaxation, it could remain unchanged.

Step 2   Again, neither of the above solutions is acceptable. We therefore continue by choosing one of these nodes for further development.

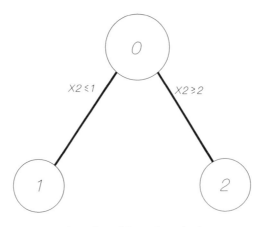

Figure 6.1   A branch in the branch-and-bound method

Which of these "waiting nodes" is chosen is again a heuristic choice. How this choice is made can again have a large effect on the total time to solve the model. This aspect is again discussed in section 7.4. For illustration, we will adopt the simple heuristic of choosing the node whose LP relaxation has best (smallest) objective value on the grounds that this may increase the chance of getting a better integer solution at a descendant node.

For the example we choose node 2 and proceed again to step 1.

Step 1 (repeated)   We choose x_1 as branching variable, observing that

$$\text{either} \quad x_1 \leqslant 2 \quad \text{or} \quad x_1 \geqslant 3. \quad (6.12)$$

Each of these constraints is individually appended to the constraints of node 2 to create IP models corresponding to nodes 3 and 4.

The full situation is illustrated in Figure 6.2. We solve the LP relaxations of the models associated with nodes 3 and 4. Associated with each node we give the solution to the corresponding LP relaxation.

Notice that at node 4 we obtain an integer solution, which we indicate by a square node, with an objective value of 20. There is no reason to believe that this solution is optimal, although in some practical applications the user might be content with this solution and stop the tree search. At node 4 there is no sense in which we can meaningfully continue to develop the node, which is therefore said to have been *fathomed*.

Step 2 (repeated)   Nodes 1 and 3 are the *waiting* nodes left to be developed (both of which have the same objective value for the associated LP relaxation). We will arbitrarily choose node 3 (depending on the data structures used this might be an easier node to recover).

Step 1 (repeated)   We branch on x_3 at node 3, creating nodes 5 and 6, the LP relaxations corresponding to which are solved.

The objective of the LP relaxation associated with node 5 is 21.5. This is worse than that of the best integer solution known to date at node 4 with an objective value of 20. Therefore, there is no virtue in developing node 5 further. It is *fathomed* for this reason.

This last observation is of great importance in practice. The objective value of the best integer solution known provides a *bound* for the optimal objective value, i.e. it cannot be worse than the bound. All waiting nodes where the LP relaxation objective is worse than the current bound are said to be *bounded* (hence the name "branch and bound") and can therefore be ignored. This consideration is further discussed in section 7.4, as it can enormously reduce the tree search.

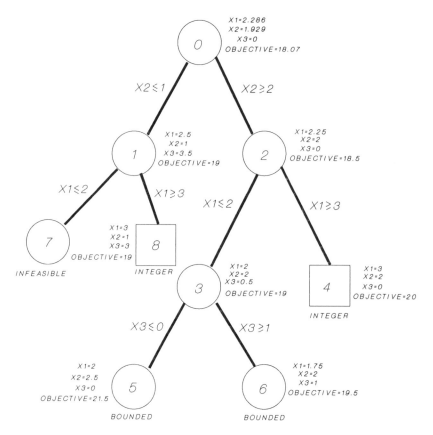

Figure 6.2 A branch-and-bound solution tree

Step 2 (repeated) Nodes 1 and 6 are now the waiting nodes and node 1 is chosen for further development. (In fact, since the objective function can only take integer values, node 6 cannot improve on node 4 and could be dropped. For mixed IP models such an observation may not be valid.)

Step 1 (repeated) We branch on x_1 at node 1, creating nodes 7 and 8, the LP relaxations of which are solved.

The LP relaxation associated with node 7 is infeasible. Therefore the associated IP model is also infeasible and *fathomed*. This is quite likely to happen at some nodes, since more and more constraints are added as we proceed down the tree.

At node 8 we obtain an even better integer solution with an objective value of 19. This node is therefore fathomed. Also node 6 can now be bounded, as its LP relaxation solution is worse than 19, and therefore fathomed.

There are now no more waiting nodes.

For our example we have therefore now *found* and *proved* that the solution at node 8 is the optimal integer solution.

General Observations

We remark on some general features of the branch-and-bound method, some of which will be considered further in Chapter 7.

  (i) The LP relaxation is solved at each node because it is computationally cheap. Other relaxations are possible (i.e. relaxing "constraints" other than the integrality conditions), some of which are discussed in sections 8.3 and 8.4. It might be worth doing a "heuristic" search around the LP relaxation solution to try to find a good integer solution that could be used as an objective bound. This is discussed in section 8.5.

 (ii) There is generally a choice of branching variable, which must be made heuristically. This is discussed further in section 7.2. For an MIP model we would, of course, only branch on the integer variables.

(iii) There is generally a choice of waiting node to be developed, which must again be made heuristically bearing in mind the solution strategy. This is discussed further in section 7.4.

(iv) Immediately after each branch the branching variable takes its imposed bound in the LP relaxation solution, e.g. $x_2 = 1$ at node 1 and $x_2 = 2$ at node 2. This will always happen immediately after a branch, but the variables could deviate from this bound below the node. For example, at node 5, x_2 takes a value >2. If, however, the integer variables are 0–1, they are obviously effectively fixed after branching on them.

 (v) If the LP relaxation is unbounded, then the IP model may be unbounded or infeasible. It is not possible for the branch-and-bound method to determine this. Example 1.18 and Figure 1.16 illustrate this.

(vi) If the feasible region of the LP relaxation is not closed (although the model is not unbounded), then there is no guarantee that the branch-and-bound method will converge. In some implementations of the branch-and-bound method, upper and lower bounds on each integer variable are demanded. Since each variable can then only take a finite number of values, only a finite number of branches is needed.

In order to demonstrate non-convergence, if the feasible region of the LP relaxation is open, a small (pathological) example is used.

Example 6.2 Non-Convergence of the Branch-and-Bound Method

$$\text{Minimise} \quad x_2 \tag{6.13}$$

subject to

$$3x_1 - 3x_2 \geqslant 1 \tag{6.14}$$

$$4x_1 - 4x_2 \leqslant 3 \tag{6.15}$$

$$x_1 \geqslant 1 \tag{6.16}$$

$$x_1, x_2 \geqslant 0 \quad \text{and integer.} \tag{6.17}$$

Step 0 The solution to the LP relaxation (node 0) is

$$x_1 = 1, \quad x_2 = \tfrac{1}{4}, \quad \text{objective} = \tfrac{1}{4}. \tag{6.18}$$

Step 1 Branching on x_2, we create nodes 1 and 2. The solutions of their LP relaxations are

Node 1:	infeasible	(6.19)
Node 2:	$x_1 = \tfrac{4}{3}, \quad x_2 = 1, \quad \text{objective} = 1$	(6.20)
	(there is an alternative solution).	

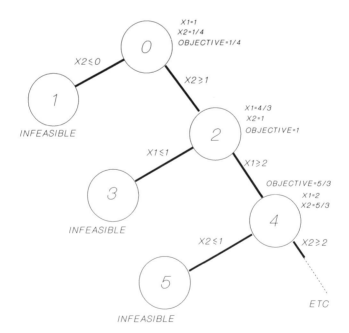

Figure 6.3 A non-convergent branch-and-bound tree

We proceed with the solution illustrated by the tree in Figure 6.3. It is apparent that the process will not terminate. Figure 6.4 illustrates the situation geometrically. The first branch creates an infeasible model (node 1) and the extra constraint B1 (node 2), giving the fractional solution at P1. The second branch gives an infeasible model (node 3) and the extra constraint B2 (node 4), giving the fractional solution at P2. Further branches and fractional solutions are illustrated. At no stage can an integer solution be found because there are none.

This is an example of an *infeasible* IP model with a *feasible* LP relaxation. Further relations between the solvability of IP models and their LP relaxations are the subject of exercise 6.6.

It is fairly easy to see that the branch-and-bound algorithm described above can take at least an exponential number of steps in the worst case. This is done through exercise 6.16.

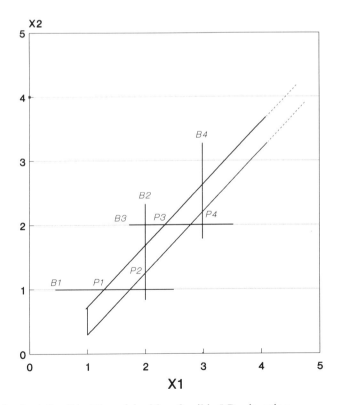

Figure 6.4 An infeasible IP model with a feasible LP relaxation

6.3 THE IMPORTANCE OF EFFICIENT FORMULATIONS

In *MBMP* much attention is paid to formulating IP models in manners that make them easier to solve. This is best illustrated in relation to specific application areas, which are beyond the scope of this book. We will, however, illustrate why one of the considerations improves ease of computation. Two aims for good IP formulation given in *MBMP* are:

 (i) To use integer variables that can be put to a good purpose in the branching process.
(ii) To make the LP relaxation as constrained as possible.

Since the first aim is best considered in relation to a specific model structure, it is not pursued here. The second aim is illustrated by an example.

Example 6.3 Creating a More Constrained LP Relaxation
An obvious observation is that the left-hand side of constraint (6.4) is divisible by 2 to produce

$$2x_1 + x_2 + x_3 \geqslant 6\tfrac{1}{2} \tag{6.21}$$

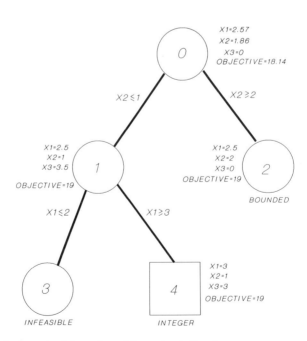

Figure 6.5 An improved branch-and-bound solution tree

which, since all variables in it are integer, implies

$$2x_1 + x_2 + x_3 \geqslant 7. \qquad (6.22)$$

Using this constraint instead or (or as well as) (6.4) in the model rules out (6.7) as a solution to the LP relaxation. Therefore, it might be hoped that it will produce an LP relaxation solution "closer" to the final IP optimal solution. Solving by the branch-and-bound method produces the solution tree shown in Figure 6.5.

It should be observed that the LP relaxation objective of $18\frac{1}{7}$ is closer to the IP optimal objective of 19 than the solution demonstrated in Figure 6.2. As a result, the right-hand branch from node 0 has appeared less attractive than before.

A more sophisticated remodelling can produce more dramatic reductions in the tree search. This is, however, best considered in the next section.

6.4 GENERATING CUTTING PLANES

It has already been pointed out that any IP model (pure or mixed) can, in principle, be reformulated in order to give the constraints defining the convex hull of feasible integer solutions. Although this is not a practicable procedure, in general (there may be an astronomical number of them), we give these constraints for Example 6.1. They were obtained (for this three-variable model) geometrically. They are

$$x_1 + 4x_2 + x_3 \geqslant 10 \qquad (6.23)$$

$$x_1 + 3x_2 + x_3 \geqslant 9 \qquad (6.24)$$

$$2x_1 + 4x_2 + x_3 \geqslant 13 \qquad (6.25)$$

$$x_1 + x_2 + x_3 \geqslant 5 \qquad (6.26)$$

$$2x_1 + x_2 + x_3 \geqslant 7 \qquad (6.27)$$

$$x_1 + 2x_2 \geqslant 5 \qquad (6.28)$$

$$2x_1 + x_2 \geqslant 4 \qquad (6.29)$$

$$x_1 + x_2 - x_3 \geqslant 0 \qquad (6.30)$$

$$x_1, x_2, x_3 \geqslant 0. \qquad (6.31)$$

Such constraints are known as *facets* of the convex hull. It can be verified that objective (6.2) with constraints (6.23) to (6.31) solved as an LP yields the optimal solution

$$x_1 = 3, \quad x_2 = 1, \quad x_3 = 3, \quad \text{objective} = 19 \tag{6.32}$$

or the alternative

$$x_1 = 6, \quad x_2 = 1, \quad x_3 = 0, \quad \text{objective} = 19. \tag{6.33}$$

Any other objective would also yield an integer LP solution. There is then no need for a computationally costly tree search.

Although it may be impracticable to generate all the facet constraints before solving the model, it is instructive to see how such facets might be derived.

Facets can be regarded as the strongest possible *cutting planes* for an IP model. Cutting planes are extra constraints that "cut off" part of the feasible region corresponding to the LP relaxation but do not cut off any feasible integer solutions. One can append them to a model, either at the beginning or during the course of optimisation, often to good effect.

It is possible to derive cutting planes (in the form of " $\geqslant$ " constraints) for PIP models by repeated use of the following three operations:

(i) Adding constraints together in suitable multiples. It is obviously only valid to take non-negative multiples of " $\geqslant$ " constraints, non-positive multiples of " $\leqslant$ " constraints and any multiple of " $=$ " constraints.
(ii) Dividing through by a common coefficient factor (e.g. dividing through (6.4) by 2).
(iii) Rounding up the RHS to the next integer for a " $\geqslant$ " constraint (rounding down for a " $\leqslant$ " constraint).

Constraint (6.22) is an example of a cutting plane devised from operations (ii) and (iii). It can be seen that it is also the facet (6.27). Facets (6.23), (6.30) and (6.31) were among the original constraints.

The cutting planes devised from (i), (ii) and (iii) are known as *Chvátal cuts*. It can be shown that all the facet constraints can be derived in this way. This is illustrated by an example.

Example 6.4 Facet Constraints from Chvátal Cuts
Derive the facet constraints (6.23) to (6.31), for Example 6.1, as Chvátal cuts.

We have already got or obtained (6.23), (6.27), (6.30) and (6.31).

Step 1   Multiplying (6.3) by 5, (6.22) by 1, " $x_3 \geqslant 0$ " by 1, adding, dividing by 7 and rounding gives (6.24).

Step 2   Multiplying (6.3) by 1, (6.22) by 3, " $x_3 \geqslant 0$ " by 3, adding, dividing by 7 and rounding gives (6.26).

Step 3 Multiplying (6.3) by 4, (6.22) by 1, (6.5) by 5, adding, dividing by 11 and rounding gives (6.28).

Step 4 Multiplying (6.22) by 1, (6.5) by 1, "$x_1 \geqslant 0$" by 1, adding, dividing by 2 and rounding gives (6.29).

Step 5 Multiplying (6.24) by 3, (6.22) by 1, (6.28) by 3, adding, dividing by 4 and rounding gives (6.25).

The disadvantage of this approach is that the order in which constraints are combined is somewhat arbitrary. Notice that some of the original constraints may need to be combined followed by roundings a number of times. For example, (6.25) arises directly in step 5 from (6.22) and indirectly through (6.24) and (6.28), which themselves depend on (6.22) through steps 1 and 3 respectively. Constraint (6.22) itself then arises from (6.4) through rounding. It can be shown that, in general, it may be necessary to add in the original constraints and round an arbitrary number of times. Further consideration of the resulting *Chvátal functions* is given in section 6.5.

In practice, the derivation of Chvátal cuts must rely on features of the structure that are specific to the application, and are beyond the scope of this book.

It is, however, possible to derive cutting planes *systematically* in the course of optimisation. This may be done by considering IP models associated with different nodes of the branch-and-bound solution tree. By adding in cuts, as well as solving the LP relaxation, we can hope to get better approximations to the IP optimum.

We can also derive cuts from the set of equations resulting from the simplex solution of the LP relaxation.

This is illustrated by means of the same model. We derive what are known as *Gomory cuts*.

Example 6.5 Derive Gomory Cuts for Example 6.1

Step 1 We solve the LP relaxation by means of the simplex algorithm, giving the final set of equations. Although this would normally be done in floating-point arithmetic, we do the calculations in fractions in order to clarify the nature of the cuts derived. This gives

$$z = \tfrac{253}{14} - \tfrac{1}{7} x_3 - \tfrac{12}{7} x_4 - \tfrac{1}{14} x_5 \qquad (6.34)$$

$$x_6 = \tfrac{59}{14} - \tfrac{11}{7} x_3 + \tfrac{1}{7} x_4 + \tfrac{3}{14} x_5 \qquad (6.35)$$

$$x_1 = \tfrac{16}{7} - \tfrac{3}{7} x_3 - \tfrac{1}{7} x_4 + \tfrac{2}{7} x_5 \qquad (6.36)$$

$$x_2 = \tfrac{27}{14} - \tfrac{1}{7} x_3 + \tfrac{2}{7} x_4 - \tfrac{1}{14} x_5. \qquad (6.37)$$

z represents the negated objective function. x_4, x_5 and x_6 are surplus variables appended to constraints (6.3) to (6.5) respectively. Clearly they can also be regarded as integer variables.

Step 2 We choose one of the basic integer variables taking a fractional value and use the corresponding equation to separate out integer parts. If we consider the first equation (6.35) we can express it as

$$x_6 - 4 + 2x_3 = \tfrac{3}{14} + \tfrac{3}{7}x_3 + \tfrac{1}{7}x_4 + \tfrac{3}{14}x_5. \tag{6.38}$$

We have deliberately subtracted off the next integer *below* the fractional coefficients on the right of equation (6.35) and moved them to the left, in order to leave *non-negative* quantities on the right in equation (6.38). Since the left-hand side of equation (6.38) represents an integer quantity, so must the right-hand side. Since the right-hand side is also strictly positive, we can assert that

$$\tfrac{3}{14} + \tfrac{3}{7}x_3 + \tfrac{1}{7}x_4 + \tfrac{3}{14}x_5 \geqslant 1 \tag{6.39}$$

i.e.

$$\tfrac{3}{7}x_3 + \tfrac{1}{7}x_4 + \tfrac{3}{14}x_5 \geqslant \tfrac{11}{14}. \tag{6.40}$$

Inequality (6.40) is expressed in terms of the non-basic variables corresponding to the optimal LP relaxation. It is possible to incorporate constraint (6.40) directly, in an equation form, into the system (6.34) to (6.37) and reoptimise. An efficient way of doing this would be the dual simplex algorithm, since we have retained dual feasibility but created a primal infeasibility. In practice this may be cumbersome with some data structures for the reasons mentioned in section 4.1. We do not pursue these considerations further, but concentrate on the IP considerations.

Instead of incorporating (6.40) in equation form, we express it in terms of the original (structural) variables for illustrative purposes. This can be done by observing that x_4 and x_5 are the surplus variables in constraints (6.3) and (6.5). Therefore

$$x_4 = -10 + x_1 + 4x_2 + x_3 \tag{6.41}$$

$$x_5 = -13 + 4x_1 + 2x_2 + 2x_3. \tag{6.42}$$

Substituting x_4 and x_5 out of (6.40) and simplifying gives

$$x_1 + x_2 + x_3 \geqslant 5. \tag{6.43}$$

Notice that this is a constraint (6.26) that we have already obtained as a Chvátal cut. In fact, Gomory cuts can always be obtained as Chvátal cuts. Multiplying (6.40) through by 14, the resulting coefficients demonstrate that (6.43) arises from multiplying "$x_3 \geqslant 0$" by 6, the inequality (6.3), in which x_4 is the logical variable, by 2, the inequality (6.4), in which x_5 is the logical variable, by 3, adding, dividing by 14 and rounding.

We could also have used constraints (6.36) and (6.37) to derive Gomory cuts. This is left to exercise 6.9. It is also possible to derive Gomory cuts by taking multiples and linear combinations of equations (6.35) to (6.37). This is the subject of exercise 6.10. The resulting set of cuts has an algebraic structure that gives rise to the cone relaxation discussed in section 8.4.

Step 3 We incorporate constraint (6.43), with surplus variable x_7, into the original model and return to step 1.

Step 1 (repeated)   Optimising the LP relaxation gives

$$z = \tfrac{55}{3} - \tfrac{5}{3} x_4 - \tfrac{1}{3} x_7 \tag{6.44}$$

$$x_3 = \tfrac{11}{6} - \tfrac{1}{3} x_4 - \tfrac{1}{2} x_5 + \tfrac{7}{3} x_7 \tag{6.45}$$

$$x_6 = \tfrac{4}{3} + \tfrac{2}{3} x_4 + x_5 - \tfrac{11}{3} x_7 \tag{6.46}$$

$$x_1 = \tfrac{3}{2} + \tfrac{1}{2} x_5 - x_7 \tag{6.47}$$

$$x_2 = \tfrac{5}{3} + \tfrac{1}{3} x_4 - \tfrac{1}{3} x_7. \tag{6.48}$$

Step 2 (repeated)   Choosing equation (6.45) we can obtain the Gomory cut

$$3x_1 + 4x_2 + 2x_3 \geqslant 15. \tag{6.49}$$

Notice that this is not a facet constraint, although it could be obtained as a Chvátal cut by multiplying (6.3) by 4, (6.4) by 3, (6.43) by 2, adding, dividing by 6 and rounding.

Step 3 (repeated)   We incorporate (6.49), with surplus variable x_8, into the model and return to step 1.

Step 1 (repeated)   Optimising the LP relaxation gives

$$z = \tfrac{55}{3} - \tfrac{5}{3} x_4 - \tfrac{1}{3} x_7 \tag{6.50}$$

$$x_3 = \tfrac{8}{3} + \tfrac{1}{3} x_4 + \tfrac{8}{3} x_7 - x_8 \tag{6.51}$$

$$x_6 = \tfrac{8}{3} - \tfrac{2}{3} x_4 - \tfrac{13}{3} x_7 + 2x_8 \tag{6.52}$$

$$x_2 = \tfrac{8}{3} + \tfrac{1}{3} x_4 - \tfrac{1}{3} x_7 \tag{6.53}$$

$$x_1 = \tfrac{8}{3} - \tfrac{2}{3} x_4 + \tfrac{4}{3} x_7 + x_8 \tag{6.54}$$

$$x_5 = \tfrac{1}{3} - \tfrac{4}{3} x_4 - \tfrac{2}{3} x_7 + 2x_8. \tag{6.55}$$

Step 2 (repeated)   Choosing equation (6.51) we can obtain the Gomory cut

$$x_1 + 2x_2 + x_3 \geqslant 7. \tag{6.56}$$

Again (with hindsight) this is a Chvátal cut obtained by multiplying (6.3) by 1, (6.43) by 2, adding, dividing by 3 and rounding.

Step 3 (repeated)   We incorporate constraint (6.56), with surplus variable x_9, into the model and return to step 1.

Step 1 (repeated)   Optimising the LP relaxation gives

$$z = \tfrac{37}{2} - \tfrac{3}{2} x_4 - \tfrac{1}{2} x_9 \tag{6.57}$$

$$x_3 = \tfrac{11}{4} - \tfrac{1}{4} x_4 - \tfrac{1}{2} x_6 + \tfrac{3}{4} x_9 \tag{6.58}$$

$$x_7 = \tfrac{1}{2} - \tfrac{1}{2} x_4 + \tfrac{3}{2} x_9 \tag{6.59}$$

$$x_2 = \tfrac{3}{2} + \tfrac{1}{2} x_4 - \tfrac{1}{2} x_9 \tag{6.60}$$

$$x_1 = \tfrac{5}{4} - \tfrac{3}{4} x_4 + \tfrac{1}{2} x_6 + \tfrac{5}{4} x_9 \tag{6.61}$$

$$x_5 = \tfrac{1}{2} - \tfrac{5}{2} x_4 + x_6 + \tfrac{11}{2} x_9 \tag{6.62}$$

$$x_8 = \tfrac{1}{4} - \tfrac{3}{4} x_4 + \tfrac{1}{2} x_6 + \tfrac{13}{4} x_9. \tag{6.63}$$

Step 2 (repeated)   Choosing equation (6.58) we can obtain the Gomory cut

$$2x_1 + 5x_2 + x_3 \geqslant 13. \tag{6.64}$$

Again this is a Chvátal cut obtained by multiplying (6.3) by 3, (6.5) by 2, (6.56) by 3, adding, dividing by 4 and rounding.

Step 3 (repeated)   We incorporate constraint (6.64), with surplus variable x_{10}, into the model and return to step 1.

Step 1 (repeated)   Optimising the LP relaxation gives

$$z = \tfrac{37}{2} - \tfrac{3}{2} x_4 - \tfrac{1}{2} x_9 \tag{6.65}$$

$$x_3 = \tfrac{5}{2} + \tfrac{1}{2} x_4 + \tfrac{3}{2} x_9 - x_{10} \tag{6.66}$$

$$x_7 = \tfrac{1}{2} - \tfrac{1}{2} x_4 + \tfrac{3}{2} x_9 \tag{6.67}$$

$$x_2 = \tfrac{3}{2} + \tfrac{1}{2} x_4 - \tfrac{1}{2} x_9 \tag{6.68}$$

$$x_1 = \tfrac{3}{2} - \tfrac{3}{2} x_4 - \tfrac{1}{2} x_9 + x_{10} \tag{6.69}$$

$$x_5 = 1 - 4x_4 + 4x_9 + 2x_{10} \tag{6.70}$$

$$x_8 = \tfrac{1}{2} - \tfrac{3}{2} x_4 + \tfrac{5}{2} x_9 + x_{10} \tag{6.71}$$

$$x_6 = \tfrac{1}{2} - \tfrac{3}{2} x_4 - \tfrac{3}{2} x_9 + 2x_{10}. \tag{6.72}$$

Step 2 (repeated)   Choosing equation (6.66) we can obtain the Gomory cut

$$x_1 + 3x_2 + x_3 \geqslant 9. \tag{6.73}$$

Notice that this is the facet constraint (6.24).

Step 3 (repeated)   We incorporate constraint (6.73), with surplus variable x_{11}, into the model and return to step 1.

Step 1 (repeated) Optimising the LP relaxation gives

$$z = 19 - x_4 - x_{11} \tag{6.74}$$

$$x_3 = \tfrac{7}{2} - x_4 - \tfrac{1}{2}x_6 + \tfrac{3}{2}x_{11} \tag{6.75}$$

$$x_7 = 2 - 2x_4 + 3x_{11} \tag{6.76}$$

$$x_2 = 1 + x_4 - x_{11} \tag{6.77}$$

$$x_1 = \tfrac{5}{2} - 2x_4 + \tfrac{1}{2}x_6 + \tfrac{5}{2}x_{11} \tag{6.78}$$

$$x_5 = 6 - 8x_4 + x_6 + 11x_{11} \tag{6.79}$$

$$x_8 = \tfrac{7}{2} - 4x_4 + \tfrac{1}{2}x_6 + \tfrac{13}{2}x_{11} \tag{6.80}$$

$$x_9 = 1 - x_4 + 2x_{11} \tag{6.81}$$

$$x_{10} = \tfrac{1}{2} + \tfrac{1}{2}x_6 + \tfrac{3}{2}x_{11} \tag{6.82}$$

Step 2 (repeated) Choosing equation (6.75) we can obtain the Gomory cut

$$x_1 + 2x_2 \geqslant 5. \tag{6.83}$$

Notice that this is the facet constraint (6.28).

Step 3 (repeated) We incorporate constraint (6.83), with surplus variable x_{12}, into the model and return to step 1.

Step 1 (repeated) Optimising the LP relaxation gives the optimal integer solution

$$x_1 = 3, \quad x_2 = 1, \quad x_3 = 3, \quad \text{objective} = 19. \tag{6.84}$$

Although the above example is untypical of large structured IP models, the solution process does exhibit general features that are typical of practical models. As many as six cuts were needed to solve this very small model. Some of these cuts were "almost parallel" to the objective plane and resulted in little or no change in the objective value.

It can be shown that, for PIP models, if we always derive the Gomory cut from the first equation in which the basic variable is fractional, then we will converge to the optimal solution in a finite number of steps. There is, however, no bound on the number of steps.

The general result is that, if we have equation

$$x_0 = b + \sum_{j=1}^{n} a_j x_j \tag{6.85}$$

where all variables x_j are non-negative integers and b is fractional, then we can derive the Gomory cut

$$\sum_{j=1}^{n} (a_j - \lfloor a_j \rfloor)x_j \geqslant 1 - (b - \lfloor b \rfloor). \qquad (6.86)$$

This can be re-expressed in terms of integer coefficients if required. Here "$\lfloor \ \rfloor$" is the operation of taking the integer less than or equal to the relevant quantity.

It is also possible to derive Gomory cuts for MIP models. These turn out to be rather weak in practice and are only used in specialist situations. We therefore give the result without further discussion. Suppose we have an equation

$$x_0 = b + \sum_{j=1}^{n} a_j x_j + \sum_{j=1}^{p} c_j y_j \qquad (6.87)$$

where all variables x_j are non-negative integers but y_j are continuous and non-negative. The resultant Gomory cut is

$$\sum_{j=1}^{n} (a_j - \lfloor a_j \rfloor)x_j + \sum_{\substack{j=1 \\ c_j > 0}}^{p} c_j y_j - \frac{1 - (b - \lfloor b \rfloor)}{b - \lfloor b \rfloor} \sum_{\substack{j=1 \\ c_j < 0}}^{p} c_j y_j \geqslant 1 - (b - \lfloor b \rfloor).$$
$$(6.88)$$

The above cuts, for an MIP model, can be introduced in the course of optimisation in the same manner as for a PIP model. It can be shown that a finite number of steps is needed if the objective function is constrained to be integer. Otherwise there is no guarantee of convergence.

6.5 DUALITY AND INTEGER PROGRAMMING

In section 2.5 it was shown that, so long as an LP model is not unbounded or infeasible, then the optimal solution to the dual model provides multipliers for the constraints, which when added together in these multiples give a strict (achievable) bound on the objective. For IP models there are no such corresponding multipliers. In general, there will be a gap between the strictest objective bound achievable by multipliers, and the optimal IP objective. This gap is known as *duality gap* and is illustrated by reconsidering Example 6.1.

Example 6.6 Duality Gaps
Obtain the minimum duality gap for Example 6.1.
The dual of the LP relaxation of Example 6.1 is

$$\text{Maximise} \quad 10y_1 + 13y_2 \qquad (6.89)$$

subject to

$$y_1 + 4y_2 + y_3 \leqslant 2 \qquad (6.90)$$

$$4y_1 + 2y_2 + y_3 \leqslant 7 \qquad (6.91)$$

$$y_1 + 2y_2 - y_3 \leqslant 2 \qquad (6.92)$$

$$y_1, y_2, y_3 \geqslant 0. \qquad (6.93)$$

By the duality theorem of LP, the optimal objective value must be the same as that of the LP relaxation of Example 6.1, namely $18\frac{1}{14}$. For completeness and future reference, however, we give the complete solution to this dual, with values given as fractions. It is

$$y_1 = \tfrac{12}{7}, \quad y_2 = \tfrac{1}{4}, \quad y_3 = y_4 = y_5 = 0, \quad y_6 = \tfrac{1}{7}, \quad \text{objective} = 18\tfrac{1}{14} \quad (6.94)$$

where y_4, y_4 and y_6 are the slack variables appended to constraints (6.90) to (6.92). If these multipliers are applied to constraints (6.3) to (6.6) respectively, we obtain the result

$$2x_1 + 7x_2 + 2x_3 \geqslant 18\tfrac{1}{14}. \qquad (6.95)$$

Whereas there exist fractional values for x_1, x_2 and x_3 satisfying (6.3) to (6.6) that make $2x_1 + 7x_2 + 2x_3$ as small as $18\frac{1}{14}$, the best we can do with integer values is the IP optimum of Example 6.1 making $2x_1 + 7x_2 + 2x_3$ as small as 19. The difference of $\frac{13}{14}$ illustrated in Figure 6.6 is the *duality gap*.

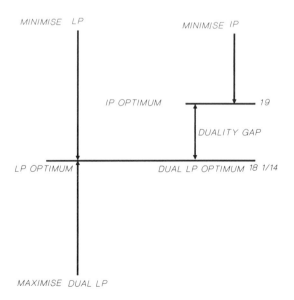

Figure 6.6   A duality gap

This difference between the optimal objective values of the IP and its LP relaxation is a measure of the difficulty of the IP.

We can, however, always close the duality gap by means of Chvátal cuts. This is again illustrated by the same example.

Example 6.7 Obtaining a Strict IP Objective Bound by Chvátal Cuts

Apply Chvátal cuts to Example 6.1 to find a strict (achievable) lower objective bound.

When Example 6.1 was solved, as an LP, subject to the facet constraints (6.23) to (6.31), either optimal solution (6.32) or (6.33) results. It can be verified, using the methods of section 2.5, that the corresponding dual multipliers applied to the facet constraints are 1 for both constraints (6.23) and (6.24) and 0 for the other constraints. Since (6.23) is the same as (6.3), the "rounded" (6.4) and "$x_3 \geqslant 0$", together with a further rounding in step 1 of Example 6.3, we can deduce and verify that

$$2x_1 + 7x_2 + 2x_3 \geqslant 19 \qquad (6.96)$$

arises from the following steps.

Step 1 Divide (6.4) by 2 and round.
Step 2 Multiply (6.3) by 12, "$x_3 \geqslant 0$" by 1, add to the result of step 1, divide by 7 and round.

Therefore we have closed the duality gap to produce a strict lower bound of 19 for the objective function.

It is of interest to observe that removing the rounding operations in the above steps would have resulted in combining (6.3), (6.4) and "$x_3 \geqslant 0$" by the optimal LP relaxation dual values (6.93) to produce the weaker lower bound of $18\frac{1}{14}$.

The operations that we have applied in steps 1 and 2 above (Chvátal cuts) can be regarded as the PIP analogy of applying dual values as multipliers and adding. It is instructive to consider these operations in the more general context of finding the value function for a PIP. This is analogous to the value function of an LP, which was considered in sections 2.2 and 2.7 and shown to be derivable from the vertices and extreme rays of the dual model. We will consider Example 6.1 with general integer RHS coefficients.

Example 6.8 The Value Function for a PIP

Find the value function for

$$\text{Minimise} \quad 2x_1 + 7x_2 + 2x_3 \qquad (6.97)$$

subject to

$$x_1 + 4x_2 + x_3 \geqslant b_1 \tag{6.98}$$

$$4x_1 + 2x_2 + 2x_3 \geqslant b_2 \tag{6.99}$$

$$x_1 + x_2 - x_3 \geqslant b_3 \tag{6.100}$$

$$x_1, x_2, x_3 \geqslant 0 \quad \text{and integer.} \tag{6.101}$$

A number of possible lower bounds for (6.97) are derivable (expressed in terms of b_1, b_2 and b_3) by applying Chvátal cuts. These are the analogies of the vertices of the dual in the LP case. The *largest* such lower bound can be shown to be strict (achievable) by the result of Chvátal. There are also, in general, feasibility conditions, which are built up in the same way as Chvátal functions. These are the analogues of the extreme rays of the dual in the LP case. For this particular example, such a condition does not arise, as the model is feasible for all b_1, b_2 and b_3.

The derivation of the value function is beyond the scope of this book. Nor would it be practicable to find the value function in general. Nevertheless, it is instructive to see, and discuss, the form that it takes for this numerical example. It is

$$\text{Max}\left(\left\lceil \frac{12}{7}b_1 + \frac{1}{7}\left\lceil \frac{b_2}{2}\right\rceil\right\rceil, \left\lceil \frac{7}{4}b_1\right\rceil, \left\lceil \frac{1}{2}\left\lceil \frac{1}{2}\left\lceil \frac{20}{3}b_1 + \frac{4}{3}b_3\right\rceil\right\rceil\right\rceil,\right.$$
$$\left.\left\lceil \frac{1}{2}\left\lceil \frac{1}{2}b_2\right\rceil\right\rceil + \left\lceil \frac{1}{2}\left\lceil \frac{1}{2}b_2\right\rceil\right\rceil\right\rceil, 2b_3, 0\right). \tag{6.102}$$

For simplicity we assume b_1, b_2 and b_3 are integers.

The form of (6.102) is known as a *Gomory function*. It is the maximum of a series of Chvátal functions. Each Chvátal function gives a "prescription" for adding together the constraints (6.98) to (6.101), in certain multiples, together with roundings to give a lower bound for the objective function (6.97). The maximum such lower bound, for a specific set of values of b_1, b_2 and b_3, is achievable by an analogy of the duality theorem for LP. For example, taking $b_1 = 10$, $b_2 = 13$, $b_3 = 0$, function (6.102) becomes

$$\text{Max}(19, 18, 17, 8, 0, 0) = 19. \tag{6.103}$$

This shows that the optimal objective value for Example 6.1 is 19, derivable from combining the constraints in the manner of the first Chvátal function in (6.102). For these specific figures this Chvátal function results from steps 1 and 2 above.

If we "relax" the Gomory function (6.102) by ignoring the rounding operation, the expression reduces to the value function for the LP relaxation, which is

$$\text{Max}(\tfrac{12}{7}b_1 + \tfrac{1}{14}b_2, \tfrac{7}{4}b_1, \tfrac{5}{3}b_1 + \tfrac{1}{3}b_3, \tfrac{1}{2}b_2, 2b_3, 0). \tag{6.104}$$

It can be verified that this arises from the vertices of the dual of the LP relaxation of Example 6.1. In general, it should not be assumed that each of the relevant Chvátal functions is a specialisation of the appropriate expression in the corresponding LP value function. Some of the Chvátal functions may "relax" to redundant expressions in the LP case. Exercise 6.15 illustrates this. It also illustrates the fact that for an n-variable IP the optimal solution may depend on more than n of the constraints (in contrast to LP). This is discussed further in section 6.6. PIP value functions are further complicated by the fact that there may be a very large number of Chvátal functions, to arbitrary levels of nesting of the roundings, which reduce to a single expression in the LP case. Exercise 6.14 illustrates this.

6.6 HISTORY, REFERENCES AND FUTURE DEVELOPMENTS

A comprehensive and up-to-date survey of the state of knowledge regarding IP is Schrijver (1986). Nemhauser and Wolsey (1988) also cover the subject thoroughly.

The first serious examination of IP was made by Gomory (1958, 1965).

Total Unimodularity and the Integrality Property

The characterisation of totally unimodular matrices as made up of network flow matrices, their duals and the special cases given in the text is due to Seymour (1981).

The Branch-and-Bound Method

The idea of branch and bound is more widely applicable than just to solving IP models. Many combinatorial and deduction problems can be approached in this way, sometimes referred to as "divide and conquer". It was Land and Doig (1960) who first suggested applying it to IP. Their version of the method is not that most widely used today. The method described here is due to Dakin (1965). A very good general account is given by Geoffrion and Marsten (1972).

The Importance of Efficient Formulations

The subject is discussed in further depth in *MBMP*. The importance of efficient formulations was stressed early on by Williams (1974, 1978). Automated reformulations were implemented by Crowder, Johnson and Padberg (1983) and Wolsey (1989).

Generating Cutting Planes

One of the earliest methods of solving PIP models is that due to Gomory (1963). It works by successively adding Gomory cuts and reoptimising the LP relaxation by the dual simplex algorithm. It has been extended to deal with the MIP case by Johnson (1974). Unfortunately, the approach has not proved to be commercially practicable, although the resultant cuts can be incorporated into a branch-and-bound method to good effect.

The result that all valid linear constraints for an IP model (therefore including the facet constraints) can be generated by Chvátal cuts is due to Chvátal (1973).

The easier derivation of cuts for certain types of IP structure (e.g. pure 0–1 models) is discussed in *MBMP* with further references. Of particular value are papers by Balas (1975), Hammer, Johnson and Peled (1975) and Wolsey (1975). Wolsey (1989) also considers the MIP case.

Duality and Integer Programming

There have been a number of attempts to define a satisfactory dual for an IP model. In particular, methods are described by Balas (1970), Shapiro (1971) and Gomory and Baumol (1960).

A survey is given by Williams (1979). The value function of a PIP in terms of Gomory functions is given by Blair and Jeroslow (1982). In general, it can be shown that the degree of nesting of " $\lceil \quad \rceil$ " functions in a Chvátal function is not a bounded function of the number of variables (see exercise 6.13), although for certain classes of model in logical inference, e.g. Hooker (1991a), there is a bound. There is no known efficient method of deriving Gomory (or Chvátal) functions for a general model. Williams (1989) derives such functions for IPs over cones.

The analogous result in IP, for the LP result that for an n-variable LP, at most n constraints are binding at the optimal solution, is due to Bell (1977). It is that at most $2^n - 1$ constraints will be binding in the IP case.

Value functions for MIP models do not take the form of Gomory functions, although consistency testers do, but are more complicated. The generalisation of Chvátal functions to the MIP case has been attempted by Cook, Kannan and Schrijver (1990).

Duality and IP is a subject deserving of further development.

6.7 EXERCISES

6.1 Solve Example 6.1 by always branching on the integer variable with value *furthest* from an integer.

6.2 Solve Example 1.14 by the branch-and-bound method.

6.3 Solve Example 1.15 by the branch-and-bound method.

6.4 Attempt to apply the branch-and-bound method to exercise 6.1 in order to enumerate *all* integer solutions. Show that the method will not terminate.

6.5 Solve Example 1.20 by the branch-and-bound method, interpreting the method geometrically.

6.6 (a) If an IP is solvable (not infeasible or unbounded), is the corresponding LP relaxation solvable?
(b) If the LP relaxation of an IP is solvable, is the IP solvable?
(c) If an IP is infeasible, is the corresponding LP relaxation infeasible?
(d) If an IP is unbounded, is the corresponding LP relaxation unbounded?
(e) If an LP relaxation of an IP is infeasible, is the corresponding IP infeasible?
(f) If an LP relaxation of an IP is unbounded, is the corresponding IP unbounded?

6.7 Generate all the facets of Example 1.20 as Chvátal cuts.

6.8 Solve Example 1.20 by successively adding Gomory cuts.

6.9 Obtain Gomory cuts from equations (6.36) and (6.37).

*6.10 By adding together equations (6.35) to (6.37) in all possible multiples, devise all possible Gomory cuts.

6.11 Obtain the value function for Example 1.20 with general right-hand sides.

*6.12 After restricting the variables in Example 2.3 to integer values, derive the value and feasibility functions. Compare these with those given for the LP relaxation.

*6.13 Show that the optimal solution to

$$\text{Maximise} \quad y$$

subject to

$$-2kx + y \leqslant 0$$
$$2kx + y \leqslant 2k$$
$$x, y \text{ integer}$$

where k is a positive integer, can only be deduced by a Chvátal function with nesting rounded to a depth of k. Hence there is no bound on the maximum number of roundings necessary for a two-variable PIP.

*6.14 Obtain the value function for the model in exercise 6.13 for general RHS coefficients.

*6.15 By geometrical means verify that the value function for

$$\text{Minimise} \quad x_2$$

subject to

$$4x_1 + 2x_2 \geqslant b_1$$
$$-4x_1 - 2x_2 \geqslant b_2$$
$$-2x_1 + 2x_3 \geqslant b_3$$
$$x_1, x_2 \text{ integer}$$

is

$$\text{Max}\left(\left\lceil \tfrac{1}{6}b_1 + \tfrac{2}{3}\left\lceil \tfrac{1}{2}b_3 \right\rceil \right\rceil, \left\lceil \tfrac{1}{6}b_1 + \tfrac{2}{3}\left\lceil \tfrac{1}{4}b_2 + \tfrac{3}{2}\left\lceil \tfrac{1}{6}b_1 + \tfrac{2}{3}\left\lceil \tfrac{1}{2}b_3 \right\rceil \right\rceil \right\rceil \right\rceil \right)$$

and that the feasibility condition is

$$\left\lceil \tfrac{1}{2}b_1 \right\rceil + \left\lceil \tfrac{1}{2}b_2 \right\rceil \leqslant 0.$$

Observe that the optimal solution may depend on more than two constraints if the second Chvátal function is operative. Why is the relaxation of this Chvátal function redundant in the LP case?

*6.16 Construct an IP model that needs an exponential number of steps to solve by the branch-and-bound method.

6.17 Show that the following knapsack IP model requires an exponential number of steps to "solve" by the branch-and-bound method based on LP relaxations:

$$\text{Maximise} \quad x_1$$

subject to

$$2x_1 + 2x_2 + \cdots + 2x_n = n$$
$$x_1, x_2, \ldots, x_n \in \{0, 1\}$$

where n is an odd integer.

*6.18 Show that a two-variable IP can have an unlimited number of facets.

Chapter 7

___ Computational Implementation of the Linear-Programming-Based Branch-and-Bound Algorithm

The branch-and-bound algorithm described in Chapter 6 is particularly simple. Its success in solving real problems depends on its implementation. Underlying this is the revised simplex algorithm, which is used repeatedly for solving the associated LP relaxations. It is, however, obviously sensible to exploit the similarity between the models associated with neighbouring nodes to avoid completely resolving relaxations of similar models. Ways of doing this are described in section 7.1. Numerical information can be produced from the LP relaxation at a node to guide (heuristically) the choices of branching variables and nodes. This is described in sections 7.2 and 7.4. In section 7.3 special ordered sets of variables, which were introduced in section 1.3, are treated as entities and the rules for dealing with integer variables generalised to deal with them. Then in section 7.4 it is shown how the numerical information defined in previous sections can be exploited in order to try to reduce the length of the tree searches. Throughout the chapter we will assume that we are using data structures, which were discussed in section 1.6.

7.1 UPDATING THE BASIS

Associated with each node, in the tree search, will be the basis corresponding to the optimal solution to the LP relaxation at that node. It is usual to store the inverse of the associated basis matrix as a product of eta vectors. If it is not stored it can, of course, be found by inverting the matrix. Once a branch is made from this node, a number of additional LP iterations will be needed to solve the LP relaxations of the resulting IPs. These are most efficiently solved using the optimal basis of the LP relaxation of the parent node as a starting basis. Example 7.1 below illustrates this. Before solving this example, however, we must pay attention to the manner in which the simplex algorithm is applied. When we branch on integer variable x, which takes the value $N + f$ where $0 < f < 1$, we stipulate that

$$\text{either} \quad x \leqslant N \quad \text{or} \quad x \geqslant N + 1. \quad (7.1)$$

Either of these extra conditions will make the solution associated with the LP relaxation of the parent node infeasible in the primal sense. It will, however, still be dual feasible. Therefore, it would be somewhat inefficient to reoptimise, from the starting basis, using the primal simplex algorithm. Instead, it would appear more efficient to use the dual simplex algorithm, so retaining dual feasibility while regaining primal feasibility. The primal simplex algorithm would, of course, destroy dual feasibility while reperforming phase I of the simplex algorithm. There is a third possibility, which is to perform parametric programming on the bound on the variable. This can be done in a number of ways, which will not be discussed here. The methods used are essentially those of the dual simplex algorithm. We therefore describe this method. The procedure is best understood through an example. We resolve Example 6.1. For convenience, we use the same notation as was used for the revised simplex algorithm in Chapter 4. Also we treat the model as a maximisation.

Example 7.1 The Branch-and-Bound Method Using the Revised Simplex Algorithm

$$\text{Maximise} \quad z$$

where

z	x_1	x_2	x_3	x_4	x_5	x_6		
1	2	7	2	0	0	0		0
0	1	4	1	−1	0	0	=	10
0	4	2	2	0	−1	0		13
0	1	1	−1	0	0	−1		0

$$(7.2)$$

LB	$-\infty$	0	0	0	0	0	0
UB	∞	∞	∞	∞	∞	∞	∞

$x_1, x_2, \ldots, x_6$ integer.

We record the initial steps of the calculation on Figure 7.1.

Step 0 We solve the LP relaxation. This produces the eta file, basis list and solution vector associated with node 0 in Figure 7.1.

Step 1 We branch on variable x_2. In the example, we are deliberately following the solution strategy exhibited in Example 6.1. More sophisticated solution strategies are discussed in section 7.4. By

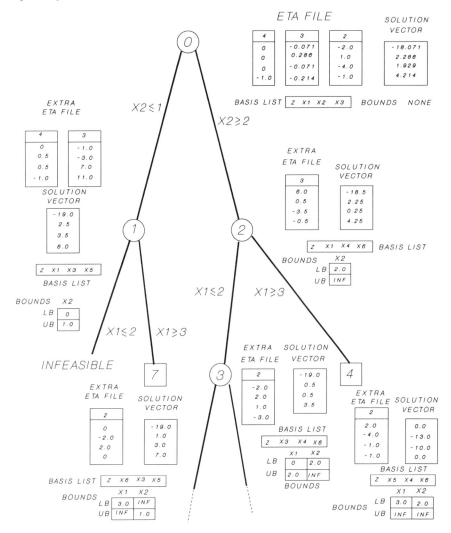

Figure 7.1 Calculations in the branch-and-bound method

branching on x_2, the current relaxed solution at node 0 becomes infeasible. Therefore we perform the dual simplex algorithm.

In order to carry out the dual simplex algorithm, we use BTRAN to update row 3 of (7.2), being the row in which x_2 is basic, to give

z	x_1	x_2	x_3	x_4	x_5	x_6	
0	0	1	0.143	-0.286	0.071	0	.

$$(7.3)$$

The updated objective row is

z	x_1	x_2	x_3	x_4	x_5	x_6
1	0	0	0.143	1.714	0.071	0

(7.4)

On the left-hand branch we wish x_2 to leave the basis, using (7.4) as pivot row, by *decreasing* it to its new upper bound of 1. We therefore (in the revised simplex form as opposed to the equation form of section 2.6) choose the variable to enter the basis as that having minimum *positive* ratio between (7.4) and (7.3). There is clearly a tie and we choose x_3 to enter, and use FTRAN to update the column for x_3 to

$$\begin{array}{|c|} \hline 0.143 \\ 0.429 \\ 0.143 \\ 1.538 \\ \hline \end{array}$$

(7.5)

The corresponding eta vector is

$$\begin{array}{|c|} \hline 3 \\ \hline -1.0 \\ -3.0 \\ 7.0 \\ 11.0 \\ \hline \end{array}$$

(7.6)

and new solution vector is

$$\begin{array}{|c|} \hline -19.0 \\ -0.5 \\ 6.5 \\ -6.0 \\ \hline \end{array}$$

(7.7)

with basis list

z	x_1	x_3	x_6

(7.8)

remembering that x_2 is non-basic at its new upper bound of 1. We are still not (primal) feasible. Therefore we perform another dual simplex iteration to drive x_6 out of the basis by pivoting on row 4. Updating row 4 by BTRAN gives

z	x_1	x_2	x_3	x_4	x_5	x_6
0	0	-11.0	0	3.0	-1.0	1.0

(7.9)

The updated objective row is

z	x_1	x_2	x_3	x_4	x_5	x_6
1.0	0	-1.0	0	2.0	0	0

$$\text{(7.10)}$$

We wish to *increase* the value of x_6 to its lower bound of 0, by pivoting in row (7.10). We choose the variable to enter the basis as that having the minimum absolute negative ratio between (7.10) and (7.9). This gives x_5 as the variable to enter. Updating the column for x_5 by FTRAN gives

$$
\begin{array}{|c|}
\hline
0 \\
-0.5 \\
0.5 \\
-1.0 \\
\hline
\end{array}
\qquad \text{(7.11)}
$$

We perform a (dual degenerate) iteration corresponding to eta vector

$$
\begin{array}{|c|}
\hline
4 \\
\hline
0 \\
0.5 \\
0.5 \\
-1.0 \\
\hline
\end{array}
\qquad \text{(7.12)}
$$

This gives the new solution vector as

$$
\begin{array}{|c|}
\hline
-19.0 \\
2.5 \\
3.5 \\
6.0 \\
\hline
\end{array}
\qquad \text{(7.13)}
$$

with basis list

$$
\begin{array}{|c|c|c|c|}
\hline
z & x_1 & x_3 & x_5 \\
\hline
\end{array}
\qquad \text{(7.14)}
$$

and x_2 at its upper bound of 1. Since this solution is feasible, we have optimised the LP relaxation associated with node 1. In Figure 7.1 these *extra* eta vectors are associated with node 1 together with additional information.

On the right-hand branch at node 0 we wish x_2 to leave the basis, using (7.3) as pivot row, by *increasing* it to its new lower bound of 2. We therefore choose the variable to enter the basis as that having minimum absolute negative ratio between (7.4) and (7.3). This gives x_4 to enter the basis. Updating the column for x_4, using the eta vectors associated with node 0, gives

$$
\begin{array}{|c|}
\hline
1.714 \\
0.143 \\
-0.286 \\
-0.143 \\
\hline
\end{array}
\cdot \qquad (7.15)
$$

The corresponding eta vector is

$$
\begin{array}{|c|}
\hline
3 \\
\hline
6.0 \\
0.5 \\
-3.5 \\
-0.5 \\
\hline
\end{array}
\qquad (7.16)
$$

and new (feasible) solution vector is

$$
\begin{array}{|c|}
\hline
-18.5 \\
2.25 \\
0.25 \\
4.25 \\
\hline
\end{array}
\qquad (7.17)
$$

with basis list

$$
\begin{array}{|c|c|c|c|}
\hline
z & x_1 & x_4 & x_6 \\
\hline
\end{array}
\qquad (7.18)
$$

remembering that x_2 is now non-basic at its lower bound of 2. At node 2 we have therefore solved the LP relaxation by one dual simplex iteration from node 0. The extra eta vector and associated information for node 2 is marked in Figure 7.1.

Step 2　We continue to follow the same tree search as in Figure 6.2, giving the resultant information obtained in Figure 7.1.

The partial development of the tree is given in Figure 7.1, producing extra eta vectors for the LP relaxations associated with each node. For any node the full associated eta file can then be obtained, if needed, by combining it with that of its parent.

One advantage of using the dual simplex algorithm to move from the LP relaxation solution at one node to that at the son or daughter is that there is a continuous non-improvement in the objective value. Generally this will be a degradation unless there is a dual degeneracy. Therefore, as frequently happens, if an LP relaxation becomes infeasible or the objective becomes worse than that of the best integer solution to date, this may manifest itself before having to solve the associated LP fully. Hence the branch can be dropped and computation saved. This happens at the left-hand branch from node 1 in Figure 7.1. If, however, the primal simplex algorithm were used, the objective value would generally degrade in phase I but improve in phase II, preventing one knowing if one could terminate the calculation before the LP relaxation was fully solved.

There are, however, disadvantages incurred by using the dual simplex algorithm. These result from the usual data structures used, in which it is cumbersome and slow to update rows of the matrix. Multiple "pricing" on rows is also slow and not usually worth while. Nevertheless, a dual simplex method, if incorporated in the package, is usually to be preferred for the reasons given.

7.2 PRIORITIES, PENALTIES AND PSEUDO-COSTS FOR BRANCHING VARIABLES

At each node the choice of variable to branch on can have a major effect on the time taken to perform the tree search. There is no easily calculated rule for finding the "best" such variable. Some useful (heuristic) data can, however, be obtained from the solution to the LP relaxation and are discussed below. Alternatively, the user can specify a *priority* order for the variables. Then the integer variable, taking a fractional value, that is highest in the priority list is chosen. This scheme has the virtue that the user should have a knowledge of which variables are more important, and no extra calculation is required to determine these variables. In this section, as in Chapter 6, we will only treat the structural variables as integer and not exploit the integrality of the logical variables in a PIP model since we are developing rules for dealing with general MIP models.

The solution tree in Figure 7.1 could be regarded as having been obtained by using the priority order x_2, x_1, x_3. Exercise 7.2 involves solving this model with a different priority order.

It is possible to use the information obtained from the LP relaxation at a node to calculate *minimum* amounts by which the objective function will be degraded through branching on a variable. These quantities are known as *penalties* and are illustrated by an example. They have the advantage over priorities in that they can be used not only to decide on which variable to branch but also to decide the favoured branching direction. Also they can be used to suggest the most desirable waiting nodes to develop, which priorities are incapable of doing.

Example 7.2 The Branch-and-Bound Method With Penalties

Solve Example 7.1 making use of penalties at each node.

We begin by considering node 0 of Figure 7.1 and the degradation caused by branching on either of the integer variables x_1 or x_2, which take fractional values.

In order to do this, we have to update, by BTRAN, rows 2 and 3 of (7.2), in which x_1 and x_2 are respectively basic, to give

z	x_1	x_2	x_3	x_4	x_5	x_6	
0	1.0	0	0.429	0.143	-0.286	0	(7.19)

and

z	x_1	x_2	x_3	x_4	x_5	x_6	
0	0	1.0	0.143	-0.286	0.071	0	(7.20)

as well as updating the objective row to

z	x_1	x_2	x_3	x_4	x_5	x_6	
1.0	0	0	0.143	0.714	0.071	0	. (7.21)

If x_1, taking the value 2.286, were to be forced down to 2, the first iteration of the dual simplex algorithm would produce a degradation of

$$0.286 \times \text{Min}\left(\frac{0.143}{0.429}, \frac{1.714}{0.143}\right) = 0.095. \tag{7.22}$$

In order to take x_1 out of the basis (at its new upper bound of 2), the integer, non-basic, variable x_3 must therefore enter the basis by a value of at least $0.286/0.429$. Since it is an integer variable, it must therefore ultimately increase by a value of at least 1. This would degrade the objective function by at least 0.143 (the reduced cost of x_3). Since this figure is larger than that in (7.22) this gives us a *down-penalty* (or left-hand penalty) for x_1.

Similarly if x_1 were to be forced up to 3, the first iteration of the dual simplex algorithm would produce a degradation of

$$0.714 \times \frac{0.071}{0.286} = 0.177. \tag{7.23}$$

For this example we will not exploit the fact that, from the structure of this particular model (because it is a PIP), the variable that would enter (x_5) is integer. The *up-penalty* on x_1 is therefore taken as 0.177.

We give the general rule for calculating penalties. If we update the row in which the branching variable taking the value $N + f$ is basic, where $0 < f < 1$, then let the updated coefficients of the non-basic variables in this row be

$$
\begin{array}{cccc}
y_1 & y_2 & \cdots & y_n \\
\hline
a_1 & a_2 & \cdots & a_n \\
\hline
\end{array}
\tag{7.24}
$$

and the updated objective corresponding to these variables be

$$
\begin{array}{cccc}
y_1 & y_2 & \cdots & y_n \\
\hline
c_1 & c_2 & \cdots & c_n \\
\hline
\end{array}.
\tag{7.25}
$$

The down-penalty will be

$$
P_D = \underset{\substack{j \\ a_j < 0}}{\text{Min}}
\begin{cases}
fc_j/|a_j|, & y_j \text{ non-integer at lower bound} \\
fc_j/a_j, & y_j \text{ non-integer at upper bound} \\
\text{Max}(c_j, fc_j/|a_j|), & y_j \text{ integer at lower bound} \\
\text{Max}(|c_j|, fc_j/a_j), & y_j \text{ integer at upper bound.}
\end{cases}
\tag{7.26}
$$

The up-penalty will be

$$
P_U = \underset{\substack{j \\ a_j > 0}}{\text{Min}}
\begin{cases}
(1-f)c_j/a_j, & y_j \text{ non-integer at lower bound} \\
(1-f)|c_j|/a_j, & y_j \text{ non-integer at upper bound} \\
\text{Max}(c_j, (1-f)c_j/a_j), & y_j \text{ integer at lower bound} \\
\text{Max}(|c_j|, (1-f)|c_j|/a_j), & y_j \text{ integer at upper bound.}
\end{cases}
\tag{7.27}
$$

Applying these results we can calculate lower and upper penalties for x_2 (taking the value of 1.929 at node 0) of

$$
P_D = \text{Max}\left(0.143, 0.929 + \frac{0.143}{0.143}\right) = 0.929
\tag{7.28}
$$

and

$$
P_U = 0.071 \times \frac{1.714}{0.286} = 0.425.
\tag{7.29}
$$

(In fact, if we exploited the integrality of x_4, we could get a better up-penalty of 1.714.) It can be observed from Figure 7.1 that the integer solutions lying down the left- and right-hand sides of the tree (nodes 7 and 4) have degradations of at least these amounts.

Penalties can be used to guide the tree search in ways that are explained in section 7.4. It is not always the case that one wishes to "aim" for the best integer solution first. For this example, however, we will use the penalties on x_1, x_2 and x_3 at each node to take the branch with least degradation. It can be verified (exercise 7.4) that this produces the tree given in Figure 7.2.

At the top of the tree we branch downwards on x_1 with the lowest penalty of 0.143. Rather than necessarily solve the LP relaxations at both son and daughter nodes, we will always develop the most promising node. It must be

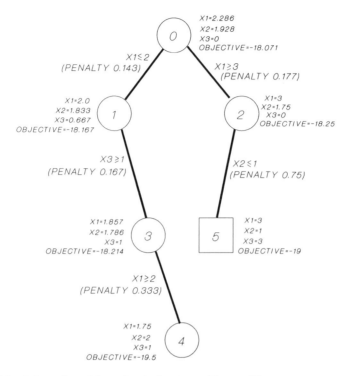

Figure 7.2 A branch-and-bound solution tree with penalties

remembered that the penalties are progressive. Hence after solving the LP relaxation at a node, we consider developing that node with a branching direction having least penalty. We do not, in this illustrative example, go back to a node and branch on a different variable, even though the penalty might be less than any other.

In the example, we obtain an integer solution in this manner at node 5. This then allows us to cut off node 4. The down-penalty on x_1 at node 3 is infinite, demonstrating an infeasible branch, which may be cut. The down-penalty on x_3 at node 1 is 3.335, demonstrating the impossibility of a better integer solution down this branch. Therefore the solution at node 5 is optimal.

Not only can penalties be used to help choose the branching variable, and waiting nodes for development, they can enable one to cut off branches. This can happen if a penalty is infinite (the corresponding ratios (7.26) or (7.27) are vacuous) or the degradation makes any possible integer solution worse than one already known. The consideration of the left-hand branches at nodes 3 and 1 in Figure 7.2 demonstrated these possibilities. It can also happen that all both up- and down-penalties associated with a node demonstrate no possibility of a better integer solution. In this case the node and all its descendants can be removed from further consideration. As explained in section 6.2, the cutting out of potential branches is what makes the branch-and-bound method viable.

The penalties described above can be improved by making use of Gomory cuts mentioned in section 6.4. References are given in section 7.5. Unfortunately, computational experience with penalties has not been as good as this small example might suggest. For realistically sized models the penalties can prove very weak and only represent *local* degradations. Some practical problems exhibit "dual degeneracy". If this occurs on the first dual simplex iteration from a node, the penalty becomes zero. They then give little useful guidance as to preferred branching variables or directions, as they do not indicate *global* effects in the tree search. In consequence they are not widely used. What is more, their calculation does require updating portions of the matrix and incurs some computational cost.

An alternative, but related, approach to penalties is to use *pseudo-costs*. These are empirically derived quantities, which suggest the degradations that will result from branching on particular variables. The hope is that these degradations will be more realistic than the gross underestimates often produced by penalties. There is an assumption that these quantities will not vary greatly from one part of the tree to another. If necessary, they can be revised during the course of the tree search. They are illustrated by considering Example 7.1 again.

Example 7.3 The Branch-and-Bound Method With Pseudo-Costs
Solve Example 7.1 making use of pseudo-costs at each node.

The pseudo-costs can be supplied by the user, possibly as a result of solving a similarly structured model in the past. Alternatively, extra calculation can be carried out at node 0 in order to calculate lower and upper pseudo-costs for each possible branching variable. We give these quantities here. Those for x_1 and x_2 can be derived from Figures 7.1 and 7.2 and those for x_3 by extra calculation later in the tree. They are defined as the degradation in objective value per unit of infeasibility removed. For this example these are:

	x_1	x_2	x_3
Lower pseudo-cost	0.335	3.248	–
Upper pseudo-cost	0.251	1.664	–

For example, in Figure 7.2 at node 0, x_1 takes the value 2.286. To remove the infeasibility of 0.286 on the left-hand branch results in an objective degradation of 0.096. The degradation by unit of infeasibility is therefore 0.335.

We are now in a position to decide on the branching variable and direction, assuming, as in Example 7.2, that we wish to "aim" for the integer optimum as quickly as possible. The resulting solution tree is given in Figure 7.3.

We estimate the lowest degradation as that resulting from branching on x_1 in a downwards direction.

At node 1 it is worth considering the branching on x_3 to calculate the

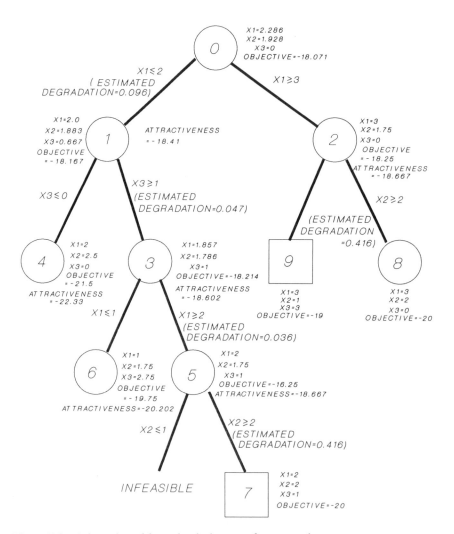

Figure 7.3 A branch-and-bound solution tree from pseudo-costs

resulting pseudo-costs for x_3. This gives:

	x_3
Lower pseudo-cost	5.0
Upper pseudo-cost	0.143

For this example we will solve the LP relaxations of both the son and the daughter nodes after each node.

We are now in a position to calculate an *attractiveness* quantity associated with each node. This is obtained by summing the degradations resulting from forcing all integer variables back in the cheapest way to a neighbouring integer value and applying this total degradation to the objective value of the LP relaxation. It gives an estimate of the ultimate objective value that might be obtained from developing the node.

For node 1:

$$\text{Attractiveness} = -18.167 - 0.117 \times 1.664 - 0.333 \times 0.143 = -18.41.$$

$$(7.30)$$

For node 2:

$$\text{Attractiveness} = -18.25 - 0.25 \times 1.667 = -18.667. \quad (7.31)$$

Node 1 therefore appears more attractive for development. We initially branch upwards on x_3. Of the waiting nodes 2, 3 and 4, node 3 appears the most attractive. The tree is developed in the manner shown in Figure 7.3 and the optimal solution found at node 9. In this example, use of pseudo-costs has not proved particularly helpful.

Nevertheless, this may result from the rather myopic use of estimated degradations and attractiveness to guide the tree search. Also we could have updated the pseudo-costs whenever possible to give more accurate estimates of degradations and attractiveness. In section 7.4 pseudo-costs are used in a rather more sophisticated manner.

7.3 BRANCHING ON SPECIAL ORDERED SETS OF VARIABLES

Special ordered sets of variables were introduced in section 1.3. For a special ordered set of type 1 (SOS1), at most one member of the set can be non-zero. For a special ordered set of type 2 (SOS2), at most two members of the set can be non-zero, and those two members must be adjacent in the ordering. The use of these sets for modelling practical problems is discussed in *MBMP*. There is great virtue in treating each set as an *entity* rather than as a collection of variables. Then it becomes possible to branch on the entity rather than the individual integer variables, to good effect.

We begin by considering the SOS1 case defined by the condition:

$$\text{At most one of } (x_1, x_2, ..., x_n) \text{ can be non-zero.} \tag{7.32}$$

This can be regarded as a generalisation (more "general" than a general integer) of a 0–1 variable. Ultimately, in a feasible solution, the non-zero variable will lie to the left, or the right, of any *marker* placed between two consecutive variables. We then say

$$\text{either} \quad \{x_1, x_2, ..., x_r\} \text{ are all zero} \tag{7.33}$$

$$\text{or} \quad \{x_{r+1}, x_{r+2}, ..., x_n\} \text{ are all zero.} \tag{7.34}$$

These two possibilities correspond to a branch in a solution tree demonstrated in Figure 7.4.

When more than one of the variables in (7.32) takes a non-zero value, the SOS1 is infeasible. We have to measure this infeasibility in a manner analogous to the fractionality of an integer variable. In order to do this we have to associate with the variables in (7.32) a monotonic set of numbers $(a_1, a_2, ..., a_n)$ known as a *reference row*. This set of numbers arises naturally in the formulation of some applications from a constraint. If it is not present, then we set $a_1 = 1, a_2 = 2, ..., a_n = n$ in order to associate each variable with its place in the ordering. We then define the following quantity known as the *fractionality* of the current value of the set

$$\sum_j a_j x_j \bigg/ \sum_j x_j. \tag{7.35}$$

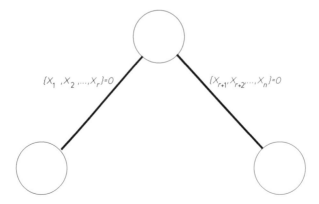

Figure 7.4   Branching on a special ordered set of type 1

If, as is frequently the case, the members of (7.32) sum to 1, then (7.35) can be regarded as the "centre of gravity" of the current value of the set. Since the numbers a_j are monotonic, there will be some a_r such that

$$a_r \leqslant \sum_j a_j x_j \Big/ \sum_j x_j < a_{r+1} \qquad (7.36)$$

indicating that the centre of gravity of the set has come out between index r and $r + 1$. If the set is still infeasible, we therefore place the branching marker between x_r and x_{r+1}.

Example 7.4 Branching on an SOS1
Find the fractionality and branching marker for the following values of an SOS1:

$$\{0.1, 0, 0.6, 0.2, 0, 0.1\}.$$

In the absence of a reference row, we take this as $(1, 2, 3, 4, 5, 6)$.

The fractionality can be calculated as 3.3. Since $3 < 3.3 < 4$, we would set the branching marker between 3 and 4. In the left-hand branch we would set $x_1 = x_2 = x_3 = 0$, and in the right-hand branch we would set $x_4 = x_5 = x_6 = 0$.

The concept of priorities, penalties and pseudo-costs can also be generalised to apply to SOS1 sets.

SOS2 sets can be dealt with in an analogous manner. Here we have the condition:

At most two adjacent members of $\{\lambda_1, \lambda_2, ..., \lambda_n\}$ can be non-zero. (7.37)

In this case, in a feasible solution, we can observe that

$$\text{either} \qquad \{\lambda_1, \lambda_2, ..., \lambda_{r-1}\} \text{ are all zero} \qquad (7.38)$$

$$\text{or} \qquad \{\lambda_{r+1}, \lambda_{r+2}, ..., \lambda_n\} \text{ are all zero.} \qquad (7.39)$$

These two possibilities correspond to a branch in the solution tree demonstrated in Figure 7.5. The branching marker, in this case, would be r.

Again, it is possible to calculate a fractionality measure associated with a set of values of the variable. Frequently there will be a reference row associated with the set since such sets commonly arise from the modelling of non-linear functions as described in *MBMP*. If there is no reference row, we again use the sequence of numbers $a_1 = 1, a_2 = 2, ..., a_n = n$. The fractionality is again defined by (7.35) with λ_j in place of x_j. Expression (7.36) is used to determine the branching marker. In this case there is ambiguity as to whether it should be r or $r + 1$. A rule has to be given to decide.

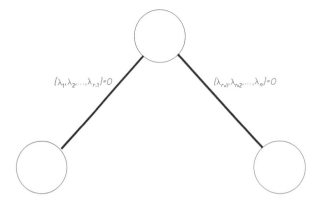

Figure 7.5 Branching on a special ordered set of type 2

The concept of priorities, penalties and pseudo-costs can again be generalised. Details of these technical calculations are not included here but can be found from references in section 7.5.

7.4 TREE SEARCH STRATEGIES

So far we have not been very precise about our aims in solving an IP model. We have loosely assumed that we wished to find the optimal solution as quickly as possible. There is, of course, a distinction between *finding* such a solution and *proving* it optimal. If we wish to do the latter, this can affect our strategy. In some cases we may be content with a "good" feasible solution.

Some of the strategies we have adopted to date have been "myopic" in the sense that we have just had regard to minimising the degradation in objective value between successive LP relaxations. Three possible (conflicting) aims that a user might have are:

(i) To obtain the proven optimal solution as quickly as possible.
(ii) To obtain a "good" integer (feasible) solution as quickly as possible and then terminate the tree search.
(iii) To obtain a large number of integer solutions in a reasonable time.

Different strategies are appropriate to these three aims.

The first aim demands that we complete the tree search. Therefore, some useless branches must still be fathomed. The higher up the solution tree this is done, the less will be the computation. It is of great advantage here to use *cut-off* values for the objective function. These are values equal to, or worse than, that of the best possible integer solution we might be interested in. Once the objective value of the LP relaxation down a branch becomes worse than this value, the branch can be terminated. If we cannot define such a value with total confidence, we may be able to define an *aspiration* level. This is an objective value that we expect to be able to achieve. If the objective value of the LP relaxation down a branch becomes worse than the value, we can *postpone* the branch. Hopefully we will later find a good integer solution whose objective value allows us to cut off this branch permanently. If the user has a reasonable knowledge of his or her model, then it is likely that he or she will be able to give cut-off or aspiration values. Otherwise there is merit in pursuing aim (ii) first in order to obtain a good cut-off value before carrying on to complete the tree search.

Besides using cut-off or aspiration values to terminate branches of the tree and so pursue aim (i), we can also use some of the measures associated with a node in pursuing this aim or other of the aims. Measures so far discussed are:

(a) The optimal objective value of the LP relaxation.
(b) The smallest/largest actual or estimated degradation associated with any possible branching variables.
(c) An attractiveness measure based on applying pseudo-costs to estimate the effect of removing all infeasibilities.

In pursuing aim (i), use can be made of (b) to choose that node with a branching variable and direction producing greatest degradation. If this degradation results from a penalty, we may be able to rule out that branching direction immediately as leading to an infeasible solution or an objective value worse than the cut-off or aspiration. Then we can make a *forced move* in the opposite direction. Even if such a forced move is not possible, there is merit on branching on this variable, in this opposite direction. Hopefully this will produce a good integer solution relatively quickly, allowing the other branch to be cut off.

If we wish to pursue aim (ii), then measure (c) could be used to try to obtain a good solution by a *depth-first* search. In many situations the user is content with such a solution and has no desire to test its optimality. Example 7.3, illustrated in Figure 7.3, made use of such an approach. An even simpler measure to use is (a). This figure is readily available and was used in Example 7.1, illustrated in Figure 7.1. In practice, such a measure is not often a good guide to the quality of the best integer solution down a branch.

The third objective is not a common one. Should one wish to obtain a large number of integer solutions, then it will be necessary to develop many waiting nodes, ignoring their measures of attractiveness. Also it will be necessary not to terminate branches where the objective value has become worse than that of the best integer solution so far found.

The choice of waiting node to develop is sometimes partly dictated by the data structures used to store the tree. In the early days the nodes of the tree were stored in a *stack*. This made it efficient to use a "last-in/first-out" (LIFO) strategy. After each LP relaxation at a node was solved, either the son or the daughter would be solved and the other placed in the stack. When backtracking up the tree, the node at the top of the stack would always be solved. With random-access computer storage it becomes unnecessary to restrict oneself in this way. The approach does, however, still have some merit since, if the eta files are stored in the manner suggested in section 7.1, less updating of the matrix will be necessary. Also, storage requirements can be reduced since nodes removed from the stack can be deleted. It is also advantageous, for this reason, to solve the LP relaxations of both the son and daughter nodes immediately on developing their parent.

Besides the choice of waiting nodes to develop, the other important choice is that of branching variable. This may be dictated by the first choice if we are using measure (b) in pursuing aim (i). There are, however, other possibilities that can be considered for the variables to branch on, such as:

(1) The highest priority variable.
(2) The variable closest/furthest from an integer value.
(3) The variable producing the smallest/largest degradation according to penalties or pseudo-costs.

Which of these choices is made will depend in part on the aims (i), (ii) or (iii). In Example 7.1 we used criterion (2), and in Examples 7.3 and 7.4 we used (3).

It is difficult to be definitive about what tree search strategy to use, since this should depend in part on one's aims but also on the structure of the model. Most computer packages give the user flexibility to choose different strategies. The methods suggested are essentially *heuristic* and their merits are measured by their success or otherwise on realistic problems. Indeed, as already explained, the branch-and-bound method is a framework within which many variations can be incorporated.

A numerical consideration should also be mentioned. It will be necessary to decide when a variable has attained an integer value. A tolerance will be needed to judge this. A common value used is 10^{-6}.

In order to illustrate some of the above considerations we will resolve Example 7.1 using an "intelligent" strategy.

Example 7.5 A Branch-and-Bound Strategy

Solve Example 7.1 using the pseudo-costs given in Example 7.3 and calculating penalties. The aim is to obtain and prove the optimal solution as quickly as possible.

The steps of the calculation are illustrated in Figure 7.6.

On the basis of penalties (or pseudo-costs), the "worst" variable and direction is the branch downwards on x_2. Therefore we branch upwards on x_2 to node 1, but simultaneously solve node 2.

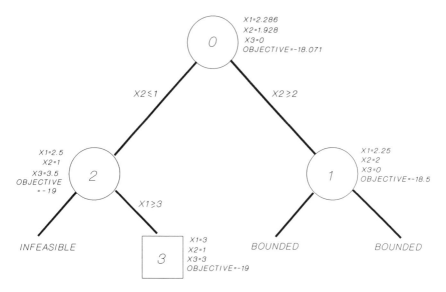

Figure 7.6 A branch-and-bound strategy

Of the two waiting nodes, branching downwards on x_1 at node 2 gives a penalty of ∞, indicating that this branch is infeasible. Therefore we are forced to branch upwards on x_1 at node 2, which we do, producing an integer solution at node 3.

The only waiting node is 1, which has downward and upward penalties that would degrade the objective to -19.0 and -20.0 respectively. Therefore this node cannot produce a better integer solution than that at node 3, which must be optimal.

7.5 HISTORY, REFERENCES AND FUTURE DEVELOPMENTS

As with LP, the computational considerations for IP are considered by Orchard-Hays (1969) and Murtagh (1981). Beale (1985) gives one of the more up-to-date surveys. Manuals associated with the more sophisticated computer packages also discuss the subject.

Updating the Basis

The material here depends on descriptions of the revised simplex and dual simplex algorithms given in references in sections 2.9 and 4.7.

Priorities, Penalties and Pseudo-Costs for Branching Variables

Penalities were devised by Driebeek (1966) and improved by Tomlin (1971). Pseudo-costs are due to Benichou et al. (1971). Beale (1979) and Mitra (1973) discuss the practical usefulness of all these ideas. A variation on pseudo-costs is to devise pseudo-shadow prices as a means of measuring the effect of altering the value of an integer variable. This is discussed by Nygreen (1991). If these qualities are to be used in solving practical models, it is desirable to experiment with them on smaller models with a similar structure in the hope that general rules will emerge.

Branching on Special Ordered Sets of Variables

Special ordered sets are due to Beale and Tomlin (1970) but are now incorporated in many computer packages. They have been generalised by Beale (1980) to deal with non-separable non-linear functions.

Tree Search Strategies

There are many papers and books reporting experimental results using different strategies with different packages on different models. Besides those given above, many ideas are contained in Forrest, Hirst and Tomlin (1974). It should be explained that the idea of a tree search strategy is not confined to optimisation problems. Where a combinatorial search is needed, IP can often be used with benefit using a "surrogate" objective to give the search a sense of direction. This aspect is considered by Williams (1987, 1990).

7.6 EXERCISES

7.1 Solve Example 1.13 by the branch-and-bound algorithm using the dual simplex algorithm between nodes, creating the necessary eta vectors at each node.

7.2 Solve Example 7.1 using the priority order x_1, x_2, x_3. Use the dual simplex algorithm between nodes and devise a suitable rule for choice of waiting node.

7.3 Calculate penalties for branching variables at each of the nodes created in exercise 7.2. Investigate if these penalties could have been used to good effect.

7.4 Verify the calculations that produce Figure 7.2.

7.5 Use the eta vectors in Figure 7.1 to create the updated matrix rows at node 1. Show that the downward branch from this node has an infinite penalty. Explain what is meant by saying that the upward branch is "dual degenerate".

7.6 Recalculate the pseudo-costs, where possible, at each node in Figure 7.3, to investigate their suitability.

***7.7** Devise a penalty calculation for branching on an SOS1 and an SOS2.

7.8 If all the variables in an SOS1 are 0–1, compare the maximum number of branches involving these variables with the maximum number of branches on the SOS1.

7.9 Solve Example 1.16 by branching on the SOS2.

7.10 Solve Example 7.1 in order to find *all* integer solutions.

Chapter 8
Specialist Methods for Integer Programming Models

The branch-and-bound method is of general applicability to integer programming (IP) models. It cannot, however, be guaranteed to be an efficient method of solving all models. Sometimes it becomes worth while to exploit the special structure of some IP models and develop specialist algorithms. The most obvious specialist structure is that of the pure 0–1 IP model. In fact, as was shown in section 1.3, any pure IP (PIP) model in bounded integer variables can be expressed in this way. Therefore, in sections 8.1 and 8.2 we give specialist methods for this type of model. The first method of implicit enumeration is also a branch-and-bound method, but not one based on the linear programming relaxation. The second method of Boolean algebra is quite different and relies on the algebra of logic. A number of well known combinatorial problems are described in section 8.3, which can be formulated as IPs but sometimes are best solved by making use of specialist algorithms.

8.1 IMPLICIT ENUMERATION FOR PURE 0–1 MODELS

We will demonstrate this method by an example. In order to do this, we have transformed Example 6.1 into a 0–1 model by the "binary expansion" given in section 1.3. It has been necessary to place bounds on the values of the integer variables x_1, x_2 and x_3 in order to do this, since, in that example, the model had an open feasible region. We have used our knowledge of the model to impose bounds that do not exclude an optimal solution (although they will obviously exclude certain feasible solutions). The following transformations have been made:

$$x_1 = y_1 + 2y_2 \tag{8.1}$$

$$x_2 = y_3 + 2y_4 \tag{8.2}$$

$$x_3 = y_5 + 2y_6 \tag{8.3}$$

where $y_j \in \{0, 1\}$.

Example 8.1 Implicit Enumeration for a Pure 0–1 Model

$$\text{Minimise} \quad 2y_1 + 4y_2 + 7y_3 + 14y_4 + 2y_5 + 4y_6 \tag{8.4}$$

subject to

$$y_1 + 2y_2 + 4y_3 + 8y_4 + y_5 + 2y_6 \geqslant 10 \tag{8.5}$$

$$4y_1 + 8y_2 + 2y_3 + 4y_4 + 2y_5 + 4y_6 \geqslant 13 \tag{8.6}$$

$$y_1 + 2y_2 + y_3 + 2y_4 - y_5 - 2y_6 \geqslant 0 \tag{8.7}$$

$$0 \leqslant y_1, y_2, y_3, y_4, y_5, y_6 \leqslant 1 \quad \text{and integer.} \tag{8.8}$$

It is convenient, when applying this algorithm, to consider all models as minimisations with all the objective coefficients non-negative. If any objective coefficient is negative, we simply complement the corresponding 0–1 variable y_j, replacing it by $1 - \bar{y}_j$, where $\bar{y}_j \in \{0, 1\}$.

The algorithm is a branch-and-bound method. It uses a tree search strategy, searching for feasible solutions down branches of a tree. When one is found, or a branch goes infeasible, or worse than the best solution to date, backtracking takes place. In this way it is similar to the branch-and-bound method for general IP models described in section 6.2. Unlike that method, however, it does not use the LP relaxation. Therefore, it can use a restricted set of arithmetical operations. If all the coefficients of the model (as is usual) are integers, then the algorithm can be performed in all-integer arithmetic with consequent savings of time and storage. The algorithm is sometimes also known as Balas' additive algorithm after its inventor, and because floating-point multiplication is not needed.

Step 1 We define three sets of indices N, J_0 and J_1 as follows: N is the set of indices of variables y_j unassigned a permanent value but temporarily assigned to 0; J_0 is the set of indices of variables y_j assigned a value of 0; and J_1 is the set of indices of variables y_j assigned a value of 1.

To begin with, all variables are assigned to N. The situation can be represented by node 0 of the tree given in Figure 8.1. J_0 and J_1 are empty sets indicated as $\emptyset$. With each node we associate

(i) the membership of N, J_0 and J_1,
(ii) the objective value, and
(iii) the total infeasibility.

Step 2 At each node we carry out a number of tests in order to reduce the potential search (and hence allow an "implicit" rather than an "explicit" enumeration of all possible values for the y_j).

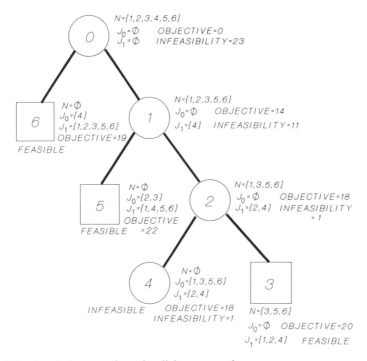

Figure 8.1 A solution tree from implicit enumeration

    Test (i) Is the solution feasible? If it is, we note it if it is better
             than the best known feasible solution and then proceed
             to step 4.
   Test (ii) We see if, by setting any unassigned variables to 1, the
             objective would become no better or worse than the best
             feasible solution. Such variables are fixed at 0 (as in a
             "forced move" in the method described in section 7.4)
             and we proceed to test (iii).
  Test (iii) We see if any variables must be fixed in order to make
             a constraint feasible and then repeat test (ii). Should
             different constraints result in contradictory assignments,
             we terminate the branch as infeasible and proceed to step
             4. Similarly, if for any constraints no feasible assign-
             ments are possible, we terminate the branch as infeasible
             and proceed to step 4. Lastly, these assignments may
             make the objective no better than the best feasible
             solution. The branch is said to be "bounded" and can be
             terminated, and we proceed to step 4. Otherwise we
             proceed to step 3.

Step 3 We choose an unassigned variable and set it to 1. The choice of variable is heuristic. A good choice is that variable which creates the greatest reduction in total infeasibility. It is therefore convenient to present this information in a table.

For the example this is done in Table 8.1, with V_j representing the infeasibility reduction resulting from assigning y_j from N to J_1. In the example, at node 0, we therefore branch on y_4, creating node 1 and return to step 2.

Step 2 (repeated)   The solution is still infeasible. None of the other tests (i), (ii) or (iii) fixes variables and we proceed to step 3.

Step 3 (repeated)   The information calculated for node 1 in Table 8.1 suggests branching on y_2, which we do, setting it to 1, to create node 2.

Step 2 (repeated)   The solution is infeasible and none of the tests fixes a variable.

Step 3 (repeated)   We branch on y_1, setting it to 1, to create node 3.

Step 2 (repeated)   The solution is now feasible with an objective value of 20. Hence we note it and proceed to step 4.

Step 4 In this step we backtrack to the previous node up the tree (a last-in/first-out strategy) and make the opposite assignment. For the example, we return to node 2 and set $y_1 = 0$, taking us to node 4.

Step 2 (repeated)   The solution is infeasible. Test (ii) shows that setting any of the unassigned variables to 1 would make the objective value at least as bad as 20, for which we already have a feasible solution. Therefore all these variables are fixed at 0 in a forced move, giving the infeasible solution at node 4, from which no further branches are possible.

Step 4 (repeated)   We backtrack to node 1 and set $y_2 = 0$, taking us to node 5.

Step 2 (repeated)   The solution is infeasible. Test (ii) shows that y_3 must

Table 8.1

Node	Objective	Infeasibility	V_1	V_2	V_3	V_4	V_5	V_6	Branching variable
0	0	23	5	10	6	12	2	4	4
1	14	11	5	10	4	–	3	6	2
2	18	1	1	–	1	–	1	1	1
3	20	0	Feasible						
4	18	1	Infeasible by fixing of variables						
5	22	0	Feasible						
6	19	0	Feasible						

be fixed at 0. Test (iii) shows that y_1, y_5 and y_6 must be fixed at 1 to make constraint 2 feasible. This results in a setting of all the variables giving a feasible solution at node 5.

Step 4 (repeated) We backtrack to node 0 and set $y_4 = 0$, taking us to node 6.

Step 2 (repeated) The solution is infeasible. Test (iii) shows that all the unassigned variables must be set to 1 in order to make constraint 1 feasible. This results in a feasible solution at node 6, which is better than that already obtained.

There being no waiting nodes, the solution at node 6 must be optimal.

Substituting this solution into (8.1), (8.2) and (8.3) gives

$$x_1 = 3, \quad x_2 = 1, \quad x_3 = 3, \quad \text{objective} = 19. \tag{8.9}$$

There are variants possible for the algorithm given here. In particular, alternative heuristics are possible for choosing the branching variable to reduce infeasibility. Degradation in the objective function, instead of infeasibility reduction, or a combination of both are possible guides. Also it is possible to backtrack to other nodes instead of LIFO strategy using heuristic measures of node attractiveness. Another possibility is to introduce "surrogate" constraints resulting from linear combinations of the original constraints. These can be used to help calculate infeasibilities resulting from variable assignments.

It is easy to construct examples (exercise 8.2) to show that, in the worst case, the number of steps needed to find the optimal solution of a pure 0–1 model by implicit enumeration is exponential in the size of the model.

8.2 BOOLEAN ALGEBRA FOR PURE 0–1 MODELS

Instead of restricting the feasible combinations of values for the 0–1 variables by linear (in)equalities, we can use Boolean algebra (sometimes known as the propositional calculus). In order to do this, it is convenient to express statements concerning combinations of the variables that *cannot* simultaneously be true. Such statements are known as *resolvents*. They are explained by means of an example.

Example 8.2 The Resolvent of a Pure 0–1 Model
Find the resolvent for the constraints of Example 8.1.

In order to do this, it is convenient to express the constraints in the " $\leqslant$ " form with all positive coefficients. This can be done by, if necessary, complementing the variables in some constraints. Also it is convenient to order the variables in each constraint so that their coefficients are in descending order of magnitude. Constraints (8.5), (8.6) and (8.7) respectively give rise to

$$8\bar{y}_4 + 4\bar{y}_3 + 2\bar{y}_2 + 2\bar{y}_6 + \bar{y}_1 + \bar{y}_5 \leqslant 8 \qquad (8.10)$$

$$8\bar{y}_2 + 4\bar{y}_1 + 4\bar{y}_4 + 4\bar{y}_6 + 2\bar{y}_3 + 2\bar{y}_5 \leqslant 11 \qquad (8.11)$$

$$2\bar{y}_2 + 2\bar{y}_4 + 2y_6 + \bar{y}_1 + \bar{y}_3 + y_5 \leqslant 6 \qquad (8.12)$$

where $\bar{y}_j = 1 - y_j$.

It is now possible to see that certain combinations of the values of the variables are infeasible. For example, $\bar{y}_3$ and $\bar{y}_4$ cannot simultaneously take the value 1, since the combined total of their coefficients exceeds the right-hand side of (8.10). In order to express this fact in Boolean algebra, we associate a *statement* Y_j with the setting $y_j = 1$ and a *statement* $\bar{Y}_j$ (meaning "not Y_j") with the setting $y_j = 0$ (i.e. $\bar{y}_j = 1$). Using "." to represent the logical connective "and", we can express our observation as

$$\bar{Y}_4 . \bar{Y}_3 \quad \text{is false.} \qquad (8.13)$$

It is possible to express all the other incompatible combinations of variables in a similar manner as *conjunctions* of statements about individual variables. For constraint (8.10), it is easy to show that the following set of conjunctions must all be false:

$$\bar{Y}_4 . \bar{Y}_3, \qquad \bar{Y}_4 . \bar{Y}_2, \qquad \bar{Y}_4 . \bar{Y}_6, \qquad \bar{Y}_4 . \bar{Y}_1, \qquad \bar{Y}_4 . \bar{Y}_5,$$
$$\bar{Y}_3 . \bar{Y}_2 . \bar{Y}_6 . \bar{Y}_1, \qquad \bar{Y}_3 . \bar{Y}_2 . \bar{Y}_6 . \bar{Y}_5. \qquad (8.14)$$

It is only necessary to state the "minimal" such combinations of incompatible variables, since the incompatibility of any larger set is then guaranteed. For example, we clearly have $\bar{Y}_4 . \bar{Y}_3 . \bar{Y}_2$ as false but implied by (8.13). Having organised the coefficients of (8.10) into descending order, it is straightforward to devise an algorithm for enumerating all the minimal conjunctions.

Since *all* conjunctions in (8.14) must be false, the *disjunction* of them also must be false. Using "∨" to represent the logical connective "or" (and reordering the statements by their indices), this is written as

$$\bar{Y}_3 . \bar{Y}_4 \vee \bar{Y}_2 . \bar{Y}_4 \vee \bar{Y}_4 . \bar{Y}_6 \vee \bar{Y}_1 . \bar{Y}_4 \vee \bar{Y}_4 . \bar{Y}_5$$
$$\vee \bar{Y}_1 . \bar{Y}_2 . \bar{Y}_3 . \bar{Y}_6 \vee \bar{Y}_2 . \bar{Y}_3 . \bar{Y}_5 . \bar{Y}_6. \qquad (8.15)$$

The compound statement (8.15) is known as the *resolvent for the constraint* (8.10). For the constraint to be satisfied it must be false. It has been written in *disjunctive normal form* as a series of *clauses* (the conjunctions) connected by "∨". Each clause is a conjunction of *literals*. A literal is either a single letter or its negation. Note that, in order to save brackets we regard the "." connective as more binding than the "∨".

In a similar manner it is possible to give resolvents for (8.11) and (8.12). These are respectively

$$\overline{Y}_1.\overline{Y}_2 \vee \overline{Y}_2.\overline{Y}_4 \vee \overline{Y}_2.\overline{Y}_6 \vee \overline{Y}_2.\overline{Y}_3.\overline{Y}_5 \vee \overline{Y}_1.\overline{Y}_4.\overline{Y}_6$$
$$\vee \overline{Y}_1.\overline{Y}_3.\overline{Y}_4.\overline{Y}_5 \vee \overline{Y}_1.\overline{Y}_3.\overline{Y}_5.\overline{Y}_6 \vee \overline{Y}_3.\overline{Y}_4.\overline{Y}_5.\overline{Y}_6 \quad (8.16)$$

and

$$\overline{Y}_1.\overline{Y}_2.\overline{Y}_4.Y_6 \vee \overline{Y}_2.\overline{Y}_3.\overline{Y}_4.Y_6 \vee \overline{Y}_2.\overline{Y}_4.Y_5.Y_6$$
$$\vee \overline{Y}_1.\overline{Y}_2.\overline{Y}_3.\overline{Y}_4.Y_5 \vee \overline{Y}_1.\overline{Y}_2.\overline{Y}_3.Y_5.Y_6 \vee \overline{Y}_1.\overline{Y}_3.\overline{Y}_4.Y_5.Y_6. \quad (8.17)$$

The fact that all constraints must be satisfied is expressed by the falsity of the *resolvent of the system*. This is the disjunction of the resolvents of the individual constraints, i.e. we connect together (8.15), (8.16) and (8.17) by "∨" connectives.

There are standard procedures for simplifying expressions, such as this, in disjunctive normal form. One method of simplification is repeatedly to apply the following operations:

(i) If exactly one literal appears negated in one clause and unnegated in another, then a new clause (known as the *consensus*) may be added to the disjunction. This clause is the conjunction of the two component clauses with the literal deleted.

(ii) If one clause is a proper subset of the other (it is said to be *subsumed*), then the larger clause may be deleted.

Both of these operations rely on results from elementary Boolean algebra. These may be found from the references in section 8.6 or verified using Venn diagrams or truth tables.

The first clause of (8.15) is subsumed by the sixth and eighth clauses of (8.16) and by the second, fourth and sixth clauses of (8.17), which may therefore all be removed.

The second clause of (8.15) is a duplicate of the second clause of (8.16) and is subsumed by the first and third clauses of (8.17), which may therefore all be removed.

The third clause of (8.15) is subsumed by the fifth clause of (8.16), which may therefore be removed.

The first clause of (8.16) is subsumed by the sixth clause of (8.15) and the fifth clause of (8.17), which may therefore be removed. (We have shown (8.17), and therefore constraint (8.7), to be redundant.)

The third clause of (8.16) is subsumed by the seventh clause of (8.15), which may therefore be removed.

These simplifications reduce the resolvent of the system to

$$\bar{Y}_3.\bar{Y}_4 \vee \bar{Y}_2.\bar{Y}_4 \vee \bar{Y}_4.\bar{Y}_6 \vee \bar{Y}_1.\bar{Y}_4 \vee \bar{Y}_4.\bar{Y}_5 \vee \bar{Y}_1.\bar{Y}_2$$
$$\vee \bar{Y}_2.\bar{Y}_6 \vee \bar{Y}_2.\bar{Y}_3.\bar{Y}_5 \vee \bar{Y}_1.\bar{Y}_3.\bar{Y}_5.\bar{Y}_6. \quad (8.18)$$

Such a resolvent is clearly a way of representing all the feasible solutions of the model.

In order to seek an optimal solution, we need also to consider the objective, which is done in the following example.

Example 8.3 Solving a Pure 0–1 Model by Boolean Algebra
Use the resolvent of Example 8.2 to solve the model.

We will place an *upper bound* on the value of the objective function in order to see if this is a value that is achievable by minimisation. For a maximisation model, we would use a lower bound. If the bound is not achievable, we progressively relax the bound until we obtain a feasible solution. Carrying out the procedure systematically enables us to find an optimal solution.

In the example, for illustration, we will try to make the objective (8.4) as small as 18. Applying a constraint to this effect, we therefore convert the objective into the following constraint, ordered in decreasing coefficient size (complementing the variables if necessary, in order to make all coefficients non-negative):

$$14y_4 + 7y_3 + 4y_2 + 4y_6 + 2y_1 + 2y_5 \leqslant 18. \quad (8.19)$$

We create the resolvent for (8.19), which is

$$Y_3.Y_4 \vee Y_2.Y_4.Y_6 \vee Y_1.Y_2.Y_4 \vee Y_2.Y_4.Y_5$$
$$\vee Y_1.Y_4.Y_6 \vee Y_4.Y_5.Y_6 \vee Y_1.Y_2.Y_3.Y_5.Y_6. \quad (8.20)$$

This resolvent is then joined by a disjunction to (8.18). The following simplifications take place.

The consensus of the second clause of (8.20) with the sixth clause of (8.18) is $\bar{Y}_1.Y_4.Y_6$, which has a consensus of $Y_4.Y_6$ with the fifth clause of (8.20). This, in turn, has a consensus of $\bar{Y}_2.Y_4$ with the seventh clause of (8.18), which combines with the second clause of (8.18) to give a consensus of $\bar{Y}_2$. By subsumation, we may now remove the second, sixth, seventh and eighth clauses of (8.18).

$\bar{Y}_2$ forms consensi with the second, third, fourth and seventh clauses of (8.20), which may then be removed by subsumation to produce the simplified system

$$\overline{Y}_3.\overline{Y}_4 \vee \overline{Y}_4.\overline{Y}_6 \vee \overline{Y}_1.\overline{Y}_4 \vee \overline{Y}_4.\overline{Y}_5 \vee \overline{Y}_1.\overline{Y}_3.\overline{Y}_5.\overline{Y}_6$$

$$\vee \, Y_3.Y_4 \vee Y_4.Y_6 \vee Y_1.Y_4 \vee Y_4.Y_5 \vee Y_1.Y_3.Y_5.Y_6 \vee \overline{Y}_2. \quad (8.21)$$

The consensus of the fifth and sixth clauses of (8.21) is $\overline{Y}_1.Y_4.\overline{Y}_5.\overline{Y}_6$, which has a consensus of $\overline{Y}_1.Y_4.\overline{Y}_5$ with the seventh clause. This in turn has a consensus of $\overline{Y}_1.\overline{Y}_5$ with the fourth clause. Combining this consensus with the ninth clause produces the consensus $\overline{Y}_1.Y_4$, which combines with the third clause to produce the consensus $\overline{Y}_1$. Similarly the consensus of $\overline{Y}_1.Y_4$ with the eighth clause is Y_4. These two consensi can be used by further consensus and subsumation to simplify the system to

$$\overline{Y}_3 \vee \overline{Y}_6 \vee \overline{Y}_1 \vee \overline{Y}_5 \vee Y_1.Y_3.Y_5.Y_6 \vee \overline{Y}_2. \quad (8.22)$$

The consensus of the first four clauses of (8.22) with the fifth is a tautology (a statement that is always true). Therefore the resolvent can never be false, demonstrating the incompatibility of objective constraint (8.19) with the other constraints.

Hence we relax the bound of 18 on the objective to 19 to give the new constraint

$$14y_4 + 7y_3 + 4y_2 + 4y_6 + 2y_1 + 2y_5 \leqslant 19. \quad (8.23)$$

This has a resolvent

$$Y_3.Y_4 \vee Y_2.Y_4.Y_6 \vee Y_1.Y_2.Y_4 \vee Y_2.Y_4.Y_5 \vee Y_1.Y_4.Y_6 \vee Y_4.Y_5.Y_6. \quad (8.24)$$

Combining this resolvent with (8.18) allows some of the steps in the simplification of (8.20) to be repeated. The resultant simplified system is

$$\overline{Y}_1 \vee \overline{Y}_2 \vee \overline{Y}_3 \vee Y_4 \vee \overline{Y}_5 \vee \overline{Y}_6. \quad (8.25)$$

No further simplification is possible. Any settings for the values of the variables that make (8.25) false will therefore produce a solution with an objective value of 19. These must all be optimal solutions. In this case the only optimal solution is

$$y_1 = y_2 = y_3 = 1, \quad y_4 = 0, \quad y_5 = y_6 = 1. \quad (8.26)$$

This corresponds (within the bounds thereby imposed on their values) by (8.1) to (8.3) to

$$x_1 = 3, \quad x_2 = 1, \quad x_3 = 3, \quad \text{objective} = 19. \quad (8.27)$$

Clearly this example demonstrates that this approach to solving pure 0–1 models can be lengthy. Exercise 8.4 is used to show that the method is not polynomially bounded. The method does, however, have the virtue of characterising *all* feasible solutions of a model. For highly restricted models with only a few feasible solutions, this may be valuable. This approach can also be used to help reformulate models. It is also closely connected with methods for solving computational logic problems arising in artificial intelligence. These considerations are discussed, with references, in section 8.6.

8.3 COMBINATORIAL PROBLEMS

In this section we describe some combinatorial problems and suitable specialist algorithms. It is, of course, always possible to treat the resultant models by the conventional IP algorithms described in Chapters 6 and 7. In most cases, however, this would be grossly inefficient, and sometimes prohibitively so.

There are many other combinatorial problems for which specialist algorithms prove worth while. Many of these are mentioned, with their applications, in *MBMP*. In particular, it is worth mentioning the quadratic assignment problem, set covering, packing and partitioning problems, facility location problems, bin packing and job shop scheduling problems. To describe specialist methods for all these problems is, however, beyond the scope of this book, whose emphasis is on general methods. Indeed, most of the specialist methods can be viewed in the framework of the general methods.

Many combinatorial optimisation problems arise in connection with graphs. These problems can usually be formulated as LP or IP models. Some of the, apparently IP, models turn out to have a special structure, which guarantees that the optimal solution to the LP relaxation is integral, so obviating the need for computationally costly IP. This was true of the minimum-cost and maximum flow models, and the shortest-path and assignment problems, which can be regarded as special cases. Therefore, they were considered as special cases of LP in Chapter 3. Nevertheless, it is sometimes worth while using specialist methods as described in that chapter.

In constrast, there are some graphical models that are genuine IP models in the sense that the LP relaxation is not generally integral. Although they can be tackled by the methods described in Chapters 6 and 7, it is more efficient to use specialist methods. One such problem concerns matching nodes on a graph. This problem is of particular computational interest since, although it is a "genuine" IP problem, there is a polynomially bounded algorithm for its solution. Therefore it is very much on the boundary between the easy (e.g. LP) and the hard (e.g. IP).

The Matching Problem

The matching problem is illustrated in Figure 8.2. We wish to "match" (or "pair") nodes together. Matched nodes must be joined by single edges of the original graph. No node may be paired with more than one other. The

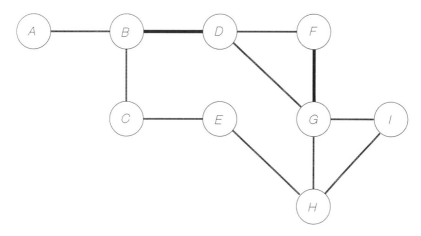

Figure 8.2 A matching of a graph

matching illustrated by bold lines in which B is matched with D and F with G is one such matching. It is not, however, a *maximum cardinality matching*, i.e. a matching corresponding to the maximum number of pairs possible. Clearly it may not be possible to make sure every node is matched (i.e. has a "mate"). Indeed, if, as in Figure 8.2, there are an odd number of nodes, such a *perfect matching* is impossible. The problem remains, however, of finding the maximum cardinality matching.

Should different possible matches (edges) be given different weights, then we may wish to find the *maximum weighted matching*.

We give IP formulations for these problems.

Example 8.4 Formulating a Matching Problem as an IP Model
Formulate the maximum cardinality matching problem of Figure 8.2 as a PIP model.

We introduce 0–1 variables x_{PQ} to indicate if P is matched with Q ($x_{PQ} = 1$) or not ($x_{PQ} = 0$). The impossibility of matching any node with more than one other gives rise to constraints corresponding to each node. Then the model is:

Maximise

$$x_{AB} + x_{BC} + x_{BD} + x_{CE} + x_{DF} + x_{DG} + x_{EH} + x_{FG} + x_{GH} + x_{GI} + x_{HI} \quad (8.28)$$

subject to

$$\text{A:} \qquad\qquad\qquad x_{AB} \leqslant 1 \qquad\qquad (8.29)$$

$$\text{B:} \qquad x_{AB} + x_{BC} + x_{BD} \leqslant 1 \qquad\qquad (8.30)$$

$$\text{C:} \qquad\qquad x_{BC} + x_{CE} \leqslant 1 \qquad\qquad (8.31)$$

$$\text{D:} \qquad x_{BD} + x_{DF} + x_{DG} \leqslant 1 \qquad\qquad (8.32)$$

$$\text{E:} \qquad x_{CE} + x_{EH} \leqslant 1 \qquad\qquad (8.33)$$

$$\text{F:} \qquad x_{DF} + x_{FG} \leqslant 1 \qquad\qquad (8.34)$$

$$\text{G:} \qquad x_{DG} + x_{FG} + x_{GH} + x_{GI} \leqslant 1 \qquad\qquad (8.35)$$

$$\text{H:} \qquad x_{EH} + x_{GH} + x_{HI} \leqslant 1 \qquad\qquad (8.36)$$

$$\text{I:} \qquad x_{GI} + x_{HI} \leqslant 1 \qquad\qquad (8.37)$$

$$x_{PQ} \geqslant 0 \quad \text{and integer for all } P \text{ and } Q. \qquad\qquad (8.38)$$

This type of model is a special case of a *packing model* as described in *MBMP*. In general, the problem is to "pack" as many of a given collection of subsets into a set of objects with no overlap. Here each of our subsets consists of exactly two objects. The objects are conveniently represented by nodes of a graph and the subsets by arcs.

That this type of model is a genuine IP model can be seen from this example. The optimal solution to the LP relaxation is

$$x_{AB} = 1, \quad x_{BC} = x_{BD} = 0, \quad x_{CE} = 1, \quad x_{DF} = x_{DG} = \tfrac{1}{2}, \quad x_{EH} = 0,$$
$$x_{FG} = \tfrac{1}{2}, \quad x_{GH} = x_{GI} = 0, \quad x_{HI} = 1, \quad \text{objective} = 4\tfrac{1}{2}. \qquad (8.39)$$

It can be verified that each node of Figure 8.2 is covered by, at most, a total of one edge, sometimes made up of two half-edges. This fractional LP solution is obviously unacceptable.

A possible approach to solving this type of mode is to add cutting planes and resolve. This type of model is one of the few types for which it is known how to characterise all of the convex hull of integer solutions.

Example 8.5 Facets of the Convex Hull of a Matching Problem

Add cuts, in the form of facets, to the IP model for Example 8.4.

If an *odd* set of $2r + 1$ arcs is considered from a graph such as that in Figure 8.2, then clearly this can contain a matching represented by at most r arcs. For example, at most one of the arcs in the set DF, DG, GF can be in any matching. In terms of an IP constraint, this is stipulated by

$$x_{DF} + x_{DG} + x_{FG} \leqslant 1. \qquad\qquad (8.40)$$

This constraint is "stronger" than any of those already stipulated as (8.29) to (8.37) in the sense that there is no reason for the LP relaxation to satisfy it. Indeed, we can verify that the solution (8.39) does not satisfy it.

Therefore, such a constraint cuts off some of the feasible region associated with the LP relaxation. It can be proved, although we do not do so here, that if we stipulate such extra constraints for *all* odd subsets of arcs then we describe, together with (8.29) to (8.37) and the non-negativity constraints, all the facets of the convex hull.

Although this is one of the few examples of a class of IP models where a simple characterisation of all the facets is known, there could be an exponential number of them. In practice, one could solve such a model by adding such facets only when needed. In the above example we need only add (8.40) to start with. Resolving the LP relaxation with this extra constraint yields the solution:

$$x_{AB} = 1, \quad x_{CE} = x_{DF} = 1, \quad x_{GH} = x_{GI} = x_{HI} = \tfrac{1}{2}, \quad \text{objective} = 4\tfrac{1}{2}. \quad (8.41)$$

This solution is still fractional and we can usefully add the facet constraint corresponding to the odd cycle GHI currently having a fractional "matching". The constraint is

$$x_{GH} + x_{GI} + x_{HI} \leqslant 1. \tag{8.42}$$

Resolving the LP relaxation with (8.40) and (8.42) appended yields the integral solution

$$x_{AB} = x_{CE} = x_{DF} = x_{GH} = 1, \quad \text{objective} = 4. \tag{8.43}$$

Hence, in this simple example, we only needed to add in two such cuts to obtain a maximum cardinality matching.

The fact that it is only necessary to add cuts corresponding to odd subsets of arcs has led to the development of a special-purpose, polynomially bounded algorithm for the maximum cardinality matching problem. This is not discussed in this book. References can be found in section 8.6.

The Minimum-Cost Spanning Tree Problem

Given a connected graph, with costs associated with the arcs, a spanning tree is a minimal subset of arcs that still connects all the nodes together. It is easy to see that, for a graph with n nodes, any spanning tree has $n - 1$ arcs. Also, it is clear that a spanning tree will not have any circuits, since they would introduce redundant arcs. A minimum-cost spanning tree is such a spanning tree with minimum total cost. Figure 8.3 illustrates a graph and a non-minimum-cost spanning tree marked with bold arcs.

As with the matching problem, the minimum-cost spanning tree problem can be formulated as an IP model. This is demonstrated by an example.

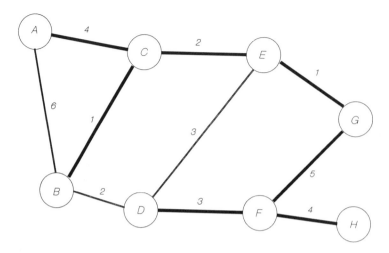

Figure 8.3 A graph and spanning tree

Example 8.6 Formulating a Minimum-Cost Spanning Tree Problem as an IP Model

Formulate the problem of finding the minimum-cost spanning tree of the graph in Figure 8.3 as an IP model.

We introduce 0–1 variables x_{PQ} to indicate which arcs are in the tree. Constraint (8.45) ensures that there are no more than seven arcs (one less than the number of nodes). Constraints (8.46) to (8.50) apply to proper subsets of three or more arcs. They prevent circuits of arcs being formed out of such subsets. In this example we have left out obviously redundant constraints. The resultant model is:

$$\text{Minimise} \quad 6x_{AB} + 4x_{AC} + x_{BC} + 2x_{BD} + 2x_{CE} + 3x_{DE}$$
$$+ 3x_{DF} + x_{EG} + 5x_{FG} + 4x_{FH} \quad (8.44)$$

subject to

$$x_{AB} + x_{AC} + x_{BL} + x_{BD} + x_{CE} + x_{DE} + x_{DF} + x_{EG} + x_{FG} + x_{FH} = 7 \quad (8.45)$$

$$x_{AB} + x_{AC} + x_{BC} \leqslant 2 \quad (8.46)$$

$$x_{AB} + x_{AC} + x_{BD} + x_{CE} + x_{DE} \leqslant 4 \quad (8.47)$$

$$x_{AB} + x_{AC} + x_{BD} + x_{CE} + x_{DF} + x_{EG} + x_{FG} \leqslant 6 \quad (8.48)$$

$$x_{BC} + x_{BD} + x_{CE} + x_{DE} \leqslant 3 \quad (8.49)$$

$$x_{DE} + x_{DF} + x_{EG} + x_{FG} \leqslant 3 \quad (8.50)$$

$$x_{PQ} \in \{0, 1\} \quad \text{for all } P, Q. \quad (8.51)$$

There are alternative IP formulations of this problem. One forms the subject of exercise 8.8.

One reason for including the IP formulation of this (easy) problem is that the formulation underlies an important IP formulation of the travelling salesman problem, which is a genuine and difficult IP problem considered in the next section.

For the above example the optimal solution is

$$x_{AB} = 1, \quad x_{AC} = 0, \quad x_{BC} = 1, \quad x_{BD} = 1, \quad x_{CE} = 1, \quad x_{DE} = 0,$$

$$x_{DF} = x_{EG} = 1, \quad x_{FG} = 0, \quad x_{FH} = 1, \quad \text{objective} = 17. \quad (8.52)$$

It is, however, quite unnecessary to use an IP model for this problem. In fact, such a model is potentially very large in view of the need to prevent circuits. There is a very simple algorithm, known as the greedy algorithm, that solves it very quickly. This is demonstrated by an example.

Example 8.7 Finding the Minimum-Cost Spanning Tree by the Greedy Algorithm
Find the minimum-cost spanning tree of the graph in Figure 8.3 by the Greedy algorithm.

Step 1 Choose one of the cheapest arcs. In the example we choose BC.
Step 2 Append a cheapest arc not yet included that connects to the existing subtree but does not create a cycle. Continue the process until all arcs are included. For example the steps of the procedure are shown in Figure 8.4.

It can be shown that in the case of a tie it does not matter which arc is chosen. If properly implemented this algorithm has a complexity of $O(n^2)$ where n is the number of vertices.

The above algorithm is referred to as "greedy" for the obvious reason that it only looks one step ahead, choosing the cheapest overall, next acceptable, arc. It is surprising that such a myopic approach does create an ultimately optimal solution. Greedy algorithms can be applied to a wide variety of other problems as heuristics that give good, but generally non-optimal, solutions. Some examples are given in section 8.5.

The Travelling Salesman and Vehicle Scheduling Problems

The travelling salesman problem (TSP) is famous because it is easily understood but notoriously difficult to solve in practice. In the example below we demonstrate how it may be formulated as an IP model.

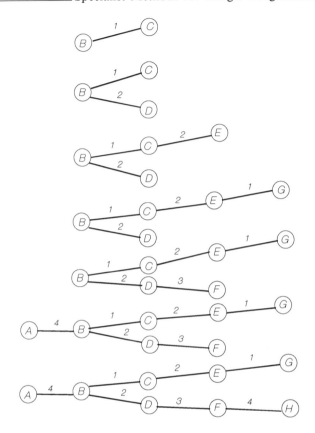

Figure 8.4 The greedy algorithm for finding a minimum-cost spanning tree

Example 8.8 Formulating an Asymmetric Travelling Salesman Problem as an IP Model

Formulate the problem of a salesman starting at one of the cities A to F, and visiting all the others, returning back to the beginning, as an IP model, where the objective is to cover the minimum distance.

Distances between cities are given in Table 8.2.

We observe that all the distances obey the *triangle inequality*, that is

Distance P to Q ≤ Distance P to R + Distance R to Q

For a distribution problem this seems a reasonable assumption. If we cannot assume such a relationship, then it can complicate certain algorithms.

This is an example of an *asymmetric TSP* because the distance from city P to city Q is not necessarily the same as the distance from Q to P. If all

Table 8.2

To From	A	B	C	D	E	F
A	0	42	62	53	96	105
B	52	0	49	29	54	84
C	70	42	0	77	65	129
D	42	35	56	0	57	56
E	105	63	81	41	0	80
F	101	93	111	72	75	0

such distances were the same, as frequently happens in distribution examples, we could specialise the formulation as is done in Example 8.9.

We introduce 0–1 variables x_{PQ} to indicate whether, or not, PQ is to be a link (directed arc) in the "tour".

It is convenient to use a concise notation to formulate the model. V will be used to represent the set of cities A, B, ..., F and c_{PQ} will be the distance between cities P and Q given in Table 8.2. Constraints (8.54) ensure that each city is entered exactly once and constraints (8.55) ensure that each city is left exactly once. Constraints (8.56) prevent *subtours*. Subtours are directed circuits among a subset of the cities as illustrated in Figure 8.5. If these constraints were ignored, the solution shown in Figure 8.5 would be feasible (and in this particular case optimal). In constraints (8.56) S is taken to represent a proper subset of the nodes and $|S|$ represents the number in this subset. The resultant model is

$$\text{Minimise} \quad \sum_{\substack{P,Q \in V \\ P \neq Q}} c_{PQ} x_{PQ} \tag{8.53}$$

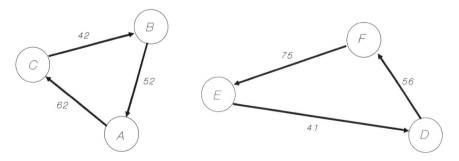

Figure 8.5 Subtours of a travelling salesman problem (total length = 328)

subject to

$$\sum_{\substack{P \in V \\ P \neq Q}} x_{PQ} = 1 \qquad \text{all } Q \in V \qquad (8.54)$$

$$\sum_{\substack{Q \in V \\ P \neq Q}} x_{PQ} = 1 \qquad \text{all } P \in V \qquad (8.55)$$

$$\sum_{\substack{P,Q \in S \\ P \neq Q}} x_{PQ} \leqslant |S| - 1 \qquad \text{all } S \subset V \qquad (8.56)$$

$$x_{PQ} \in \{0, 1\} \qquad \text{all } P, Q \in V, P \neq Q \qquad (8.57)$$

where " $\subset$ " represents strict inclusion.

The number of constraints (8.56) is an exponential function of the number of cities. This renders this *full* formulation impracticable for realistic problems. An alternative formulation is given in *MBMP* and another formulation forms the subject of exercise 8.11. The formulation given here is, however, useful in illustrating the solution method given in Example 8.10. Before doing this, however, we formulate the symmetric TSP as an IP model, as this specialisation has a structure that suggests another solution method.

Example 8.9 Formulating a Symmetric Travelling Salesman Problem as an IP Model

In Example 8.8, assume the distance from Q to P, where Q is after P on the listing of cities (represented by "$Q \geqslant P$"), is the same as that given for P to Q. Produce a more concise formulation.

We now let the 0–1 variables x_{PQ} indicate whether arc PQ (irrespective of direction) is a link in the tour. Constraints (8.54) and (8.55) can be combined in (8.59), which enforces exactly two arcs to be incident to each city. The resultant model is

$$\text{Minimise} \quad \sum_{\substack{P,Q \in V \\ P < Q}} c_{PQ} x_{PQ} \qquad (8.58)$$

subject to

$$\sum_{\substack{P \in V \\ P \neq Q}} x_{PQ} = 2 \qquad \text{all } Q \in V \qquad (8.59)$$

$$\sum_{\substack{P,Q \in S \\ P \neq Q \\ P < Q}} x_{PQ} \leqslant |S| - 1 \qquad \text{all } S \subset V \qquad (8.60)$$

$$x_{PQ} \in \{0, 1\} \qquad \text{all } P, Q \in V, P < Q. \qquad (8.61)$$

As the above formulations of both the asymmetric and symmetric travelling salesman problems have an exponential number of constraints, it would be impracticable to use them in their full form. Instead, we can exploit their special structure to use *relaxations* other than the (large) LP relaxation as part of the solution process. We first illustrate this by the problem in Example 8.9.

Example 8.10 Solving a Travelling Salesman Problem by the Assignment Relaxation
Solve the problem given in Example 8.8 by relaxing it to an assignment problem.

In section 6.2 we based the branch-and-bound method on the familiar *LP relaxation*. That is, we dropped the integrality conditions (constraints) at different stages in order to solve a much easier LP model. Other relaxations are possible. We can, as an alternative, drop some of the (in)equality constraints. As with an LP relaxation, the result will be to obtain an upper, or lower, bound on the optimal objective value of the original model, depending on whether the model is a maximisation or a minimisation.

For the formulation given in Example 8.8 a rather obvious relaxation is to ignore the subtour elimination constraints (8.56). The resultant model is an *assignment problem*. This type of model was discussed in section 3.2. Especially efficient methods (e.g. the Hungarian algorithm) exist for its solution. We illustrate the method through this example.

We incorporate the relaxation within a branch-and-bound framework. It is important to emphasise that there are many branch-and-bound methods that can be applied with this relaxation. We give one. Others can be found from the references in section 8.6.

Step 1 Solve the assignment relaxation.

For the example we ignore constraints (8.56) and the resultant solution is that given in figure 8.5.

If we now imposed a subtour elimination constraint, of the type (8.56), to remove the subtour BACB (say), we would no longer have an assignment problem. Therefore we would have to use a genuine IP algorithm. If we used the branch-and-bound method based on LP relaxations, the integrality property of the assignment problem would be lost. This would seem wasteful. Instead, we will branch in a different way, which allows us to remove the current subtours but does not rely on the LP relaxation.

Step 2 We observe that the following set of possibilities are exclusive and exhaustive:

$$x_{BA} = 0$$

or $\qquad x_{BA} = 1 \qquad$ and $\qquad x_{AC} = 0 \qquad\qquad$ (8.62)

or $\qquad x_{BA} = 1 \qquad$ and $\qquad x_{AC} = 1 \qquad$ and $\qquad x_{CB} = 0.$

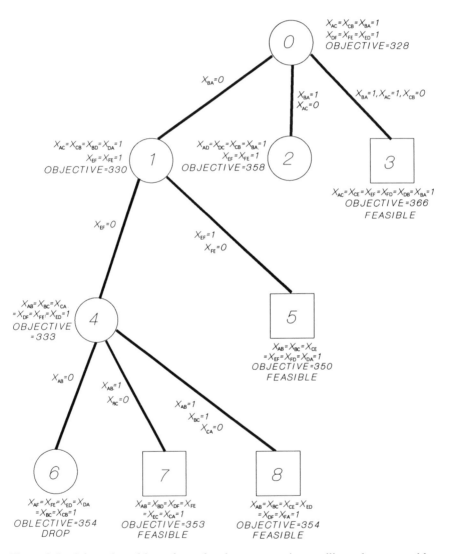

Figure 8.6 A branch-and-bound tree for the asymmetric travelling salesman problem using the assignment relaxation

Our branch-and-bound tree will allow more than two branches to emanate from nodes as indicated in Figure 8.6. We therefore create the three subproblems indicated from node 0. Each of these can be solved as an assignment problem by excluding and including the arcs shown. (If necessary, they can respectively be given large or zero costs.)

Step 3 We resolve each of the models corresponding to nodes 1, 2 and 3.

These are illustrated in Figure 8.7. Whereas the solutions at nodes 1 and 2 represent subtours, that at node 3 is a total tour. There is, of course, no guarantee that it is optimal, although the objective value does provide an upper bound on the optimal tour length. This branch of the tree is therefore fathomed.

We repeat step 3, branching in the same manner at nodes where subtours have been found.

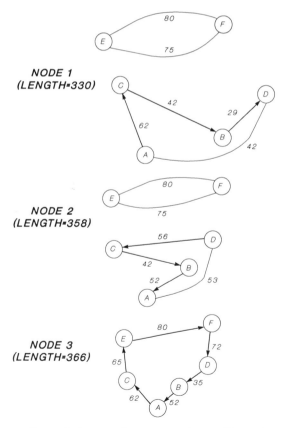

Figure 8.7 Intermediate solutions to the asymmetric travelling salesman problem

Notice that we find a total tour at node 5 of length 350. This enables us to drop the branch from node 2, which is also therefore fathomed.

The optimal tour is that found at node 5, which is illustrated in Figure 8.8. It was, however, necessary to develop node 4 before this could be proved.

The symmetric TSP could, of course, be treated as a special case of the general TSP and the assignment relaxation used as in Example 8.10. This is not, in practice, a very efficient method, as it is likely to result in very small subtours consisting of loops around two cities. If the assignment problem is regarded as a special case of the matching problem, then it is possible to generalise the matching problem to give a useful relaxation. Instead of insisting that at most one arc intersects each node, constraints (8.59) suggest that we relax this to at most *two* arcs intersecting each node. The resultant problem is known as the two-matching problem. We do not pursue this relaxation here. This and other approaches are referenced in section 8.6.

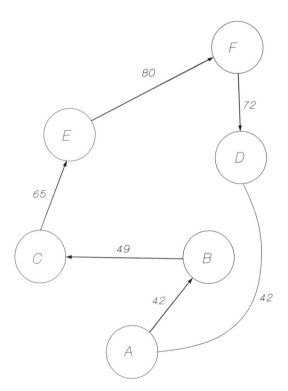

Figure 8.8 Optimal solution to the asymmetric travelling salesman problem (length = 350)

A powerful relaxation to use for the symmetric TSP results from an observation of the connection between this problem and the minimum-cost spanning tree problem. If one of the arcs is omitted from a TSP tour, we have a (particularly simple) spanning tree. It therefore seems profitable to consider spanning trees with one extra arc as a relaxation of a TSP tour. Such generalisations are known as *spanning one-trees*. The problem of finding a minimum-cost spanning one-tree can be formulated as an IP model by modifying the type of minimum-cost spanning tree formulation illustrated in Example 8.6. From the following example it will be clear that this is a relaxation of the TSP IP formulation given in Example 8.9.

Example 8.11 Relaxing a Symmetric Travelling Salesman Problem by a Minimum-Cost Spanning One-Tree
Relax the problem given in Example 8.9 to a minimum-cost spanning one-tree problem.

Step 1 We arbitrarily choose one city (known as the "root") and retain the constraint (8.59) relating to it.

For the example we will choose city A, so setting $Q = A$ in (8.59) to give

$$x_{AB} + x_{AC} + x_{AD} + x_{AE} + x_{AF} = 2. \qquad (8.63)$$

Step 2 We combine (so relaxing) all the other constraints (8.59) by adding them together. If there are n cities, then the resultant right-hand side will be $2(n-2)$. Each variable (apart from those in (8.63) that will have been eliminated) has a coefficient of 2. Therefore we can divide the constraint through by 2 to result in a constraint summing these variables to be equal to $n - 2$.

For the example we have

$$\sum_{\substack{P,Q \in V \\ P < Q \\ P,Q \neq A}} x_{PQ} = 4. \qquad (8.64)$$

Constraints (8.63) and (8.64) should be contrasted with the constraint that would result from the minimum-cost spanning tree formulation. This would be

$$\sum_{\substack{P,Q \in V \\ P < Q}} x_{PQ} = 5. \qquad (8.65)$$

We also need to remove all subtour elimination constraints involving the root node (city A in the example). Apart from this, the (large number of) other subtour elimination constraints will remain and be the same as those which would appear in the formulation of the minimum-cost spanning tree version of this example.

We postpone describing how to solve this symmetric TSP through the relaxation until section 8.4, since it can be regarded as a special case of a concept known as Lagrangean relaxation. Solving a minimum-cost spanning one-tree problem is, however, straightforward. It is not necessary to use explicitly the (large) IP formulation. The greedy algorithm, demonstrated through Example 8.7, can be used to find the minimum-cost spanning tree for the graph obtained by excluding the root node and its incident arcs. Then the two cheapest nodes incident to the root node are appended to give a one-tree.

For the example the resultant one-tree is shown in Figure 8.9.

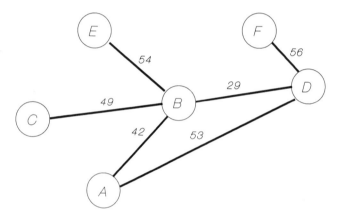

Figure 8.9 Minimum-cost spanning one-tree rooted at node A (length = 283)

In spite of the advantages of using specialist algorithms for *optimising* the TSP, the algorithms are still of exponential complexity. As a result of the discussion in section 1.7, it seems very unlikely that any polynomially bounded optimising algorithm will ever be found. Polynomially bounded heuristics can be found for finding sub-optimal solutions. Some are discussed in section 8.5.

The vehicle scheduling problem is closely related to the TSP. It is the problem of assigning delivery vehicles to customers and then routeing these vehicles. Rather surprisingly, it can be regarded as a special case of the TSP, as is demonstrated by the following example.

Example 8.12 Formulating a Vehicle Scheduling Problem as a Travelling Salesman Problem
Given three vehicles, based at city A, which must be used, formulate this problem, using the cities in Example 8.8, as a TSP.

In order to do this we split the base city into as many "dummy" cities as there are vehicles. The distances between these dummy cities are regarded as infinite. All other distances are as before. This problem, with the extra dummy cities, is now regarded as a TSP. Since there is an infinite distance between the dummy cities, the minimum-length tour will never go between them.

In the example, for illustration, we show in Figure 8.10 the optimal tour that can be obtained by one of the methods mentioned.

In practice, vehicle scheduling problems have extra conditions, only some of which can be satisfactorily tackled by an IP model. The two most common extra considerations are:

(i) Limited vehicle capacities, which limit the customers that can be visited by one vehicle.
(ii) "Time windows" for customer deliveries, which restrict the order in which they can be visited.

These extra considerations encourage the use of heuristic algorithms in conjunction with IP methods. They are discussed further in section 8.5.

The Chinese Postman Problem

This problem, at first sight, appears similar to the TSP but is genuinely

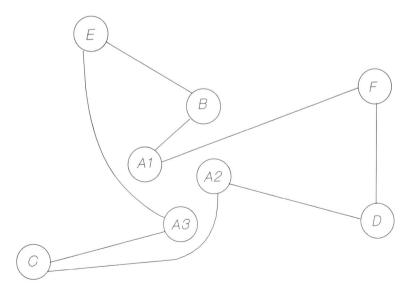

Figure 8.10 Optimal vehicle scheduling tour as a travelling salesman tour

different and somewhat easier. Given a connected graph of nodes (cities) and arcs, it is the problem of going along all the *arcs* and returning to the origin. This is in contrast to the TSP, which is the problem of visiting all the *nodes*.

For simplicity we will only consider the symmetric case in which the distance between *P* and *Q* is the same as that between *Q* and *P*. The arcs may therefore be regarded as undirected. As would be expected, the directed case is more difficult to solve. In order to illustrate the method, we use an example.

Example 8.13 Finding a Chinese Postman Tour
Find the shortest tour along all the edges of the graph in Figure 8.3.

A major observation is that, if a node has an *odd* number of arcs intersecting it, then at least one of these arcs must be traversed more than once. This is because each node is *left* as many times as it is *entered*. Therefore we have:

Step 1 Find all nodes of odd degree.

For the example, nodes B, C, D, E, F and H have odd degree. Therefore some of the arcs intersecting these nodes must be used more than once.

Another important observation is that there must be an *even* number of such odd-degree nodes. This is because each arc intersects two nodes, making for a grand total of an even number of node–arc intersections in the graph.

Given that we must traverse all arcs at least once, we wish to minimise the total *extra* distance we have to travel by duplicating arcs traversed. This may be done by matching the odd-degree nodes by the shortest paths between pairs.

Step 2 Find the minimum-cost matching of the odd-degree nodes. In order to do this we can use an IP model or the method mentioned (but not demonstrated) in section 8.3.

For the small example, one of the minimum-cost matchings is easily seen to be that in Figure 8.11.

Step 3 We duplicate the arcs in the paths corresponding to the matching in order to obtain a graph in which each node is of even degree.

For the example, the resultant graph is shown in Figure 8.12.

A graph with all nodes of even degree is known as Eulerian. It is fairly straightforward to show that an *Eulerian tour* is possible, i.e. a tour that traverses each arc exactly once.

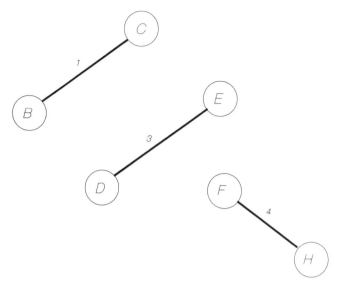

Figure 8.11 Minimum-cost matching for odd-degree nodes in the Chinese postman problem

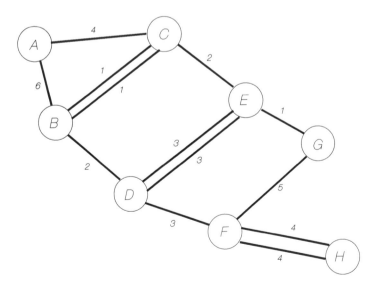

Figure 8.12 Chinese postman problem after duplicating arcs in the matching

Step 4 We start at any node and traverse an arc intersecting the node, arriving at another node. This process is continued. Each time we traverse an arc and a node we "rub it out", but must immediately check that we do not disconnect any part of the graph in so doing. If we do, then we must reinstate the arc and node and take an alternative arc out of the current node.

For the example, we can start at node A and proceed to B. We then (arbitrarily) go to C. If we were then to go to A, we would have disconnected nodes D, E, F, G and H. Therefore, we return instead to B along the other arc. We can proceed from there to D to E (avoiding going to C) to G to F (avoiding going to D) to H to F to D to E to C to A. A Chinese postman tour has now been created.

The complexity of this method is dominated by the minimum-cost (equivalent to maximum weighted) matching step. It can therefore be implemented in $O(n^3)$ steps, where n is the number of nodes.

The Knapsack Problem

This is the name given to a pure IP model with only one constraint; that is, a model of the form

$$\text{Maximise} \quad p_1 x_1 + p_2 x_2 + \cdots + p_n x_n \quad (8.66)$$

subject to

$$a_1 x_1 + a_2 x_2 + \cdots + a_n x_n \leqslant b \quad (8.67)$$

$$x_1, x_2, \ldots, x_n \geqslant 0. \quad (8.68)$$

We can assume that all coefficients are integers. Variants of the model with simple bounds on the variables, or where the variables are all 0–1, are regarded as special cases.

Instead of solving such models by general methods, it is more efficient to use dynamic programming as described in section 3.3. There, it was pointed out that the formulation of a deterministic problem as a dynamic programme amounts to representing it as a shortest-path model through an acyclic network. Therefore, instead of representing such a model using the somewhat off-putting notation of dynamic programming, we will directly represent it as a shortest-path model. In practice, such a representation would be *implicit* within a suitable data structure. A numerical example is used.

Example 8.14 Representing a Knapsack Problem as a Shortest- (Longest-) Path Problem

Represent the following as a shortest-path model:

$$\text{Maximise} \quad 7x_1 + 5x_2 + 3x_3 \qquad (8.69)$$

subject to

$$4x_1 + 3x_2 + 2x_3 \leqslant 9 \qquad (8.70)$$

$$x_1, x_2, x_3 \geqslant 0 \quad \text{and integer.} \qquad (8.71)$$

Since this model is a maximisation, it is convenient to consider it as a longest-path problem. We also include a slack variable x_4.

Nodes of a network are created corresponding to integers from 0 to the right-hand side value.

From the example we will have 10 nodes, which are conveniently labelled $0, 1, ..., 9$.

The longest-path problem from node 0 to a particular node corresponds to the knapsack problem with the number of this node as right-hand side. Directed arcs are introduced between nodes with numerical differences equal to coefficients in the constraint and costs equal to the corresponding objective coefficients.

For the example the network is shown in Figure 8.13.

The traversing of an arc corresponds to increasing the value of the corresponding variable by 1. A path from 0 to another node corresponds to a solution to the knapsack problem with the node number as right-hand side.

For example, if (8.70) had a right-hand side of 7, the (non-optimal) path

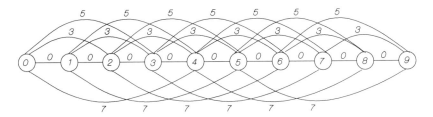

Figure 8.13 Shortest-path representation of a knapsack problem

0–4–6–7 of length 10 would correspond to the solution $x_1 = 1$, $x_2 = 0$, $x_3 = 1$, $x_4 = 0$. The path 0–3–6–7 of length 10 would correspond to the solution $x_1 = 0$, $x_2 = 2$, $x_3 = 0$, $x_4 = 0$.

Dynamic programming uses the principle of optimality to obtain the optimal path in terms of the optimal paths to preceding nodes. We illustrate its application by an example.

Example 8.15 Solving a Knapsack Problem as a Longest-Path Problem by Dynamic Programming

Apply dynamic programming to finding the longest path from 0 to 9 in Figure 8.13.

Using the method described in section 3.3, we produce the following table of longest distances $d(i)$ from node 0 to node i and the predecessor $p(i)$ of node i.

i	0	1	2	3	4	5	6	7	8	9
$d(i)$	0	0	3	5	7	8	10	12	14	15
$p(i)$	–	0	0	0	0	3	3	4	4	7

This demonstrates that the longest path is of length 15. Since $p(9) = 7$, $p(7) = 4$ and $p(4) = 0$, the corresponding path is 0–4–7–9. This uses one link between nodes of difference 4 (corresponding to x_1), one link between nodes of difference 3 (corresponding to x_2) and one link between nodes of difference 2 (corresponding to x_3). Therefore an optimal solution to this knapsack problem is

$$x_1 = x_2 = x_3 = 1, \quad \text{objective} = 15. \tag{8.72}$$

8.4 LAGRANGEAN, SURROGATE AND CONE RELAXATIONS

The version of the branch-and-bound method described in section 6.2 relied on solving the LP relaxation of an IP model at each node. Solving such a relaxation has three virtues:

(i) The LP relaxation is easier to solve than the IP model.
(ii) It might produce an integer solution, so obviating the need for further investigation down the current branch of the solution tree.
(iii) It will (if solvable) provide a *bound* on the optimal objective value, i.e. an upper bound for a maximisation model and a lower bound for a

minimisation model. This often enables one to truncate further search down a branch. The branch is then said to have been "fathomed".

The LP relaxation is not the only possible one to use in such a branch-and-bound framework, as was demonstrated in relation to the TSP. In this section we describe three alternative general relaxations that could be used. It is sometimes valuable to use them outside a branch-and-bound framework, but we confine ourselves to this approach in this section.

Lagrangean Relaxation

In section 2.5 we described the dual of an LP. The optimal dual solution provides a set of multipliers (*Lagrange multipliers*) for the constraints which give a tight bound for the optimal LP objective value. In section 6.5 we showed that there will, in general, be no such multipliers for the constraints of an IP model which provide a *tight* bound, i.e. there will be a *duality gap*. Nevertheless, any set of multipliers, of appropriate sign depending on whether they correspond to "$\leqslant$" or "$\geqslant$" constraints, will provide a bound.

If we apply a set of multipliers to *some* of the constraints of an IP (pure or mixed) model, and add them together in these multiples, we obtain such a bound. This may be subtracted from the objective function, and the corresponding constraints removed, to provide an easier IP model. Such a model is known as a *Lagrangean relaxation*.

It is worth pointing out that the assignment relaxation of the travelling salesman problem discussed in section 8.3 could be regarded as an especially simple case of Lagrangean relaxation. There, the multipliers for the subtour elimination constraints are 0. An improved algorithm can, however, be obtained by, at each stage, applying non-zero multipliers to the constraints corresponding to subtours and incorporating them in the objective function. This forms the subject of exercise 8.17.

In order to illustrate Lagrangean relaxation, we will solve the symmetric travelling salesman example for which we gave the one-tree relaxation example in Example 8.11. It is still, in general, advantageous to incorporate this in a branch-and-bound solution method. Again we could choose one of a number of possible branch-and-bound methods.

Example 8.16 Solving a Symmetric Travelling Salesman Problem by a Lagrangean One-Tree Relaxation
Attach multipliers to the constraints removed in Example 8.11 and substract the constraints, in these multiples, from the objective function in order to create a Lagrangean relaxation. Solve the model by means of this relaxation.

Step 1   We will begin with multipliers of 0, so obtaining the relaxation whose optimal solution is given in Figure 8.9.

Step 2   We attach multipliers to the constraints (8.59), which are violated by the solution shown in Figure 8.9. These constraints correspond to nodes that are intersected by more than or less than two arcs.

In this example node B is intersected by four arcs, node D by three arcs and nodes C, E and F by one arc. The corresponding relaxed constraints are

$$x_{AB} + x_{BC} + x_{BD} + x_{BE} + x_{BF} = 2 \tag{8.73}$$

$$x_{AD} + x_{BD} + x_{CD} + x_{DE} + x_{DF} = 2 \tag{8.74}$$

$$x_{AC} + x_{BC} + x_{CD} + x_{CE} + x_{CF} = 2 \tag{8.75}$$

$$x_{AE} + x_{BE} + x_{CE} + x_{DE} + x_{EF} = 2 \tag{8.76}$$

$$x_{AF} + x_{BF} + x_{CF} + x_{DE} + x_{EF} = 2. \tag{8.77}$$

We want the effect of multipliers on these constraints to *discourage* arcs intersecting B and D and to *encourage* arcs intersecting C, E and F. There is a systematic way, known as *subgradient optimisation*, of adjusting the multipliers to counteract the infeasibility resulting from leaving out the constraints. References to this are given in section 8.6.

For this example, we will begin by choosing multipliers of -20 and -10 respectively for (8.73) and (8.74) and 10 for (8.75), (8.76) and (8.77), in proportion to the amount by which the number of incident arcs to the node exceeds, or falls below, 2. The factor of 10 has been chosen to be of comparable magnitude to typical differences between costs of arcs. Applying these multipliers and subtracting the constraints from the objective function transforms the cost matrix to Table 8.3.

The spanning one-tree corresponding to this cost matrix is given in Figure 8.14, although original costs are entered in the figure. We incorporate extra multipliers to discourage arcs at C and to encourage arcs at F. In the example, the resultant one-tree is given in Figure 8.15. This is clearly a total tour and therefore the optimal solution.

Table 8.3

	B	C	D	E	F
A	62	52	63	86	95
B		59	59	64	94
C			77	45	109
D				57	56
E					60
F					

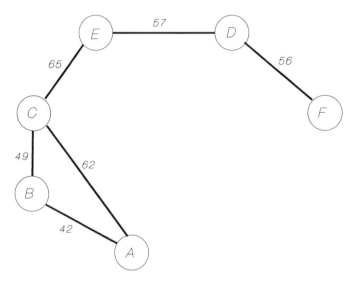

Figure 8.14 Second spanning one-tree from Lagrangean relaxation of symmetric travelling salesman problem (length = 331)

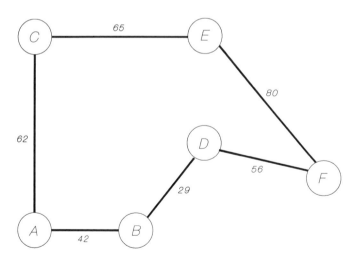

Figure 8.15 Third spanning one-tree from Lagrangean relaxation of symmetric travelling salesman problem (length = 334)

Although Lagrangean relaxation based on spanning one-trees are very powerful, they may still fail to produce an optimal solution. In that case a branch-and-bound method has to be used. There are many possible forms that this may take, which may be considered through the references in section 8.6.

Surrogate Relaxation

This relaxation consists of adding together all, or some, of the constraints of an IP model (pure or mixed) to create a replacement *surrogate* constraint. The effect of adding constraints together is generally to weaken their effect and so produce a relaxation. In the case of Lagrangean relaxation, this surrogate constraint is removed and incorporated in the objective function. Here, however, it is retained.

We illustrate surrogate relaxation by using the small numerical example of Example 6.1.

Example 8.17 Creating and Solving a Surrogate Relaxation of an IP Model
Apply multipliers to all (apart from non-negativity) constraints of the IP model of Example 6.1 to create a surrogate relaxation.

Clearly the significance lies in the ratios of the multipliers, not their absolute values.

For illustration, we will take all the multipliers as 1 to produce the knapsack constraint:

$$6x_1 + 7x_2 + 2x_3 \geqslant 23. \tag{8.78}$$

Using the objective function (6.2) to solve the model by dynamic programming gives the solution:

$$x_1 = 4, \quad x_2 = x_3 = 0, \quad \text{objective} = 8.$$

This is clearly infeasible according to the constraint (6.3), but provides a lower bound on the optimal objective value.

A better choice of multipliers would be the dual values associated with the LP relaxation. For constraints (6.2), (6.3) and (6.4) these are respectively $25/14$, 0 and $1/14$, giving the knapsack constraint:

$$25x_1 + 97x_2 + 23x_3 \geqslant 240. \tag{8.79}$$

This gives the solution

$$x_1 = 0, \quad x_2 = 2, \quad x_3 = 2, \quad \text{objective} = 18. \tag{8.80}$$

These are not the best set of multipliers in the sense of producing the tightest bound. Finding them is the subject of exercise 8.19. As with Lagrangean relaxation, it is seldom worth the effort to find the best. While the best Lagrangean relaxation always produces a bound at least as good as the LP relaxation, the best surrogate relaxation can be shown to be at least as good as a Lagrangean relaxation.

The Cone Relaxation

In section 6.5 the number of binding constraints for the optimal solution of an IP model was contrasted with the number for an LP model. For the latter case, in a model with n structural variables, it can be shown that at most n constraints (including non-negativity constraints if present) will be binding at an optimal solution. For a PIP model, however, this number can be as large as $2^n - 1$. By "binding" we mean that removal would alter the optimal solution (see exercise 6.15). Intuitively, however, it might seem plausible to assume that the same n constraints will be binding at the IP optimum as are binding for the optimum of the LP relaxation. Therefore we could ignore all but these n constraints in the IP model. By so doing we produce a relaxation. The optimal solution to this relaxation will produce a lower or upper bound on the objective function for the original model depending on whether it is a minimisation or a maximisation.

The resulting relaxed IP model is known as an *integer programme over a cone*. If we assume that the optimal solution to the LP relaxation of the original model is a vertex solution and ignore all constraints apart from those which are binding (and therefore intersect this vertex), we have constraints giving rise to a pointed cone (exercise 8.20 illustrates this geometrically). The relaxed IP model involves searching for the optimal integer lattice point within this cone.

It turns out that an IP model over a cone is particularly easy to solve. This is illustrated by Example 8.19. Before doing that, however, we will demonstrate the cone relaxation for our numerical example. We restrict ourselves to pure IP models, although the approach can be generalised to mixed IP models.

Example 8.18 The Cone Relaxation of an IP Model
For Example 6.1 create the cone relaxation associated with the optimal solution to LP relaxation.

The original model is

$$\text{Minimise} \quad 2x_1 + 7x_2 + 2x_3 \tag{8.81}$$

subject to

$$x_1 + 4x_2 + x_3 \geqslant 10 \tag{8.82}$$

$$4x_1 + 2x_2 + 2x_3 \geqslant 13 \tag{8.83}$$

$$x_1 + x_2 - x_3 \geqslant 0 \tag{8.84}$$

$$x_1, x_2, x_3 \geqslant 0 \quad \text{and integer.} \tag{8.85}$$

The optimal solution to the LP relaxation is

$$x_1 = 2\tfrac{2}{7}, \quad x_2 = \tfrac{13}{14}, \quad x_3 = 0, \quad \text{objective} = 18\tfrac{1}{4}. \tag{8.86}$$

The binding constraints can easily be seen to be (8.82), (8.83) and the non-negativity constraint on x_3. Therefore the cone relaxation is

$$\text{Minimise} \quad 2x_1 + 7x_2 + 2x_3 \tag{8.87}$$

subject to

$$x_1 + 4x_2 + x_3 \geqslant 10 \tag{8.88}$$

$$4x_1 + 2x_2 + 2x_3 \geqslant 13 \tag{8.89}$$

$$x_3 \geqslant 0 \tag{8.90}$$

$$x_1, x_2, x_3 \text{ integer.} \tag{8.91}$$

Notice that we are ignoring constraints (8.84) and the non-negativity constraints on x_1 and x_2 (the basic structural variables).

There are a number of efficient methods of solving the above type of model, which are referenced in section 8.6. The slightly unconventional approach that we adopt here relies on Fourier–Motzkin elimination, as described in section 2.2. Since the IP models of the type above have, by design, LP relaxations with only one vertex, Fourier–Motzkin elimination will not result in the usual explosive growth in inequalities. It will still, however, be necessary to modify the method to deal with the integrality of the variables. We describe this by means of an example.

Example 8.19 Solving the Cone Relaxation of an IP Model
Solve the cone relaxation created in Example 8.18.

Step 1   We convert the model into the "standard" form described in section 2.2.

$$\text{Minimise} \quad z \tag{8.92}$$

subject to

$$-2x_1 - 7x_2 - 2x_3 + z \geqslant 0 \tag{8.93}$$

$$x_1 + 4x_2 + x_3 \geqslant 10 \tag{8.94}$$

$$4x_1 + 2x_2 + 2x_3 \geqslant 13 \tag{8.95}$$

$$x_3 \geqslant 0. \tag{8.96}$$

Step 2   We eliminate a variable between all pairs of inequalities in which it has opposite sign. In so doing we are ignoring its integrality and thereby may ultimately attain a non-integer optimal solution. This can be rectified by adjusting the optimal value of z as described in step 4. Eliminating x_1 gives

$$x_2 + z \geqslant 20 \tag{8.97}$$

$$-12x_2 - 2x_3 + 2z \geqslant 13 \tag{8.98}$$

$$x_3 \geqslant 0. \tag{8.99}$$

Step 2 (repeated)   We eliminate x_2 to give

$$-2x_3 + 14z \geqslant 253 \tag{8.100}$$

$$x_3 \geqslant 0. \tag{8.101}$$

Step 2 (repeated)   We eliminate x_3 to give

$$14z \geqslant 253. \tag{8.102}$$

Step 3   Since z must be integral, (8.102) gives

$$z \geqslant 19. \tag{8.103}$$

Step 4   We back-substitute to obtain integral values for x_3, x_2 and x_1. Should such integral values not be obtainable, we must relax the value of z given by (8.103) and repeat the back-substitution. In this case, that is not necessary. Back-substitution yields the following solutions to the cone relaxation:

$$x_3 = 0, \quad x_2 = 1, \quad x_1 = 6, \quad \text{objective} = 19 \tag{8.104}$$

$$x_3 = 1, \quad x_2 = 1, \quad x_1 = 5, \quad \text{objective} = 19 \tag{8.105}$$

$$x_3 = 2, \quad x_2 = 1, \quad x_1 = 4, \quad \text{objective} = 19 \tag{8.106}$$

$$x_3 = 3, \quad x_2 = 1, \quad x_1 = 3, \quad \text{objective} = 19 \tag{8.107}$$

$$x_3 = 4, \quad x_2 = 1, \quad x_1 = 2, \quad \text{objective} = 19 \tag{8.108}$$

$$x_3 = 5, \quad x_2 = 1, \quad x_1 = 1, \quad \text{objective} = 19 \tag{8.109}$$

$$x_3 = 6, \quad x_2 = 1, \quad x_1 = 0, \quad \text{objective} = 19. \tag{8.110}$$

Step 5   We check if any of the optimal solutions produced to the cone relaxation are feasible with regard to the original model. If so, they are optimal with regard to this model. In this particular case, solutions (8.107) to (8.110) are all feasible and therefore optimal.

Step 6   Should the cone relaxation produce no feasible solutions to the original model, a branch-and-bound procedure can be applied. A reference to one such method is given in section 8.6.

8.5 HEURISTIC AND LOCAL SEARCH METHODS

The inherent difficulty of solving IP models, as compared with LP models, has been stressed in earlier sections. Theoretical as well as experimental results suggest that there will always be some models where optimisation will be prohibitively expensive. For such models, we will have to resort to sub-optimal methods. *Heuristics* is the name adopted for such approaches. A reasonable definition of heuristics (or heuristic methods) is:

> *Simple procedures, often guided by common sense, that are meant to provide good, but not necessarily optimal, solutions to difficult problems easily and quickly.*

It should be pointed out that the common usage of the word differs slightly from the Greek derivation of *"heuriskein"*, meaning "to discover".

Heuristics are widely used in practice, but it is only fairly recently that they have been studied in general (as opposed to problem-specific) terms.

Computational speed is not the only reason for using heuristics. A fuller set of reasons (including this one) is as follows:

(i) Optimisation may require prohibitive amounts of computer time and storage.
(ii) The data in some models are sufficiently imprecise that the expense and time for optimisation is unwarranted.
(iii) A heuristic is easier to understand. This may seem a strong reason but it can make it more acceptable to non-technical users.
(iv) Heuristics can often be incorporated within optimisation procedures (e.g. branch and bound) to good effect. A feasible solution to a model obtained by a heuristic provides a lower (upper) bound on the optimal objective value if the model is a maximisation (minimisation). This is in contrast to a *relaxation*, as considered in sections 6.2, 6.3 and 8.4, which provides an upper (lower) bound if the model is a maximisation (minimisation). Should it be possible to close the gap completely between these bounds, then we have the optimal objective value.

Heuristics are usually *problem-specific*. This makes it difficult to give them a general treatment. Nevertheless, there are a few general principles. It is possible to apply these principles to general IP models, although in practice greater specialisation is worth while.

Problem-specific heuristics have been developed (and in some cases analysed) for a number of combinatorial optimisation problems. In particular, facility location, quadratic assignment, job shop scheduling and lot sizing problems have been considered. To describe these would be beyond the scope of this book, whose emphasis is on *general* LP and IP models. Nonetheless, references are given in section 8.6. We will illustrate heuristics in this section by application to the travelling salesman problem as a well defined specific application to illustrate the generality of the concepts.

Two aims in finding a good solution heuristically are (a) to find a *first feasible solution* and (b) to find *improving solutions*. These are illustrated by examples.

First Feasible Solution Heuristics

Example 8.20 Finding a First Feasible Solution to the Travelling Salesman Problem by the Nearest-Neighbour Method

Find a heuristic solution to the problem stated in Example 8.8 using the nearest-neighbour method.

The method we describe is an example of a *greedy algorithm*. Such an approach was used on the minimum-cost spanning tree problem in Example 8.7 to produce an optimal solution. In general, as with the travelling salesman problem, greedy algorithms are heuristics, which cannot be guaranteed to produce optimal solutions.

Step 1   We start anywhere. For illustration, we choose city A.
Step 2   We go to the the nearest unvisited city. In this case this is city B.
Step 2   (repeated)   We then go to city D followed by C, E and F.
Step 3   When all cities have been visited we return to the beginning. In this case this is city A. The resultant tour is illustrated in Figure 8.16.

This tour is clearly not optimal when compared with that in Figure 8.8. It is, however, very quick to obtain. The number of computer operations required is analysed in Example 8.22. Also, a measure of the quality of the solutions produced by this method is given.

It should be apparent why this method cannot be guaranteed to be optimal. The greedy approach is myopic and takes no account of the indirect effects of going to the nearest city. Eventually we may end up a long way from the origin.

Greedy heuristics can be invented for almost any specific optimisation problem. Some references are given in section 8.6.

Having found a first feasible solution to a model, heuristics can also be used to improve this solution. Again some heuristics will be described through examples.

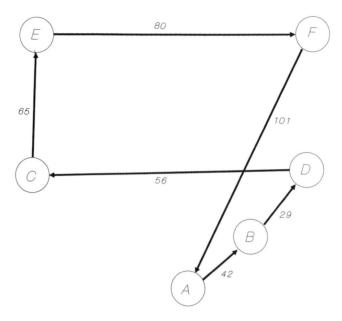

Figure 8.16 Heuristic solution to the asymmetric travelling salesman problem by the nearest-neighbour method (total length = 373)

Locally Improving Heuristics

For a general IP model, we could examine all neighbouring integer solutions to an initial feasible solution (or to the LP relaxation solution) to see if they improve the solution. If none of them do, then we may wish to stop. There is, however, no guarantee that we have achieved optimality if this happens.

There is clearly an analogy with non-linear programming as discussed in section 5.2. Although our solution space is not continuous, the concept of a *local optimum* still applies, where we allow discrete changes of at most 1 in the integer values. Therefore, using neighbourhood search methods, we can become "trapped" at such local optima. Two possible ways out of this, apart from complete enumeration or general IP methods, are known as *tabu search* and *simulated annealing*. These are discussed below. Before doing this, however, we apply a neighbourhood search to try to improve the heuristic solution to the travelling salesman problem given in Example 8.20.

Example 8.21 Finding a Locally Improving Solution to the Travelling Salesman Problem by Two-Interchanges
Improve the solution given to Example 8.20 by replacing two arcs by two new arcs to produce another tour.

We consider each pair of used arcs in turn to see if we can improve the solution by removing them and reconnecting the disconnected cities in a different manner.

For the example, we begin by considering removing AB and DC, replacing them by AD and BC and reversing the path from B to D to produce the tour ADBCEFA. This has length 383, which is longer. Therefore the change is not made.

We continue by considering all other possible two-interchanges. It turns out to be worth interchanging DC and FA with DF and CA and reversing the path from F to C to produce the tour ABDFECA of length 353. No other two-interchanges produce an improvement.

It can be seen that this is not the optimal tour shown in Figure 8.8.

When, as in this example, distances are geographical, then the only worthwhile two-interchanges will be for arcs that cross, such as DC and FA in Figure 8.12. For general travelling salesman problems, however, this will not be the case.

In general, such two-optimal tours will only be locally optimal in the sense described above. To improve them requires either allowing degradations by further interchanges as described under tabu search and simulated annealing or allowing k-interchanges where $k > 2$. Clearly if k were allowed to be the same as the number of cities, the method would amount to complete enumeration and be guaranteed to produce the optimal solution, but, in general, at enormous computational cost.

Tabu search is a method of allowing neighbourhood changes that may produce a degradation in objective value. From one such solution we move in turn to the best neighbourhood solution. In order to prevent "cycling", the most recent solutions considered are declared "tabu". The tabu list is kept within a certain size by releasing solutions from the list after a sufficient number of moves. This approach is a very flexible one, allowing for a compromise between complete enumeration and the over-restrictive moves that only allow objective improvements.

Measuring the Quality and Complexity of Heuristics

The value of a heuristic clearly depends on both its speed (and computer storage requirements) and the quality of the solution it develops. This latter aspect can be difficult to measure. On average a heuristic may produce near-optimal solutions, but can we rely on this? A common measure to use is the *maximum relative error* produced by the heuristic. This is

$$\left| \frac{\text{Objective value from heuristic } - \text{ Optimal objective value}}{\text{Optimal objective value}} \right|. \quad (8.111)$$

This measure has only been evaluated for a small class of simple heuristics. The evaluation of such measures is often quite difficult. References are given in section 8.6. Like measures of computational complexity discussed in section 1.7, it considers the worst case (which may be rare) as the determinant of quality.

Results have also tended to concentrate on heuristics for the travelling salesman problem in view of its interest. All results assume that the triangle inequality holds. For the nearest-neighbour method, illustrated in Example 8.21, the ratio (8.111) can be shown to be $\frac{1}{2} \lceil \ln(n) \rceil - \frac{1}{2}$ for a problem with n cities; " $\lceil \quad \rceil$ " represents integer rounding. This ratio demonstrates that (in the worst case) the method can be arbitrarily bad, as it increases with the value of n.

The quality of the solutions produced by improvement heuristics obviously depends on those produced by the first feasible solution.

The analysis of the number of computational steps required by a heuristic is usually quite straightforward. We do this for the nearest-neighbour method by an example.

Example 8.22 Finding the Number of Computer Operations for the Nearest-Neighbour Method for the Travelling Salesman Problem

For a problem with n cities, having arbitrarily chosen a starting city, we then make a choice from the remaining $n - 1$ cities. This leaves $n - 2$ cities to choose from. Repeating this argument, the number of operations is

$$(n - 1) + (n - 2) + \cdots + 1 = n(n - 1)/2. \tag{8.112}$$

Using the notation described in section 1.7, we have a complexity of $O(n^2)$. Therefore this is a polynomially bounded method, unlike all known optimising methods for this problem, which are of exponential, or worse, complexity.

Example 8.22 therefore demonstrates a very fast method but one of poor quality, producing an arbitrarily bad relative error depending on the size of the model.

By means of an example below we describe a method for the symmetric travelling salesman problem that is polynomially bounded and produces the smallest known relative error for this problem.

Example 8.23 Finding a Heuristic Solution to the Symmetric Travelling Salesman Problem by Christofides' Method and Analysing the Relative Error and Number of Operations

Find a solution to the problem stated in Example 8.9 using Christofides' method.

Step 1   We find the minimum-cost spanning tree associated with the (undirected) graph of distances using the greedy heuristic. This takes $O(n^2)$ operations. For the example, the result is given in Figure 8.17.

Step 2   In the graph resulting from the spanning tree, there will be an even number of nodes having odd degree. These are *matched* using the shortest distances between them. Since we are assuming the triangle inequality holds, these distances will be the lengths of the direct arcs. The algorithm for minimum-cost matching was mentioned (but not described) in section 8.3. It has complexity $O(n^3)$. For this simple example there are four odd-degree nodes to be matched, i.e. A, C, E and F. It is easy to see that the minimum-cost matching is that shown in Figure 8.18.

The result of adding the arcs associated with the matching is to produce a graph where each node has even degree. As with the Chinese postman problem, it can be shown that such a graph will have an Eulerian tour, i.e. a tour in which each arc is covered exactly once. For the example, the resultant graph and an Eulerian tour are shown in Figure 8.19. Such a tour may well be improved by short-circuiting cities that are visited twice.

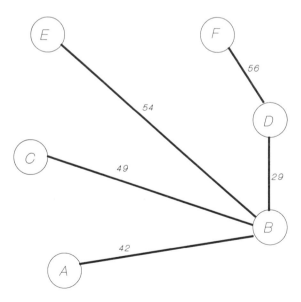

Figure 8.17   Minimum-cost spanning tree associated with a symmetric travelling salesman problem (length = 230)

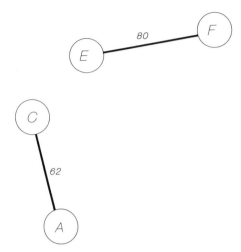

Figure 8.18 Minimum-cost matching of odd-degree nodes for minimum-cost spanning tree associated with a symmetric travelling salesman problem

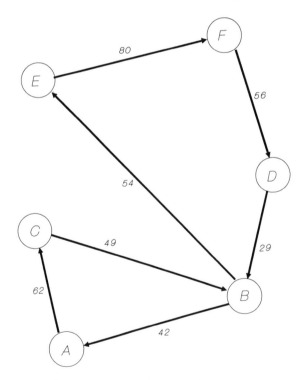

Figure 8.19 Graph of tour resulting from Christofides' method applied to the symmetric travelling salesman problem (length = 372)

In the example, we can go directly from C to E to produce the tour ACEFDBA of length 334. For this (small) example, we have the optimal solution shown in Figure 8.15.

In general, Christofides' method will not produce the optimal solution. Its complexity is dominated by that of the minimum-cost matching problem. Therefore the number of computational steps is $O(n^3)$.

The (worst-case) relative error of a solution produced by Christofides' method is easy to calculate. We can assert

Length of minimum-cost spanning tree $\leqslant$ Length of optimal tour. (8.113)

This is because the optimal tour is itself a spanning one-tree. If all arcs have positive length, then the inequality in (8.113) is strict.

We can also assert

$$\left.\begin{array}{l}\textit{Cost of minimum-cost matching}\\ \textit{among odd-degree nodes}\end{array}\right\} \leqslant \tfrac{1}{2} \times \textit{length of optimal tour.} \quad (8.114)$$

This is because the optimal tour could be regarded as made up of two matchings, plus one extra arc if there are an odd number of nodes.

Figure 8.20 demonstrates this for a general tour. One matching is marked

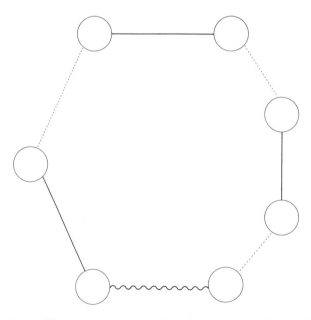

Figure 8.20 A travelling salesman tour resulting from two matchings and an extra arc

by bold arcs and the other by dotted arcs. The extra arc has a wavy line. Therefore, any such matching must obey inequality (8.114). Adding (8.113) and (8.114) gives a relative error bound of 1/2 for Christofides' method.

Probabilistic Methods: Simulated Annealing

The possibility of "local" optima being obtained when searches are only allowed in the neighbourhood of a solution has been pointed out. A compromise between stopping at such local optima and completely enumerating all other possibilities is to allow some neighbourhood solutions with an inferior objective value. As before, the idea of a neighbourhood is not confined to neighbouring solutions in an IP model. Problem-specific neighbourhoods are more useful, e.g. solutions obtainable by a two-interchange for the travelling salesman problem or other small rearrangements in other problems.

There is a useful analogy between allowing deteriorations in objective value with a controlled (small) probability and a physical system. *Annealing* is the name given to the controlled cooling of a material to a crystalline solid. Rapid cooling tends to produce lots of small crystals and results in a solid at a relatively high energy state. Slower cooling produces a lower energy state. When the liquid cools the tendency is for the molecules to slow down. Individual molecules may, however, speed up (go to a higher energy). Whether a molecule speeds up or slows down can be predicted only probabilistically. The probability is given by a formula that depends on the current temperature. As the temperature drops, the probability becomes smaller. In order to mirror this cooling in solving combinatorial problems, we use such a formula. At each stage we allow a neighbourhood improvement but only allow a neighbourhood degradation with such a declining probability. The "temperature" of the system falls as the computation progresses. The formula usually used takes the form

$$p(\delta) = \exp(-\delta/kt) \qquad (8.115)$$

where δ represents the degradation, t the current temperature and k is a constant. This change will only be admitted with probability $p(\delta)$. We can implement it by generating a random number between 0 and 1, and only allowing the degradation if it falls above $p(\delta)$. The formula (8.115) is that used in thermodynamics and known as Boltzmann's law. The "temperature" conveniently represents how far we are from the estimated termination of the calculation.

In practice, it may be better to use other probability distributions, which experience has shown to be best with a particular class of problem. For example, in the travelling salesman problem, if we know the type of distribution that represents the number of tours of a given length, we can use a probability distribution that reflects this.

8.6 HISTORY, REFERENCES AND FUTURE DEVELOPMENTS

Implicit Enumeration for Pure 0–1 Models

The method described here is due to Balas (1965). It is often referred to as "Balas' additive algorithm" since it can be executed in additive integer arithmetic with great economy in data storage and execution time. A more easily understood explanation of the method was provided by Glover (1965), who also showed how to add extra redundant ("surrogate") constraints to speed the solution process.

Boolean Algebra for Pure 0–1 Models

The method described here is due to Granot and Hammer (1972). Quine (1952, 1955) described the logic simplification method that is used. In practice, this method of IP only works well when the model is highly constrained with few feasible solutions. Use can be made of a method described by Hooker (1991b) for economically simplifying the resolvent obtained by appending resolvents for successively more constrained objective functions. The Boolean algebra approach has proved of more value in helping to *reformulate* models for solution by other algorithms.

There are close connections between IP and computational logic, which are surveyed in Williams (1991) and Hooker (1988). A widely used method of solving logical problems arising in artificial intelligence and expert systems is resolution due to Robinson (1965). This is, in fact, the logical dual of Quine's method of consensus. Another method due to Davis and Putnam (1960) uses a branch-and-bound approach. There is great merit in producing hybrid methods based on both traditional logic and MP approaches.

Combinatorial Problems

The formulation of combinatorial problems as IPs is described in *MBMP* and in Nemhauser and Wolsey (1988).

The analysis of matching problems and models was done by Edmonds (1965). A description of specialist algorithms is given in Lawler (1976).

The greedy algorithm given, for finding the minimum-cost spanning tree, is due to Kruskal (1956). Another greedy algorithm is due to Prim (1957).

A full coverage of many aspects of the travelling salesman and vehicle scheduling problems is covered in Lawler et al. (1985).

The Chinese postman problem is discussed by Edmonds and Johnson (1973). The algorithm for finding an Eulerian tour is known as Fleury's algorithm, and is given in standard texts on graph theory.

The knapsack problem and connected problems are discussed in Martello and Toth (1990). The application of dynamic programming to the knapsack problem is due to Bellman (1957).

Lagrangean, Surrogate and Cone Relaxations

A comprehensive discussion of LP, Lagrangean and surrogate relaxations was given by Geoffrion (1974). Specific applications of Lagrangean relaxation are reported for many applications. The application to the travelling salesman problem using one-trees was developed by Held and Karp (1970, 1971). An iterative method of refining the multipliers is known as subgradient optimisation. It was first applied to the travelling salesman problem by Held, Wolfe and Crowder (1974). References can be found in Nemhauser and Wolsey (1988).

Bradley (1971) applied surrogate relaxation to reduce pure IP models to knapsack models, and Forgo (1974) used this idea to create analogies to shadow prices.

The cone relaxation is more usually referred to as the *group relaxation*, since the resulting model can be expressed as the problem of optimising over a finite Abelian group with non-negative variables. There are especially simple methods for solving such models. The approach was pioneered by Gomory (1969) and further developed by Johnson (1974).

Heuristic and Local Search Methods

Many general papers have been written on heuristics, for example Zanakis and Evans (1981), and Silver, Vidal and De Werra (1980). Geoffrion and Van Roy (1979) give some cautionary advice. Muller-Merbach (1974) gives a general discussion of heuristics in operational research. Papadimitriou and Stieglitz (1982) cover the subject in relation to IP, as does Glover (1977).

Tabu search is an idea due to Glover (1989).

A discussion and analysis of heuristics for the travelling salesman problem is given by Rosencrantz, Stearns and Lewis (1974) and Golden et al. (1980). The idea of interchanges is due to Lin (1965).

A discussion of principles behind worst-case analysis of heuristic algorithms is given by Fisher (1980). The method described for the symmetric travelling salesman problem, which currently is the polynomially bounded method with least error bound, is due to Christofides (1975b).

A general discussion of the subject of simulated annealing is given by Kirkpatrick, Gellatt and Vecchi (1983) and Burkhard and Rendl (1984). Golden and Skiscim (1986) describe the results of experiments in applying this approach to distribution problems.

8.7 EXERCISES

8.1 Solve Example 1.19 by implicit enumeration.

8.2 Construct a class of pure 0–1 IP models where implicit enumeration takes an exponential number of steps.

8.3 Solve Example 1.19 by the Boolean algebra method. Why is this inefficient?

8.4 Construct a class of pure 0–1 IP models where the Boolean algebra method takes an exponential number of steps.

8.5 Find a maximum cardinality matching for the nodes in Figure 8.3.

8.6 Using a computer package, find a maximum weighted matching for the nodes of the graph in Figure 8.3.

8.7 Find the *maximum*-cost spanning tree for the graph in Figure 8.3.

8.8 Formulate the minimum-cost spanning tree problem in Example 8.6 as an IP model by introducing constraints to create at least one arc between any subset and its complement, as an alternative formulation.

8.9 Show, by an example, that the minimum-cost spanning tree IP formulation does not have the integrality property.

8.10 Using a package, solve Example 8.8 through the branch-and-bound method based on the LP relaxation described in section 6.2, using the formulation described in *MBMP*.

8.11 For Example 8.8 specify subtour elimination constraints by excluding arcs between subsets and their complements.

8.12 Solve the assignment relaxation of Example 8.10 by the Hungarian algorithm of section 3.2.

8.13 For Example 8.11 find the minimum-cost spanning one-tree rooted at node B.

8.14 Show that the number of steps needed to find a minimum-cost spanning tree on a graph of n nodes is $O(n^2)$.

8.15 Solve the following knapsack problem by dynamic programming:

$$\text{Maximise} \quad 4x_1 + 3x_2 + x_3$$

subject to

$$2x_1 + 2x_2 + x_3 \leqslant 7$$
$$x_1, x_2, x_3 \geqslant 0 \quad \text{and integer.}$$

8.16 For a knapsack problem with n variables and right-hand side b, show that the number of computational steps is $O(nb)$. Why is this not a polynomially bounded algorithm?

8.17 Resolve Example 8.10 using Lagrangean relaxation by applying suitable multipliers to the removed constraints.

8.18 Solve the symmetric travelling salesman problem given in Example 8.9 by Lagrangean relaxation based on the assignment relaxation. Observe the nature of some of the subtours.

8.19 For Example 6.1, find the set of multipliers for the constraints that minimises the surrogate duality gap.

8.20 Illustrate the cone relaxation for Example 1.20 geometrically. Does this give the optimal solution to the original model?

8.21 Devise a method of extending implicit enumeration, as described in section 8.1, to deal with minimax objectives.

8.22 Devise a method of extending the Boolean algebra method, as described in section 8.2, to deal with minimax objectives.

8.23 The cheapest insertion heuristic for the travelling salesman problem starts with the cheapest loop around two cities and inserts extra cities, one at a time, in the cheapest way. Apply this method to find a solution to Example 8.8.

8.24 Analyse the complexity of the method of exercise 8.23.

References

Balas, E. (1965), An additive algorithm for solving linear programs with zero–one variables, *Oper. Res.*, **13**, 517–46.

Balas, E. (1970), Duality in Discrete Programming, Reprint No. 519, Graduate School of Industrial Administration, Carnegie–Mellon University, Pittsburgh, PA.

Balas, E. (1975), Facets of the knapsack polytope, *Math. Prog.*, **8**, 146–64.

Bartels, R. H. and G. H. Golub (1969), The simplex method of linear programming using L\U decomposition, *Commun. Assoc. Comput. Mach.*, **12**, 266–8 and 275–8.

Beale, E. M. L. (1955), Cycling in the dual simplex algorithm, *Naval Res. Logist. Q.*, **2**, 269–76.

Beale, E. M. L. (1968), *Mathematical Programming in Practice*, Pitman, London.

Beale, E. M. L. (1979), Branch and bound methods for mathematical programming systems, *Annals of Discrete Mathematics*, North-Holland, Amsterdam, Vol. 5, pp. 201–19.

Beale, E. M. L. (1980), Branch and bound methods for numerical optimisation of non-convex functions, in M. M. Barritt and D. Wishart (Eds), *COMPSTAT 80: Proceedings in Computational Statistics*, Physica Verlag, Wien, pp. 11–20.

Beale, E. M. L. (1985), Integer programming, in K. Schittkowski (Ed.), *Computational Mathematical Programming*, Springer-Verlag, Berlin.

Beale, E. M. L. and J. A. Tomlin (1970), Special facilities in a general mathematical programming system for non-convex problems using ordered sets of variables, in J. Lawrence (Ed.), *Proceedings of the 5th International Conference in Operational Research*, Tavistock Publications, London.

Bell, D. E. (1977), A theorem concerning the integer lattice, *Stud. Appl. Math.*, **56**, 187–8.

Bellman, R. E. (1957), *Dynamic Programming*, Princeton University Press, Princeton, NJ.

Bellman, R. E. (1958), On a routing problem, *Q. Appl. Math.*, **16**, 87–90.

Benichou, M., J. M. Gauthier, G. Hentges and G. Ribiere (1971), Experiments in mixed integer linear programming, *Math. Prog.*, **1**, 76–94.

Blair, C. E. and R. G. Jeroslow (1982), The value function of an integer programme, *Math. Prog.*, **23**, 237–73.

Bland, R. G. (1977), New finite privoting rules for the simplex method, *Math. Oper. Res.*, **2**, 103–7.

Bradley, G. H. (1971), Transformation of integer programs to knapsack problems, *Discrete Math.*, **1**, 29–45.

Bradley, G. H. (1975), Survey of deterministic networks, *AIIE Trans.*, **7**, 222–34.

Bradley, G. H., G. Brown and G. Graves (1977), Design and implementation of large scale primal transshipment algorithms, *Manage. Sci.*, **24**, 1–34.

Brayton, R. K., F. G. Gustavson and R. A. Willoughby (1969), Some Results on Sparse Matrices, Report No. RC-2332, IBM Research Centre, Yorktown Heights, NY.

Brearley, A. L., G. Mitra and H. P. Williams (1978), Analysis of mathematical programming problems prior to applying the simplex algorithm, *Math. Prog.*, **8**, 54–83.

Burkhard, R. E. and F. Rendl (1984), A thermodynamically motivated simulation procedure for combinatorial optimization problems, *Eur. J. Oper. Res.*, **17**, 169–74.

Christofides, N. (1975a), *Graph Theory, An Algorithmic Approach*, Academic Press, London.

Christofides, N. (1975b), Worst-Case Analysis of a New Heuristic for the Travelling Salesman Problem, Report No. 388, Graduate School of Industrial Administration, Carnegie–Mellon University, Pittsburgh, PA.

Chvátal, V. (1973), Edmonds polytopes and hierarchy of combinatorial problems, *Discrete Math.*, **4**, 305–37.

Chvátal, V. (1983), *Linear Programming*, W. H. Freeman, New York.

Cohn, P. M. (1958), *Linear Equations*, Routledge and Kegan Paul, London.

Cook, S. A. (1971), The complexity of theorem-proving procedures, *Proceedings of the 3rd Annual ACM Symposium of Theory of Computing Machinery*, pp. 151–8.

Cook, W., R. Kannan and A. Schrijver (1990), Chvátal closures for mixed integer programming problems, *Math. Prog.*, **47**, 155–74.

Crowder, H. P., E. L. Johnson and M. W. Padberg (1983), Solving large-scale zero–one linear programming problems, *Oper. Res.*, **31**, 803–34.

Cunningham, W. H. and J. G. Klincewicz (1983), On cycling in the network simplex method, *Math. Prog.*, **26**, 182–9.

Dakin, R. J. (1965), A tree search algorithm for mixed integer programming problems, *Comput. J.*, **9**, 250–5.

Dantzig, G. B. (1951), Application of the simplex method to a transportation problem, in T. C. Koopmans (Ed.), *Activity Analysis of Production and Allocation*, Wiley, New York, pp. 359–73.

Dantzig, G. B. (1955), Upper bounds, secondary constraints and block triangularity in linear programming, *Econometrica*, **23**, 174–83.

Dantzig, G. B. (1963), *Linear Programming and Extensions*, Princeton University Press, Princeton, NJ.

Dantzig, G. B. (1974), On the need for a systems optimization laboratory, in R. W. Cottle and J. Krarup (Eds), *Optimisation Methods*, English Universities Press, London.

Dantzig, G. B. and W. Orchard-Hays (1953), Notes on Linear Programming: Part V— Alternative Algorithm for the Revised Simplex Method Using Product Form for the Inverse, Research Memorandum No. RM-1268, The Rand Corporation.

Davis, M. and H. Putnam (1960), A computing procedure for quantification theory, *J. Assoc. Comput. Mach.*, **7**, 201–15.

Descartes, R. (1637), Discours de la Méthode pour bien Conduire sa Raison, et Chercher la Vérité dans les Sciences.

Dijkstra, E. W. (1959), A note on two problems in connexion with graphs, *Numer. Math.*, **1**, 269–71.

Dorfman, R. P. A., P. A. Samuelson and R. M. Solow (1958), *Linear Programming and Economic Analysis*, McGraw-Hill, New York.

Driebeek, N. J. (1966), An algorithm for the solution of mixed integer programming problems, *Manage. Sci.*, **12**, 576–87.

Duff, I. S., A. M. Erisma and J. K. Reid (1986), *Direct Methods for Sparse Matrices*, Clarendon Press, Oxford.

Dyer, M. E. and L. G. Proll (1977), An algorithm for determining all extreme points of a convex polytope, *Math. Prog.*, **12**, 81–96.

Edmonds, J. (1965), Paths, trees and flowers, *Can. J. Math.*, **17**, 449–67.

Edmonds, J. and E. L. Johnson (1973), Matching Euler tours and the Chinese postman, *Math. Prog.*, **5**, 88–124.

Fisher, M. L. (1980), Worst-case analysis of heuristic algorithms, *Manage. Sci.*, **25**, 1–17.

Fletcher, R. (1987), *Practical Methods of Optimisation*, Wiley, Chichester.

Ford, L. W. and D. R. Fulkerson (1962), *Flowers in Networks*, Princeton University Press, Princeton, NJ.

Forgo, F. (1974), Shadow Prices and Decomposition for Integer Programs, Report No. DM74-6, Department of Mathematics, Karl Marx University of Economics, Budapest.

Forrest, J. J. H., J. P. H. Hirst and J. A. Tomlin (1974), Practical solution of large mixed integer programming problems with UMPIRE, *Manage. Sci.*, **20**, 763–73.

Forrest, J. J. H. and J. A. Tomlin (1972), Updating triangular factors of the basis to maintain sparsity in the product form simplex method, *Math. Prog.*, **2**, 263–78.

Fourier, J. B. J. (1826), Solution d'une question particulière du calcul des inégalités, *Oevres II*, Paris, pp. 317–28.

Gale, D., H. W. Kuhn and A. W. Tucker (1951), Linear programming and the theory of games, in T. C. Koopmans (Ed.), *Activity Analysis of Production and Allocation*, Wiley, New York, pp. 317–29.

Garey, M. R. and D. S. Johnson (1979), *Computers and Intractability*, W. H. Freeman, San Francisco.

Gauss, C. F. (1809), *Theoria Motus Corporum Coolestium in Sectionitus Conicis Solem Ambientium*, F. Perthes and J. H. Besser, Hombury.

Geoffrion, A. M. (1974), Lagrangean relaxation for integer programming, *Math. Prog. Study*, **2**, 82–114.

Geoffrion, A. M. and R. E. Marsten (1972), Integer programming algorithms: a framework and state-of-the-art survey, *Manage. Sci.*, **18**, 465–91.

Geoffrion, A. M. and T. J. Van Roy (1979), Caution: common sense planning methods can be hazardous to your corporate health, *Sloan Manage. Rev.*, **20**, 31–42.

Gill, P. E., W. Murray, M. A. Saunders, J. A. Tomlin and M. H. Wright (1986), On projected Newton barrier methods for linear programming, *Math. Prog.*, **36**, 183–209.

Glover, F. (1965), A multiphase-dual algorithm for the zero–one integer programming problem, *Oper. Res.*, **13**, 879–919.

Glover, F. (1977), Heuristics for integer programming using surrogate constraints, *Decis. Sci.*, **8**, 156–66.

Glover, F. (1990), TabuSearch: A Tutorial, *Interface*, **20**, 74–94.

Glover, F. and D. Klingman (1974), Real World Applications of Network Related Problems and Breakthrough in Solving them Efficiently, Research Report No. CCS 159, Center for Cybernetic Studies, University of Texas, Austin, TX.

Gödel, K. (1931), Uber Formal Unentscheidbare Satze der Principia Mathematica und Verwandter System I, *Monatsh. Math. Phys.*, **28**, 173–98.

Golden, B. L., L. Bodin, T. Doyle and W. Stewart (1980), Approximate travelling salesman algorithms, *Oper. Res.*, **28**, 694–711.

Golden, B. L. and C. C. Skiscim (1986), Using simulated annealing to solve routing and location problems, *Naval Res. Logist. Q.*, **33**, 261–79.

Gomory, R. E. (1958), Outline of an algorithm for integer solutions to linear programs, *Bull. Am. Math. Soc.*, **64**, 275–78.

Gomory, R. E. (1963), An all-integer programming algorithm, in J. F. Muth and G. L. Thomson (Eds), *Industrial Scheduling*, Prentice-Hall, Englewood Cliffs, NJ, pp. 193–206.

Gomory, R. E. (1965), On the relation between integer and non-integer solutions to linear programs, *Proc. Nat. Acad. Sci. USA*, **53**, 260–5.

Gomory, R. E. (1969), Some polyhedra related to combinatorial problems, *Lin. Alg. Applic.*, **2**, 451–8.

Gomory, R. E. and W. J. Baumol (1960), Integer programming and pricing, *Econometrica*, **28**, 521–50.

Granot, F. and P. L. Hammer (1972), On the use of Boolean functions in 0–1 programming, *Meth. Oper. Res.*, **12**, 154–84.

Hammer, P. L., E. L. Johnson and U. N. Peled (1975), Facets of regular 0–1 polytopes, *Math. Prog.*, **8**, 179–206.

Harris, P. M. J. (1973), Pivot selection methods of the Devex LP code, *Math. Prog.*, **5**, 1–28.

Held, M. and R. M. Karp (1970), The travelling salesman problem and minimum spanning trees, *Oper. Res.*, **18**, 1138–62.

Held, M. and R. M. Karp (1971), The travelling salesman problem and minimal spanning trees; Part II, *Math. Prog.*, **1**, 6–25.

Held, M., P. Wolfe and H. P. Crowder (1974), Validation of subgradient optimization, *Math. Prog.*, **6**, 62–88.

Hellerman, E. and D. Rarick (1971), Reinversion with the preassigned pivot procedure, *Math. Prog.*, **1**, 195–216.

Hooker, J. N. (1988), A quantitative approach to logical inference, *Decis. Support Syst.*, **4**, 45–69.

Hooker, J. N. (1989), Input proofs and rank one cutting planes, *ORSA J. Comput.*, **1**, 137–45.

Hooker, J. N. (1991), Solving the Incremental Satisfiability Problem, Working Paper No. 1991-9, Graduate School of Industrial Administration, Carnegie–Mellon Univerity, Pittsburgh, PA.

Jeroslow, R. (1972), There cannot be any algorithm for integer programming with quadratic constraints, *Oper. Res.*, **21**, 221–4.

Jeroslow, R. (1973), The simplex algorithm with the pivot rule of maximizing criterion improvement, *Discrete Math.*, **4**, 367–77.

Jeroslow, R. (1989), Logic-based decision support; mixed integer model formulation, *Annals of Discrete Mathematics*, North-Holland, Amsterdam, Vol. 40.

Johnson, E. L. (1974), On the group problem for mixed integer programming, *Math. Prog. Study*, **2**, 137–79.

Kalan, J. E. (1971), Aspects of large-scale in-core linear programming, *Proceedings of ACM Conference*, Chicago, pp. 304–13.

Kantorovitch, L. V. (1942), On the translocation of masses, *C. R. Acad. Sci. URSS*, **37**, 199–201.

Karmarkar, N. (1984), A new polynomial time algorithm for linear programming, *Combinatorica*, **4**, 375–95.

Karp, R. M. (1972), Reducibility among combinatorial problems, in R. E. Miller and J. W. Thatcher (Eds), *Complexity of Computer Computations*, Plenum Press, New York, pp. 85–103.

Karush, W. (1939), Minima of Functions of Several Variables with Inequalities as Side Constraints, M.Sc. Dissertation, Department of Mathematics, University of Chicago.

Karwan, M. H., V. Lotfi, J. Telgen and S. Zionts (Eds) (1983), *Redundancy in Mathematical Programming*, Springer-Verlag, Berlin.

Kirkpatrick, S., C. D. Gellatt and M. P. Vecchi (1983), Optimisation by simulated annealing, *Science*, **220**, 671–80.

Klee, V. and G. J. Minty (1972), How good is the simplex algorithm, in O. Shisha (Ed.), *Inequalities-III*, Academic Press, New York, pp. 159–75.

Knuth, D. E. (1979), *The Art of Computer Programming*, Vol. I, *Fundamental Algorithms*, Addison-Wesley, Reading, MA.

Koopmans, T. C. and S. Reiter (1951), A model of transportation in T. C. Koopmans (Ed.), *Activity Analysis of Production and Allocation*, Wiley, New York, pp. 222–59.

Kruskal, J. B. (1956), On the shortest spanning subtree of a graph and the travelling salesman problem, *Proc. Am. Math. Soc.*, **7**, 48–50.

Kuhn, H. W. (1955), The Hungarian method for the assignment problem, *Naval Res. Logist. Q.*, **2**, 83–97.

Kuhn, H. W. and A. W. Tucker (1951), Nonlinear programming, in J. Neyman (Ed.), *Proceedings of the Second Berkeley Symposium on Mathematical Statistics and Probability*, University of California Press, Berkeley, CA.

Land, A. H. and A. G. Doig (1960), An automatic method for solving discrete programming problems, *Econometrica*, **28**, 497–520.

Lawler, E. L. (1976), *Combinatorial Optimization: Networks and Matroids*, Holt, Rinehart and Winston, New York.

Lawler, E. L., J. K. Lenstra, A. H. G. Rinnooy Kan and D. B. Shmoys (Eds) (1985), *The Travelling Salesman Problem: A Guided Tour of Combinatorial Optimization*, Wiley, Chichester.

Legendre, A. M. (1805), *Nouvelles Méthodes pour la Détermination des Orbites de Comètes*, F. Didot, Paris.

Lemke, C. E. (1954), The dual method of solving the linear programming problem, *Naval Res. Logist. Q.*, **1**, 36–47.

Lemke, C. E. (1970), Recent results on complementarity problems, in J. B. Rosen, O. L. Mangasarian and K. Ritter (Eds), *Non-Linear Programming*, Academic Press, New York.

Leontief, W. (1951), *The Structure of the American Economy, 1919–1931*, Oxford University Press, New York.

Lin, S. (1965), Computer solutions of the travelling salesman problem, *Bell Syst. Tech. J.*, **44**, 2245–69.

McMullen, P. (1970), The maximum number of faces of a convex polytope, *Mathematica*, **17**, 179–84.

Markowitz, H. M. (1957), The elimination form of the inverse and its application to linear programming, *Manage. Sci.*, **3**, 255–69.

Martello, S. and P. Toth (1990), *Knapsack Problems: Algorithms and Computer Implementations*, Wiley, Chichester.

Mattheiss, T. H. and B. K. Schmidt (1980), Computational results on an algorithm for finding all vertices of a polytope, *Math. Prog.*, **18**, 308–29.

Miller, C. E. (1963), The simplex method for local separable programming, in R. G. Graves and P. Wolfe (Eds), *Recent Advances in Mathematical Programming*, McGraw-Hill, New York, pp. 89–110.

Mitra, G. (1973), Investigations of some branch and bound strategies for the solution of mixed integer linear programs, *Math. Prog.*, **4**, 155–70.

Motzkin, T. S. (1936), Beitrage zur Theorie der Linearm Ungleichangen, Dissertation, University of Basel.

Müller-Merbach, H. (1974), Heuristic methods: structures, applications, computational experience, in R. Cottle and J. Krarup (Eds), *Optimisation Methods for Resource Allocation*, English Universities Press, London, pp. 401–16.

Mulvey, J. (1978), Pivot strategies for primal-simplex network codes, *J. Assoc. Comput. Mach.*, **25**, 266–70.

Murtagh, B. A. (1981), *Advanced Linear Programming: Computation and Practice*, McGraw-Hill, New York.

Nemhauser, G. L. and L. A. Wolsey (1988), *Integer and Combinatorial Optimization*, Wiley, Chichester.

Nygreen, B. (1991), Branch and bound with estimation based on pseudo-shadow prices, *Math. Prog.*, **52**, 59–70.

Orchard-Hays, W. (1969), *Advanced Linear Programming Computing Techniques*, McGraw-Hill, New York.

Papadimitriou, C. H. and K. Stieglitz (1982), *Combinatorial Optimization: Algorithms and Complexity*, Prentice-Hall, Englewood Cliffs, NJ.

Powell, M. J. D. (1981), *Nonlinear Optimisation*, Academic Press, London.

Prim, R. C. (1957), Shortest connection networks and some generalizations, *Bell Syst. Tech. J.*, **36**, 1389–401.

Quine, W. V. (1952), The problem of simplifying truth functions, *Am. Math. Monthly*, **59**, 521–31.

Quine, W. V. (1955), A way to simplify truth functions, *Am. Math. Monthly*, **62**, 627–31.

Robinson, J. A. (1965), A machine-oriented logic based on the resolution principle, *J. Assoc. Comput. Mach.*, **12**, 23–41.

Rockafellar, R. T. (1970), *Convex Analysis*, Princeton University Press, Princeton, NJ.

Rosencrantz, D. J., R. E. Stearns and P. M. Lewis (1974), Approximate algorithms for the travelling salesman problem, *Proceedings of the 15th IEEE Symposium on Switching and Automata Theory*, pp. 33–42.

Schrijver, A. (1986), *Theory of Linear and Integer Programming*, Wiley, Chichester.

Seymour, P. D. (1981), Recognising graphic matroids, *Combinatorica*, **1**, 75–78.

Shamir, R. (1987), The efficiency of the simplex method: a survey, *Manag. Sci.*, **3**, 301–34R.

Shapiro, J. F. (1971), Generalised Lagrange multipliers in integer programming, *Oper. Res.*, **19**, 68–76.

Shapiro, J. F. (1979), *Mathematical Programming: Structures and Algorithms*, Wiley, New York.

Sherali, H. D. and C. M. Shetty (1980), *Optimization with Disjunctive Constraints*, Springer-Verlag, Berlin.

Silver, E. A., R. V. V. Vidal and D. De Werra (1980), A tutorial on heuristic methods, *Eur. J. Oper. Res.*, **5**, 153–62.

Smale, S. (1983), On the average speed of the simplex method of linear programming, *Math. Prog.*, **27**, 241–62.

Strassen, V. (1969), Gaussian elimination is not optimal, *Numer. Math.*, **13**, 354–6.

Tarjan, R. E. (1983), *Data Structures and Network Algorithms*, SIAM Publications, Philadelphia.

Todd, M. J. (1989), Recent developments and new directions in linear programming, in M. Iri and K. Tanabe (Eds), *Mathematical Programming: Recent Developments and Applications*, Kluwer Academic, Dordrecht, pp. 109–57.

Tomlin, J. A. (1971), An improved branch and bound method for integer programming, *Oper. Res.*, **19**, 1070–5.

Tomlin, J. A. (1987), An experimental approach to Karmarkar's projective method for linear programming, *Math. Prog.*, **31**, 175–91.

Von Neumann, J. and O. Morgenstern (1947), *Theory of Games and Economic Behaviour*, Princeton University Press, Princeton, NJ.

Williams, H. P. (1974), Experiments in the formulation of integer programming problems, *Math. Prog. Study*, **2**, 180–97.

Williams, H. P. (1978), The reformulation of two mixed integer programming problems, *Math. Prog.*, **14**, 325–31.

Williams, H. P. (1979), The economic interpretation of duality of practical mixed integer programming problems, in A. Prekopa (Ed.), *Survey of Mathematical Programming*, North-Holland, Amsterdam, pp. 567–86.

Williams, H. P. (1984), Restricted vertex generation applied as a crashing procedure for linear programming, *Comput. Oper. Res.*, **11**, 401–7.

Williams, H. P. (1986), Fourier's method of linear programming and its dual, *Am. Math. Monthly*, **93**, 681–94.

Williams, H. P. (1987), Linear and integer programming applied to the propositional calculus, *Int. J. Syst. Res. Inf. Sci.*, **2**, 81–100.

Williams, H. P. (1989), Constructing the value function for an integer linear programme over a cone, Report OR 19, Faculty of Mathematical Studies, University of Southampton, UK.

Williams, H. P. (1990a), *Model Building in Mathematical Programming*, 3rd Edn, Wiley, Chichester (referred to simply as *MBMP* in the text).

Williams, H. P. (1990b), Optimisation and operational research, *IMA Bull.*, **26**, 76–85.

Williams, H. P. (1991), Computational logic and integer programming: connections between the methods of logic, AI and OR, *Ann. Oper. Res.*, to appear.

Wolfe, P. (1963), A technique for resolving degeneracy in linear programming, *J. Soc. Ind. Appl. Math.*, **11**, 205–11.

Wolsey, L. A. (1975), Faces for a linear inequality in 0–1 variables, *Math. Prog.*, **8**, 165–78.

Wolsey, L. A. (1989), Strong formulations for mixed integer programming: a survey, *Math. Prog.*, **45**, 173–91.

Zanakis, S. H. and J. R. Evans (1981), Heuristic optimization: why, when and how to use it, *Interfaces*, **11**, 84–91.

Author Index

Subject Index